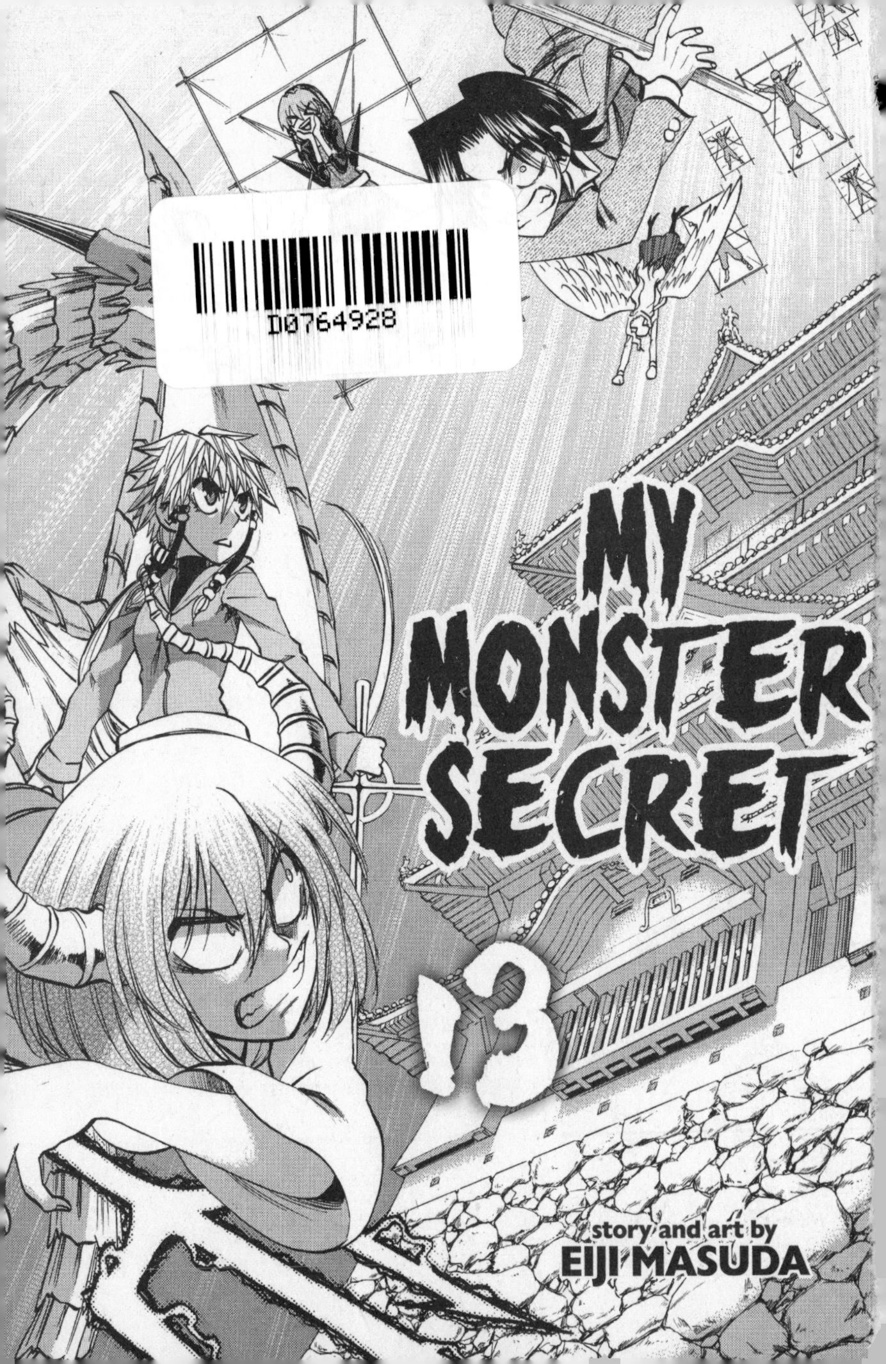
MY MONSTER SECRET
13
story and art by
EIJI MASUDA

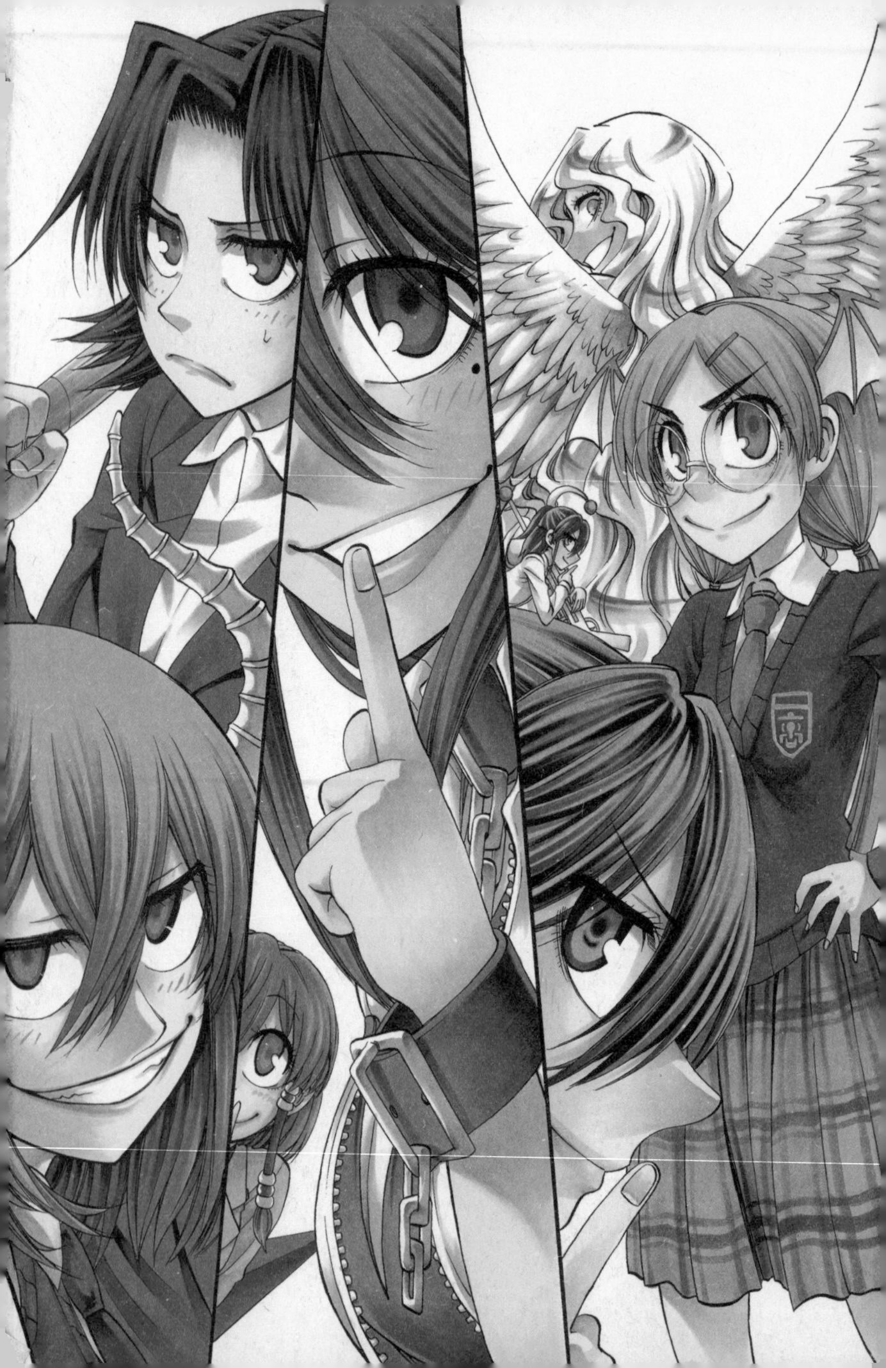

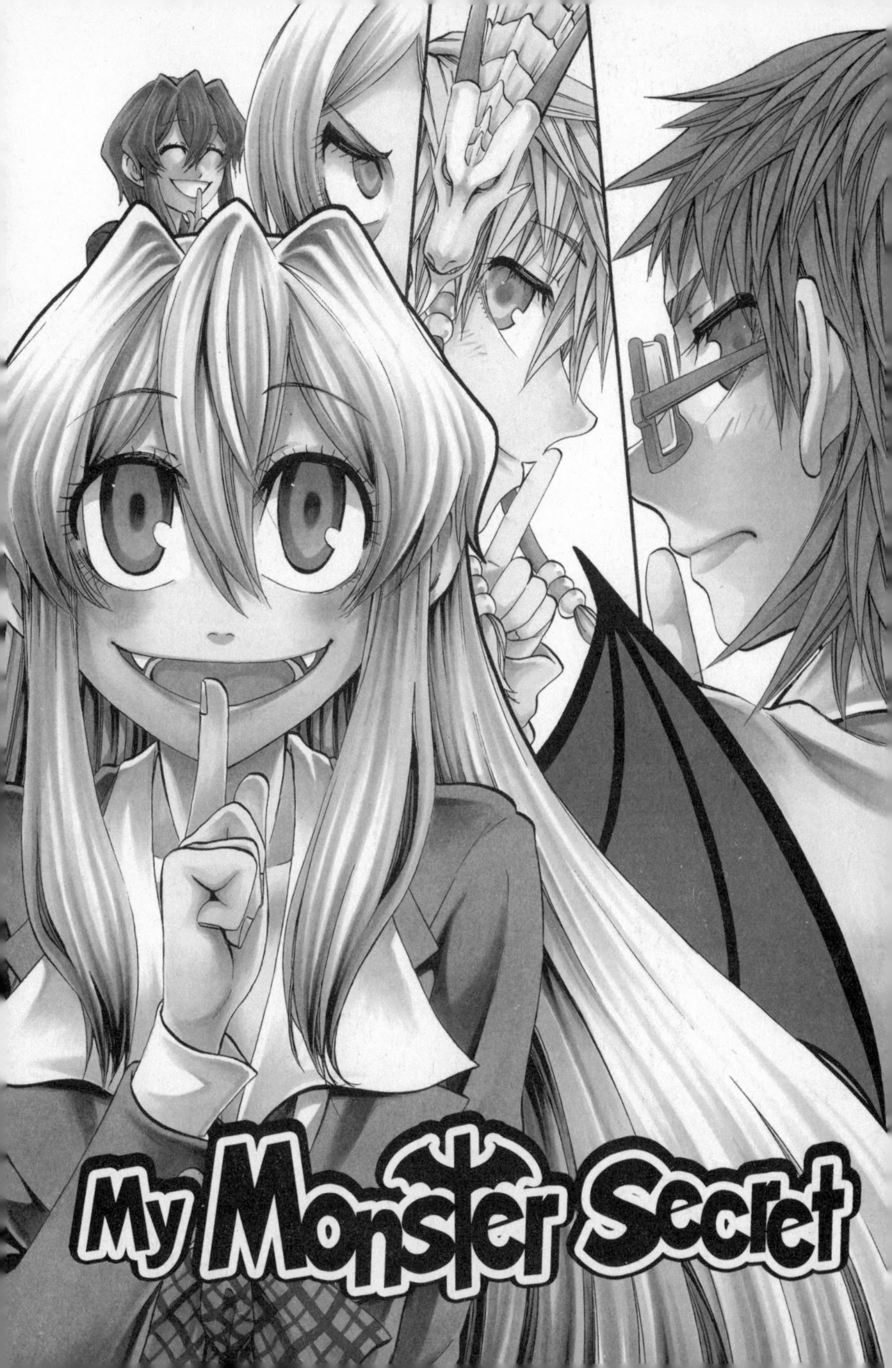
My Monster Secret

Story & Characters

My Monster Secret "Actually, I am..."

After school one day, Kuromine Asahi opened the door to his classroom to confess his love to his crush Shiragami Youko...and discovered that she's actually a vampire! His goal was to tell Shiragami that he loved her, but he instead resolved to keep her secret--as a friend. It means they can continue to go to school together, but their problems are only beginning...

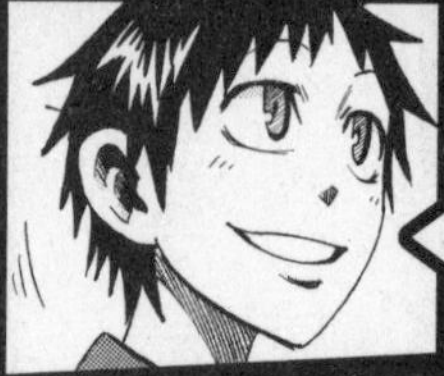

KUROMINE ASAHI

THE HOLEY SIEVE

The man with the worst poker face in the world, he's known as ***The Sieve with a Hole in It...*** because secrets slide right out of him. Now he has to hide the fact that Shiragami-san--the girl he's in love with--is a vampire.

SHIRAGAMI YOUKO

ACTUALLY A VAMPIRE

She's attending a human high school under the condition that she'll ***stop going immediately*** if her true identity is discovered. Asahi found out (whoops), but she believes him when he says he'll keep her secret, and the two are now friends.

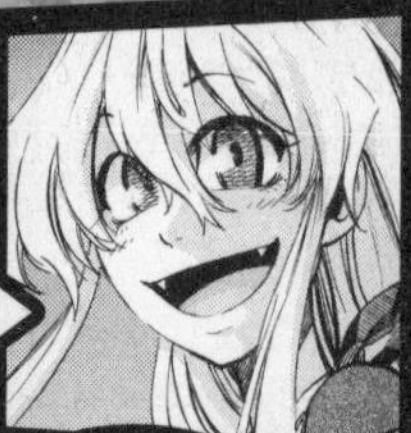

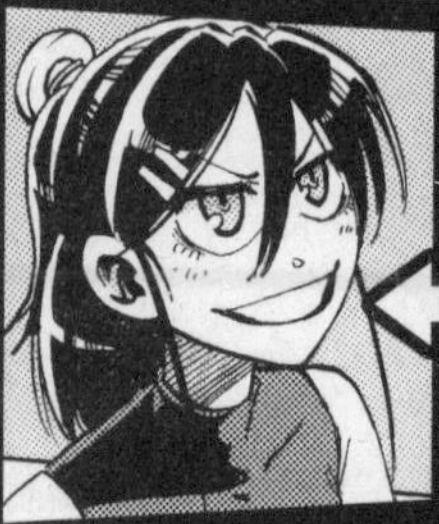

AIZAWA NAGISA

ACTUALLY AN ALIEN

Currently investigating Earth as a class representative, she once mercilessly tore Asahi to shreds before he could confess his love, but she now harbors an unrequited crush on him. Her true (tiny) form emerges from the screw-shaped cockpit on her head. Her brother **Aizawa Ryo** is also staying on Earth.

AKEMI MIKAN

THE QUEEN OF PURE EVIL

Editor-in-chief of the school newspaper and a childhood friend of Asahi's. Currently straying from the path of villainy since her favorite pair of glasses became the **Goddess of Fortune, Fuku-chan.**

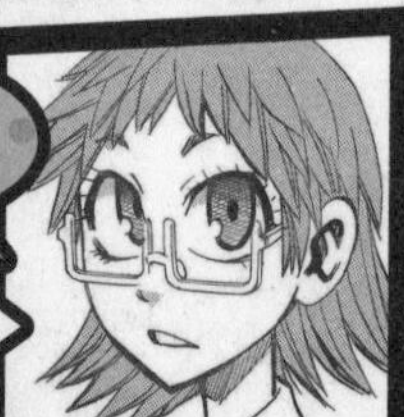

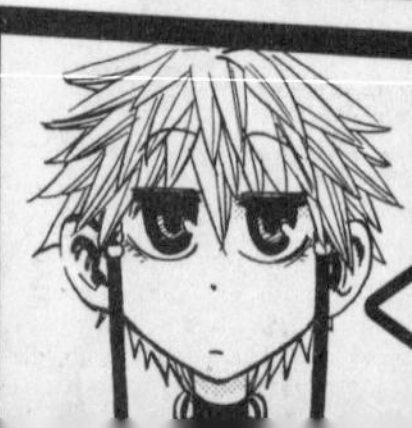

KIRYUIN RIN

ACTUALLY FROM THE FUTURE

Came from fifty years in the future to save the world from the clutches of a nympho tyrant. Now she's a refugee who can't return home because she told Asahi (among others) about the future. Asahi's granddaughter.

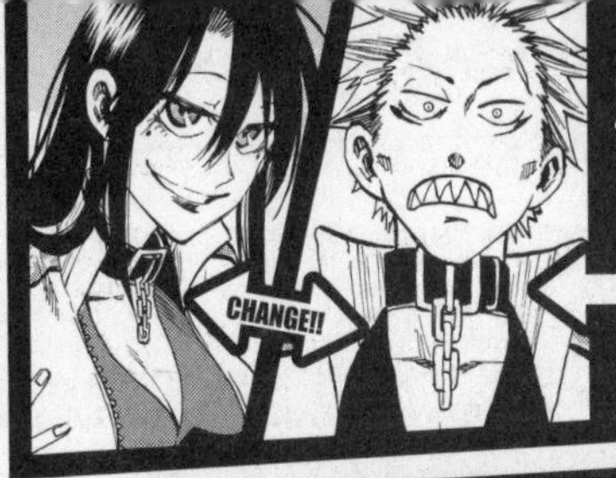
CHANGE!!

SHISHIDO SHIHO ♀
SHISHIDO SHIROU ♂

This childhood friend of Youko's is a nympho. When she sees the moon, she transforms into the wolfman Shishido Shirou (male body and all), and that dude is in love with Youko. Her mother is a nympho icon.

ACTUALLY A WOLFMAN

KOUMOTO AKANE

HORNED DEVIL

The principal of Asahi's high school looks adorable, but she's actually a **millennia-old devil.** The great-great-grandmother of Asahi's homeroom teacher, Koumoto-sensei. Her true weakness is junk food.

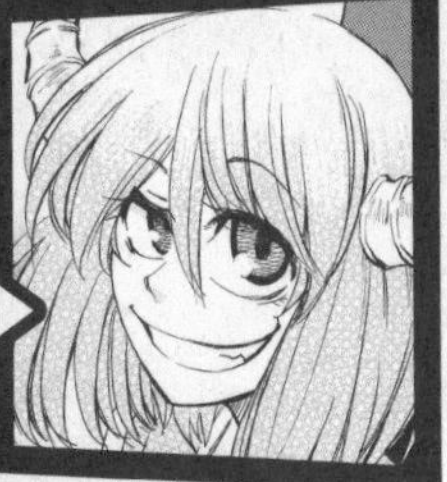

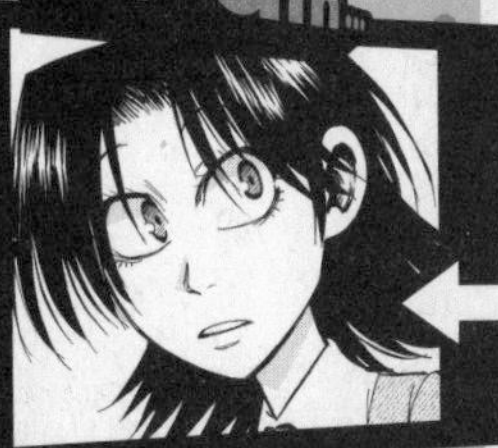

KOUMOTO AKARI

FORMER GANGSTER

The teacher in charge of Asahi's class. Although she's a descendant of Principal Akane, she has no demon powers of her own. Formerly a gangster, currently single.

SHIROGANE KAREN

ACTUALLY AN ANGEL

The student council president of Asahi's school. She lost her halo to one of the principal's practical jokes and thus became a (self-proclaimed) **fallen angel.** Was a classmate of Shiragami-san's parents.

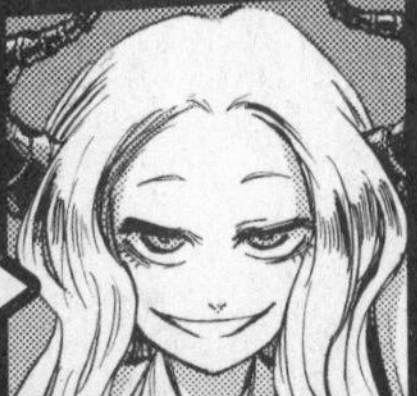

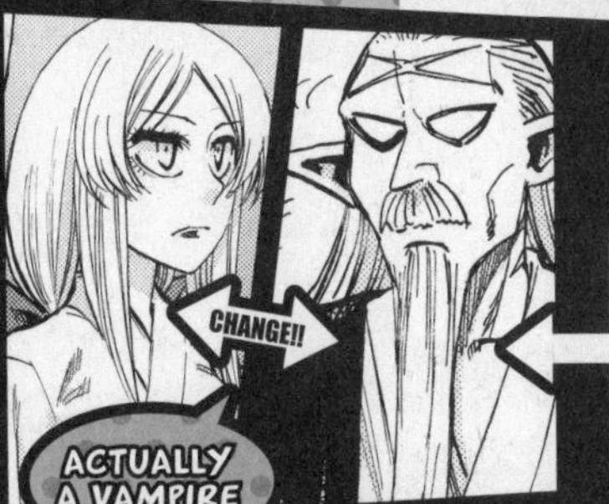
CHANGE!!
ACTUALLY A VAMPIRE

RYOKUENZAKA YUMI
SHIRAGAMI GENJIROU

A full-blooded vampire and Shiragami-san's **father.** Worried about Shiragami-san, he has transformed into Ryokuenzaka-sensei and infiltrated the school as the **assistant teacher** of Asahi's class.

THEM

ASAHI'S WORTHLESS FRIENDS

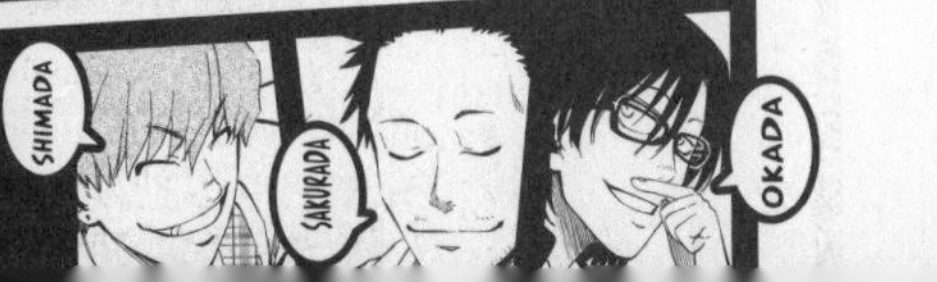
SHIMADA
SAKURADA
OKADA

SEVEN SEAS ENTERTAINMENT PRESENTS

My Monster Secret
"Actually, I am..."

story and art by Eiji Masuda
VOLUME 13

TRANSLATION
Alethea and Athena Nibley

ADAPTATION
Rebecca Scoble

LETTERING AND RETOUCH
Annaliese Christman

LOGO DESIGN
Karis Page

COVER DESIGN
Nicky Lim

PROOFREADER
Shanti Whitesides
Danielle King

EDITOR
Jenn Grunigen

PRODUCTION ASSISTANT
CK Russell

PRODUCTION MANAGER
Lissa Pattillo

EDITOR IN CHIEF
Adam Arnold

PUBLISHER
Jason DeAngelis

JITSUHA WATASHIHA Volume 13
© EIJI MASUDA 2015
Originally published in Japan in 2015 by Akita Publishing Co., Ltd.
English translation rights arranged with Akita Publishing Co., Ltd.
through TOHAN CORPORATION, Tokyo.

Seven Seas books may be purchased in bulk for promotional, educational, or
business use. Please contact your local bookseller or the Macmillan Corporate
and Premium Sales Department at 1-800-221-7945, extension 5442, or by
e-mail at MacmillanSpecialMarkets@macmillan.com.

Seven Seas and the Seven Seas logo are trademarks of
Seven Seas Entertainment, LLC. All rights reserved.

ISBN: 978-1-626929-20-3

Printed in Canada

First Printing: October 2018

10 9 8 7 6 5 4 3 2 1

FOLLOW US ONLINE: www.sevenseasentertainment.com

READING DIRECTIONS

This book reads from *right to left*, Japanese style.
If this is your first time reading manga, you start
reading from the top right panel on each page and
take it from there. If you get lost, just follow the
numbered diagram here. It may seem backwards at
first, but you'll get the hang of it! Have fun!!

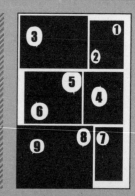

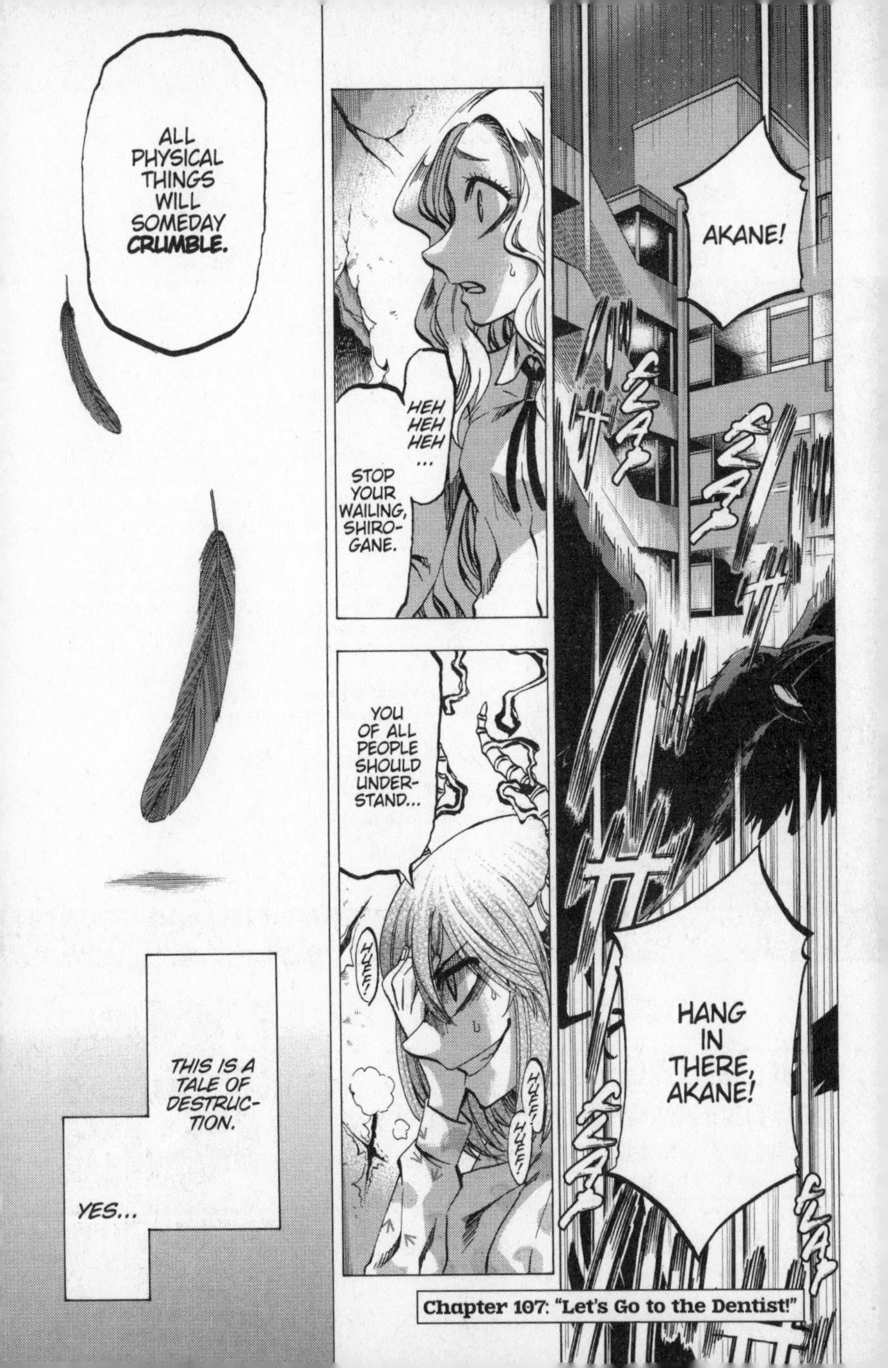
AKANE!
FLAP
FLAP
HANG IN THERE, AKANE!
FLAP
FLAP
FLAP
Chapter 107: "Let's Go to the Dentist!"
HEH HEH HEH ...
STOP YOUR WAILING, SHIRO-GANE.
YOU OF ALL PEOPLE SHOULD UNDER-STAND...
HUFF!
HUFF! HUFF!
ALL PHYSICAL THINGS WILL SOMEDAY CRUMBLE.
THIS IS A TALE OF DESTRUC-TION.
YES...

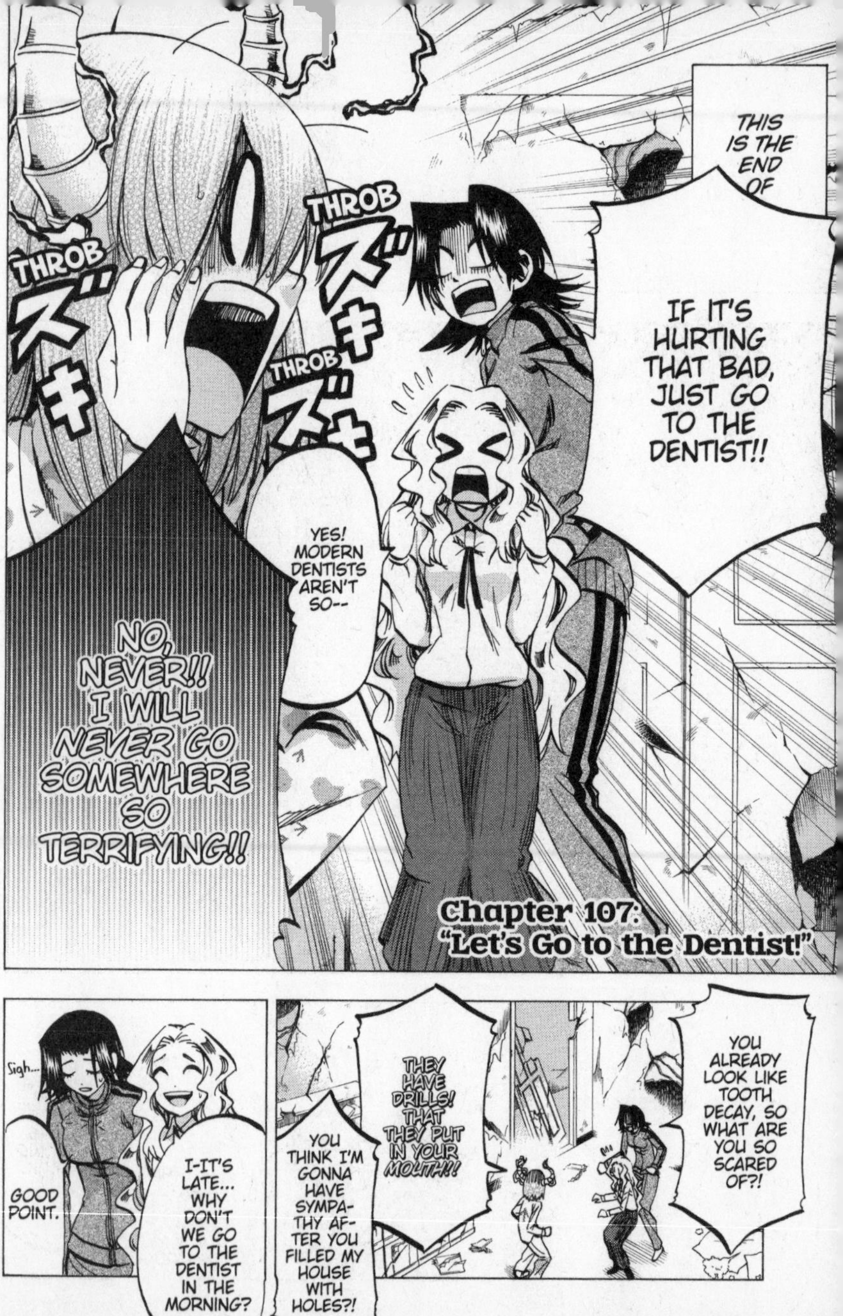
THIS IS THE END OF
IF IT'S HURTING THAT BAD, JUST GO TO THE DENTIST!!
THROB
THROB
THROB
YES! MODERN DENTISTS AREN'T SO--
NO, NEVER!! I WILL NEVER GO SOMEWHERE SO TERRIFYING!!
Chapter 107: "Let's Go to the Dentist!"
YOU ALREADY LOOK LIKE TOOTH DECAY, SO WHAT ARE YOU SO SCARED OF?!
THEY HAVE DRILLS! THAT THEY PUT IN YOUR MOUTH!!
YOU THINK I'M GONNA HAVE SYMPATHY AFTER YOU FILLED MY HOUSE WITH HOLES?!
I-IT'S LATE... WHY DON'T WE GO TO THE DENTIST IN THE MORNING?
Sigh...
GOOD POINT.

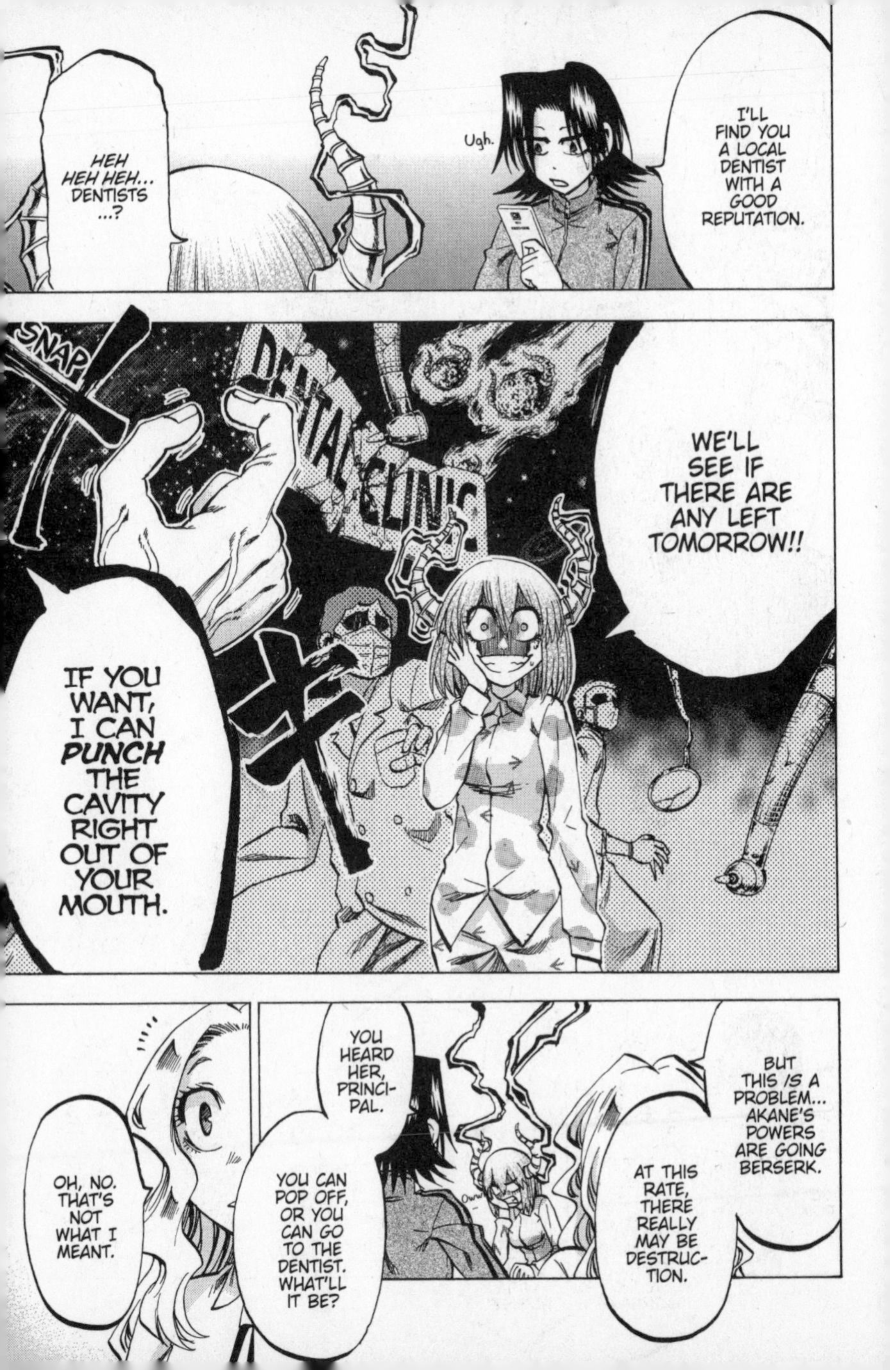
I'LL FIND YOU A LOCAL DENTIST WITH A GOOD REPUTATION.
Ugh.
HEH HEH HEH... DENTISTS ...?
WE'LL SEE IF THERE ARE ANY LEFT TOMORROW!!
DENTAL CLINIC
SNAP
IF YOU WANT, I CAN *PUNCH* THE CAVITY RIGHT OUT OF YOUR MOUTH.
BUT THIS *IS* A PROBLEM... AKANE'S POWERS ARE GOING BERSERK.
AT THIS RATE, THERE REALLY MAY BE DESTRUCTION.
YOU HEARD HER, PRINCIPAL.
Oww
YOU CAN POP OFF, OR YOU CAN GO TO THE DENTIST. WHAT'LL IT BE?
OH, NO. THAT'S NOT WHAT I MEANT.

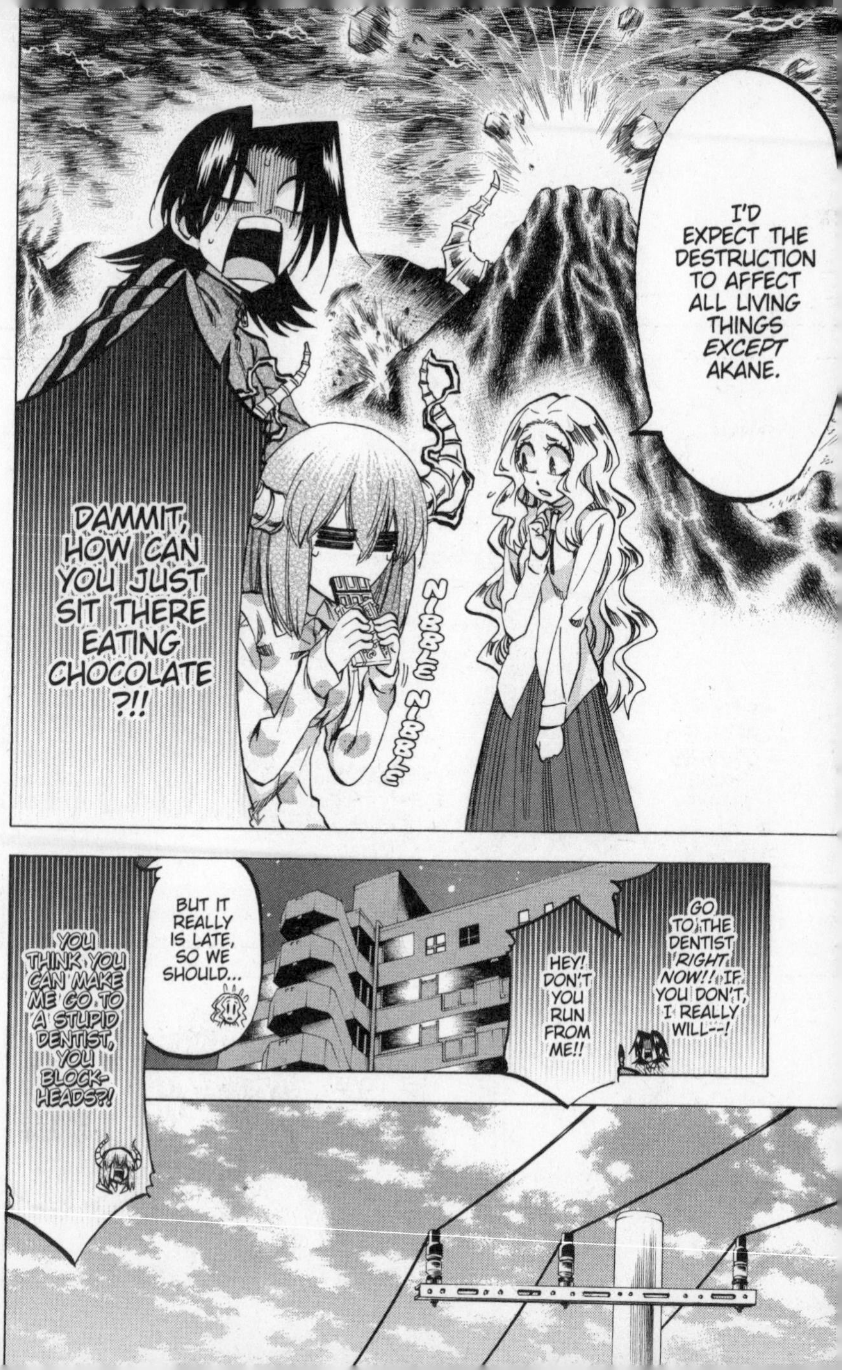
I'D EXPECT THE DESTRUCTION TO AFFECT ALL LIVING THINGS *EXCEPT* AKANE.
NIBBLE NIBBLE
DAMMIT, HOW CAN YOU JUST SIT THERE EATING CHOCOLATE ?!!
GO TO THE DENTIST *RIGHT NOW!!* IF YOU DON'T, I REALLY WILL--!
HEY! DON'T YOU RUN FROM ME!!
BUT IT REALLY IS LATE, SO WE SHOULD...
YOU THINK YOU CAN MAKE ME GO TO A STUPID DENTIST, YOU BLOCK-HEADS?!

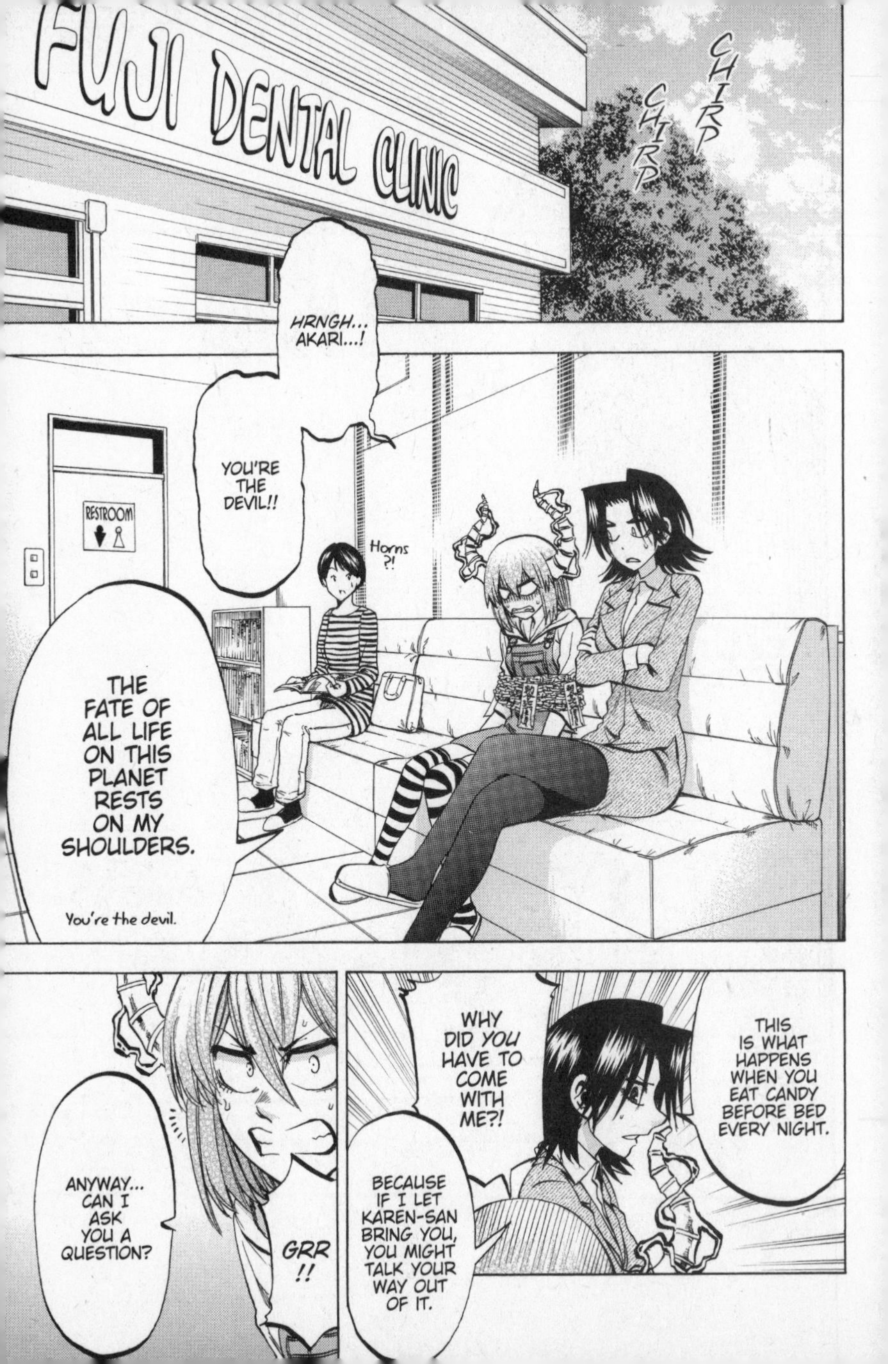
CHIRP
CHIRP
FUJI DENTAL CLINIC
HRNGH... AKARI...!
YOU'RE THE DEVIL!!
Horns ?!
RESTROOM
THE FATE OF ALL LIFE ON THIS PLANET RESTS ON MY SHOULDERS.
You're the devil.
THIS IS WHAT HAPPENS WHEN YOU EAT CANDY BEFORE BED EVERY NIGHT.
WHY DID YOU HAVE TO COME WITH ME?!
BECAUSE IF I LET KAREN-SAN BRING YOU, YOU MIGHT TALK YOUR WAY OUT OF IT.
GRR !!
ANYWAY... CAN I ASK YOU A QUESTION?

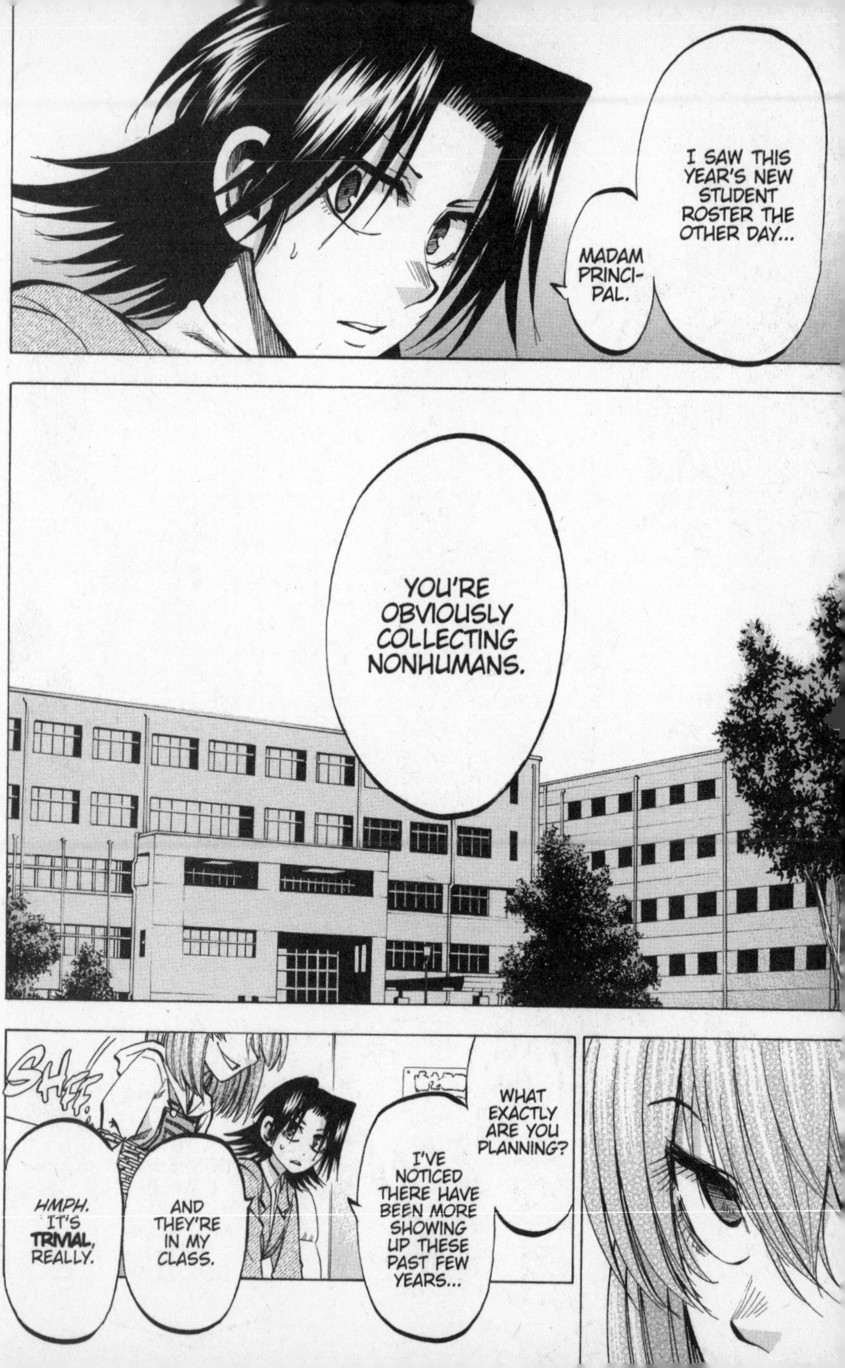
I SAW THIS YEAR'S NEW STUDENT ROSTER THE OTHER DAY...
MADAM PRINCIPAL.
YOU'RE OBVIOUSLY COLLECTING NONHUMANS.
WHAT EXACTLY ARE YOU PLANNING?
I'VE NOTICED THERE HAVE BEEN MORE SHOWING UP THESE PAST FEW YEARS...
AND THEY'RE IN MY CLASS.
SHFF.
HMPH. IT'S TRIVIAL, REALLY.

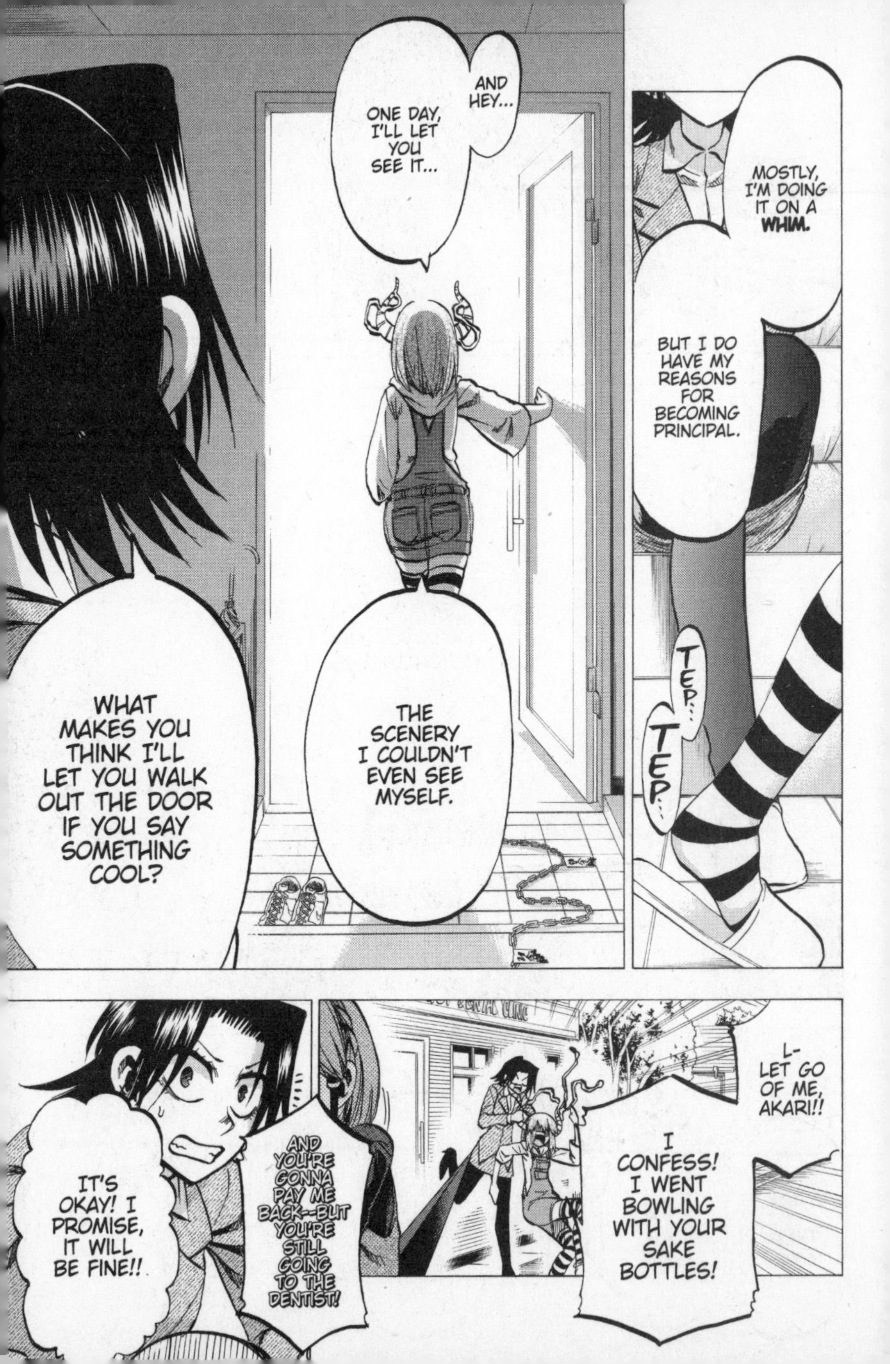

MOSTLY, I'M DOING IT ON A WHIM.
BUT I DO HAVE MY REASONS FOR BECOMING PRINCIPAL.
TEP...
TEP...
AND HEY...
ONE DAY, I'LL LET YOU SEE IT...
THE SCENERY I COULDN'T EVEN SEE MYSELF.
WHAT MAKES YOU THINK I'LL LET YOU WALK OUT THE DOOR IF YOU SAY SOMETHING COOL?
L- LET GO OF ME, AKARI!!
I CONFESS! I WENT BOWLING WITH YOUR SAKE BOTTLES!
AND YOU'RE GONNA PAY ME BACK--BUT YOU'RE STILL GOING TO THE DENTIST!
IT'S OKAY! I PROMISE, IT WILL BE FINE!!

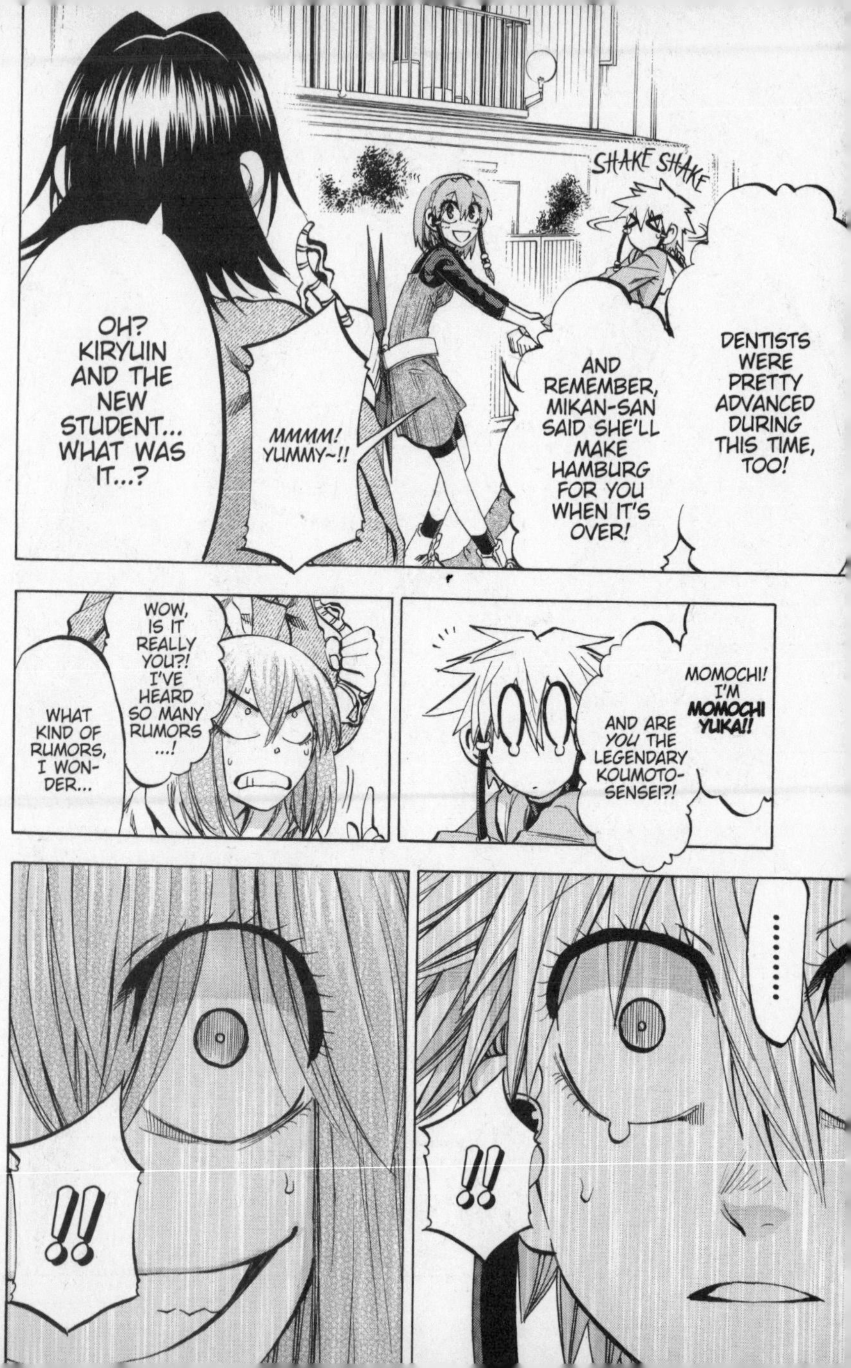
SHAKE SHAKE
DENTISTS WERE PRETTY ADVANCED DURING THIS TIME, TOO!
AND REMEMBER, MIKAN-SAN SAID SHE'LL MAKE HAMBURG FOR YOU WHEN IT'S OVER!
MMMM! YUMMY~!!
OH? KIRYUIN AND THE NEW STUDENT... WHAT WAS IT...?
MOMOCHI! I'M **MOMOCHI YUKA!!**
AND ARE *YOU* THE LEGENDARY KOUMOTO-SENSEI?!
WOW, IS IT REALLY YOU?! I'VE HEARD SO MANY RUMORS ...!
WHAT KIND OF RUMORS, I WONDER...
......
!!
!!

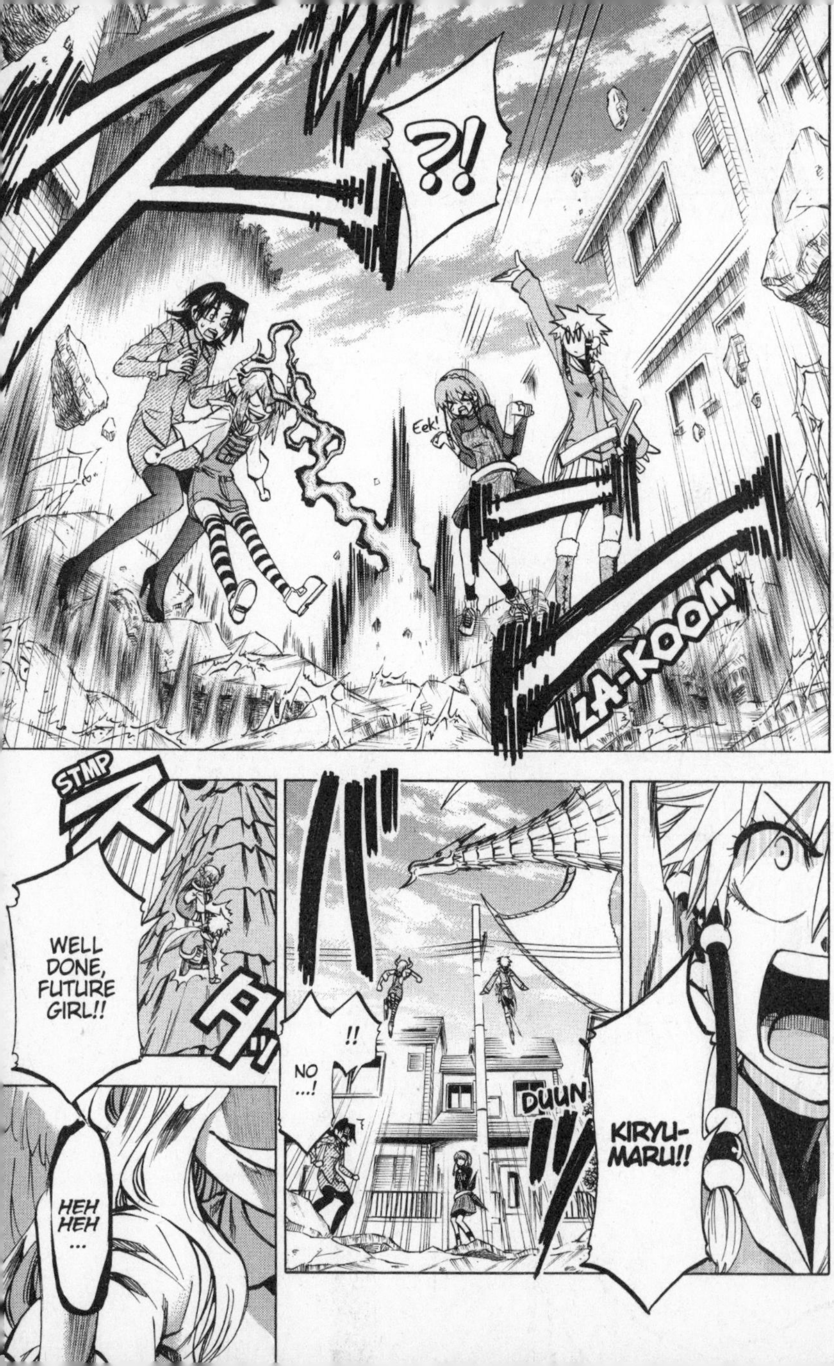

?!
Eek!
ZA-KOOM
KIRYU-MARU!!
!!
NO ...!
DUUN
STMP
WELL DONE, FUTURE GIRL!!
HEH HEH ...

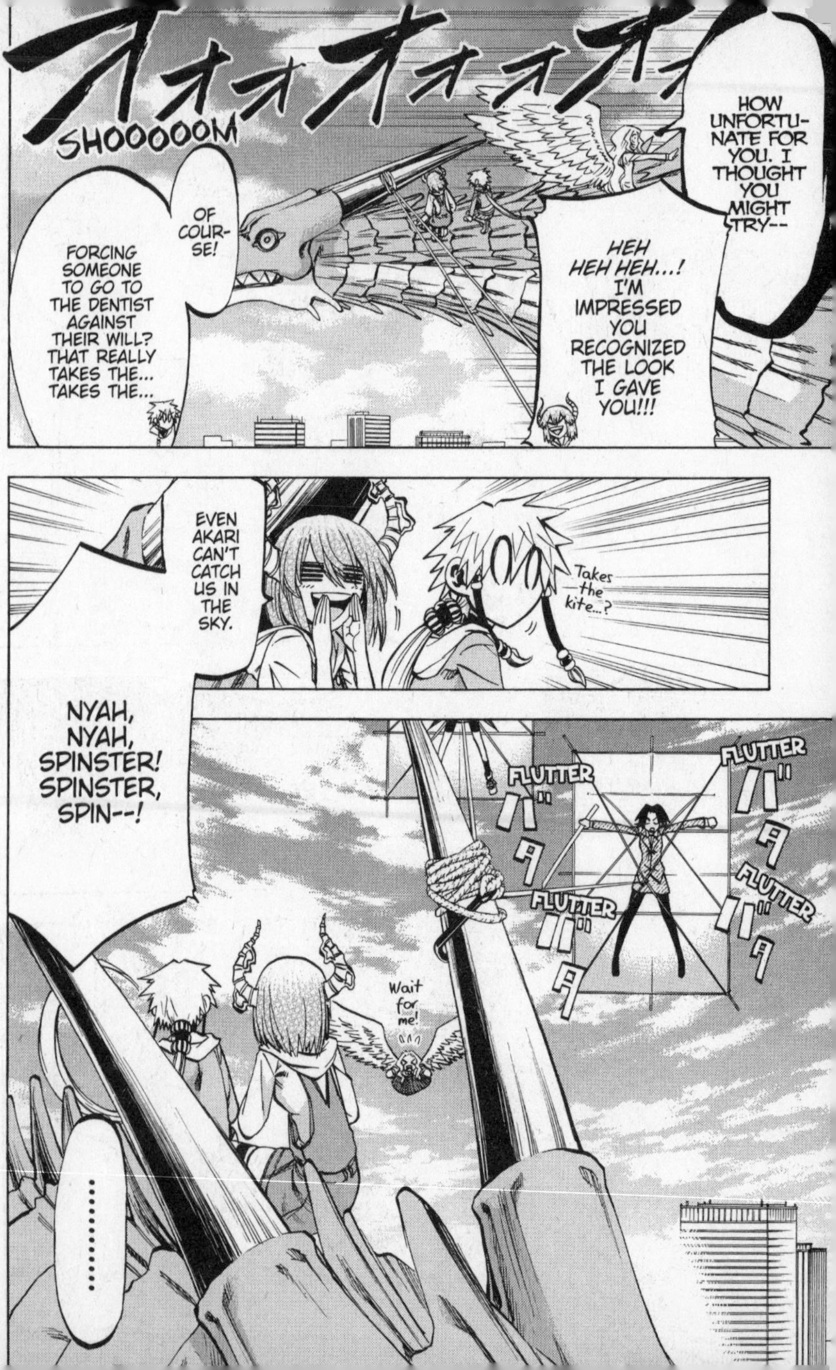
HOW UNFORTUNATE FOR YOU. I THOUGHT YOU MIGHT TRY--
オォォオォォオ
SHOOOOOM
HEH HEH HEH...! I'M IMPRESSED YOU RECOGNIZED THE LOOK I GAVE YOU!!!
OF COURSE!
FORCING SOMEONE TO GO TO THE DENTIST AGAINST THEIR WILL? THAT REALLY TAKES THE... TAKES THE...
Takes the kite...?
EVEN AKARI CAN'T CATCH US IN THE SKY.
FLUTTER
FLUTTER
FLUTTER
FLUTTER
NYAH, NYAH, SPINSTER! SPINSTER, SPIN--!
Wait for me!
....

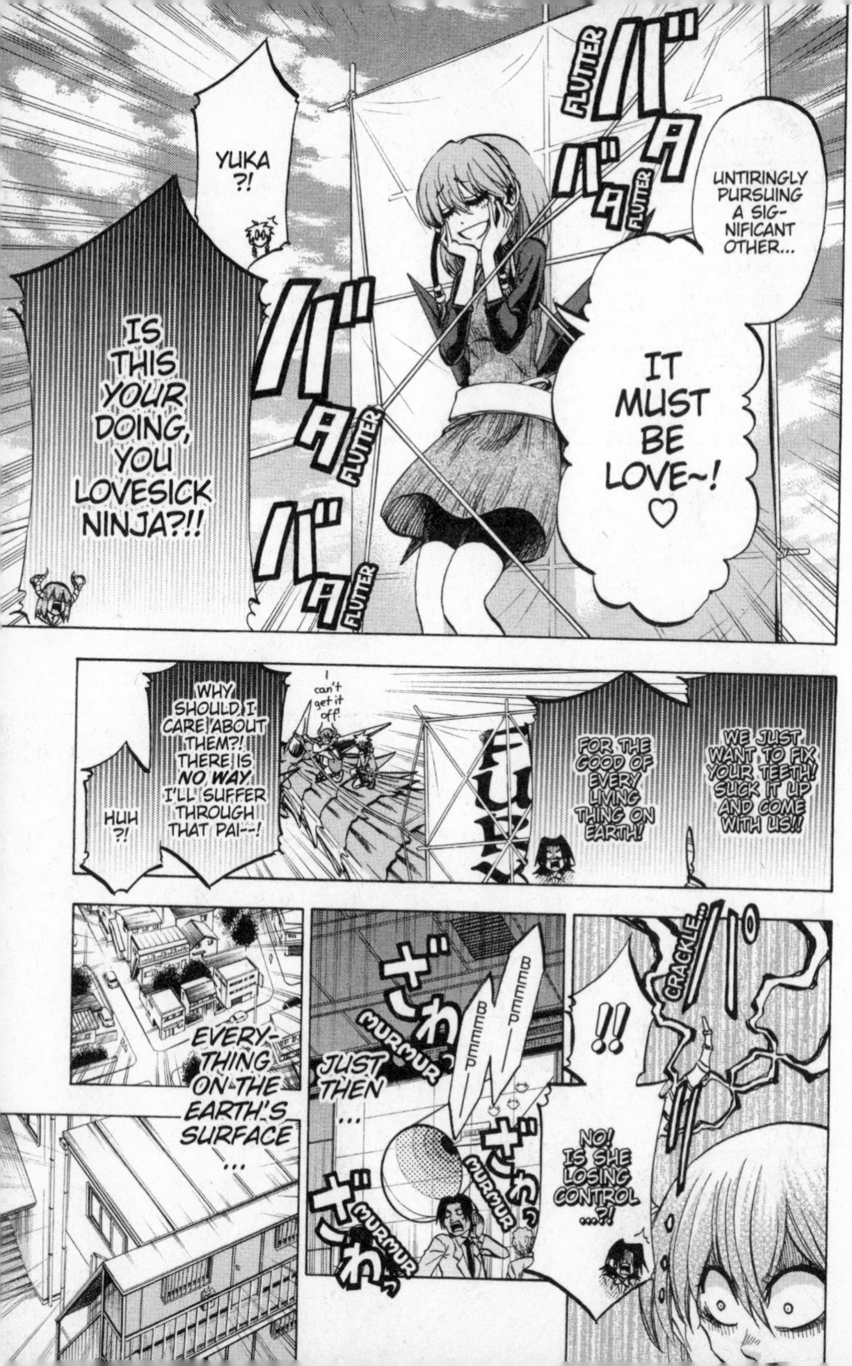
FLUTTER
FLUTTER
UNTIRINGLY PURSUING A SIGNIFICANT OTHER...
IT MUST BE LOVE~! ♡
FLUTTER
FLUTTER
YUKA ?!
IS THIS *YOUR* DOING, YOU LOVESICK NINJA?!!
WE JUST WANT TO FIX YOUR TEETH! SUCK IT UP AND COME WITH US!!
FOR THE GOOD OF EVERY LIVING THING ON EARTH!
I can't get it off!
WHY SHOULD I CARE ABOUT THEM?! THERE IS ***NO WAY*** I'LL SUFFER THROUGH THAT PAI--!
HUH ?!
CRACKLE...
!!
NO! IS SHE LOSING CONTROL...?!
BEEEP
BEEEP
MURMUR
JUST THEN...
MURMUR
MURMUR
EVERYTHING ON THE EARTH'S SURFACE...

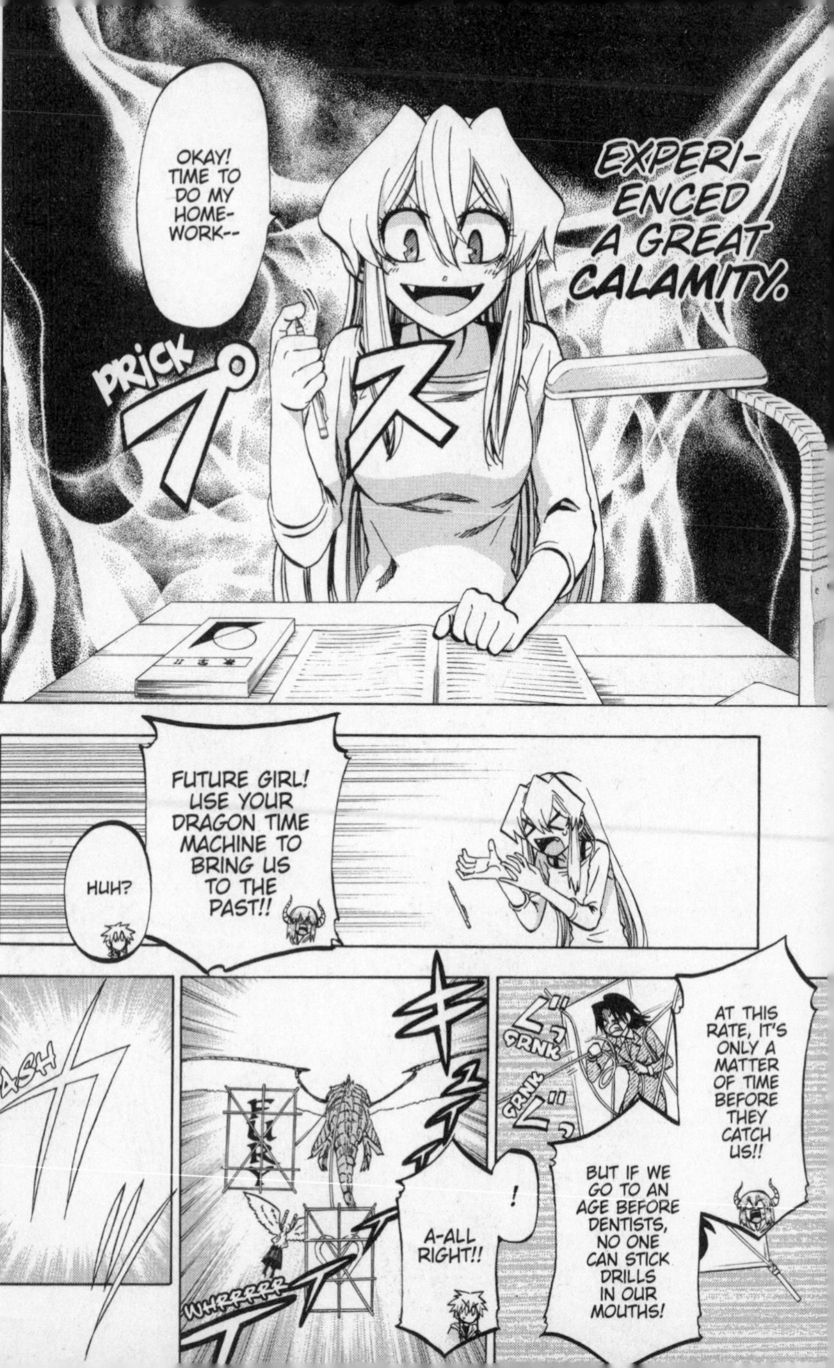

EXPERI-ENCED A GREAT CALAMITY.
OKAY! TIME TO DO MY HOME-WORK--
PRICK
FUTURE GIRL! USE YOUR DRAGON TIME MACHINE TO BRING US TO THE PAST!!
HUH?
AT THIS RATE, IT'S ONLY A MATTER OF TIME BEFORE THEY CATCH US!!
GRNK
GRNK
BUT IF WE GO TO AN AGE BEFORE DENTISTS, NO ONE CAN STICK DRILLS IN OUR MOUTHS!
!
A-ALL RIGHT!!
WHRRRRR
FLASH

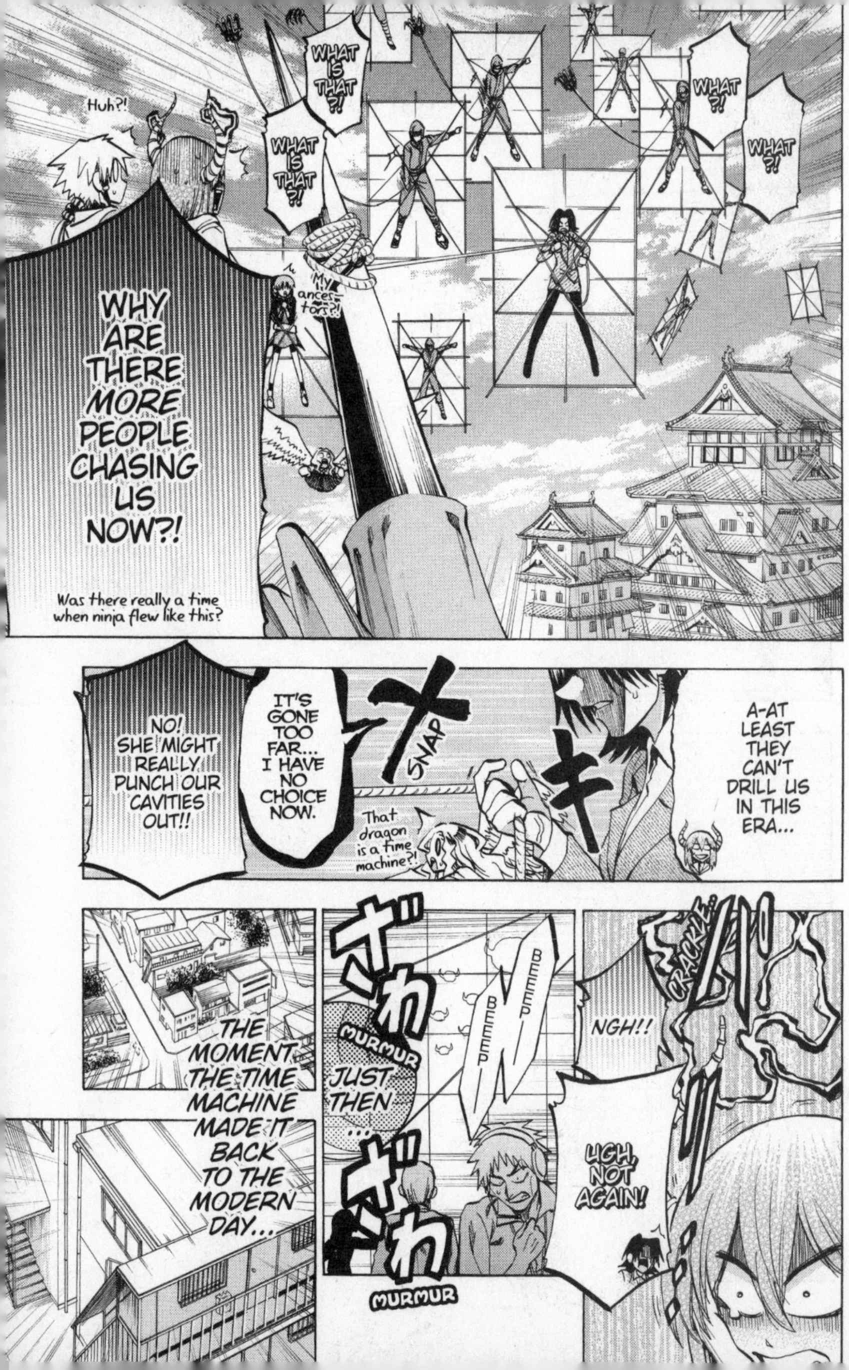
WHAT ?!
WHAT ?!
WHAT IS THAT ?!
WHAT IS THAT ?!
Huh?!
My ancestors?!
WHY ARE THERE MORE PEOPLE CHASING US NOW?!
Was there really a time when ninja flew like this?
A-AT LEAST THEY CAN'T DRILL US IN THIS ERA...
SNAP
That dragon is a time machine?!
IT'S GONE TOO FAR... I HAVE NO CHOICE NOW.
NO! SHE MIGHT REALLY PUNCH OUR CAVITIES OUT!!
CRACKLE
NGH!!
UGH, NOT AGAIN!
BEEEP
BEEEP
ざわ
MURMUR
JUST THEN...
ざわ
MURMUR
THE MOMENT THE TIME MACHINE MADE IT BACK TO THE MODERN DAY...

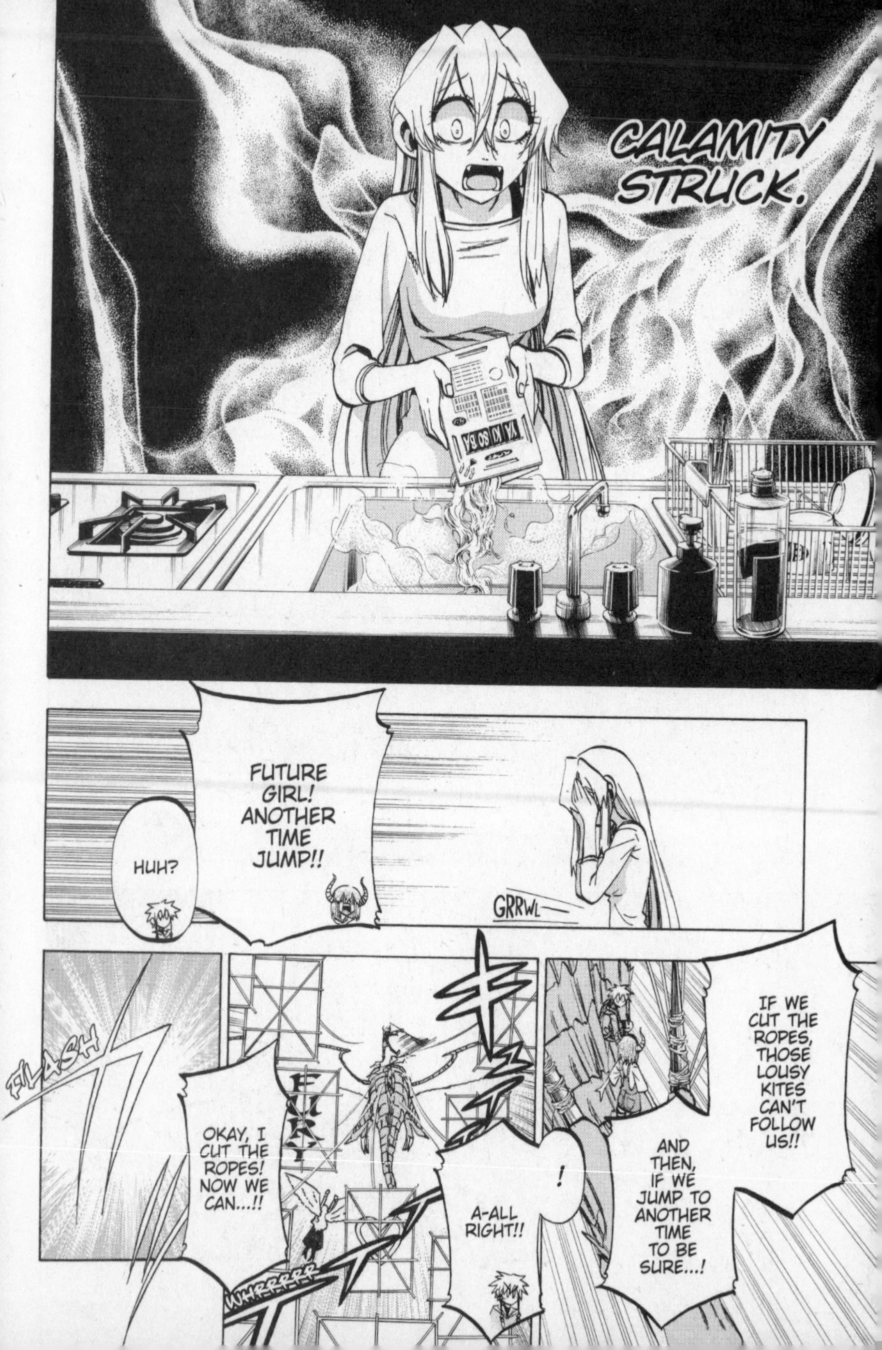
CALAMITY STRUCK.
YA KI SO BA
GRRWL
FUTURE GIRL! ANOTHER TIME JUMP!!
HUH?
IF WE CUT THE ROPES, THOSE LOUSY KITES CAN'T FOLLOW US!!
AND THEN, IF WE JUMP TO ANOTHER TIME TO BE SURE...!
A-ALL RIGHT!!
!
FURY
OKAY, I CUT THE ROPES! NOW WE CAN...!!
WHRRRRR
FLASH

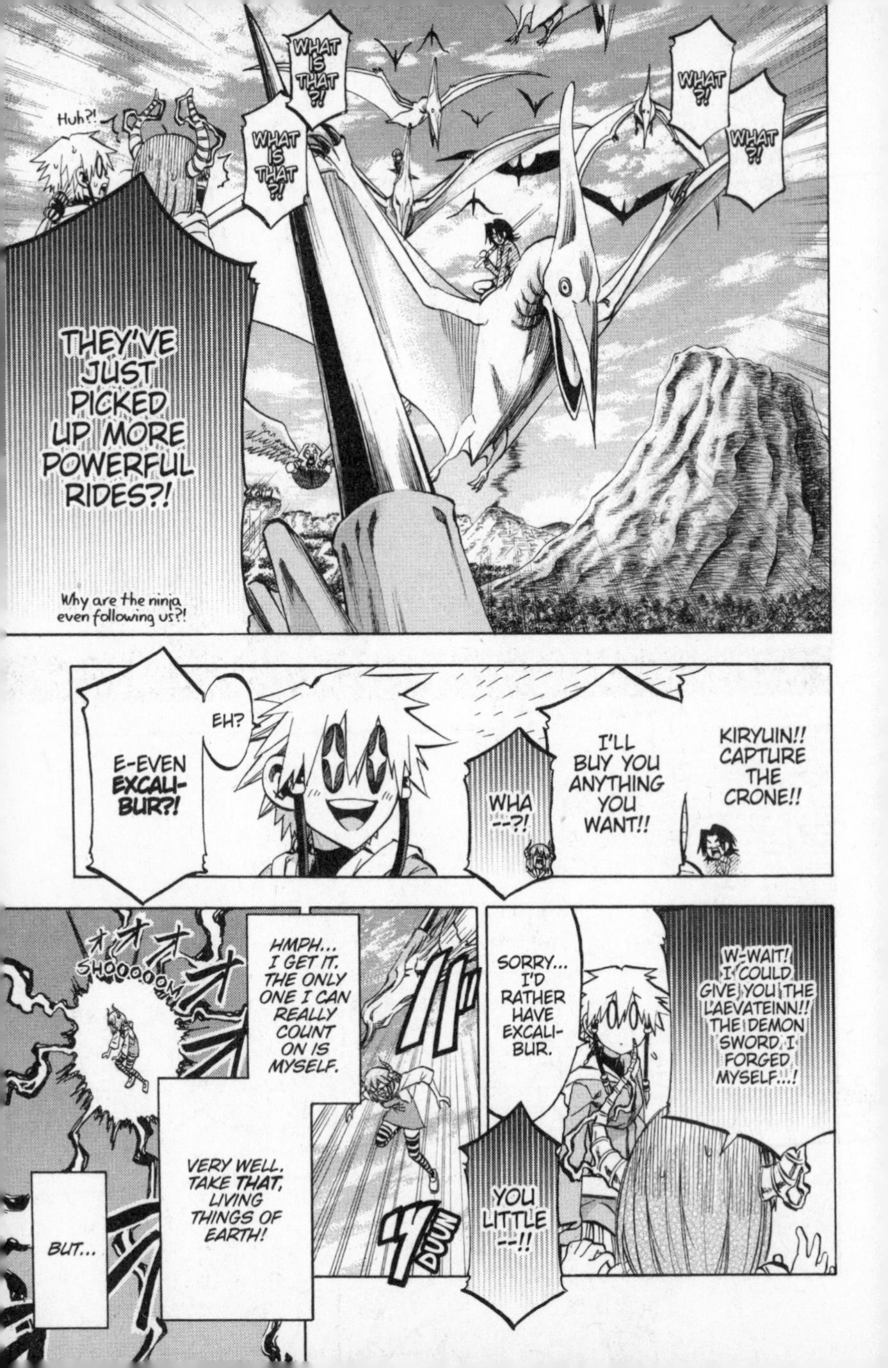
WHAT?!
WHAT?!
WHAT IS THAT?!
WHAT IS THAT?!
Huh?!
THEY'VE JUST PICKED UP MORE POWERFUL RIDES?!
Why are the ninja even following us?!
KIRYUIN!! CAPTURE THE CRONE!!
I'LL BUY YOU ANYTHING YOU WANT!!
WHA--?!
EH?
E-EVEN EXCALIBUR?!
W-WAIT! I COULD GIVE YOU THE LAEVATEINN!! THE DEMON SWORD I FORGED MYSELF...!
SORRY... I'D RATHER HAVE EXCALIBUR.
YOU LITTLE--!!
HMPH... I GET IT. THE ONLY ONE I CAN REALLY COUNT ON IS MYSELF.
DUUN
VERY WELL. TAKE THAT, LIVING THINGS OF EARTH!
オオオオ
SHOOOOOM
BUT...

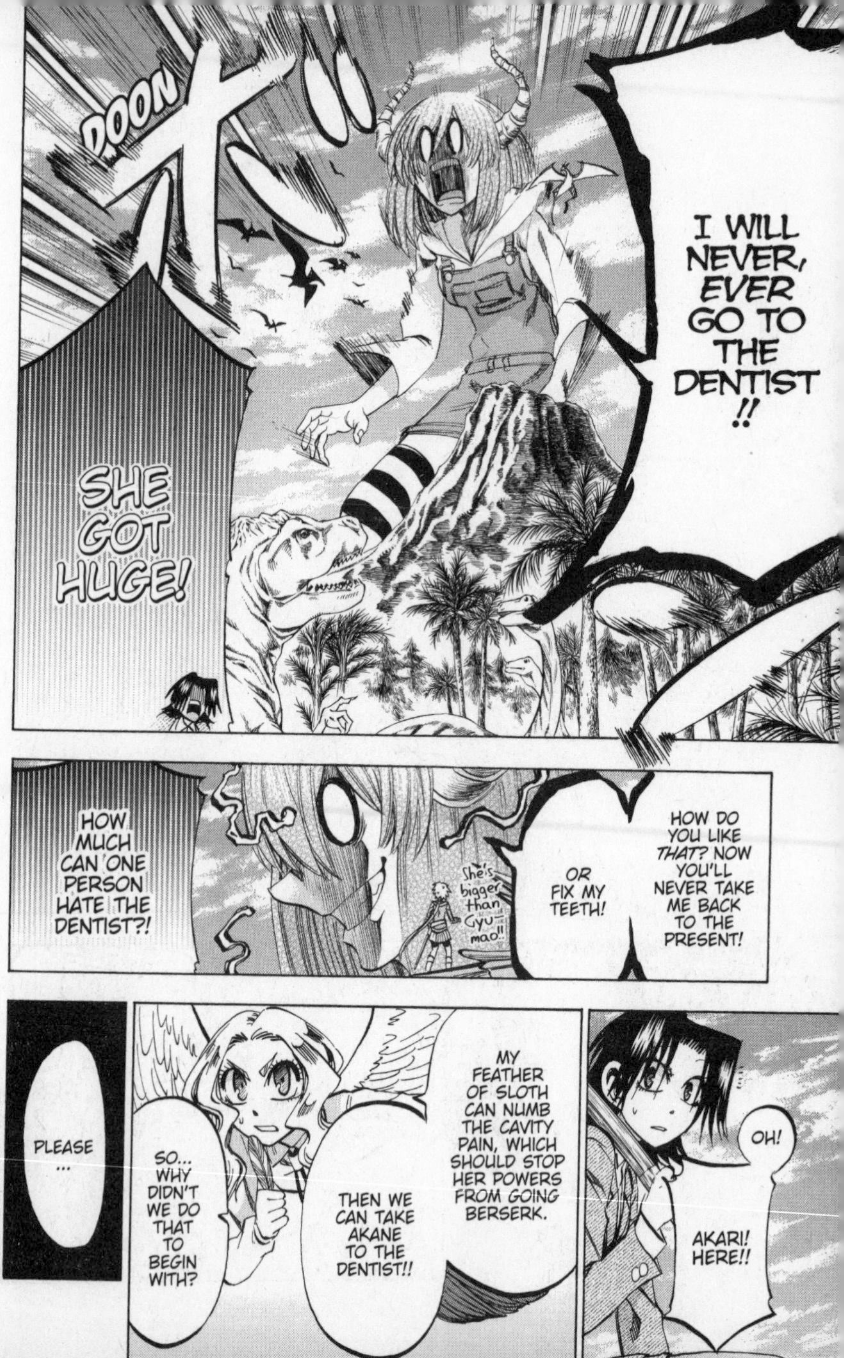
I WILL NEVER, *EVER* GO TO THE DENTIST!!
DOON
SHE GOT HUGE!
HOW DO YOU LIKE *THAT*? NOW YOU'LL NEVER TAKE ME BACK TO THE PRESENT!
OR FIX MY TEETH!
She's bigger than Gyu-mao!!
HOW MUCH CAN ONE PERSON HATE THE DENTIST?!
OH!
AKARI! HERE!!
MY FEATHER OF SLOTH CAN NUMB THE CAVITY PAIN, WHICH SHOULD STOP HER POWERS FROM GOING BERSERK.
THEN WE CAN TAKE AKANE TO THE DENTIST!!
SO... WHY DIDN'T WE DO THAT TO BEGIN WITH?
PLEASE ...

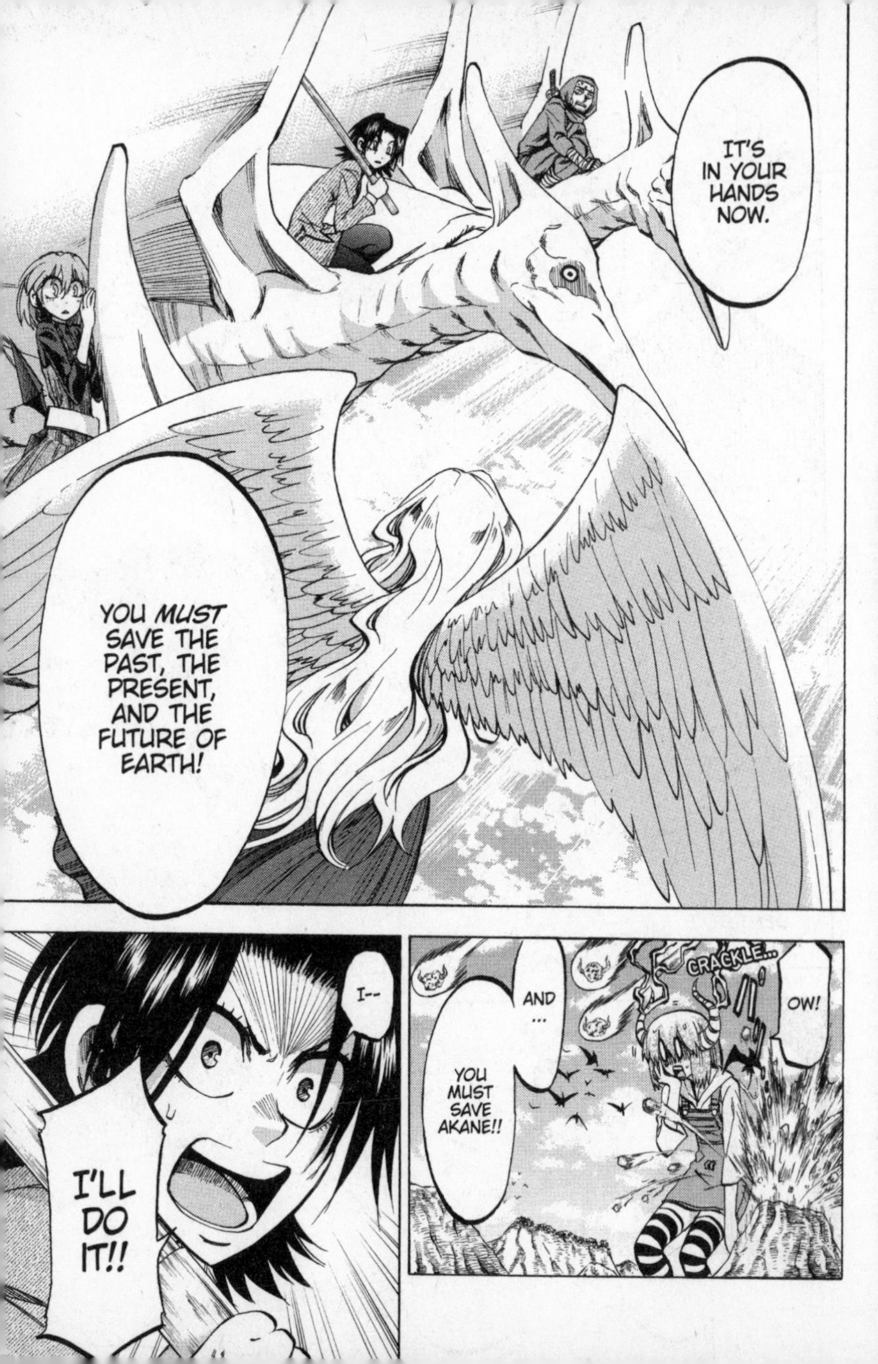
IT'S IN YOUR HANDS NOW.
YOU MUST SAVE THE PAST, THE PRESENT, AND THE FUTURE OF EARTH!
CRACKLE...
OW!
AND ...
YOU MUST SAVE AKANE!!
I--
I'LL DO IT!!

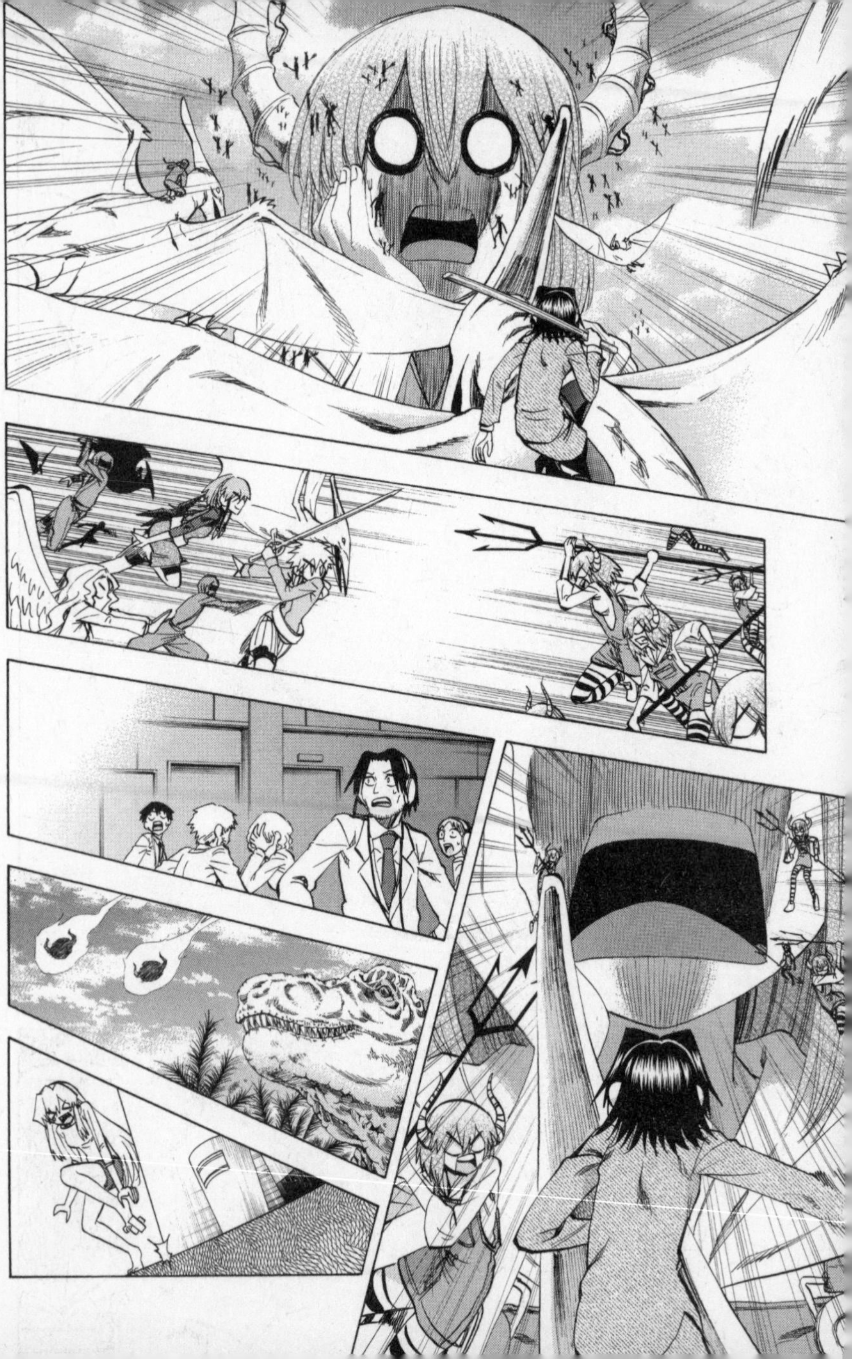

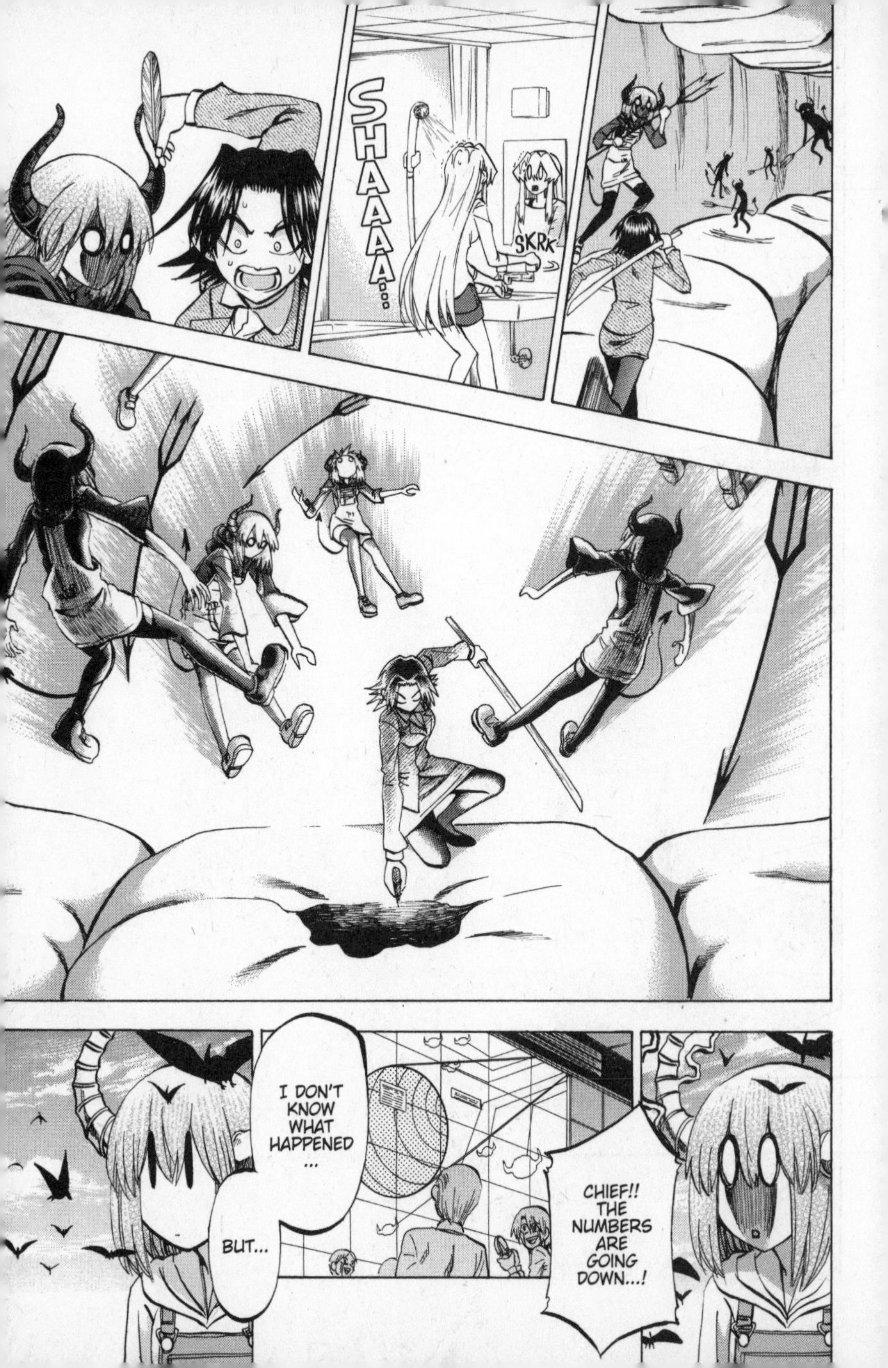
SHAAAA...
SKRK
CHIEF!! THE NUMBERS ARE GOING DOWN...!
I DON'T KNOW WHAT HAPPENED ...
BUT...

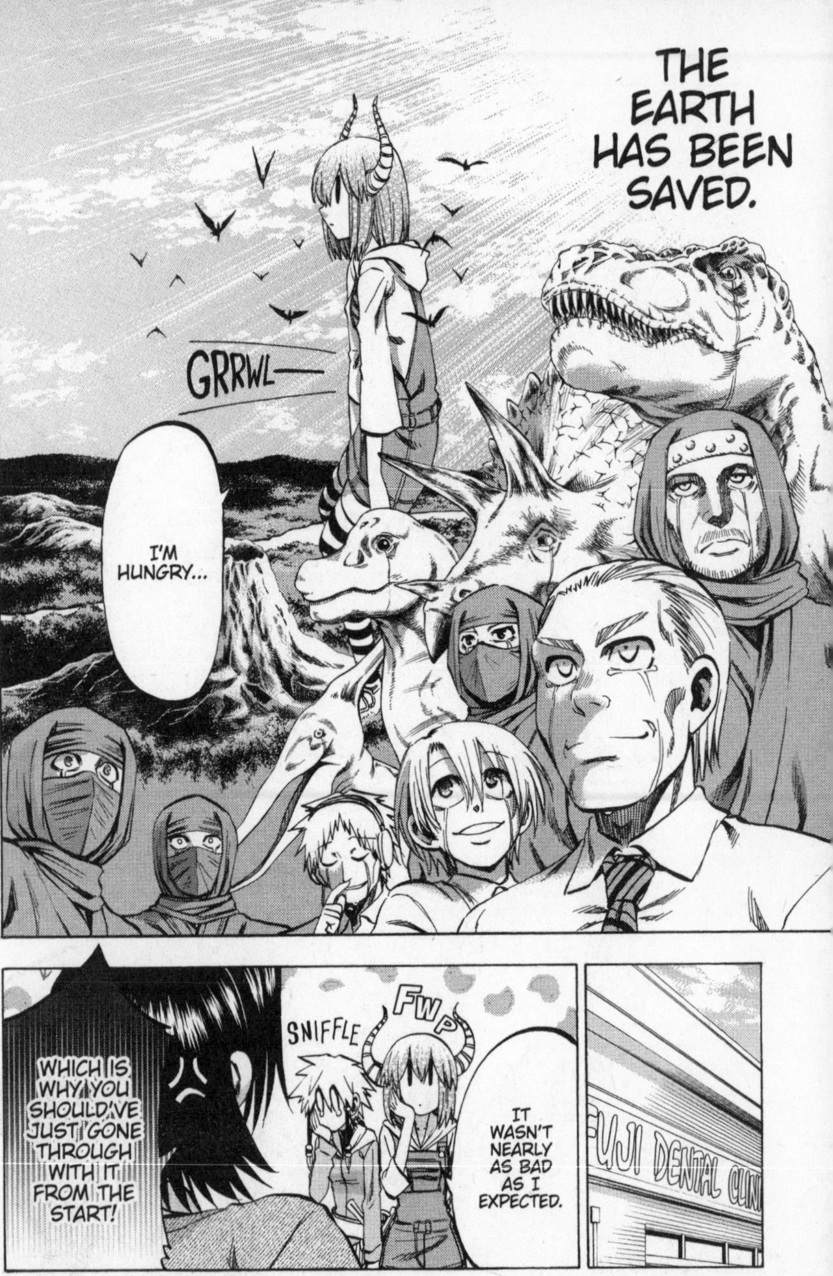
THE EARTH HAS BEEN SAVED.
GRRWL—
I'M HUNGRY...
FUJI DENTAL CLIN
FWP
SNIFFLE
IT WASN'T NEARLY AS BAD AS I EXPECTED.
WHICH IS WHY YOU SHOULD'VE JUST GONE THROUGH WITH IT FROM THE START!

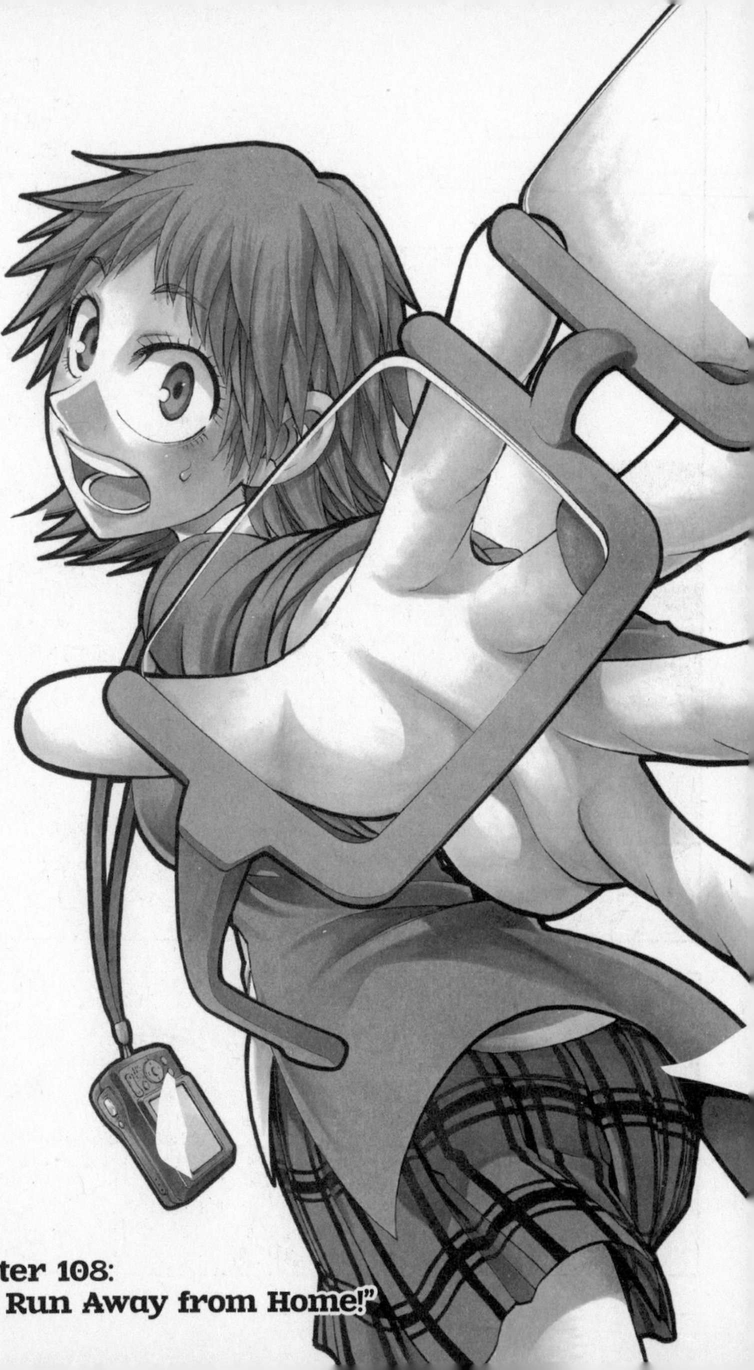

Chapter 108:
“Let’s Run Away from Home!”

TOP SECRET

My Monster Secret 13

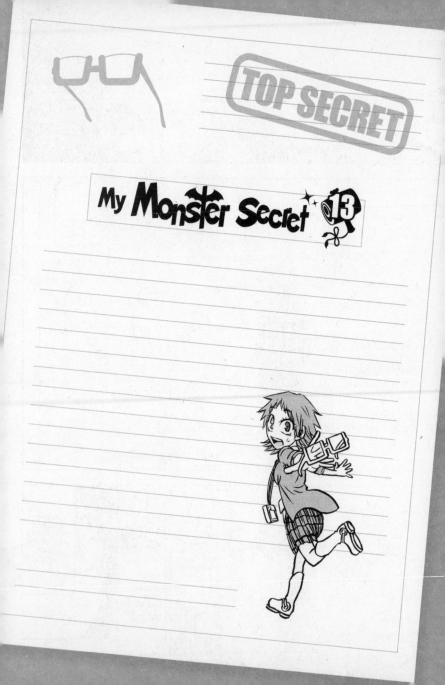

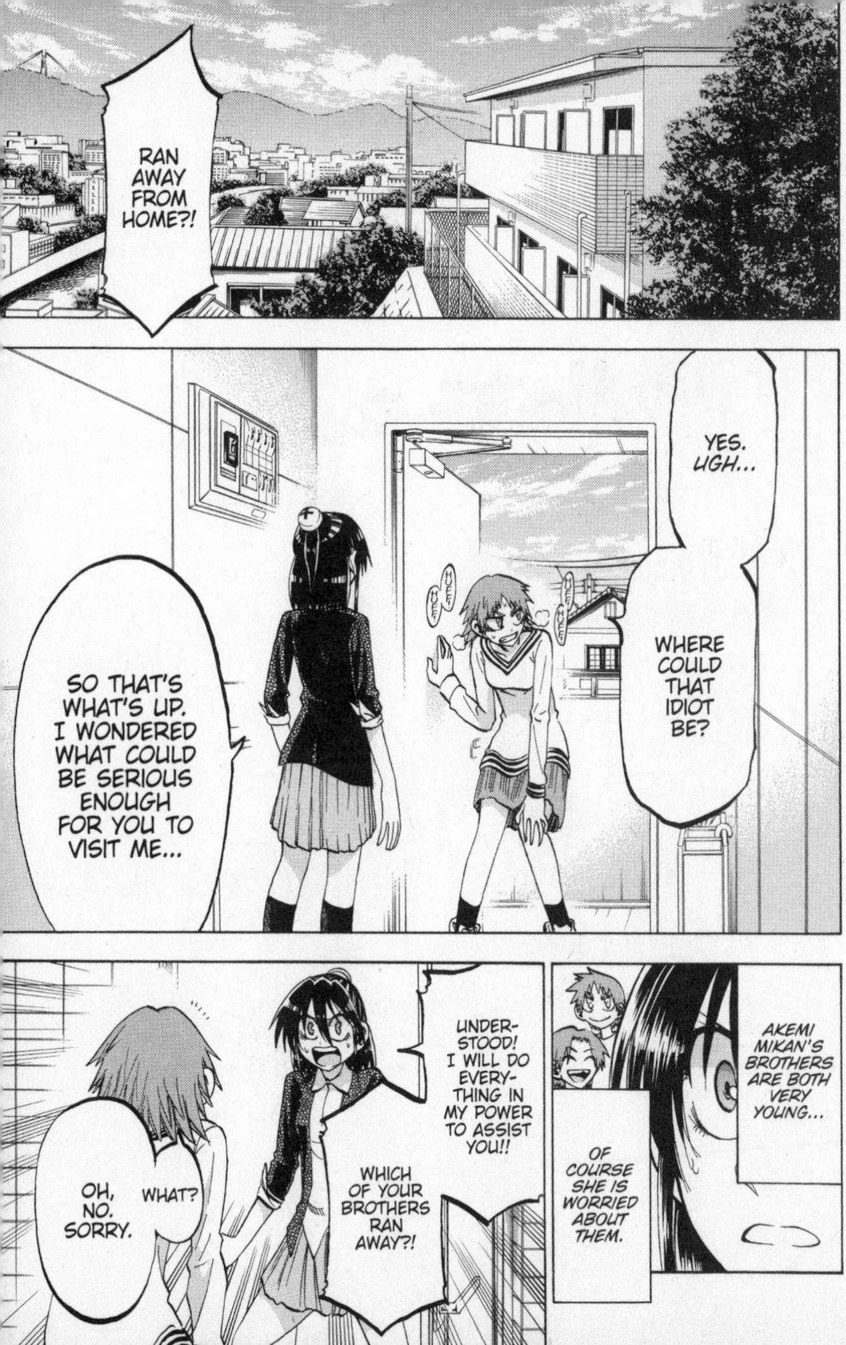

RAN AWAY FROM HOME?!
YES. UGH...
WHERE COULD THAT IDIOT BE?
HUFF HUFF
HUFF HUFF
SO THAT'S WHAT'S UP. I WONDERED WHAT COULD BE SERIOUS ENOUGH FOR YOU TO VISIT ME...
AKEMI MIKAN'S BROTHERS ARE BOTH VERY YOUNG...
OF COURSE SHE IS WORRIED ABOUT THEM.
UNDER-STOOD! I WILL DO EVERY-THING IN MY POWER TO ASSIST YOU!!
WHICH OF YOUR BROTHERS RAN AWAY?!
WHAT?
OH, NO. SORRY.

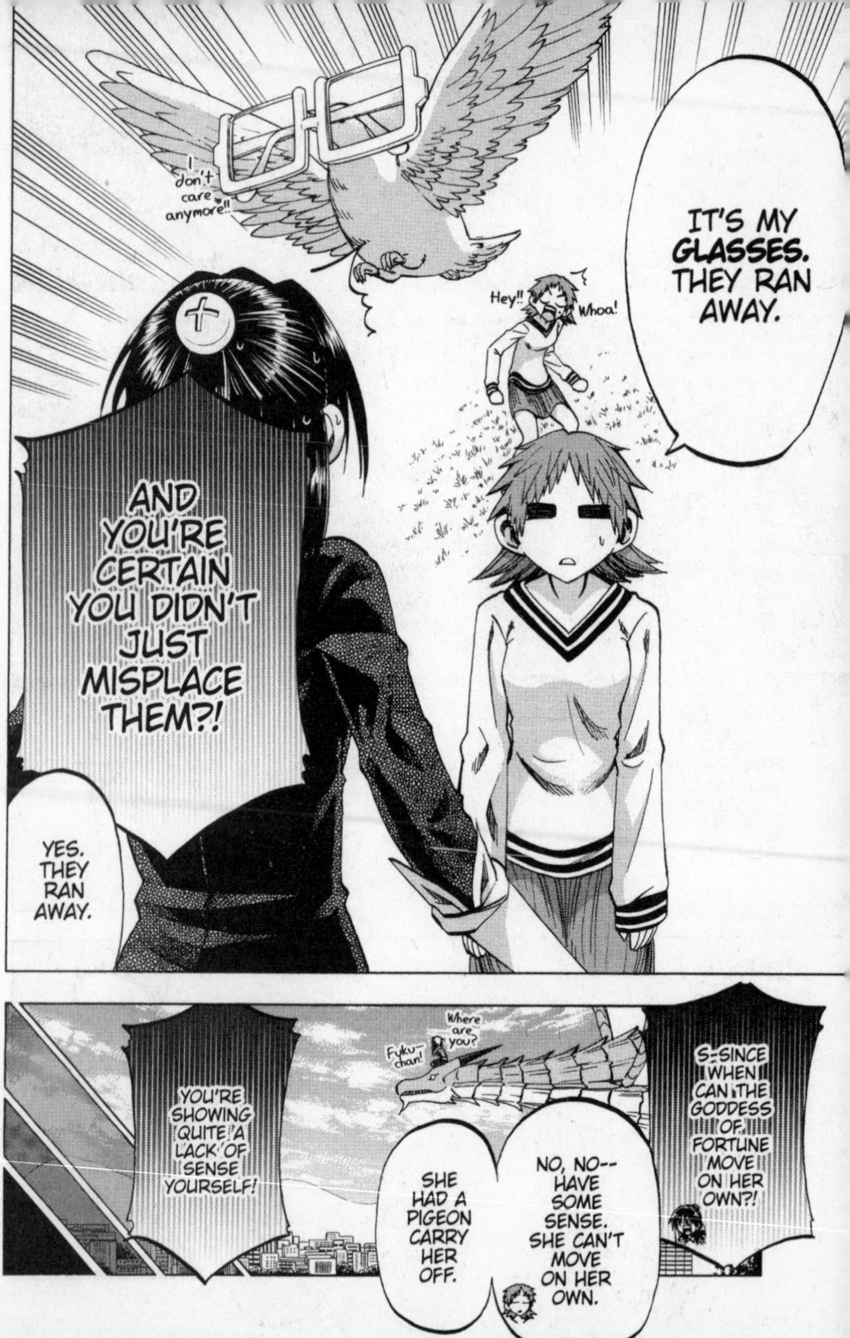
IT'S MY GLASSES. THEY RAN AWAY.
I don't care anymore!!
Whoa!
Hey!!
AND YOU'RE CERTAIN YOU DIDN'T JUST MISPLACE THEM?!
YES. THEY RAN AWAY.
S-SINCE WHEN CAN THE GODDESS OF FORTUNE MOVE ON HER OWN?!
NO, NO-- HAVE SOME SENSE. SHE CAN'T MOVE ON HER OWN.
SHE HAD A PIGEON CARRY HER OFF.
Where are you?
Fuku-chan!
YOU'RE SHOWING QUITE A LACK OF SENSE YOURSELF!

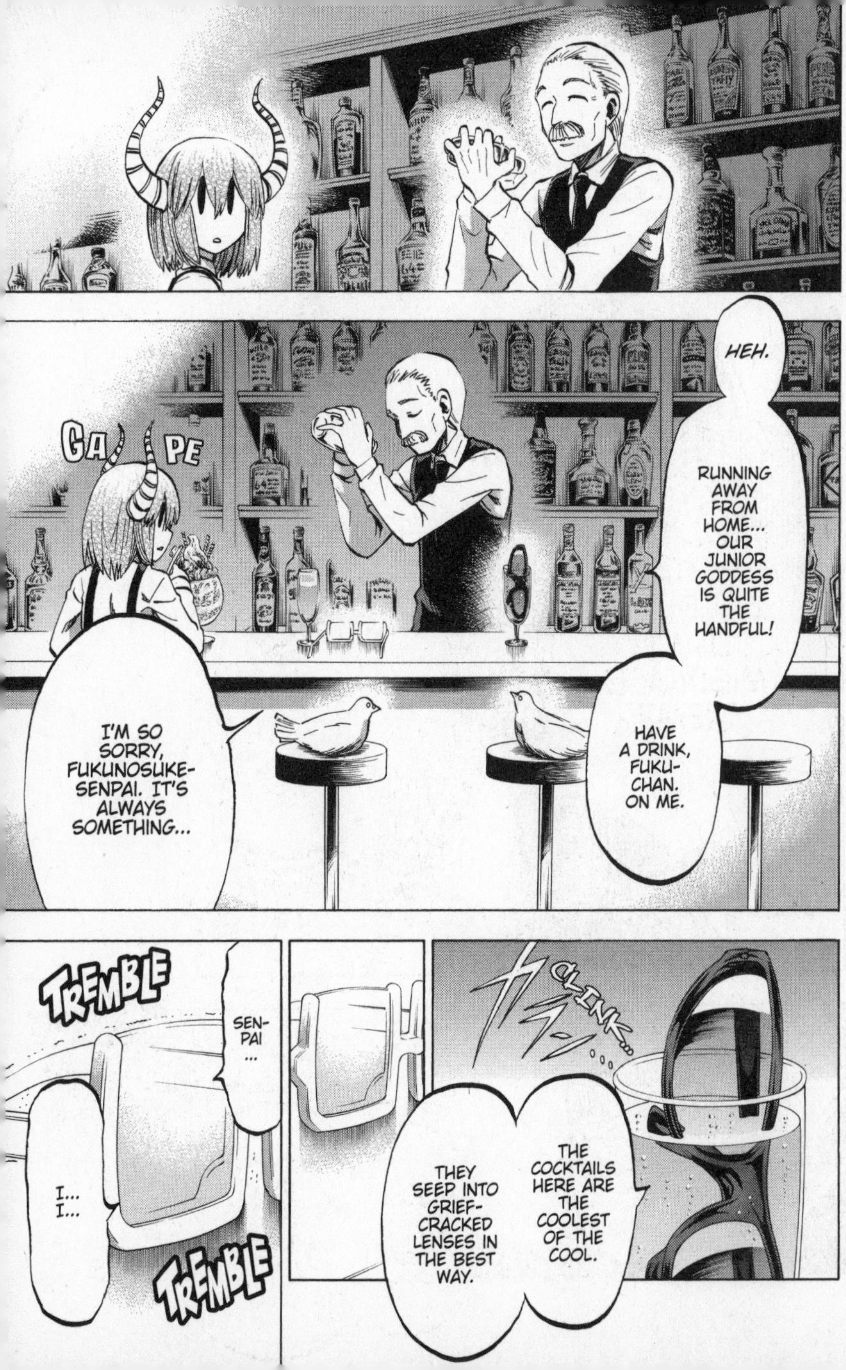
HEH.
RUNNING AWAY FROM HOME... OUR JUNIOR GODDESS IS QUITE THE HANDFUL!
HAVE A DRINK, FUKU-CHAN. ON ME.
GAPE
I'M SO SORRY, FUKUNOSUKE-SENPAI. IT'S ALWAYS SOMETHING...
CLINK...
THE COCKTAILS HERE ARE THE COOLEST OF THE COOL.
THEY SEEP INTO GRIEF-CRACKED LENSES IN THE BEST WAY.
TREMBLE
SEN-PAI...
I... I...
TREMBLE

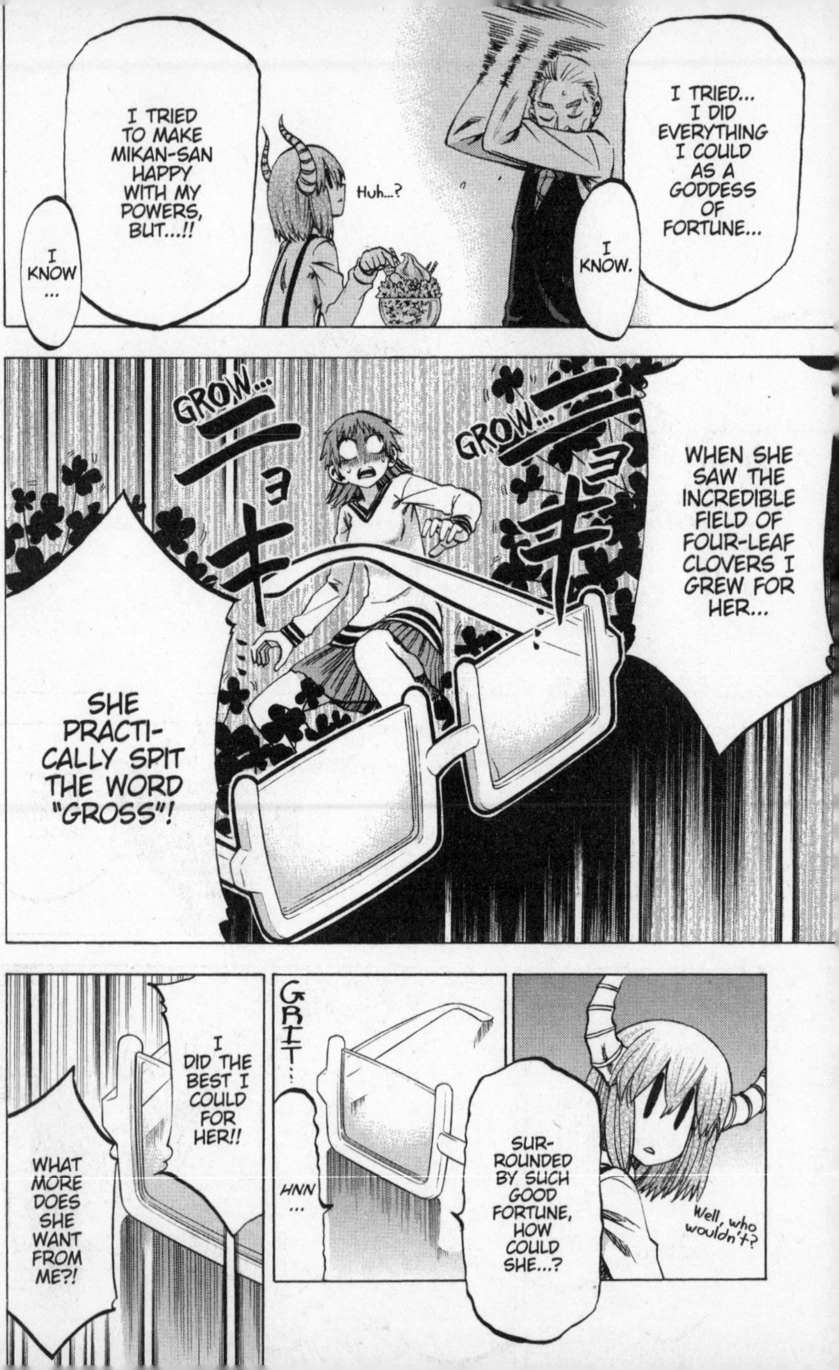
I TRIED... I DID EVERYTHING I COULD AS A GODDESS OF FORTUNE...
I KNOW.
Huh...?
I TRIED TO MAKE MIKAN-SAN HAPPY WITH MY POWERS, BUT...!!
I KNOW...
WHEN SHE SAW THE INCREDIBLE FIELD OF FOUR-LEAF CLOVERS I GREW FOR HER...
GROW...
GROW...
SHE PRACTICALLY SPIT THE WORD "GROSS"!
SUR-ROUNDED BY SUCH GOOD FORTUNE, HOW COULD SHE...?
Well, who wouldn't?
GRIT...
HNN...
I DID THE BEST I COULD FOR HER!!
WHAT MORE DOES SHE WANT FROM ME?!

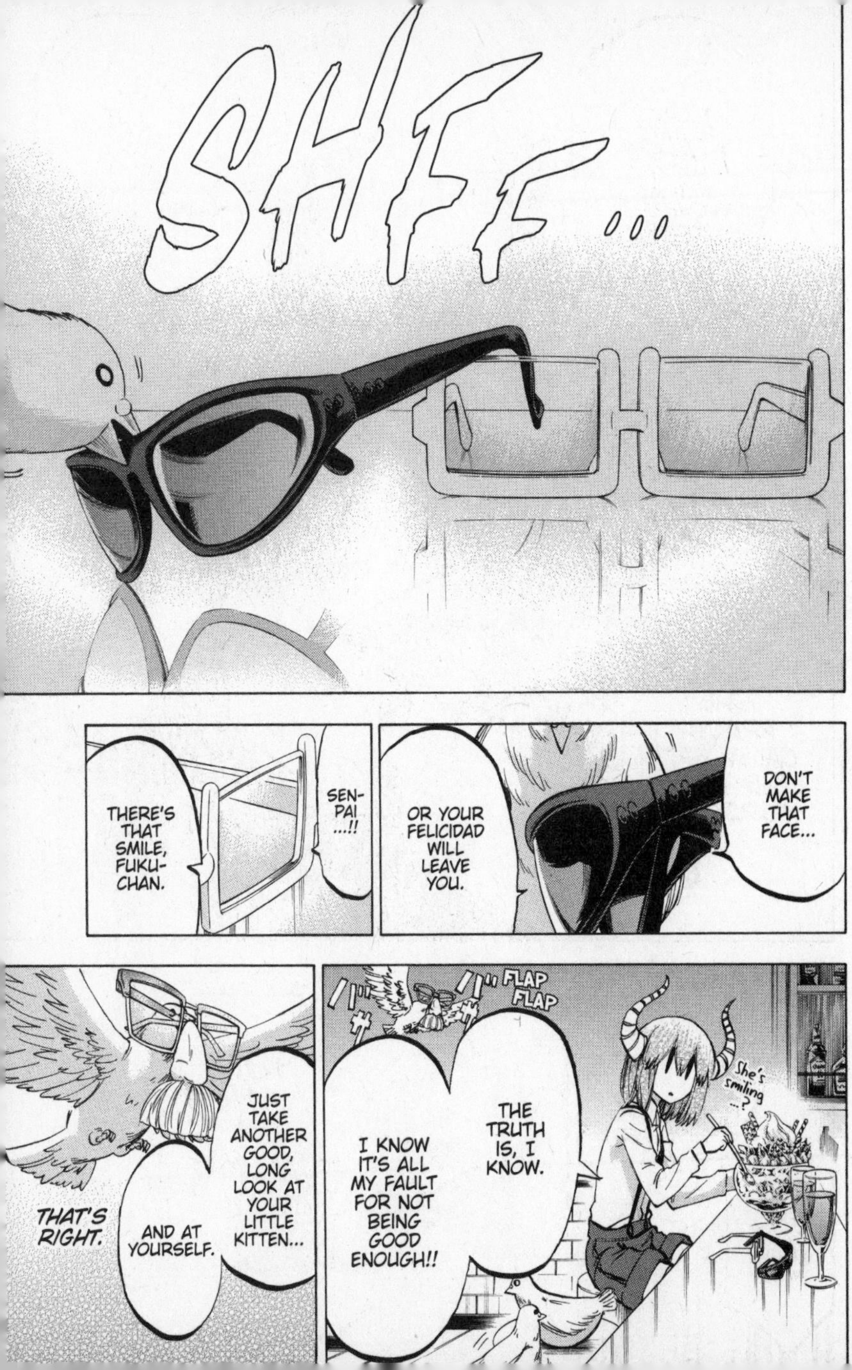
SHFF...
DON'T MAKE THAT FACE...
OR YOUR FELICIDAD WILL LEAVE YOU.
SEN-PAI ...!!
THERE'S THAT SMILE, FUKU-CHAN.
FLAP FLAP
She's smiling...?
THE TRUTH IS, I KNOW.
I KNOW IT'S ALL MY FAULT FOR NOT BEING GOOD ENOUGH!!
JUST TAKE ANOTHER GOOD, LONG LOOK AT YOUR LITTLE KITTEN...
AND AT YOURSELF.
THAT'S RIGHT.

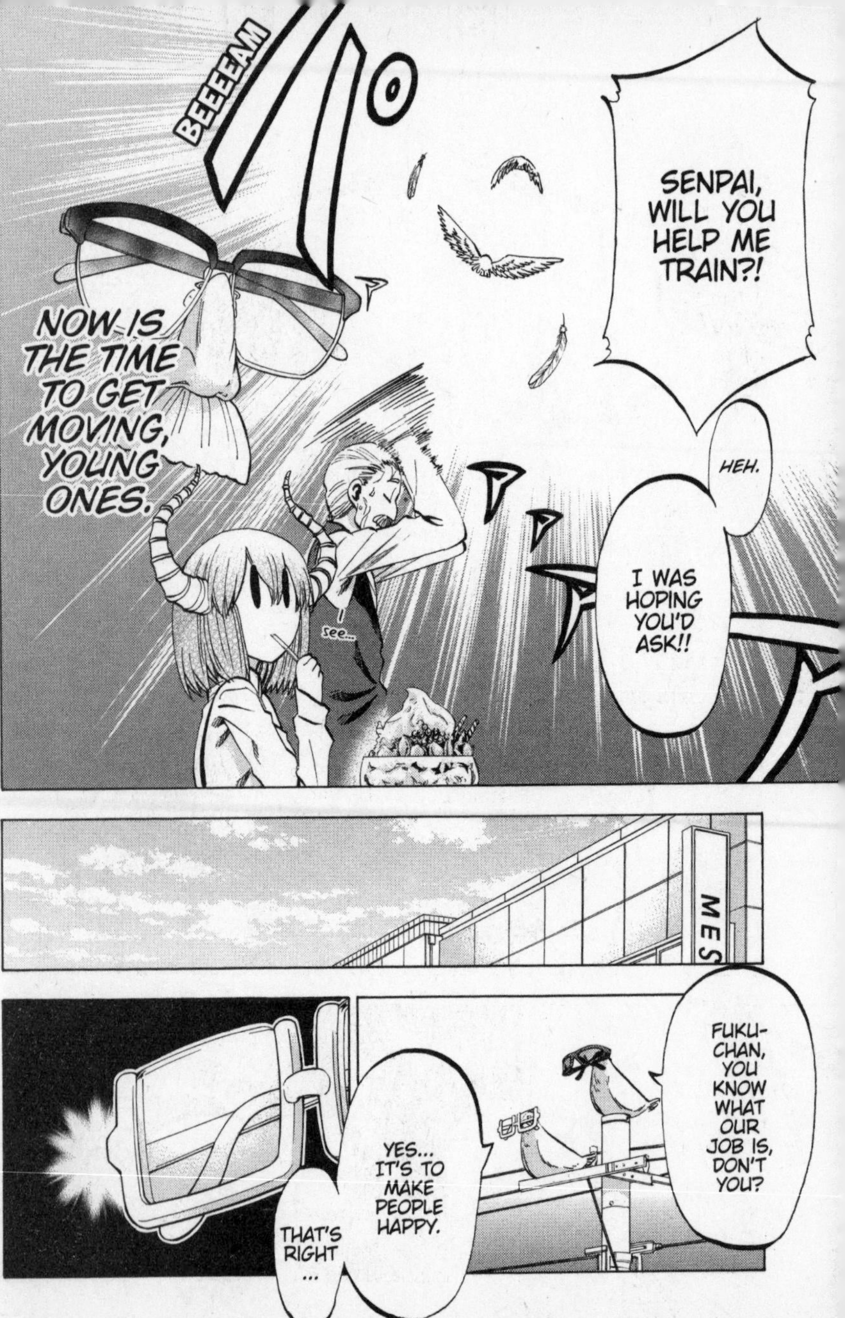
SENPAI, WILL YOU HELP ME TRAIN?!
BEEEEAM
HEH.
I WAS HOPING YOU'D ASK!!
NOW IS THE TIME TO GET MOVING, YOUNG ONES.
I see...
MES
FUKU-CHAN, YOU KNOW WHAT OUR JOB IS, DON'T YOU?
YES... IT'S TO MAKE PEOPLE HAPPY.
THAT'S RIGHT ...

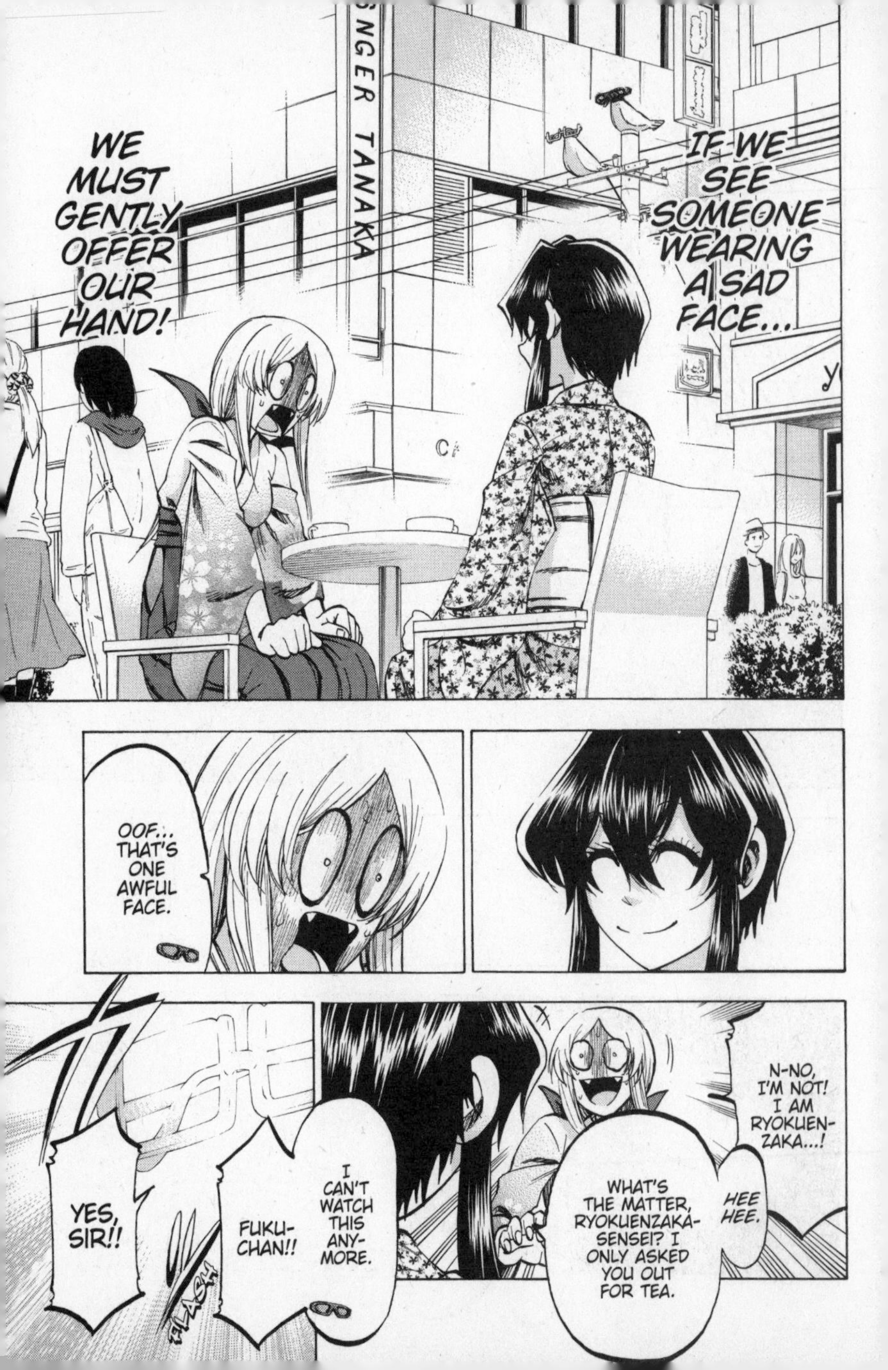
NGER TANAKA
IF WE SEE SOMEONE WEARING A SAD FACE...
WE MUST GENTLY OFFER OUR HAND!
OOF... THAT'S ONE AWFUL FACE.
N-NO, I'M NOT! I AM RYOKUEN-ZAKA...!
HEE HEE.
WHAT'S THE MATTER, RYOKUENZAKA-SENSEI? I ONLY ASKED YOU OUT FOR TEA.
I CAN'T WATCH THIS ANYMORE.
FUKU-CHAN!!
YES, SIR!!
FLASH

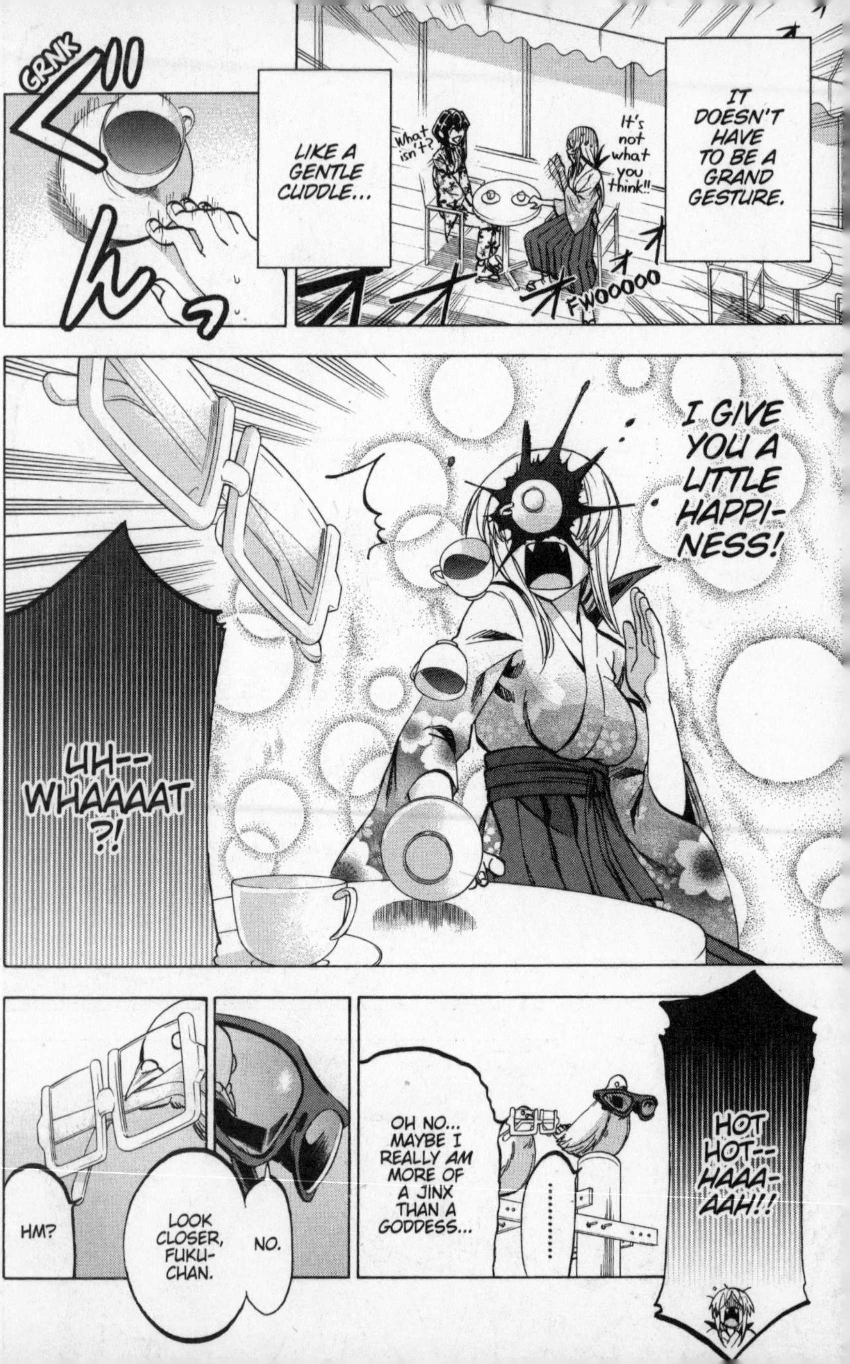
IT DOESN'T HAVE TO BE A GRAND GESTURE.
It's not what you think!!
What isn't?
LIKE A GENTLE CUDDLE...
FWOOOOO
GRNK
I GIVE YOU A LITTLE HAPPI-NESS!
UH--WHAAAAT?!
HOT HOT--HAAA-AAH!!
OH NO... MAYBE I REALLY AM MORE OF A JINX THAN A GODDESS...
......
NO.
LOOK CLOSER, FUKU-CHAN.
HM?

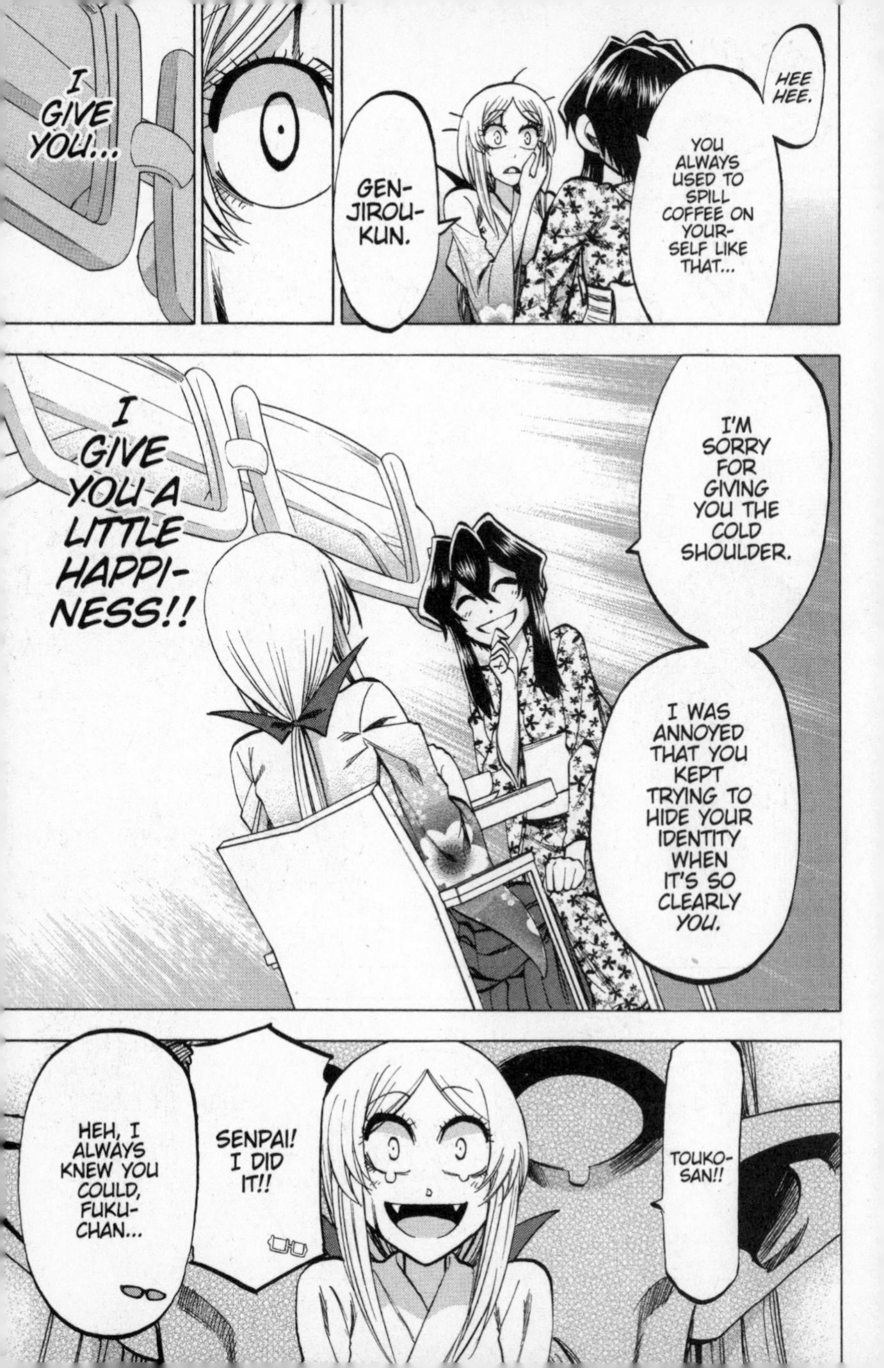
HEE HEE.
YOU ALWAYS USED TO SPILL COFFEE ON YOURSELF LIKE THAT...
GEN-JIROU-KUN.
I GIVE YOU...
I'M SORRY FOR GIVING YOU THE COLD SHOULDER.
I WAS ANNOYED THAT YOU KEPT TRYING TO HIDE YOUR IDENTITY WHEN IT'S SO CLEARLY YOU.
I GIVE YOU A LITTLE HAPPINESS!!
TOUKO-SAN!!
SENPAI! I DID IT!!
HEH, I ALWAYS KNEW YOU COULD, FUKU-CHAN...

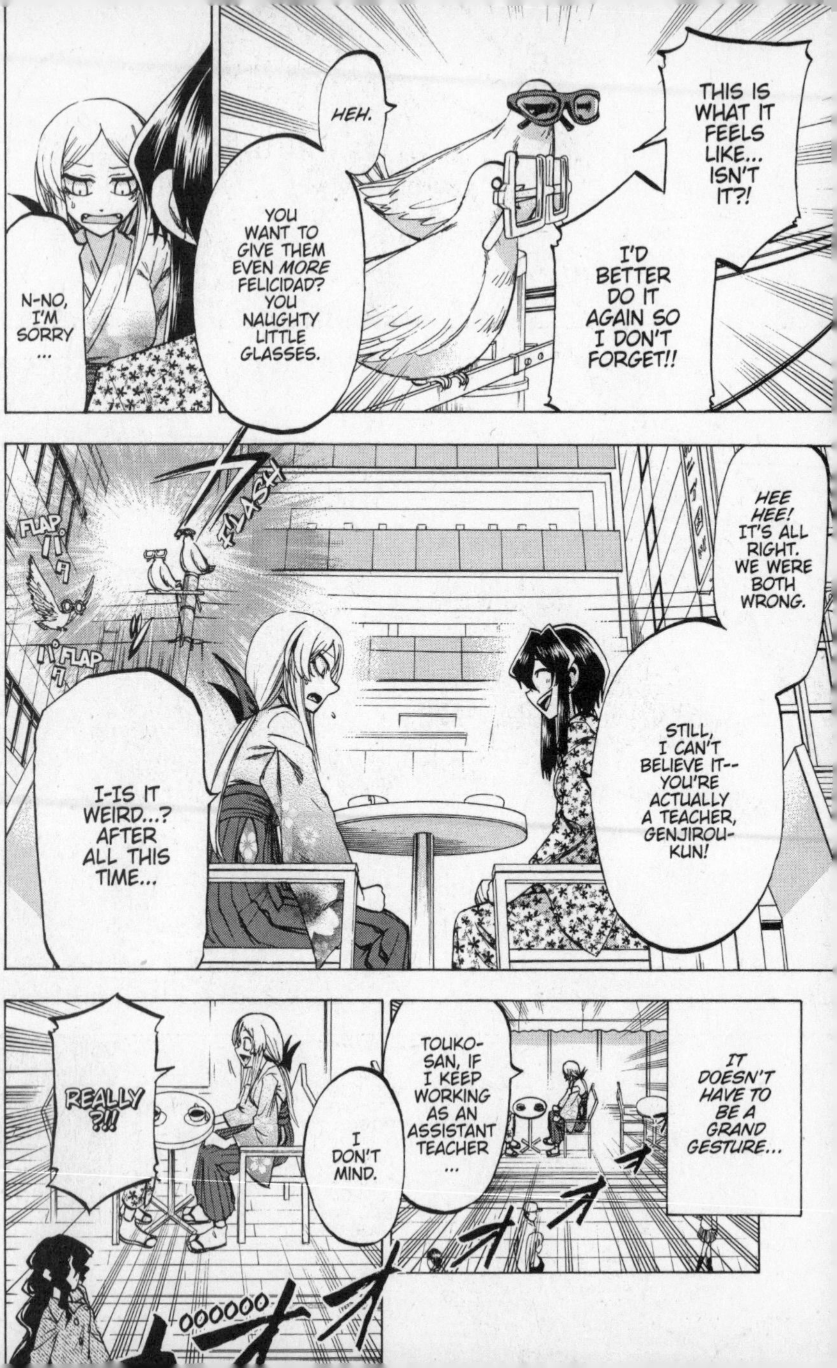
THIS IS WHAT IT FEELS LIKE... ISN'T IT?!
I'D BETTER DO IT AGAIN SO I DON'T FORGET!!
HEH.
YOU WANT TO GIVE THEM EVEN *MORE* FELICIDAD? YOU NAUGHTY LITTLE GLASSES.
N-NO, I'M SORRY ...
FLASH
FLAP
FLAP
HEE HEE! IT'S ALL RIGHT. WE WERE BOTH WRONG.
STILL, I CAN'T BELIEVE IT-- YOU'RE ACTUALLY A TEACHER, GENJIROU-KUN!
I-IS IT WEIRD...? AFTER ALL THIS TIME...
IT DOESN'T HAVE TO BE A GRAND GESTURE...
TOUKO-SAN, IF I KEEP WORKING AS AN ASSISTANT TEACHER ...
I DON'T MIND.
REALLY ?!!
OOOOOO

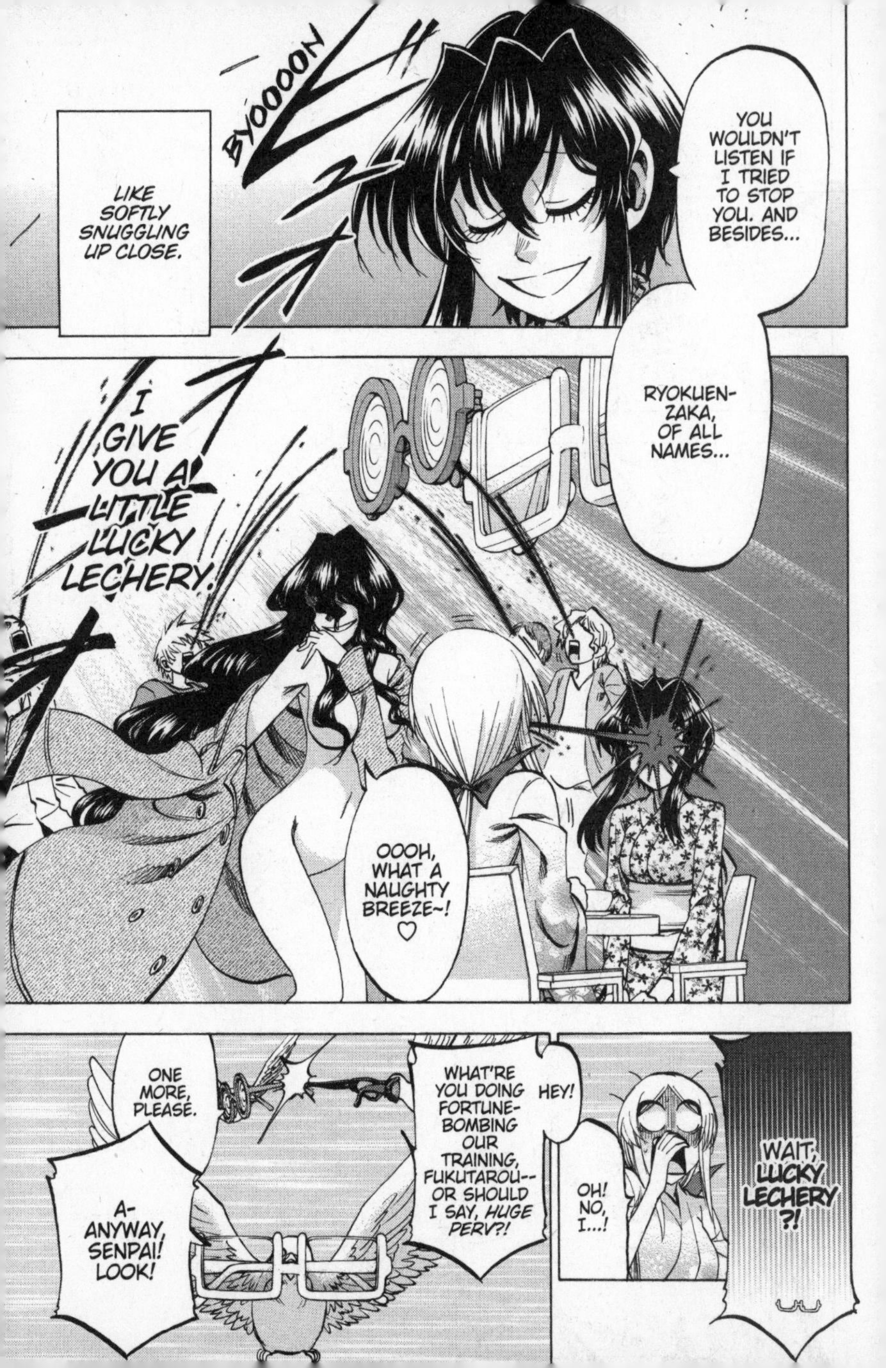

YOU WOULDN'T LISTEN IF I TRIED TO STOP YOU. AND BESIDES...
BYOOOON
LIKE SOFTLY SNUGGLING UP CLOSE.
RYOKUEN-ZAKA, OF ALL NAMES...
I GIVE YOU A LITTLE LUCKY LECHERY!
OOOH, WHAT A NAUGHTY BREEZE~! ♡
WAIT, LUCKY LECHERY?!
OH! NO, I...!
HEY!
WHAT'RE YOU DOING FORTUNE-BOMBING OUR TRAINING, FUKUTAROU--OR SHOULD I SAY, *HUGE PERV*?!
ONE MORE, PLEASE.
A-ANYWAY, SENPAI! LOOK!

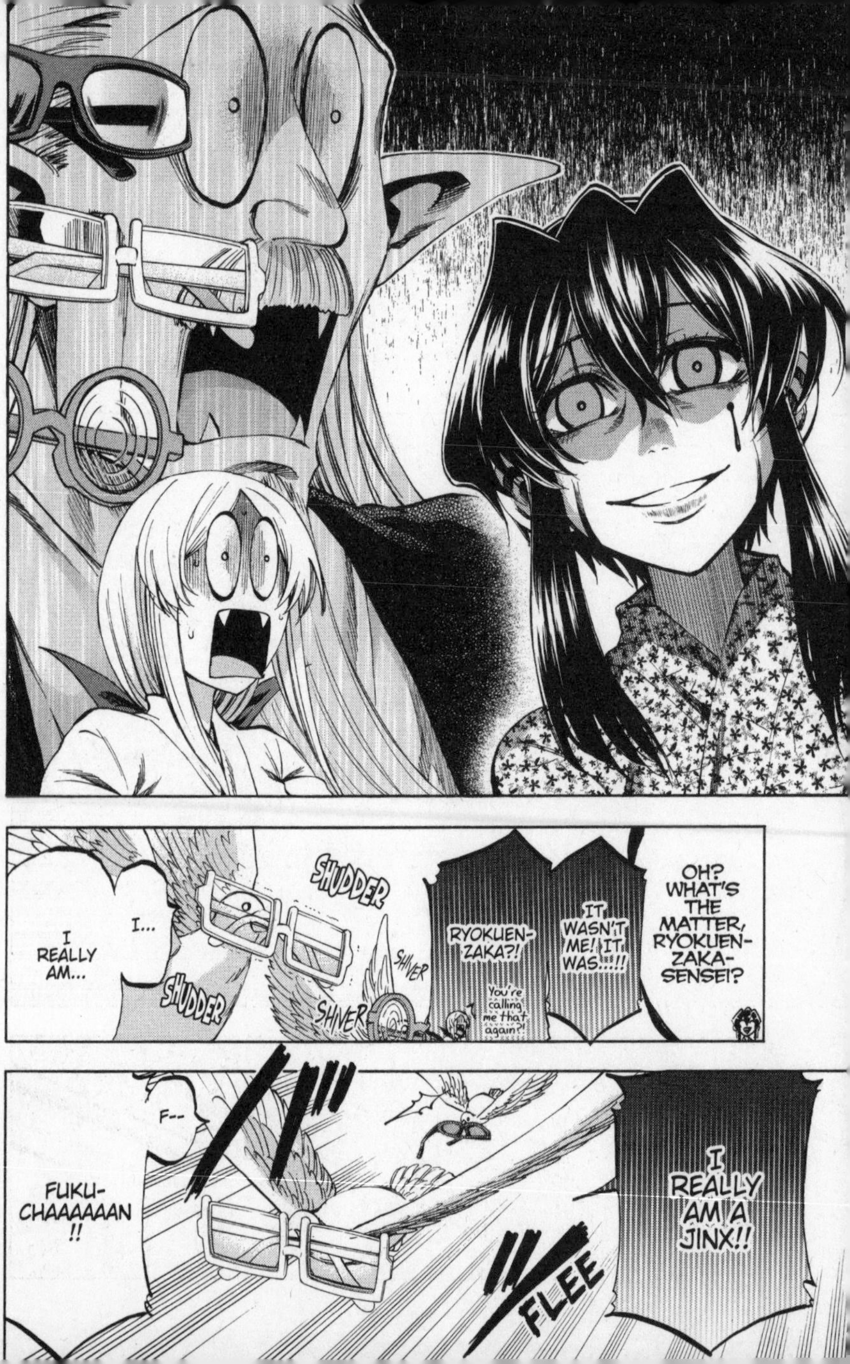
OH? WHAT'S THE MATTER, RYOKUEN-ZAKA-SENSEI?
IT WASN'T ME! IT WAS...!!
RYOKUEN-ZAKA?!
You're calling me that again?!
SHIVER
SHIVER
SHUDDER
SHUDDER
I...
I REALLY AM...
I REALLY AM A JINX!!
FLEE
F--
FUKU-CHAAAAAAN!!

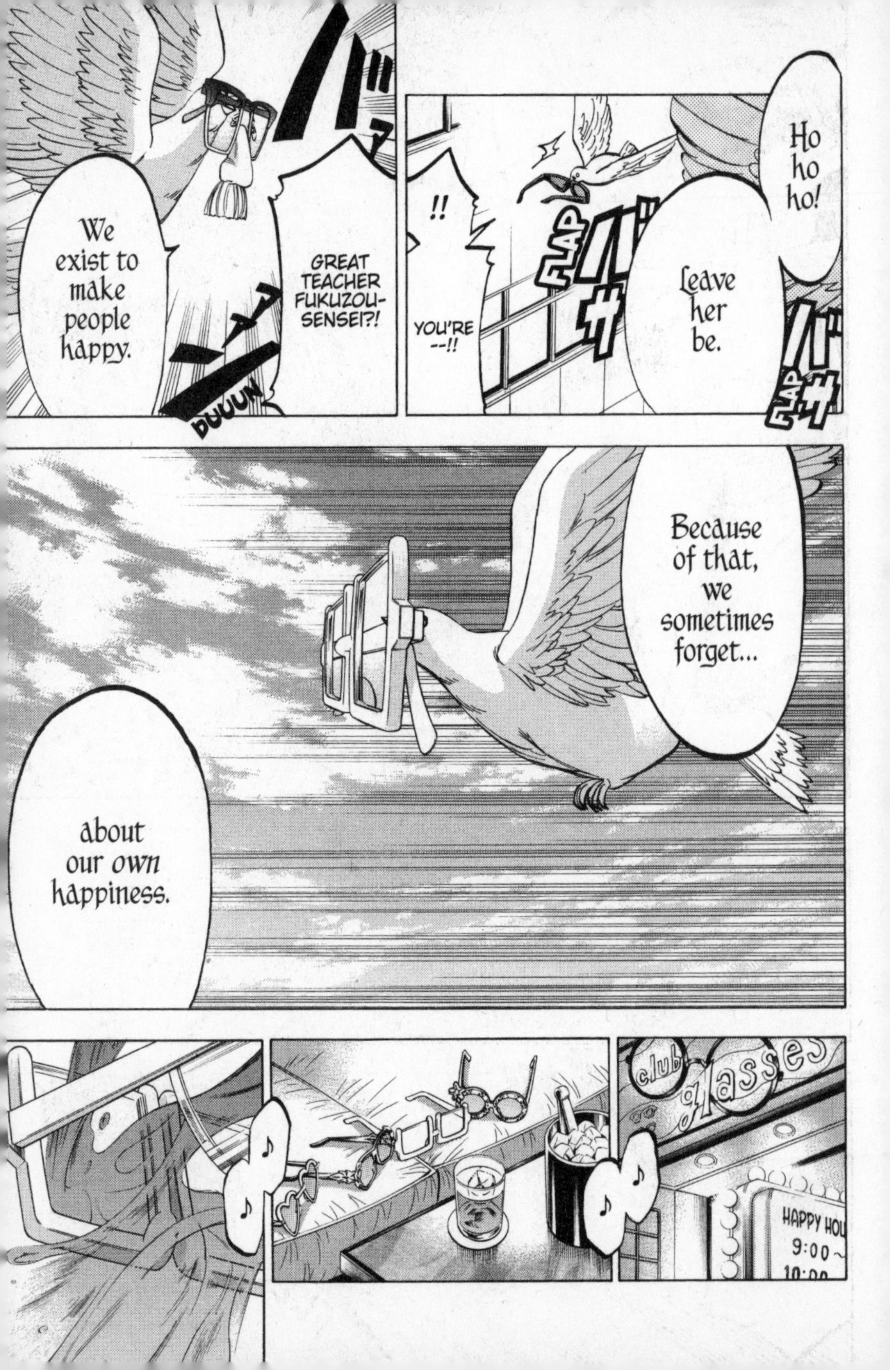
Ho ho ho!
Leave her be.
FLAP
FLAP
!!
YOU'RE --!!
GREAT TEACHER FUKUZOU-SENSEI?!
We exist to make people happy.
DUUUN
Because of that, we sometimes forget...
about our *own* happiness.
club glasses
HAPPY HOU
9:00~

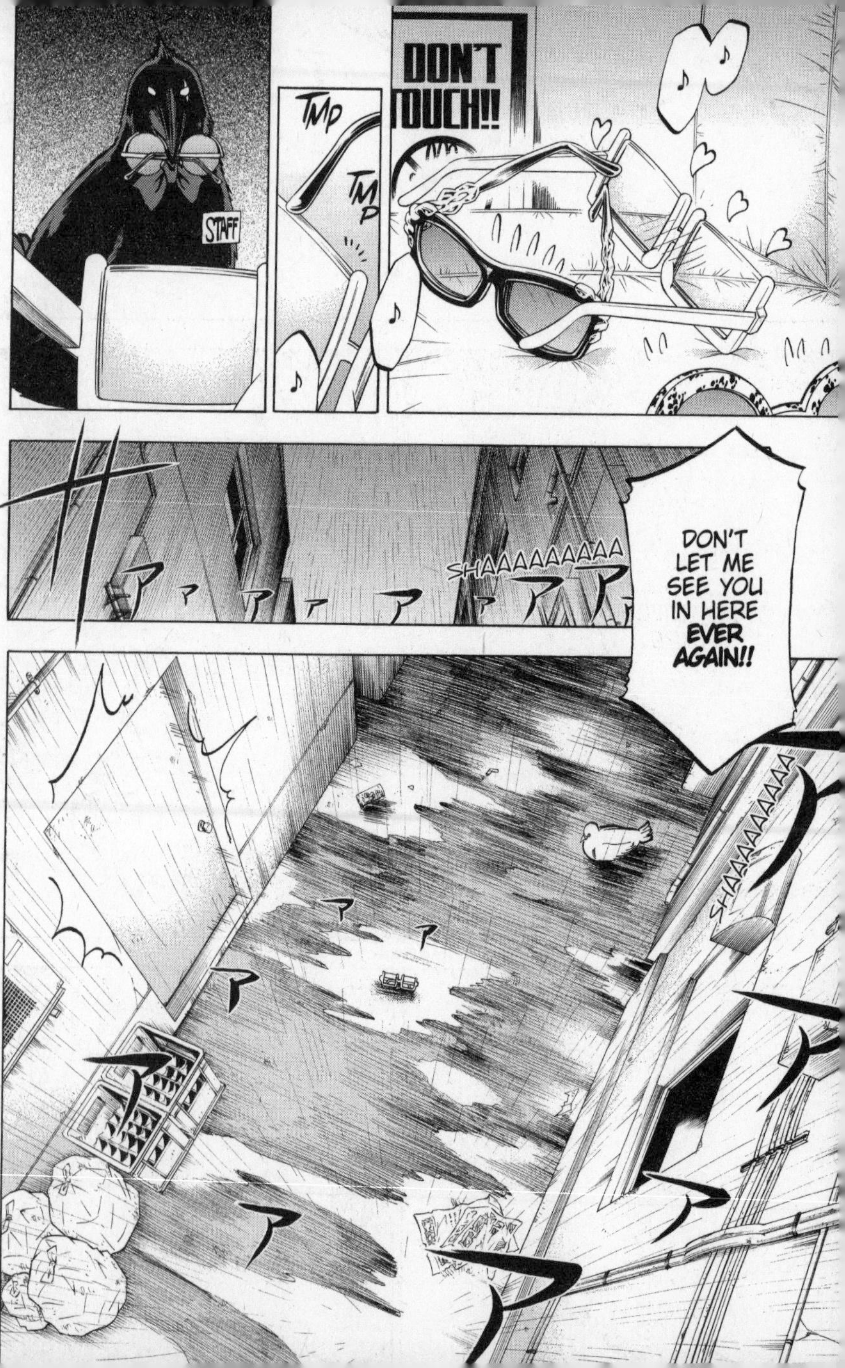
DON'T TOUCH!!
TMP
TMP
STAFF
DON'T LET ME SEE YOU IN HERE **EVER AGAIN!!**
SHAAAAAAAAAA
SHAAAAAAAAAA

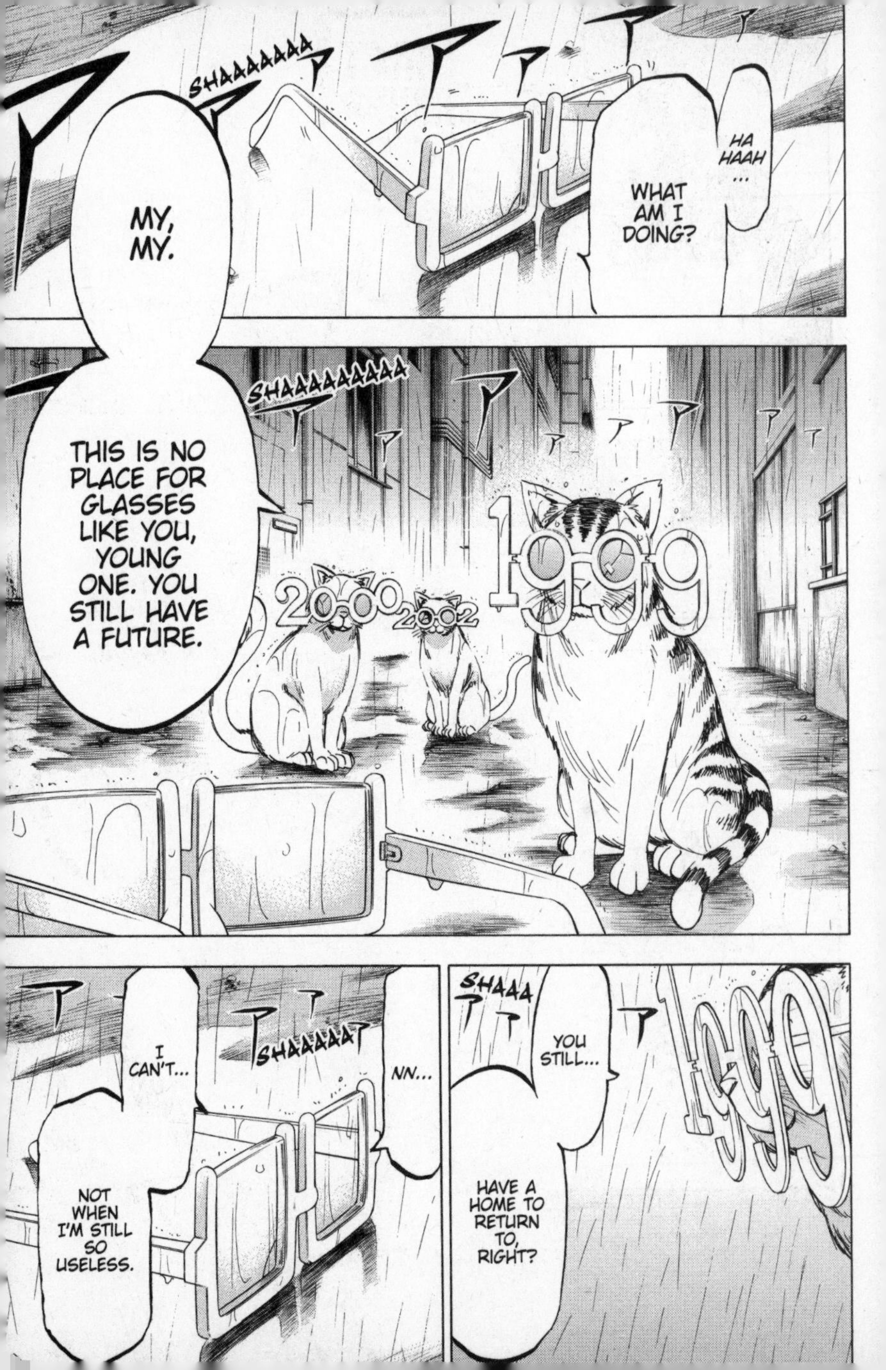
HA HAAH ...
WHAT AM I DOING?
SHAAAAAAA
MY, MY.
SHAAAAAAAAA
THIS IS NO PLACE FOR GLASSES LIKE YOU, YOUNG ONE. YOU STILL HAVE A FUTURE.
SHAAA
YOU STILL...
HAVE A HOME TO RETURN TO, RIGHT?
NN...
SHAAAAAA
I CAN'T...
NOT WHEN I'M STILL SO USELESS.

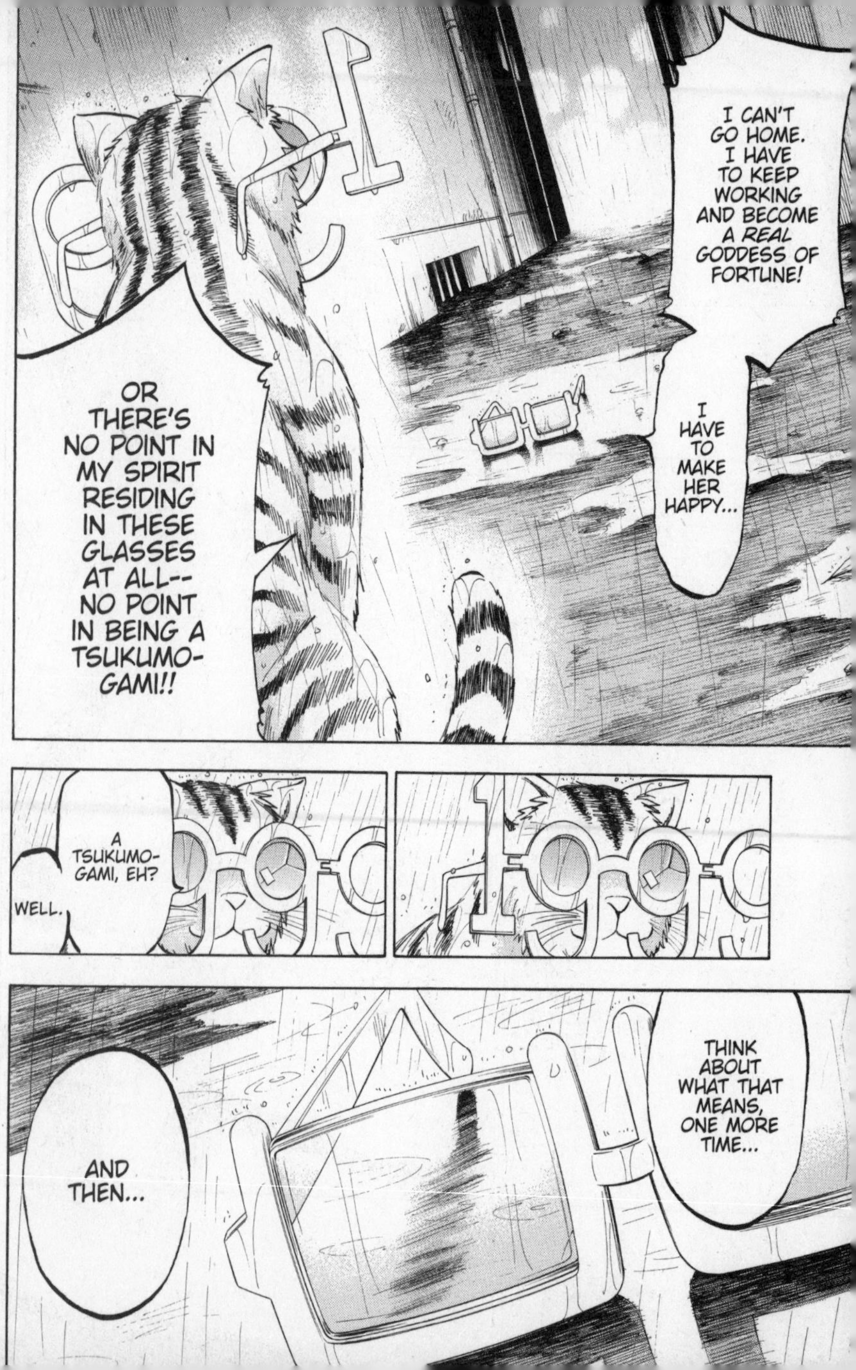
I CAN'T GO HOME. I HAVE TO KEEP WORKING AND BECOME A *REAL* GODDESS OF FORTUNE!
I HAVE TO MAKE HER HAPPY...
OR THERE'S NO POINT IN MY SPIRIT RESIDING IN THESE GLASSES AT ALL-- NO POINT IN BEING A TSUKUMO-GAMI!!
A TSUKUMO-GAMI, EH?
WELL.
THINK ABOUT WHAT THAT MEANS, ONE MORE TIME...
AND THEN...

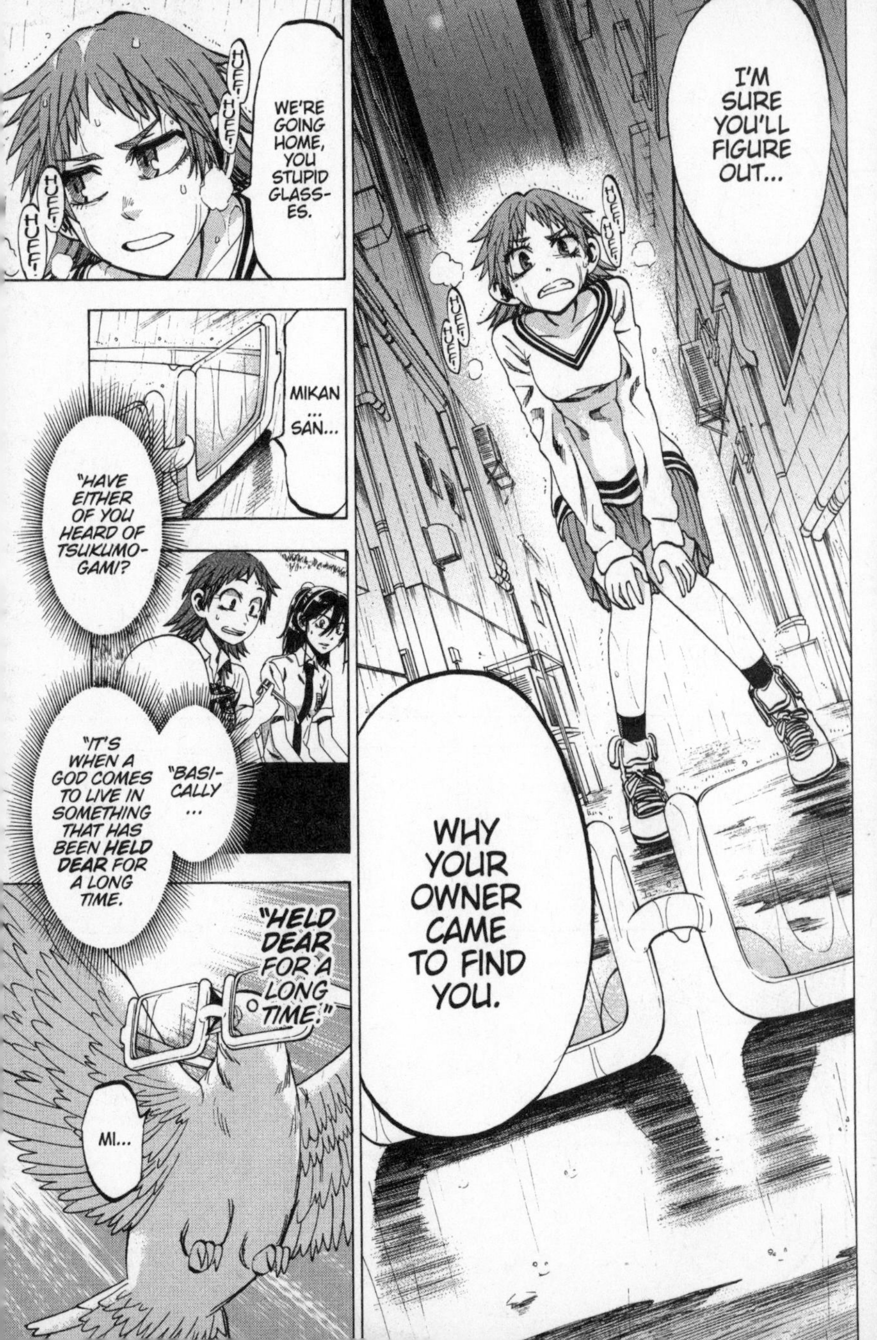
I'M SURE YOU'LL FIGURE OUT...
HUFF! HUFF!
HUFF! HUFF!
WHY YOUR OWNER CAME TO FIND YOU.
HUFF! HUFF!
WE'RE GOING HOME, YOU STUPID GLASS-ES.
HUFF! HUFF!
MIKAN ... SAN...
"HAVE EITHER OF YOU HEARD OF TSUKUMO-GAMI?
"BASI-CALLY ...
"IT'S WHEN A GOD COMES TO LIVE IN SOMETHING THAT HAS BEEN HELD DEAR FOR A LONG TIME.
"HELD DEAR FOR A LONG TIME."
MI...

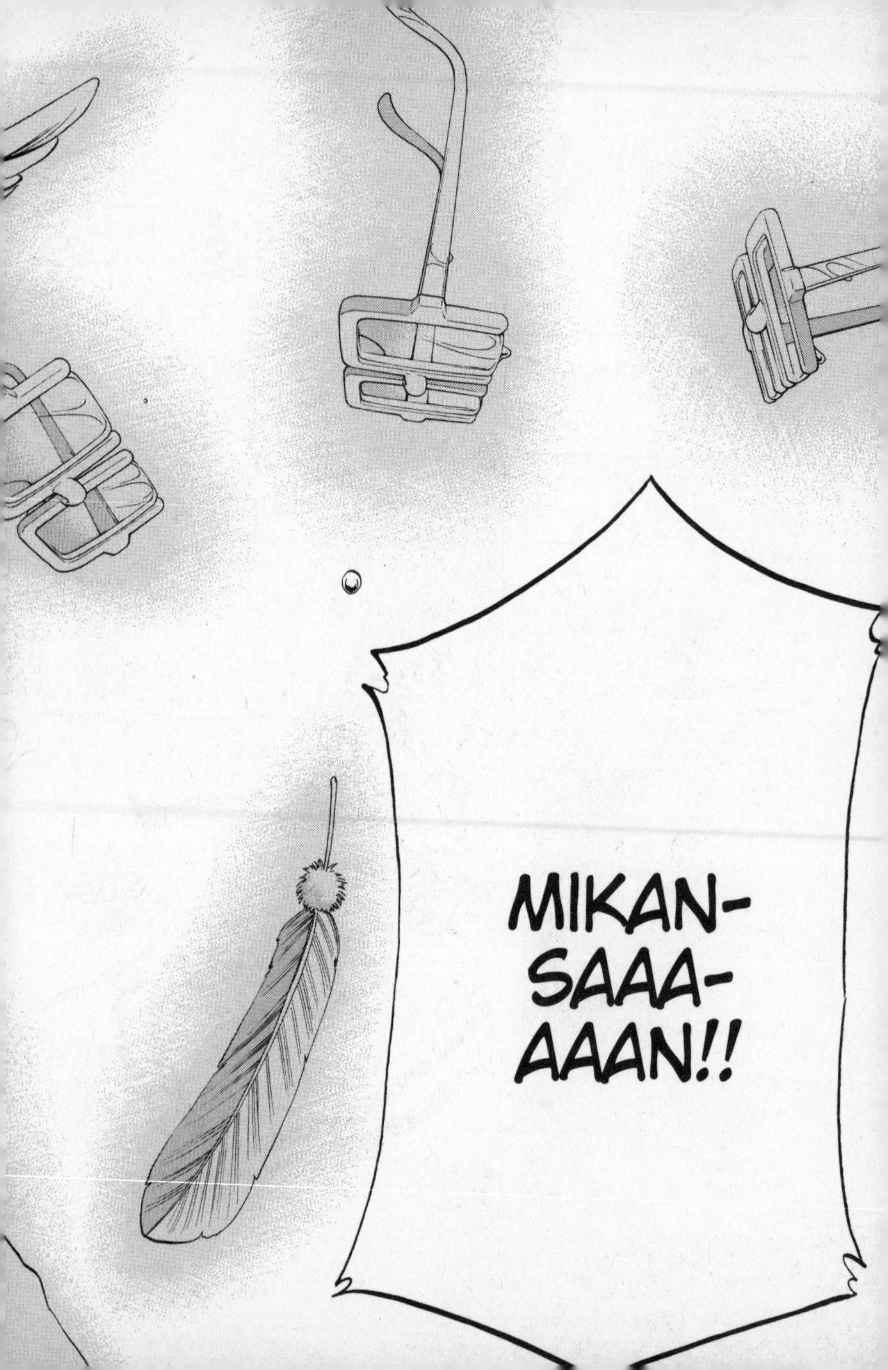
MIKAN-SAAAA-AAAN!!

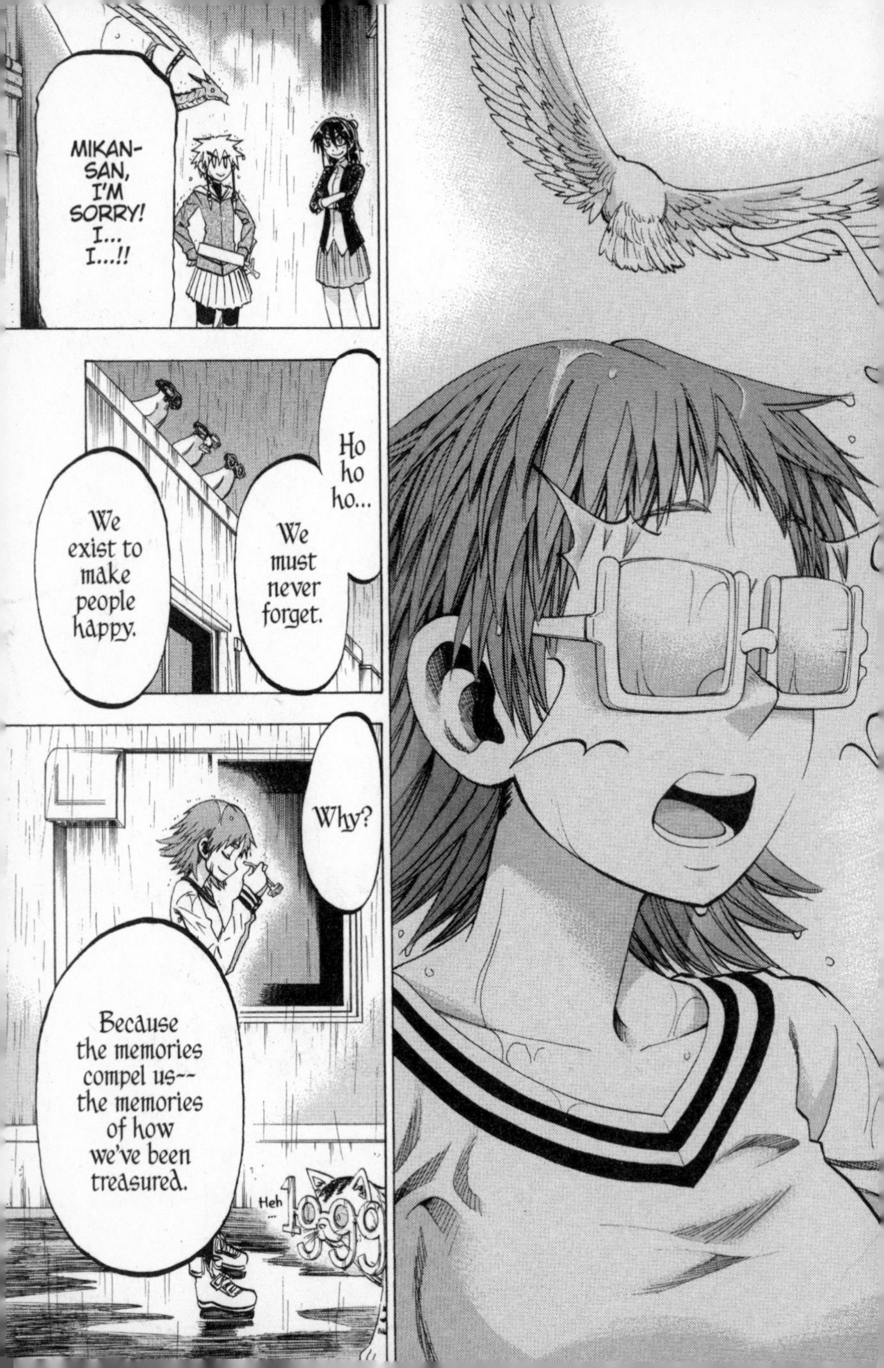
MIKAN-SAN, I'M SORRY! I... I...!!
Ho ho ho...
We must never forget.
We exist to make people happy.
Why?
Because the memories compel us-- the memories of how we've been treasured.
Heh...

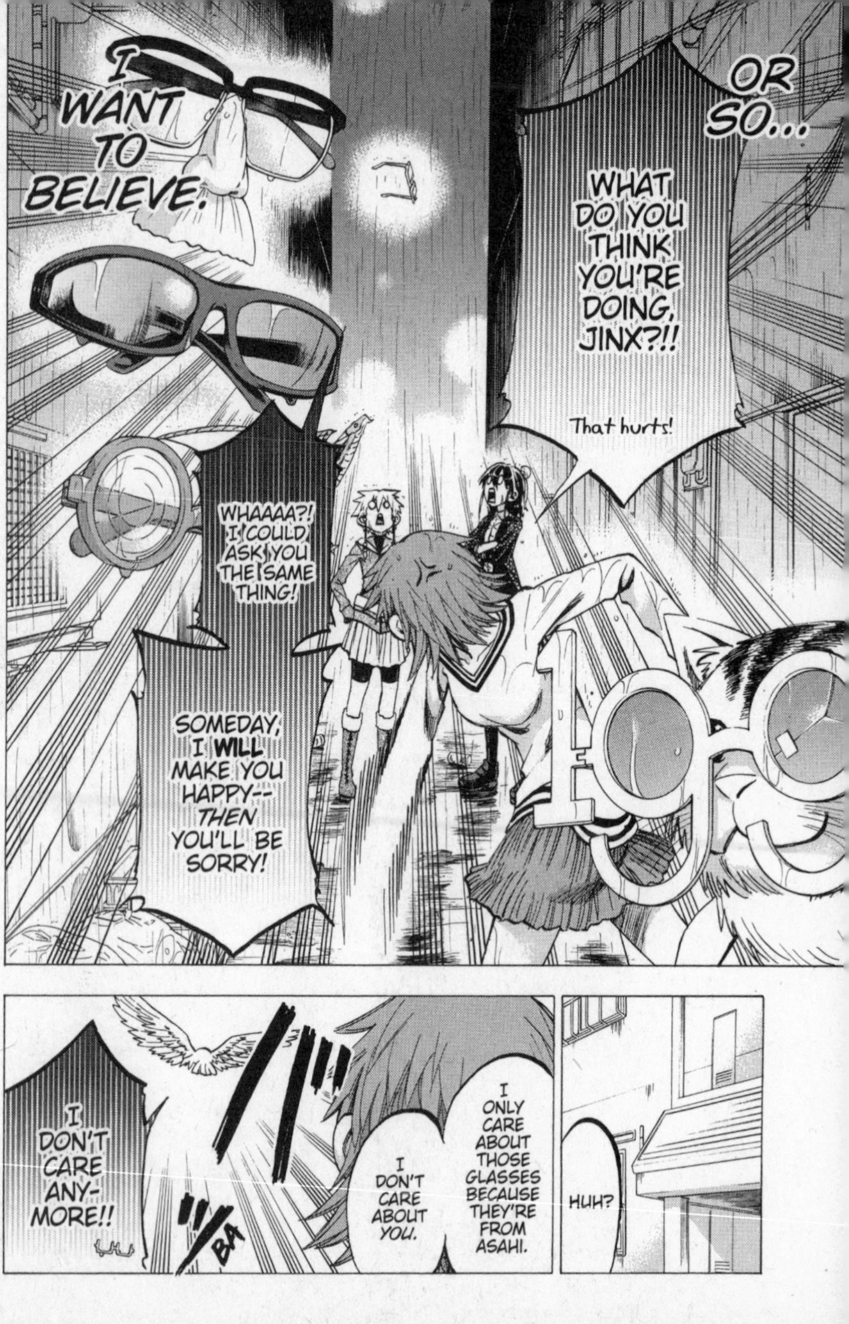
I WANT TO BELIEVE.
OR SO...
WHAT DO YOU THINK YOU'RE DOING, JINX?!!
That hurts!
WHAAAA?! I COULD ASK YOU THE SAME THING!
SOMEDAY, I **WILL** MAKE YOU HAPPY-- THEN YOU'LL BE SORRY!
HUH?
I ONLY CARE ABOUT THOSE GLASSES BECAUSE THEY'RE FROM ASAHI.
I DON'T CARE ABOUT YOU.
BA
I DON'T CARE ANYMORE!!

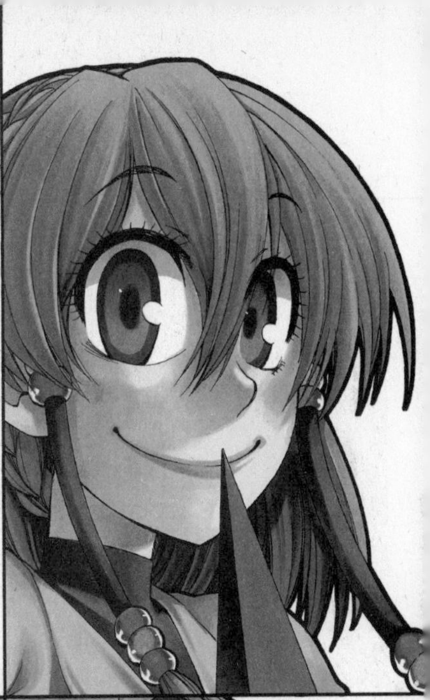

Chapter 109: "Let's Reclaim Our Pride!"

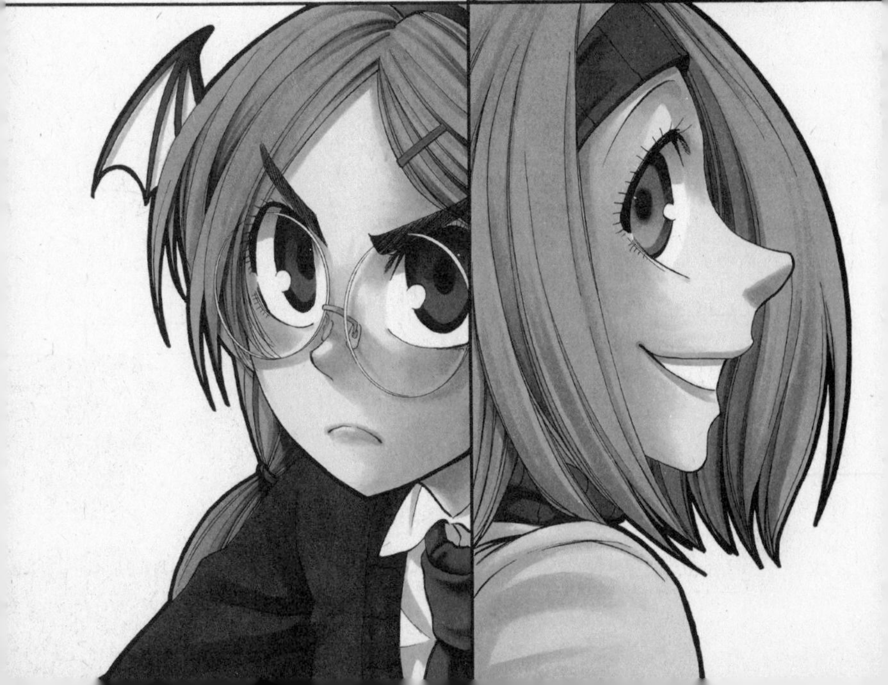

TOP SECRET

My Monster Secret 13

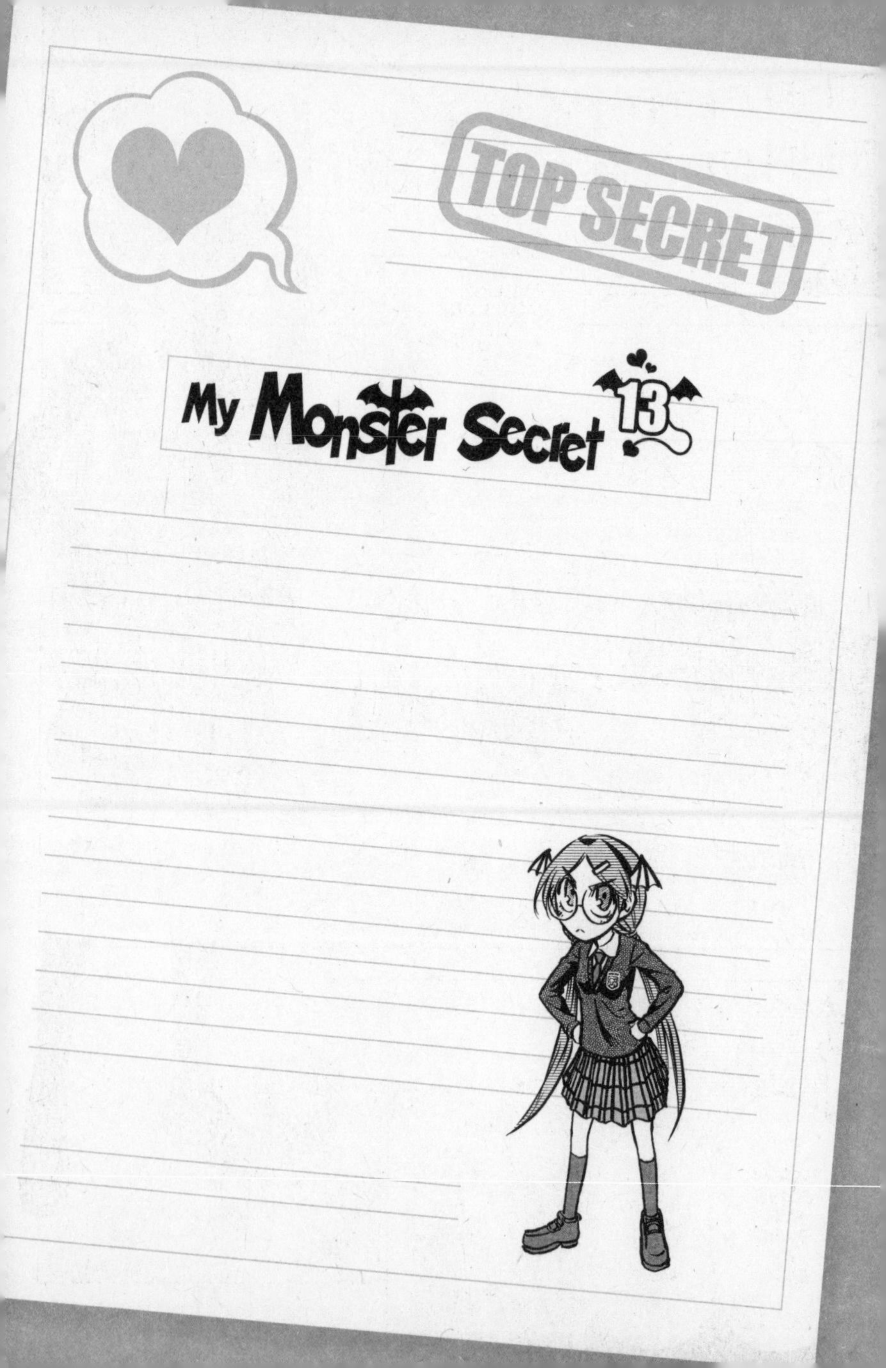

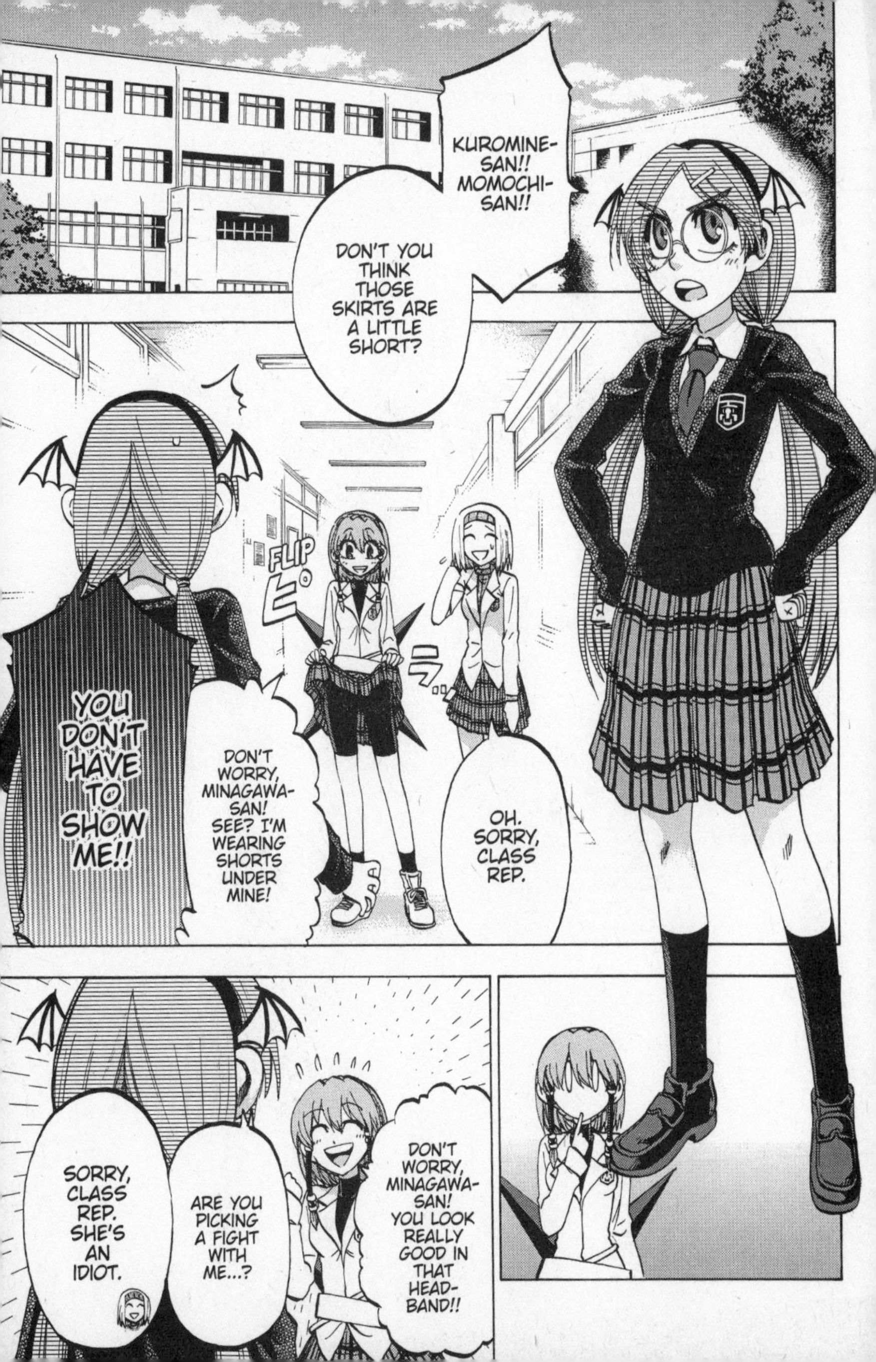
KUROMINE-SAN!! MOMOCHI-SAN!!
DON'T YOU THINK THOSE SKIRTS ARE A LITTLE SHORT?
FLIP
DON'T WORRY, MINAGAWA-SAN! SEE? I'M WEARING SHORTS UNDER MINE!
YOU DON'T HAVE TO SHOW ME!!
OH. SORRY, CLASS REP.
DON'T WORRY, MINAGAWA-SAN! YOU LOOK REALLY GOOD IN THAT HEAD-BAND!!
ARE YOU PICKING A FIGHT WITH ME...?
SORRY, CLASS REP. SHE'S AN IDIOT.

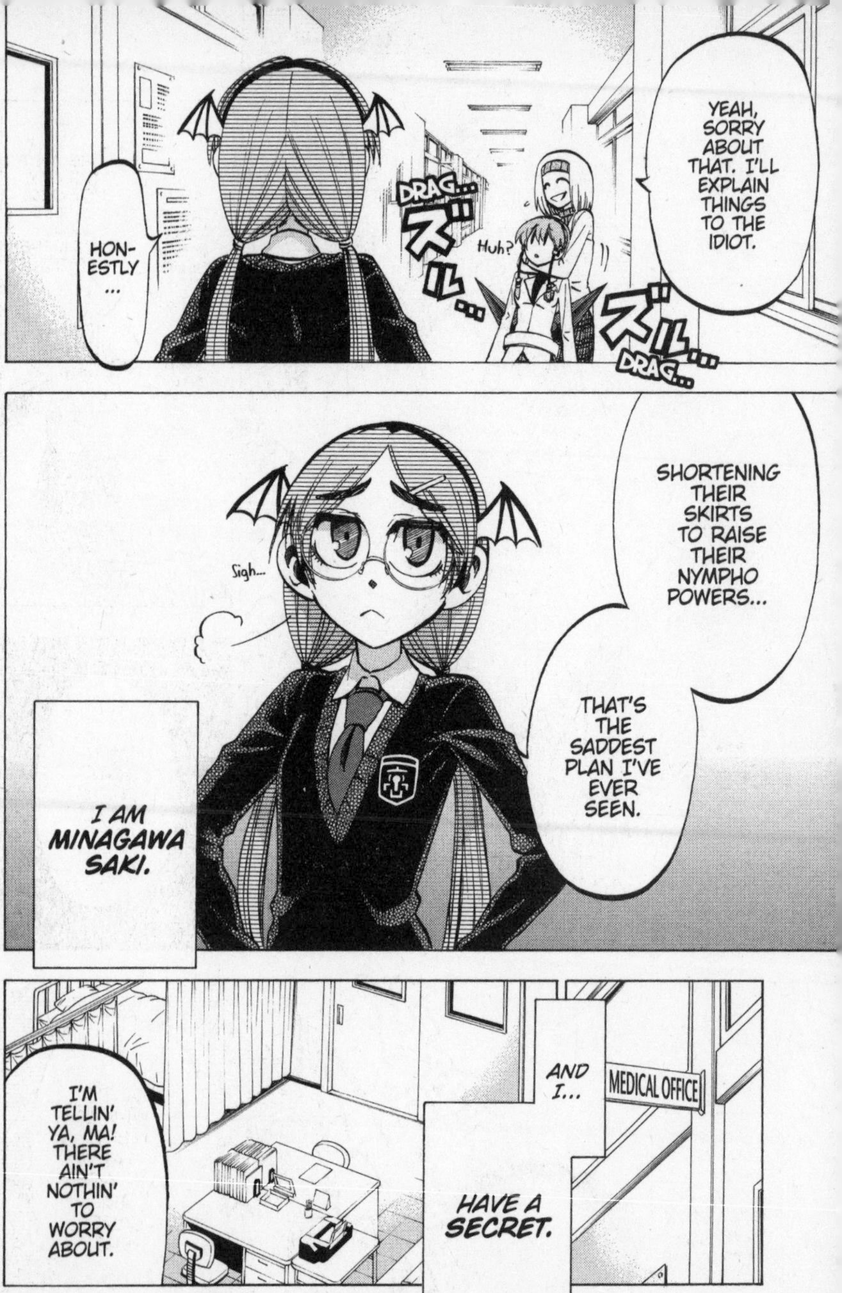
YEAH, SORRY ABOUT THAT. I'LL EXPLAIN THINGS TO THE IDIOT.
ズル… DRAG…
Huh?
ズル… DRAG…
HON-ESTLY…
SHORTENING THEIR SKIRTS TO RAISE THEIR NYMPHO POWERS…
THAT'S THE SADDEST PLAN I'VE EVER SEEN.
Sigh…
I AM MINAGAWA SAKI.
MEDICAL OFFICE
AND I…
HAVE A SECRET.
I'M TELLIN' YA, MA! THERE AIN'T NOTHIN' TO WORRY ABOUT.

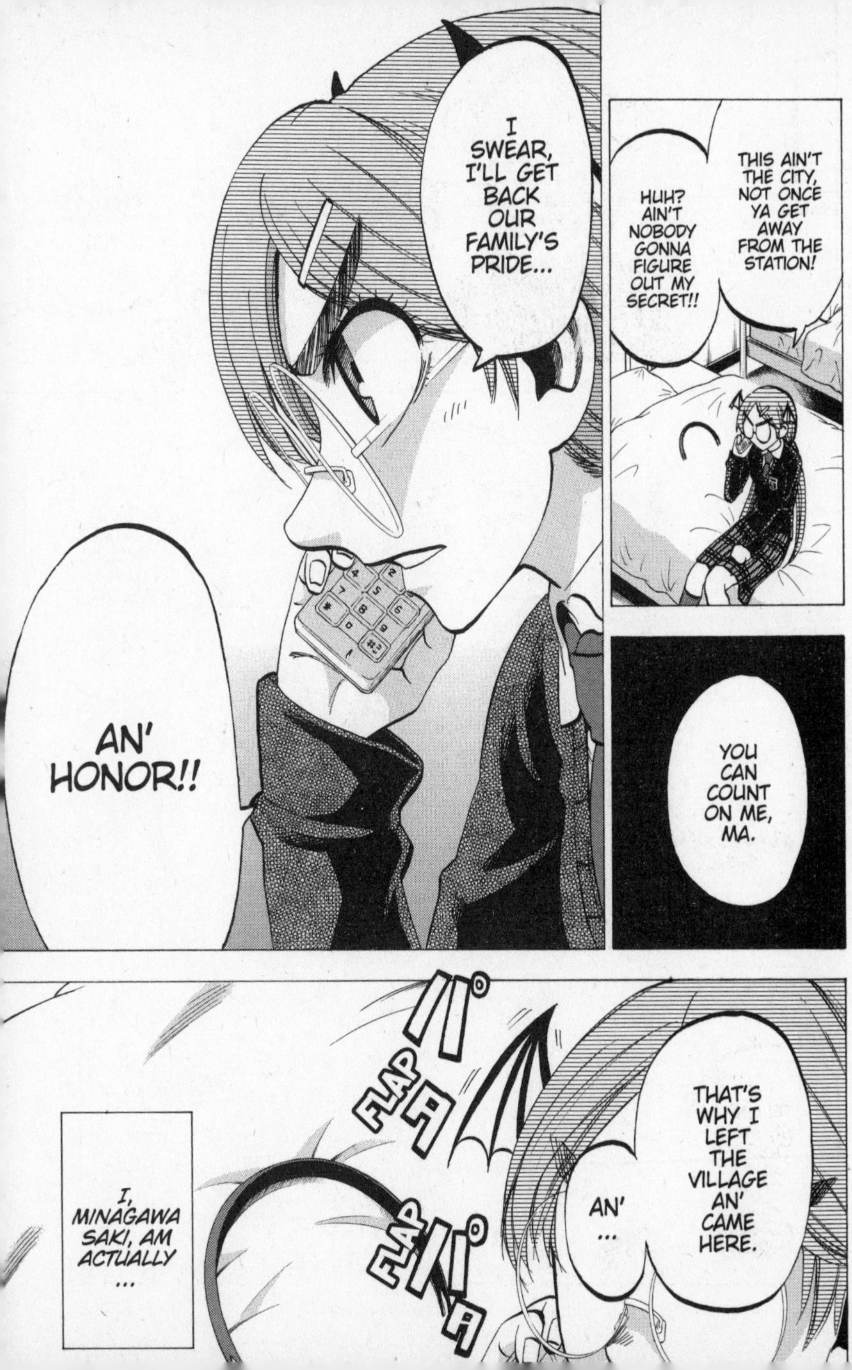
THIS AIN'T THE CITY, NOT ONCE YA GET AWAY FROM THE STATION!
HUH? AIN'T NOBODY GONNA FIGURE OUT MY SECRET!!
YOU CAN COUNT ON ME, MA.
I SWEAR, I'LL GET BACK OUR FAMILY'S PRIDE...
AN' HONOR!!
THAT'S WHY I LEFT THE VILLAGE AN' CAME HERE.
AN' ...
FLAP
FLAP
I, MINAGAWA SAKI, AM ACTUALLY ...

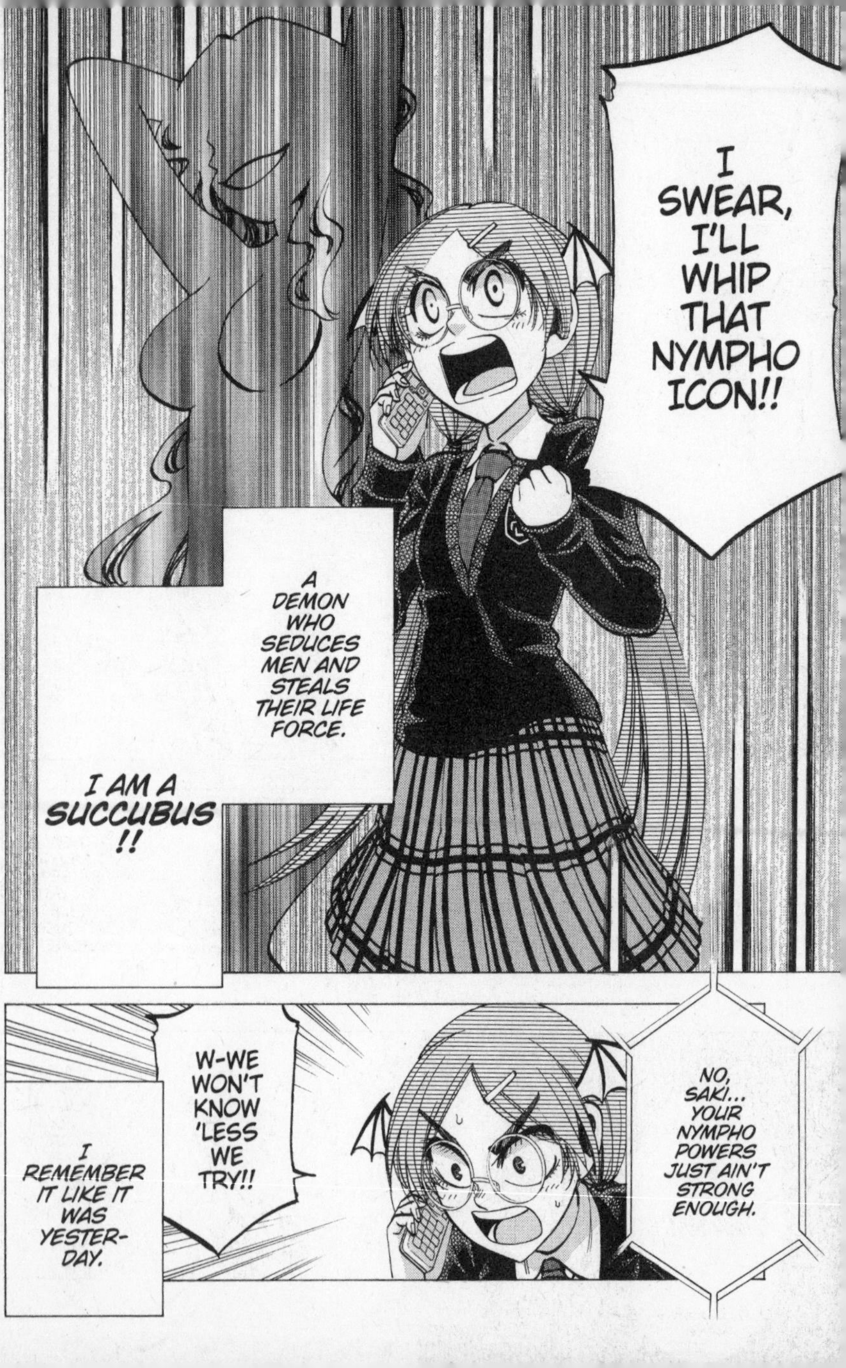
I SWEAR, I'LL WHIP THAT NYMPHO ICON!!
A DEMON WHO SEDUCES MEN AND STEALS THEIR LIFE FORCE.
I AM A SUCCUBUS!!
NO, SAKI... YOUR NYMPHO POWERS JUST AIN'T STRONG ENOUGH.
W-WE WON'T KNOW 'LESS WE TRY!!
I REMEMBER IT LIKE IT WAS YESTER-DAY.

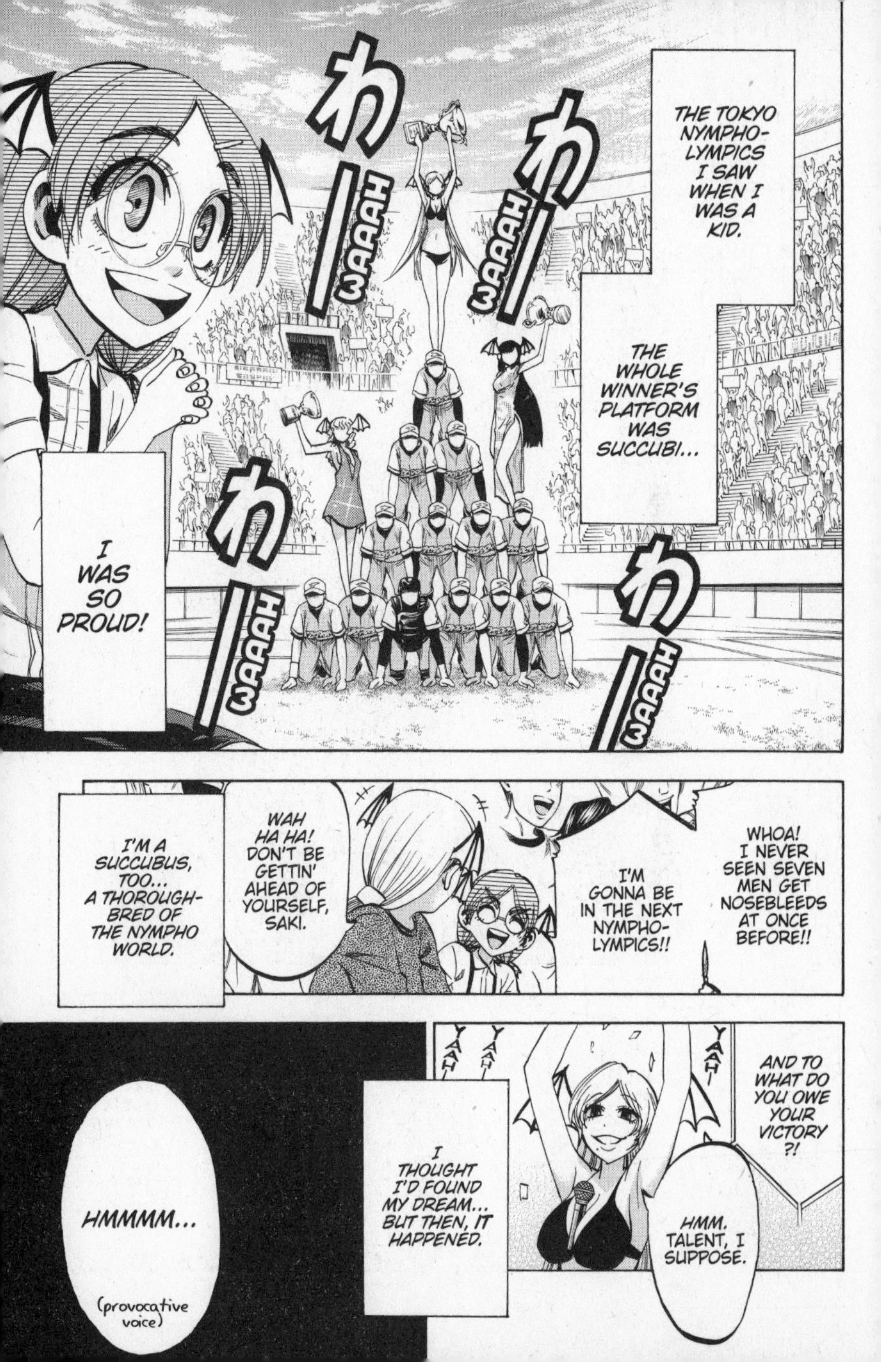
THE TOKYO NYMPHO-LYMPICS I SAW WHEN I WAS A KID.
わー WAAAAH
わー WAAAAH
THE WHOLE WINNER'S PLATFORM WAS SUCCUBI...
わー WAAAAH
わー WAAAAH
I WAS SO PROUD!
WHOA! I NEVER SEEN SEVEN MEN GET NOSEBLEEDS AT ONCE BEFORE!!
I'M GONNA BE IN THE NEXT NYMPHO-LYMPICS!!
WAH HA HA! DON'T BE GETTIN' AHEAD OF YOURSELF, SAKI.
I'M A SUCCUBUS, TOO... A THOROUGHBRED OF THE NYMPHO WORLD.
YAAH!
AND TO WHAT DO YOU OWE YOUR VICTORY?!
YAAH!
YAAH!
HMM. TALENT, I SUPPOSE.
I THOUGHT I'D FOUND MY DREAM... BUT THEN, IT HAPPENED.
HMMMM...
(provocative voice)

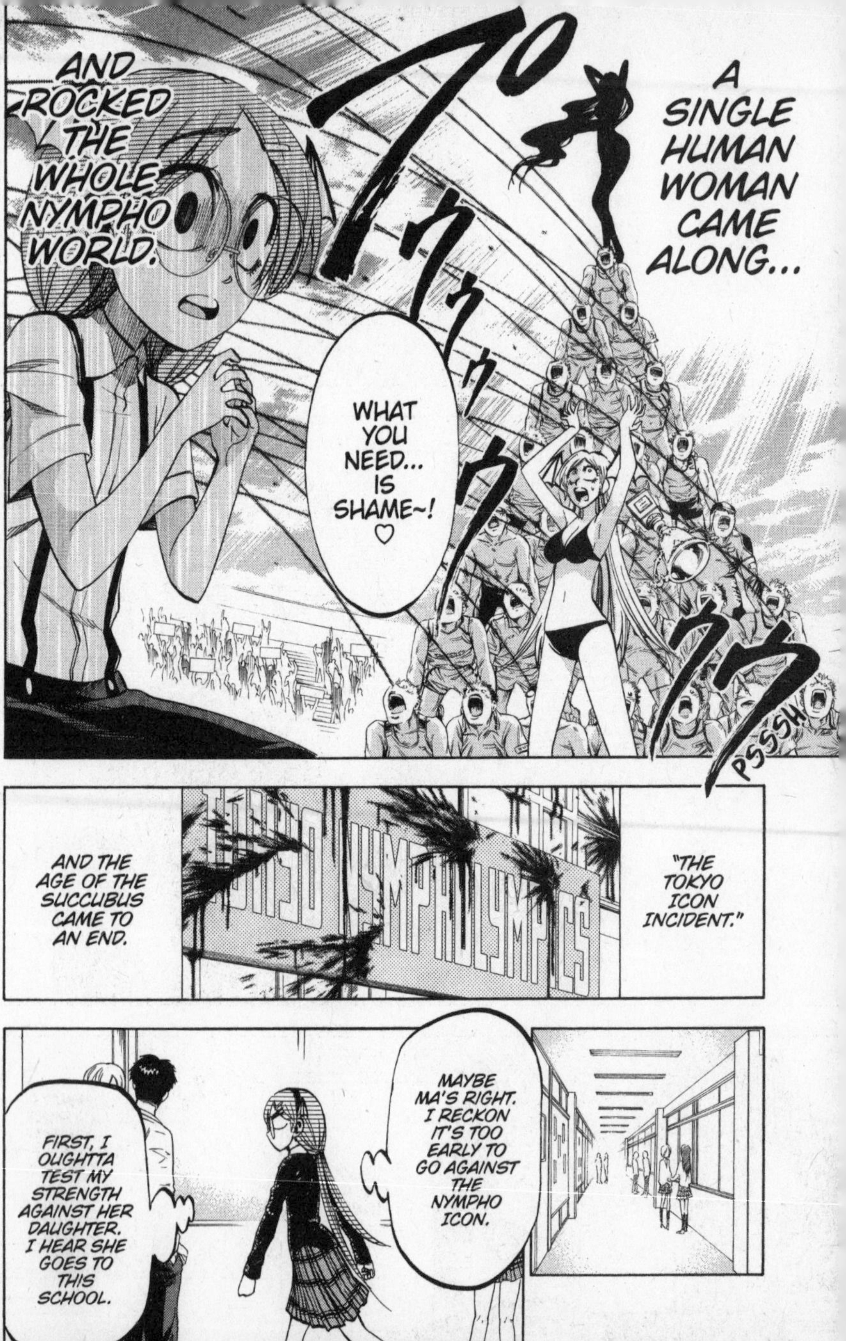
A SINGLE HUMAN WOMAN CAME ALONG...
WHAT YOU NEED... IS SHAME~! ♡
AND ROCKED THE WHOLE NYMPHO WORLD.
PSSSH
"THE TOKYO ICON INCIDENT."
AND THE AGE OF THE SUCCUBUS CAME TO AN END.
MAYBE MA'S RIGHT. I RECKON IT'S TOO EARLY TO GO AGAINST THE NYMPHO ICON.
FIRST, I OUGHTTA TEST MY STRENGTH AGAINST HER DAUGHTER. I HEAR SHE GOES TO THIS SCHOOL.

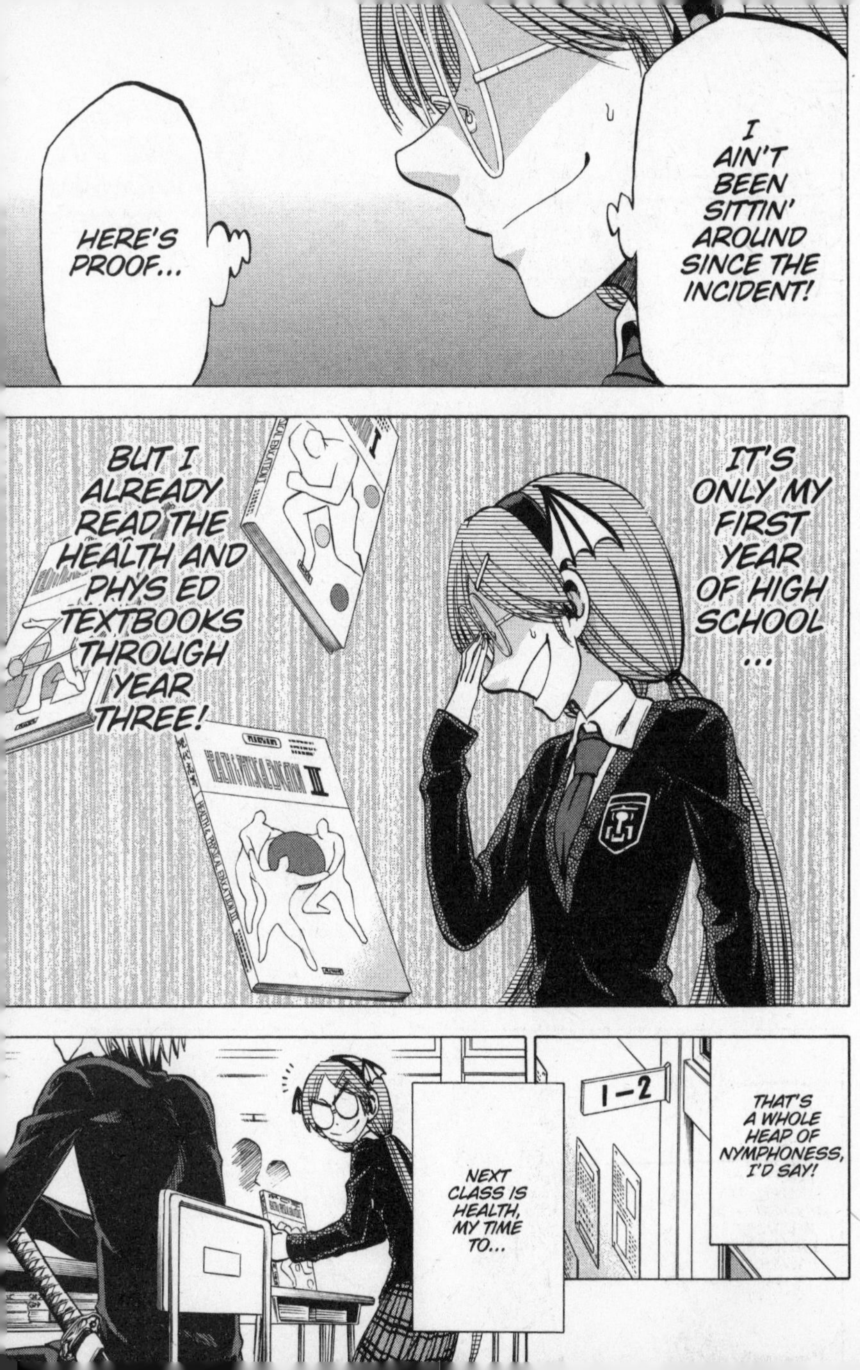
I AIN'T BEEN SITTIN' AROUND SINCE THE INCIDENT!
HERE'S PROOF...
IT'S ONLY MY FIRST YEAR OF HIGH SCHOOL...
BUT I ALREADY READ THE HEALTH AND PHYS ED TEXTBOOKS THROUGH YEAR THREE!
THAT'S A WHOLE HEAP OF NYMPHONESS, I'D SAY!
1-2
NEXT CLASS IS HEALTH, MY TIME TO...

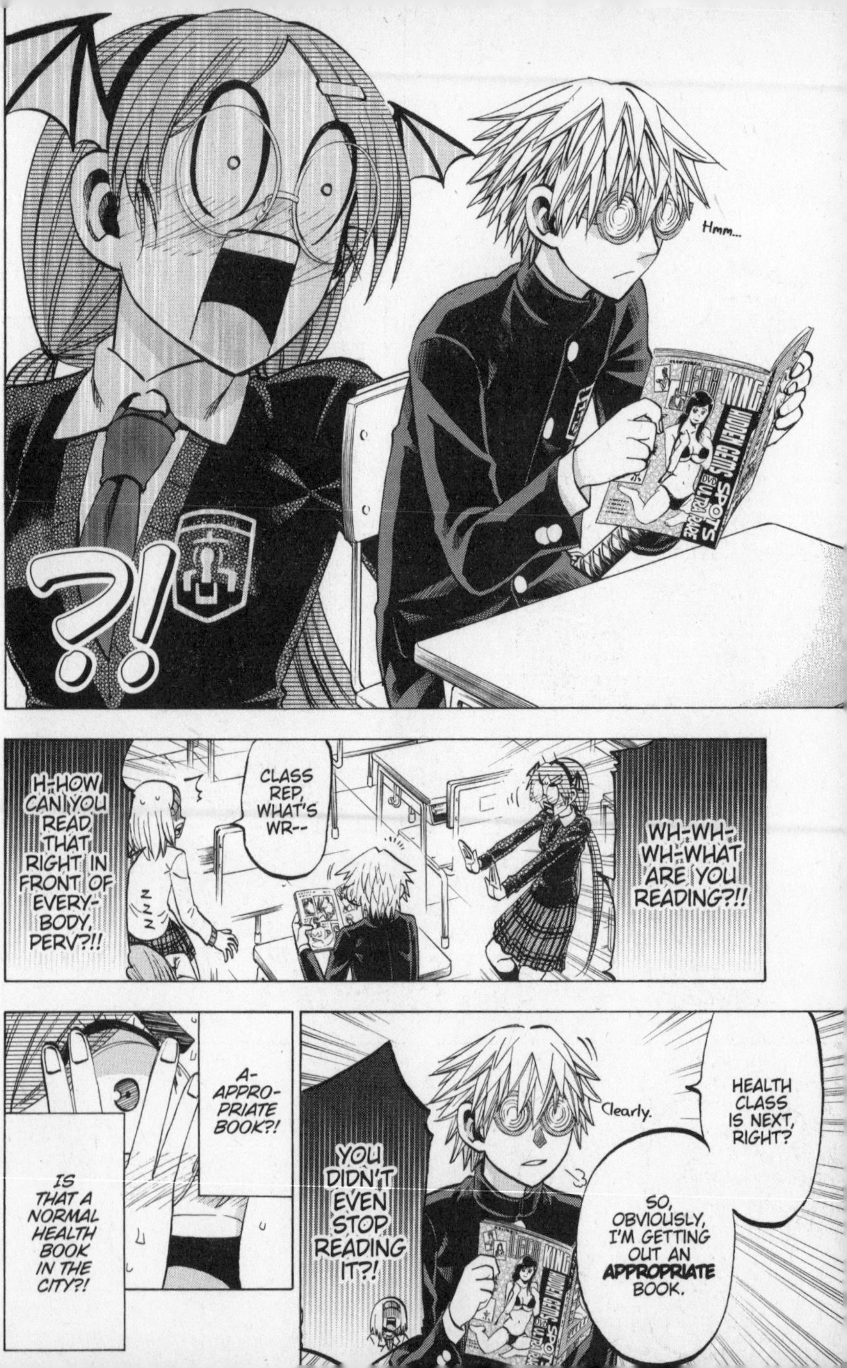
Hmm...
LEECH KING
HIDDEN GEMS
SPOTS
DVD
ULTRA RARE
?!
WH-WH-WH-WHAT ARE YOU READING?!!
CLASS REP, WHAT'S WR--
H-HOW CAN YOU READ THAT RIGHT IN FRONT OF EVERYBODY, PERV?!!
ZZZ
HEALTH CLASS IS NEXT, RIGHT?
SO, OBVIOUSLY, I'M GETTING OUT AN **APPROPRIATE** BOOK.
Clearly.
YOU DIDN'T EVEN STOP READING IT?!
A-APPROPRIATE BOOK?!
IS THAT A NORMAL HEALTH BOOK IN THE CITY?!

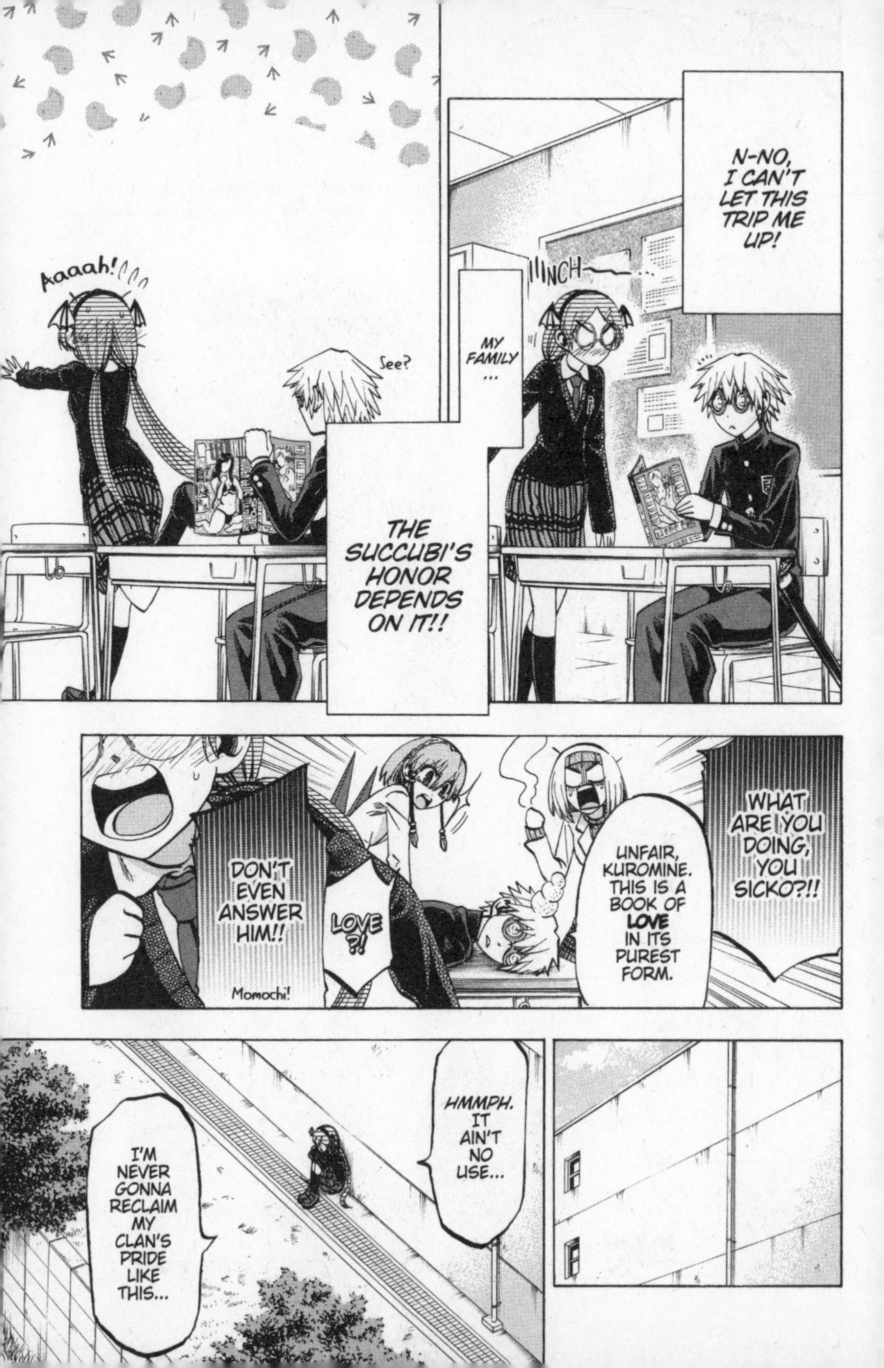
N-NO, I CAN'T LET THIS TRIP ME UP!
IIINCH
MY FAMILY...
THE SUCCUBI'S HONOR DEPENDS ON IT!!
See?
Aaaah!
WHAT ARE YOU DOING, YOU SICKO?!!
UNFAIR, KUROMINE. THIS IS A BOOK OF **LOVE** IN ITS PUREST FORM.
LOVE?!
DON'T EVEN ANSWER HIM!!
Momochi!
HMMPH. IT AIN'T NO USE...
I'M NEVER GONNA RECLAIM MY CLAN'S PRIDE LIKE THIS...

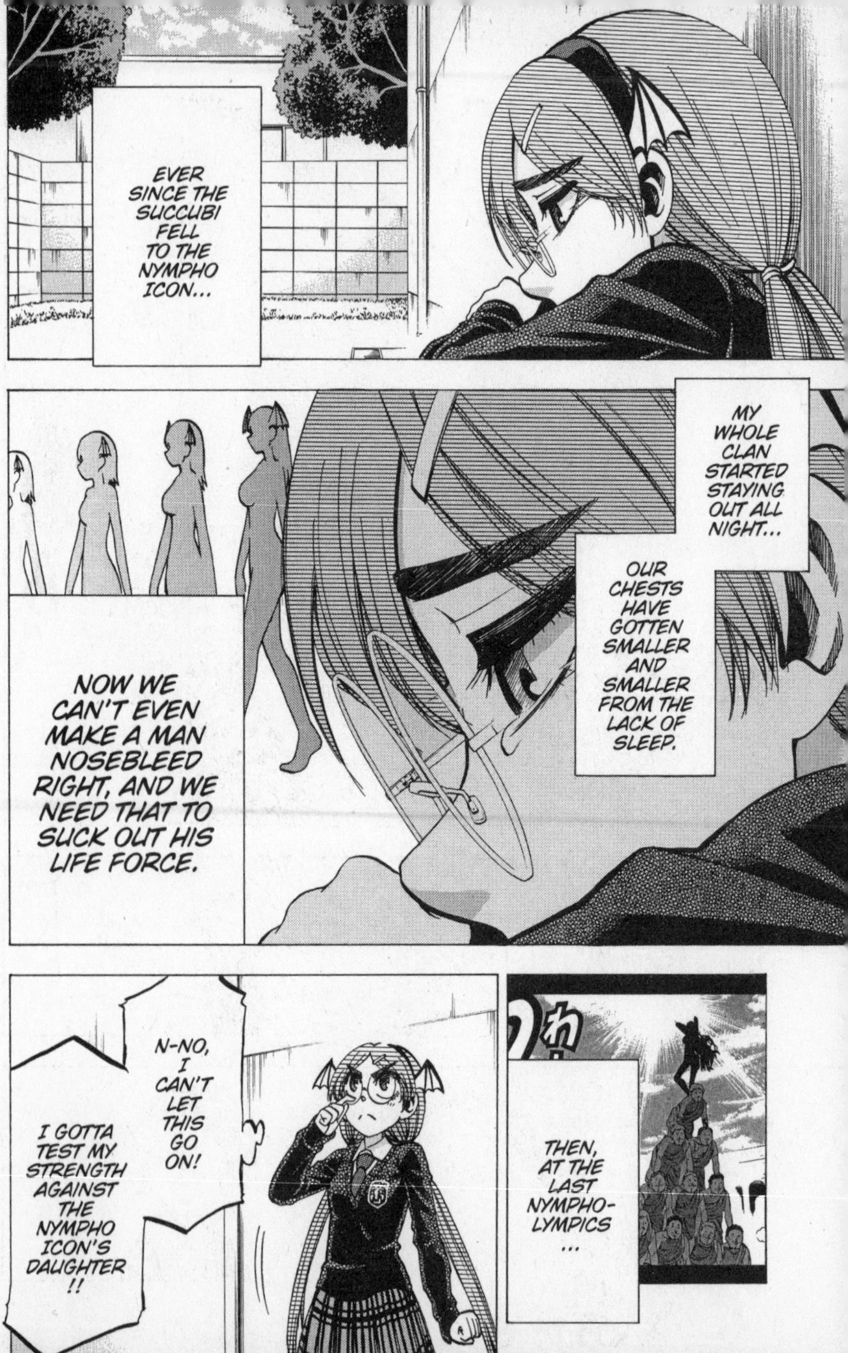
EVER SINCE THE SUCCUBI FELL TO THE NYMPHO ICON...
MY WHOLE CLAN STARTED STAYING OUT ALL NIGHT...
OUR CHESTS HAVE GOTTEN SMALLER AND SMALLER FROM THE LACK OF SLEEP.
NOW WE CAN'T EVEN MAKE A MAN NOSEBLEED RIGHT, AND WE NEED THAT TO SUCK OUT HIS LIFE FORCE.
THEN, AT THE LAST NYMPHO-LYMPICS ...
N-NO, I CAN'T LET THIS GO ON!
I GOTTA TEST MY STRENGTH AGAINST THE NYMPHO ICON'S DAUGHTER !!

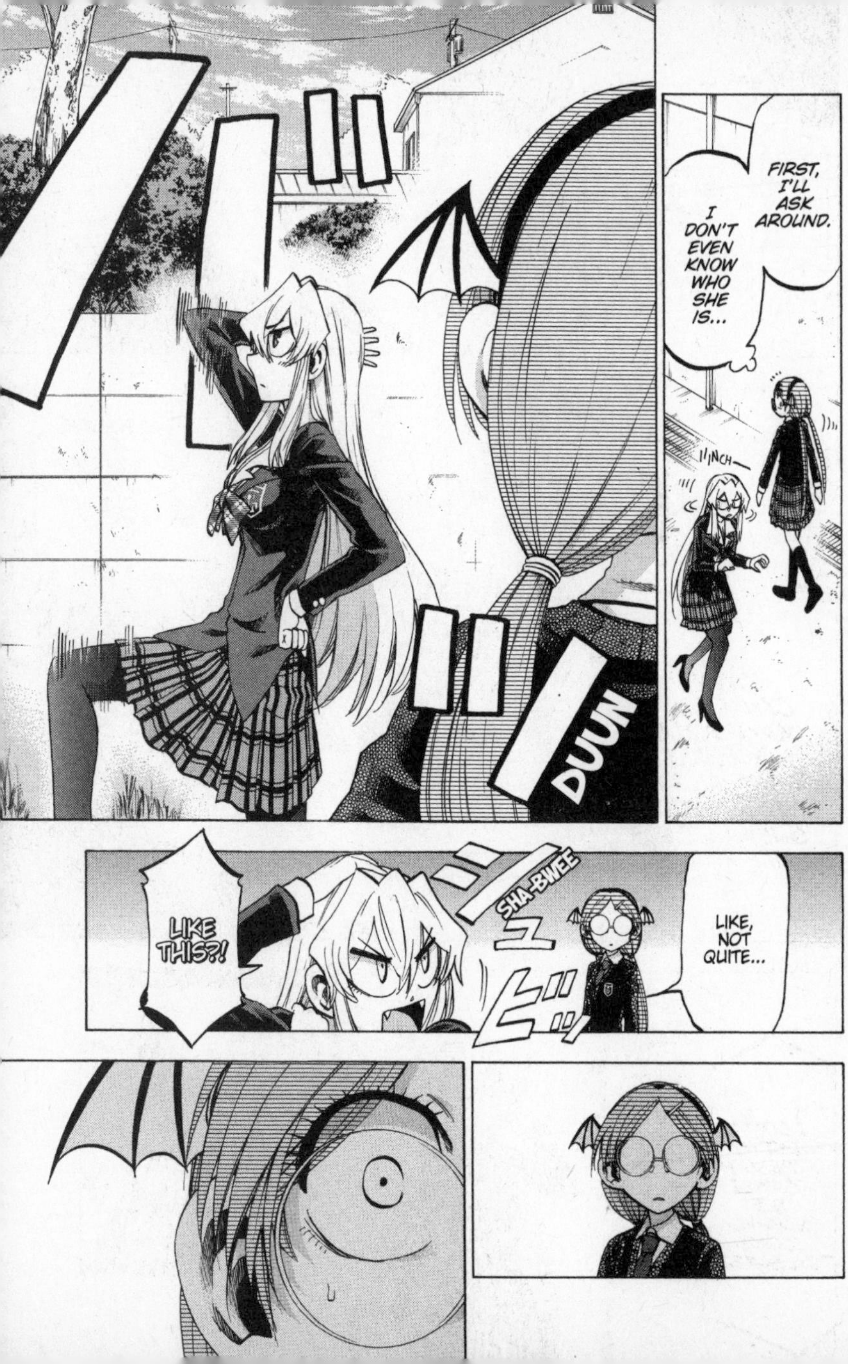
FIRST, I'LL ASK AROUND.
I DON'T EVEN KNOW WHO SHE IS...
FLINCH—
DUUN
LIKE, NOT QUITE...
SHA-BWEE
LIKE THIS?!

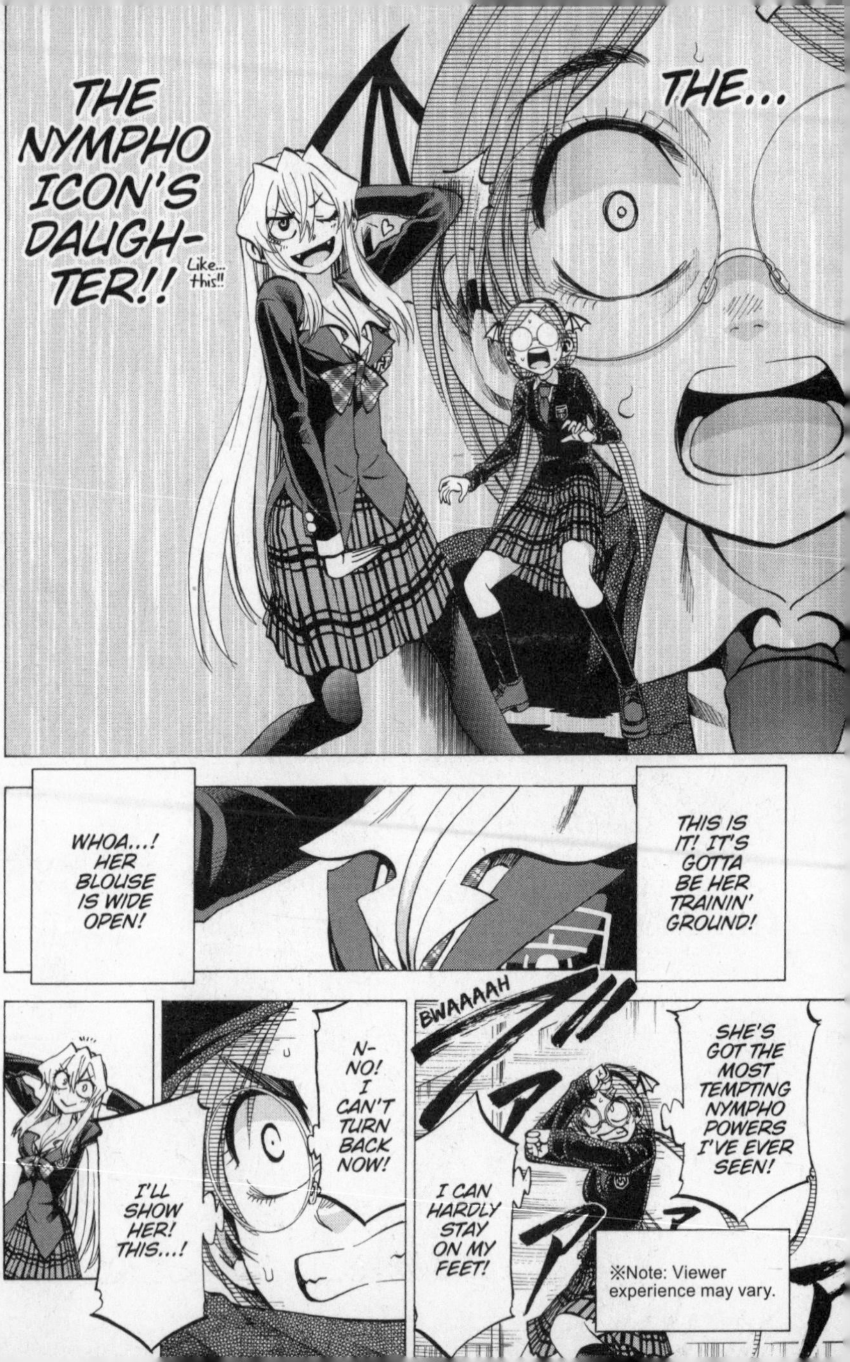
THE...
THE NYMPHO ICON'S DAUGHTER!!
Like... this!!
THIS IS IT! IT'S GOTTA BE HER TRAININ' GROUND!
WHOA...! HER BLOUSE IS WIDE OPEN!
SHE'S GOT THE MOST TEMPTING NYMPHO POWERS I'VE EVER SEEN!
BWAAAAH
I CAN HARDLY STAY ON MY FEET!
※Note: Viewer experience may vary.
N-NO! I CAN'T TURN BACK NOW!
I'LL SHOW HER! THIS...!

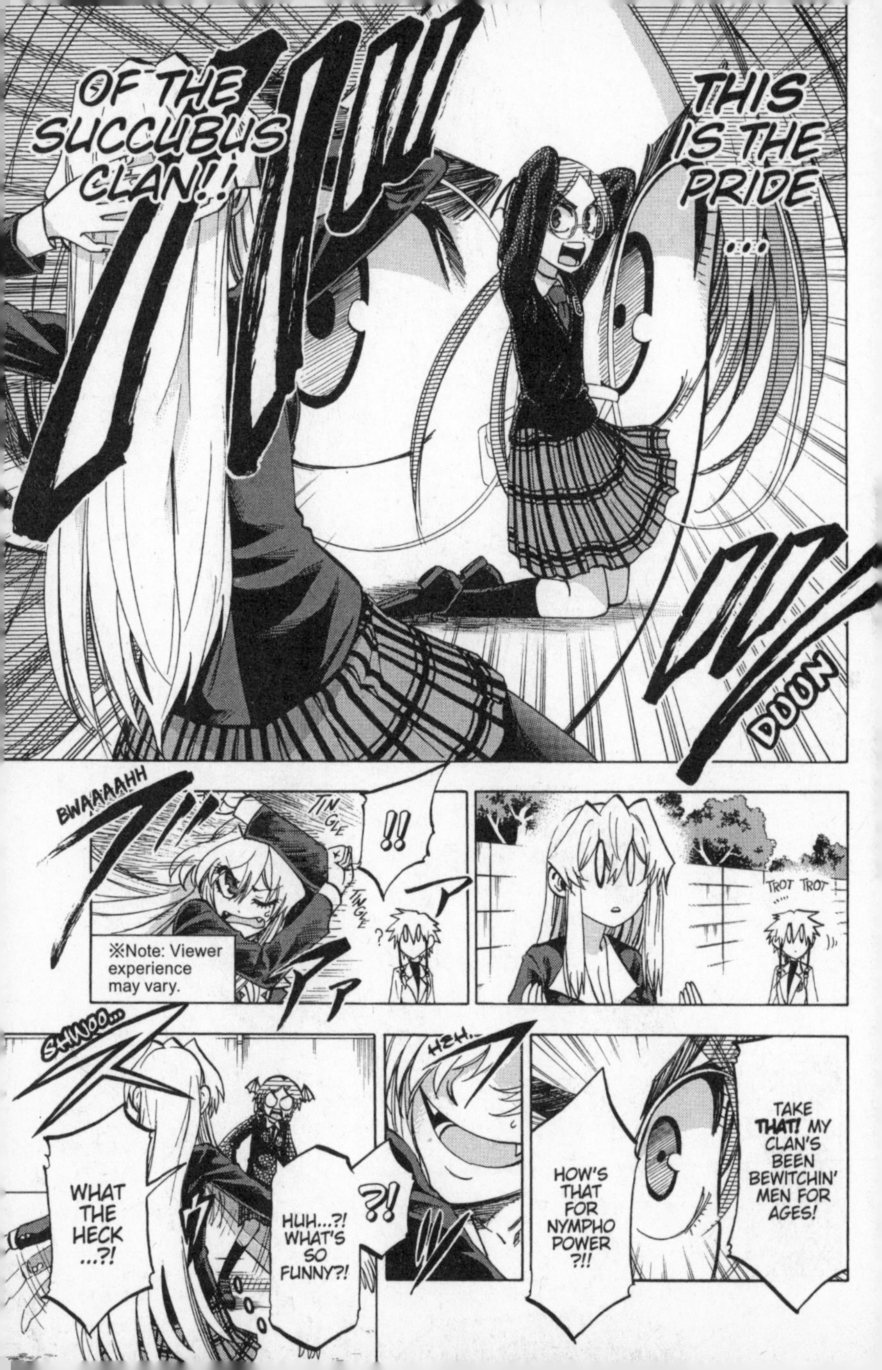
THIS IS THE PRIDE ...
OF THE SUCCUBUS CLAN!!
DUUN
TROT TROT
!!
TINGLE
TINGLE
BWAAAAHH
?
※Note: Viewer experience may vary.
TAKE THAT! MY CLAN'S BEEN BEWITCHIN' MEN FOR AGES!
HOW'S THAT FOR NYMPHO POWER ?!!
HEH...
?!
HUH...?! WHAT'S SO FUNNY?!
SHWOO...
WHAT THE HECK ...?!

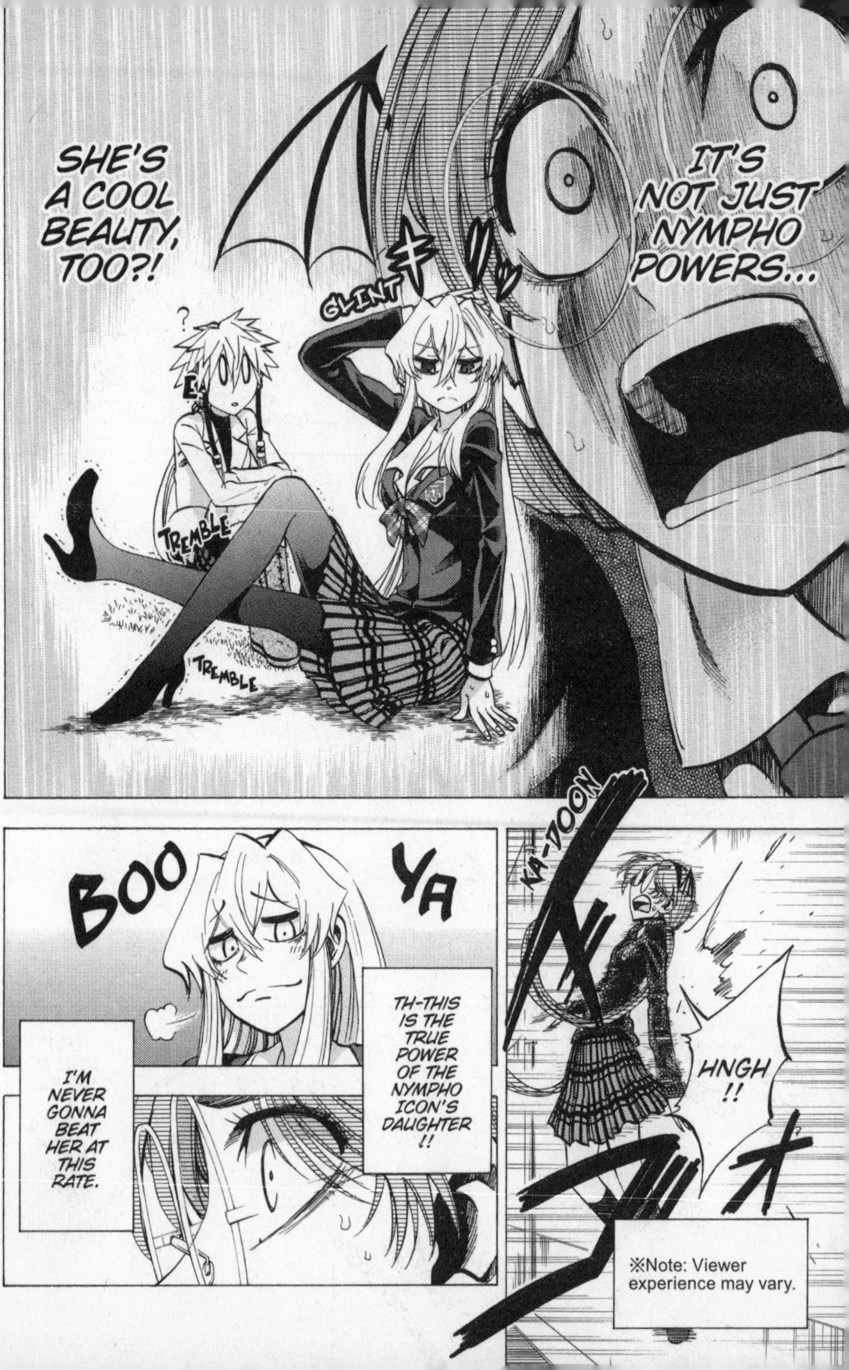
IT'S NOT JUST NYMPHO POWERS...
SHE'S A COOL BEAUTY, TOO?!
GLINT
TREMBLE
TREMBLE
KA-DOON
HNGH !!
※Note: Viewer experience may vary.
BOO
YA
TH-THIS IS THE TRUE POWER OF THE NYMPHO ICON'S DAUGHTER !!
I'M NEVER GONNA BEAT HER AT THIS RATE.

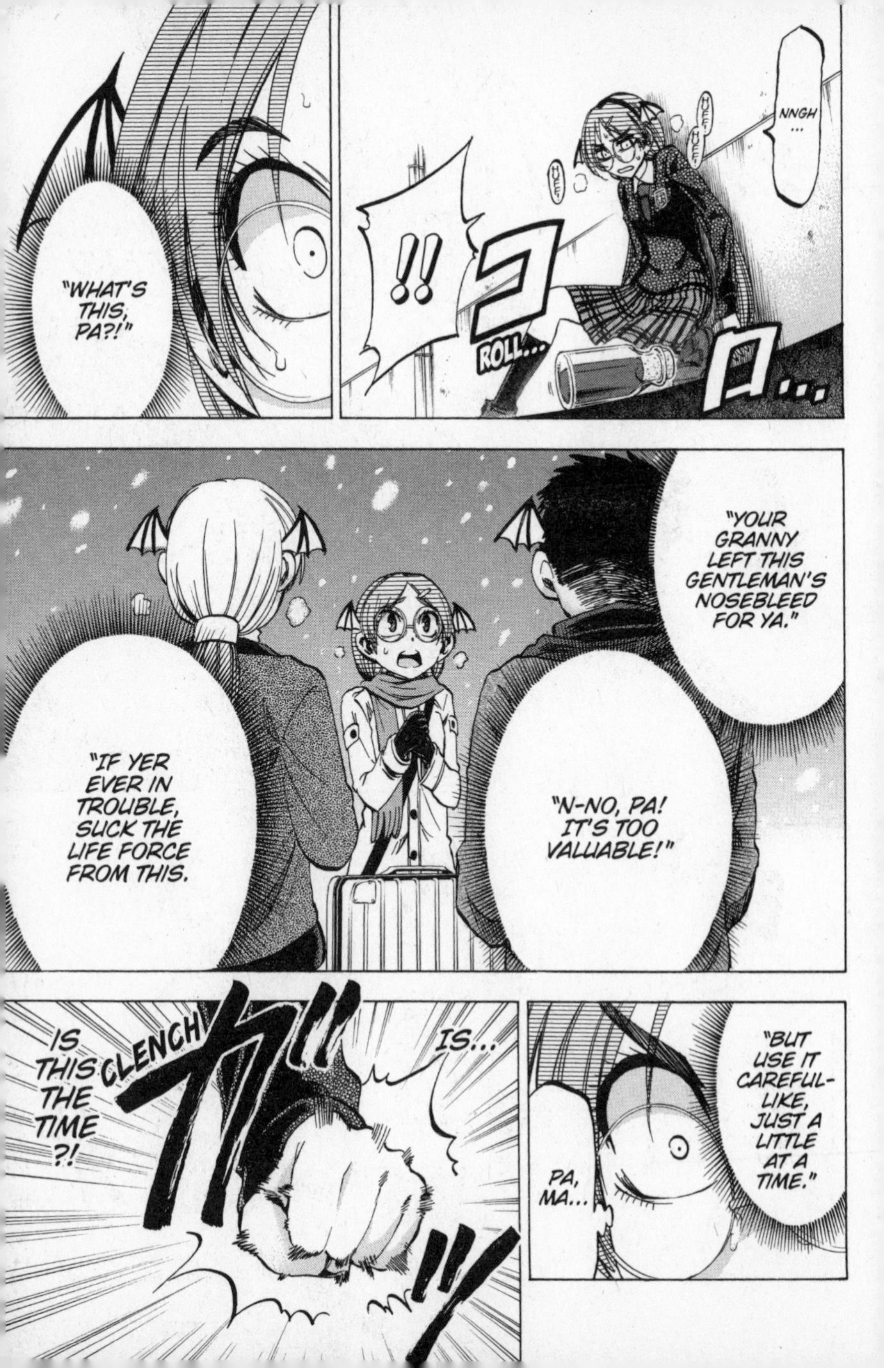
NNGH...
HUFF HUFF
HUFF
!!
ROLL...
"WHAT'S THIS, PA?!"
"YOUR GRANNY LEFT THIS GENTLEMAN'S NOSEBLEED FOR YA."
"N-NO, PA! IT'S TOO VALUABLE!"
"IF YER EVER IN TROUBLE, SUCK THE LIFE FORCE FROM THIS.
"BUT USE IT CAREFUL-LIKE, JUST A LITTLE AT A TIME."
PA, MA...
IS...
IS THIS THE TIME?!
CLENCH

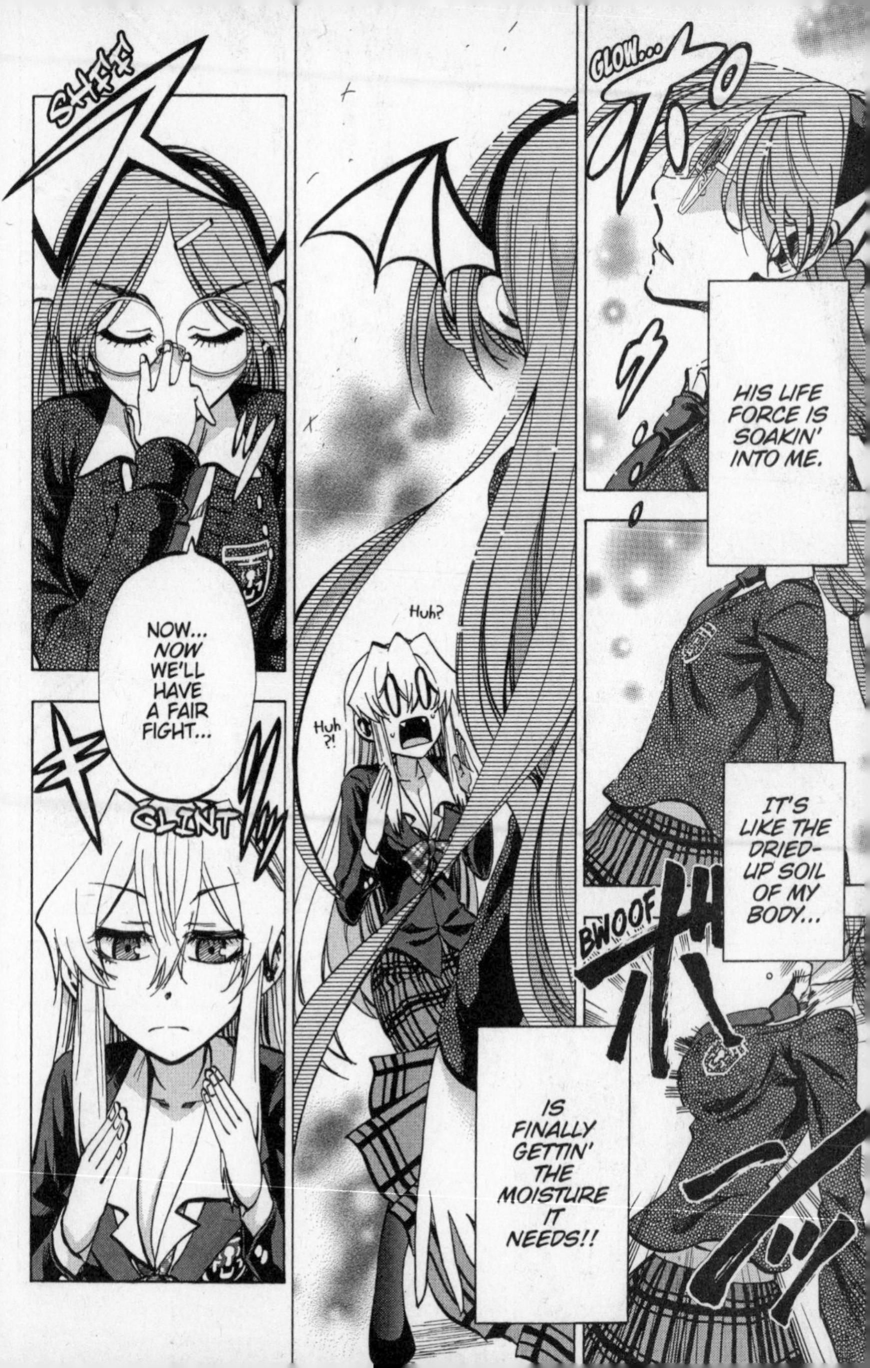
GLOW...
HIS LIFE FORCE IS SOAKIN' INTO ME.
IT'S LIKE THE DRIED-UP SOIL OF MY BODY...
BWOOF
IS FINALLY GETTIN' THE MOISTURE IT NEEDS!!
Huh?
Huh ?!
SHFF
NOW... NOW WE'LL HAVE A FAIR FIGHT...
GLINT

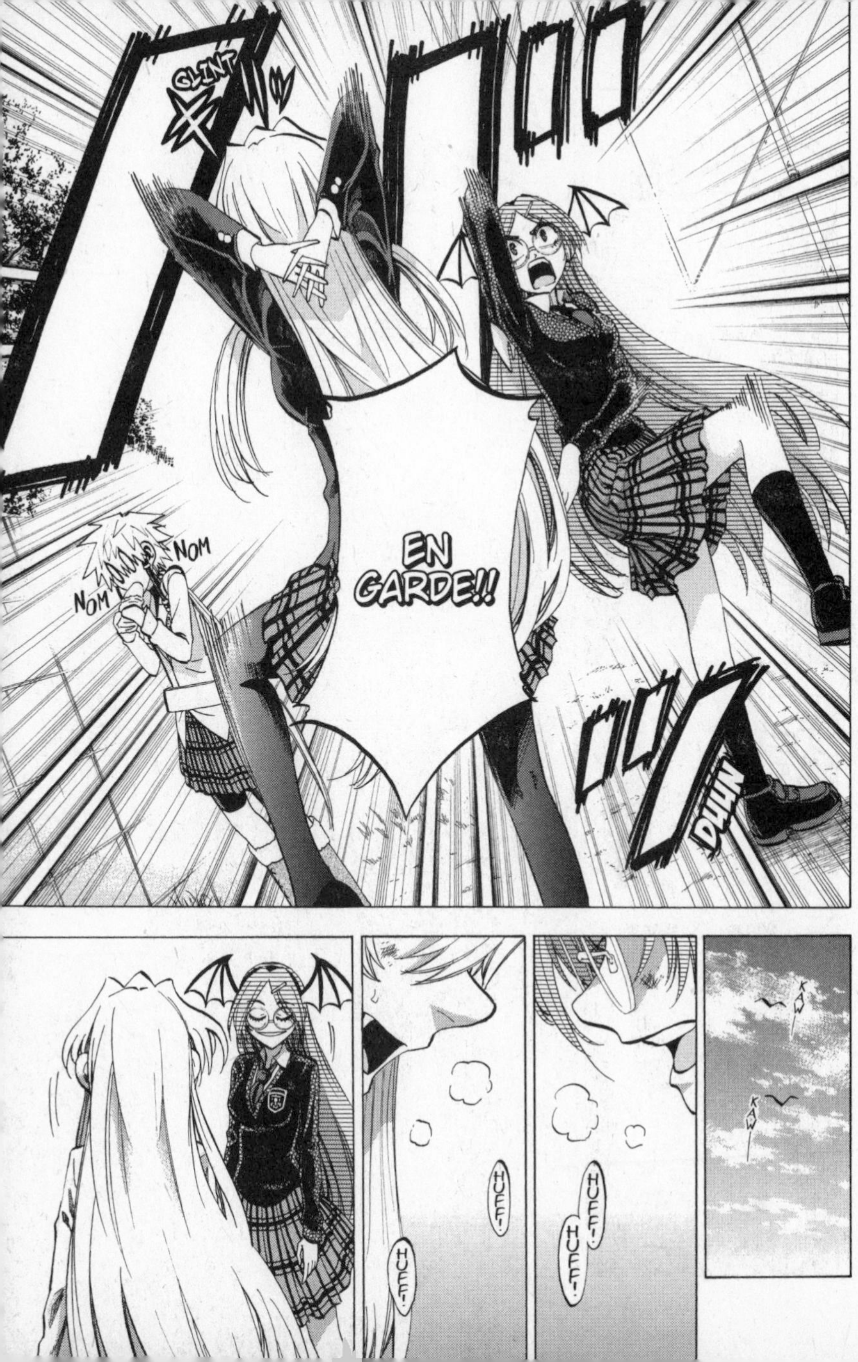
GLINT
EN GARDE!!
NOM
NOM
DUHN
KAW
KAW
HUFF!
HUFF!
HUFF!
HUFF!
HUFF!

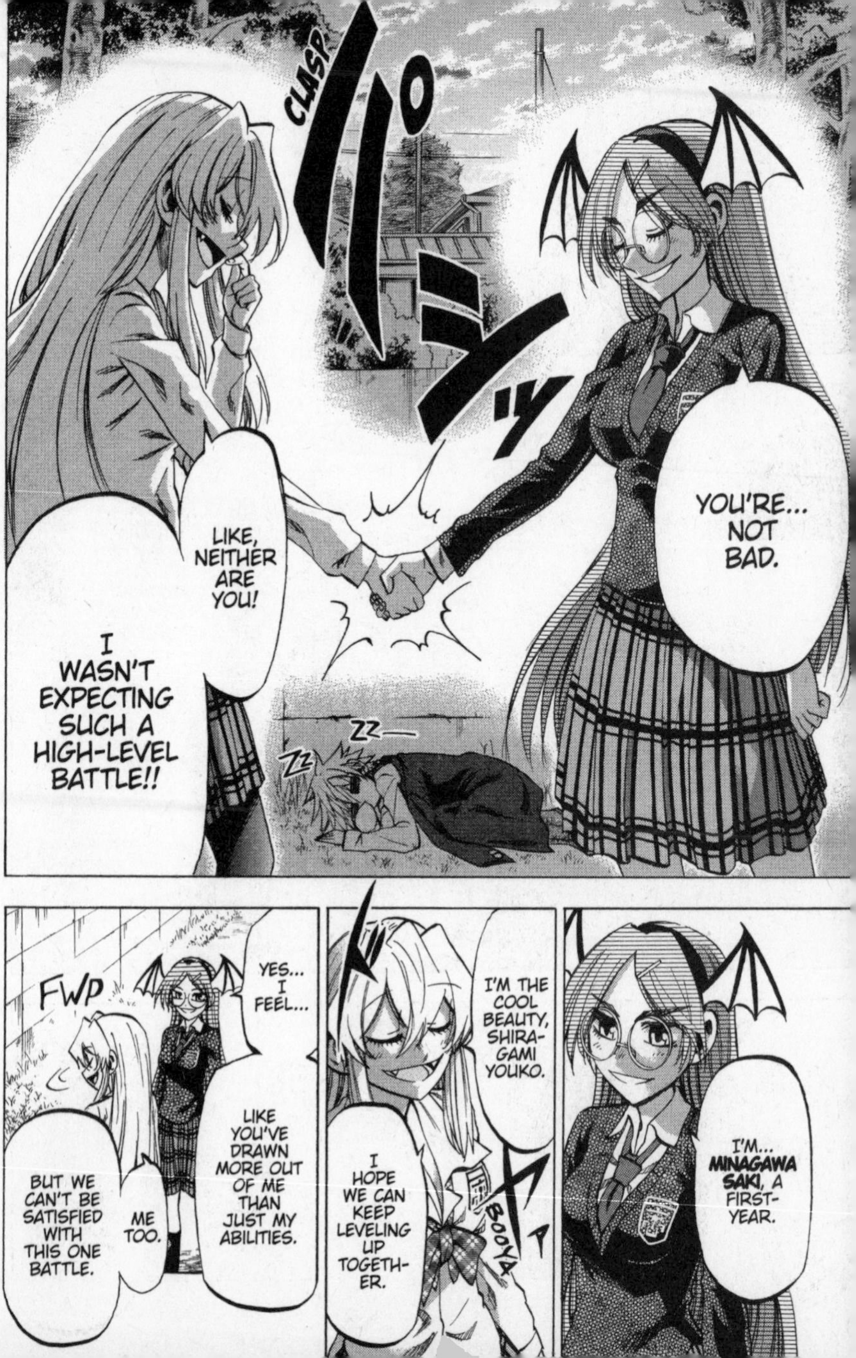
CLASP
YOU'RE... NOT BAD.
LIKE, NEITHER ARE YOU!
I WASN'T EXPECTING SUCH A HIGH-LEVEL BATTLE!!
ZZ—
ZZ
I'M... MINAGAWA SAKI, A FIRST-YEAR.
I'M THE COOL BEAUTY, SHIRA-GAMI YOUKO.
I HOPE WE CAN KEEP LEVELING UP TOGETH-ER.
BOOYA
YES... I FEEL...
LIKE YOU'VE DRAWN MORE OUT OF ME THAN JUST MY ABILITIES.
FWP
ME TOO.
BUT WE CAN'T BE SATISFIED WITH THIS ONE BATTLE.

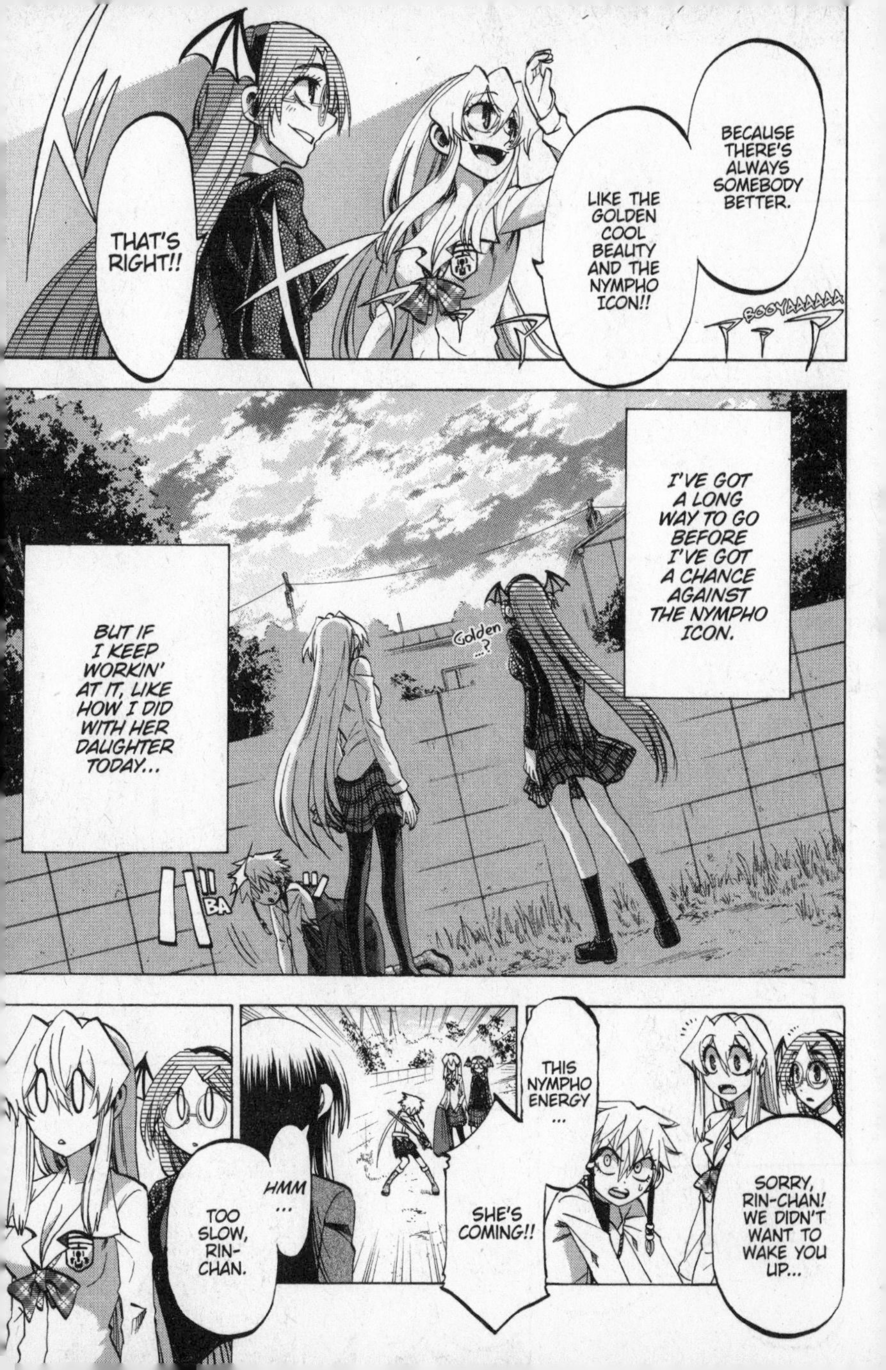
BECAUSE THERE'S ALWAYS SOMEBODY BETTER.
LIKE THE GOLDEN COOL BEAUTY AND THE NYMPHO ICON!!
BOOYAAAAAA
THAT'S RIGHT!!
I'VE GOT A LONG WAY TO GO BEFORE I'VE GOT A CHANCE AGAINST THE NYMPHO ICON.
Golden ...?
BUT IF I KEEP WORKIN' AT IT, LIKE HOW I DID WITH HER DAUGHTER TODAY...
BA
SORRY, RIN-CHAN! WE DIDN'T WANT TO WAKE YOU UP...
THIS NYMPHO ENERGY ...
SHE'S COMING!!
HMM ...
TOO SLOW, RIN-CHAN.

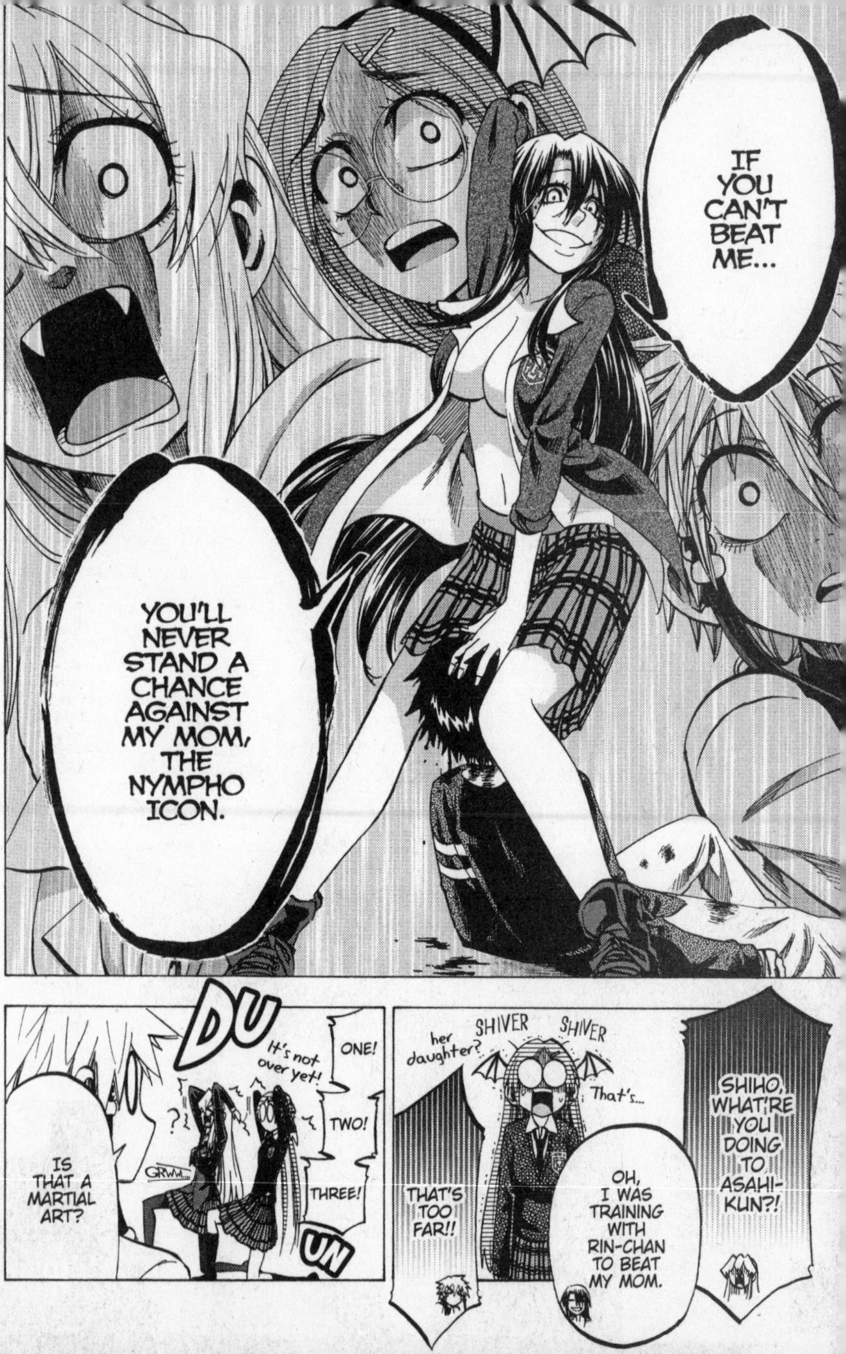
IF YOU CAN'T BEAT ME...
YOU'LL NEVER STAND A CHANCE AGAINST MY MOM, THE NYMPHO ICON.
SHIHO, WHAT'RE YOU DOING TO ASAHI-KUN?!
SHIVER SHIVER
her daughter?
That's...
OH, I WAS TRAINING WITH RIN-CHAN TO BEAT MY MOM.
THAT'S TOO FAR!!
DU
ONE!
It's not over yet!
TWO!
THREE!
UN
IS THAT A MARTIAL ART?

Chapter 110: "Let's Think About Our Future Careers!"

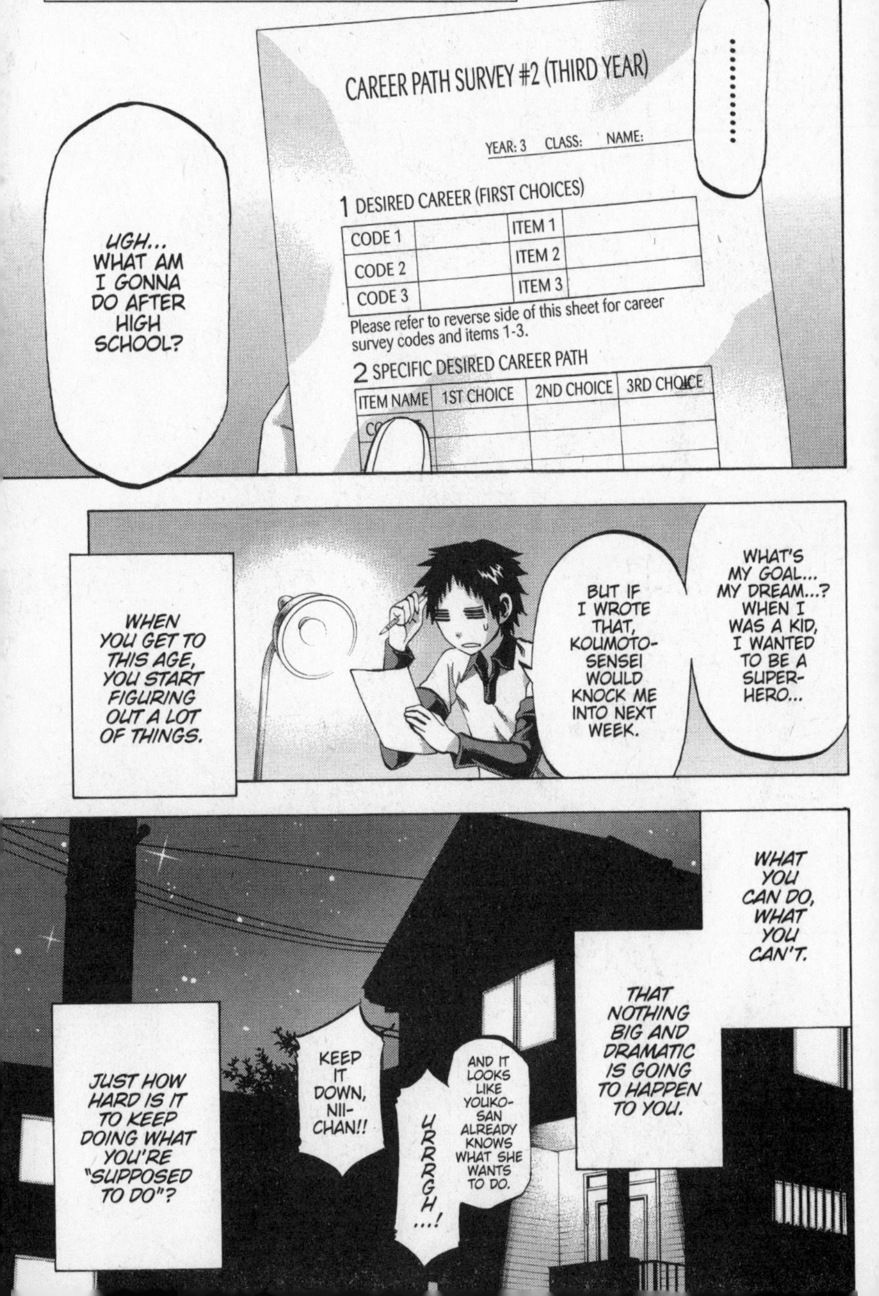
....
CAREER PATH SURVEY #2 (THIRD YEAR)
YEAR: 3 CLASS: NAME:
1 DESIRED CAREER (FIRST CHOICES)
CODE 1 ITEM 1
CODE 2 ITEM 2
CODE 3 ITEM 3
Please refer to reverse side of this sheet for career survey codes and items 1-3.
2 SPECIFIC DESIRED CAREER PATH
ITEM NAME 1ST CHOICE 2ND CHOICE 3RD CHOICE
UGH... WHAT AM I GONNA DO AFTER HIGH SCHOOL?
WHAT'S MY GOAL... MY DREAM...? WHEN I WAS A KID, I WANTED TO BE A SUPER-HERO...
BUT IF I WROTE THAT, KOUMOTO-SENSEI WOULD KNOCK ME INTO NEXT WEEK.
WHEN YOU GET TO THIS AGE, YOU START FIGURING OUT A LOT OF THINGS.
WHAT YOU CAN DO, WHAT YOU CAN'T.
THAT NOTHING BIG AND DRAMATIC IS GOING TO HAPPEN TO YOU.
AND IT LOOKS LIKE YOUKO-SAN ALREADY KNOWS WHAT SHE WANTS TO DO.
URRRGH...!
KEEP IT DOWN, NII-CHAN!!
JUST HOW HARD IS IT TO KEEP DOING WHAT YOU'RE "SUPPOSED TO DO"?

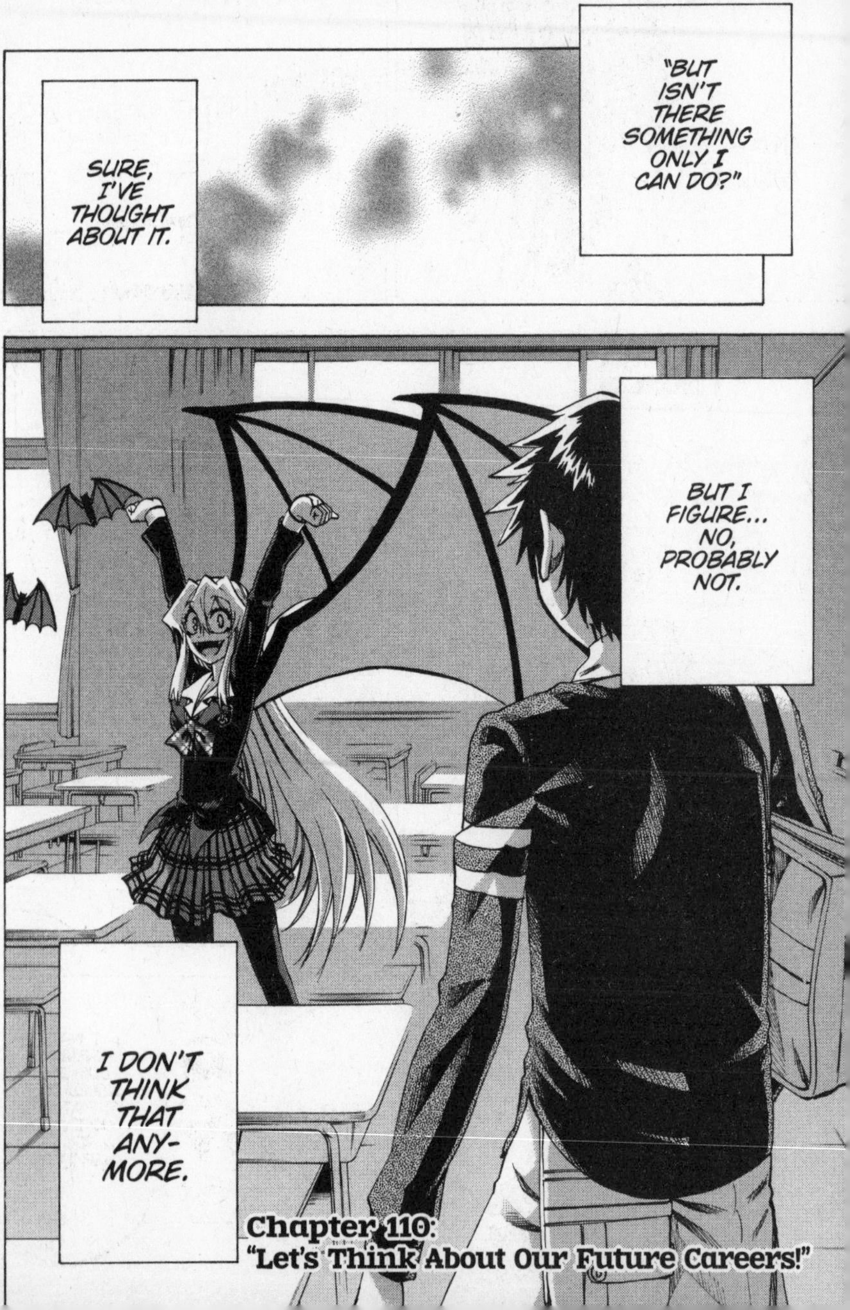
"BUT ISN'T THERE SOMETHING ONLY I CAN DO?"
SURE, I'VE THOUGHT ABOUT IT.
BUT I FIGURE... NO, PROBABLY NOT.
I DON'T THINK THAT ANY-MORE.
Chapter 110:
"Let's Think About Our Future Careers!"

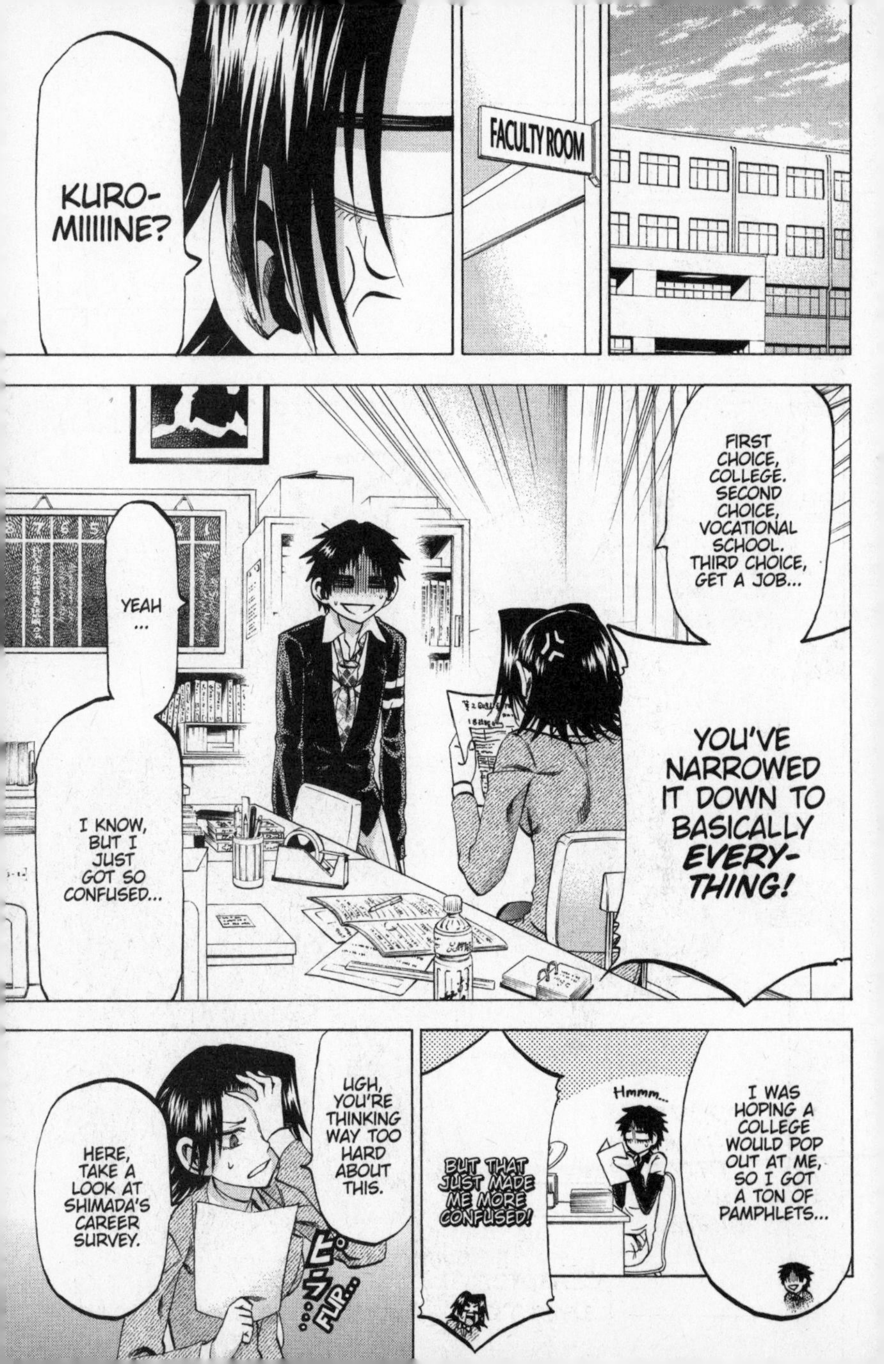
FACULTY ROOM
KURO-MIIIIINE?
FIRST CHOICE, COLLEGE. SECOND CHOICE, VOCATIONAL SCHOOL. THIRD CHOICE, GET A JOB...
YOU'VE NARROWED IT DOWN TO BASICALLY EVERYTHING!
YEAH ...
I KNOW, BUT I JUST GOT SO CONFUSED...
I WAS HOPING A COLLEGE WOULD POP OUT AT ME, SO I GOT A TON OF PAMPHLETS...
Hmmm...
BUT THAT JUST MADE ME MORE CONFUSED!
UGH, YOU'RE THINKING WAY TOO HARD ABOUT THIS.
HERE, TAKE A LOOK AT SHIMADA'S CAREER SURVEY.
FLIP...

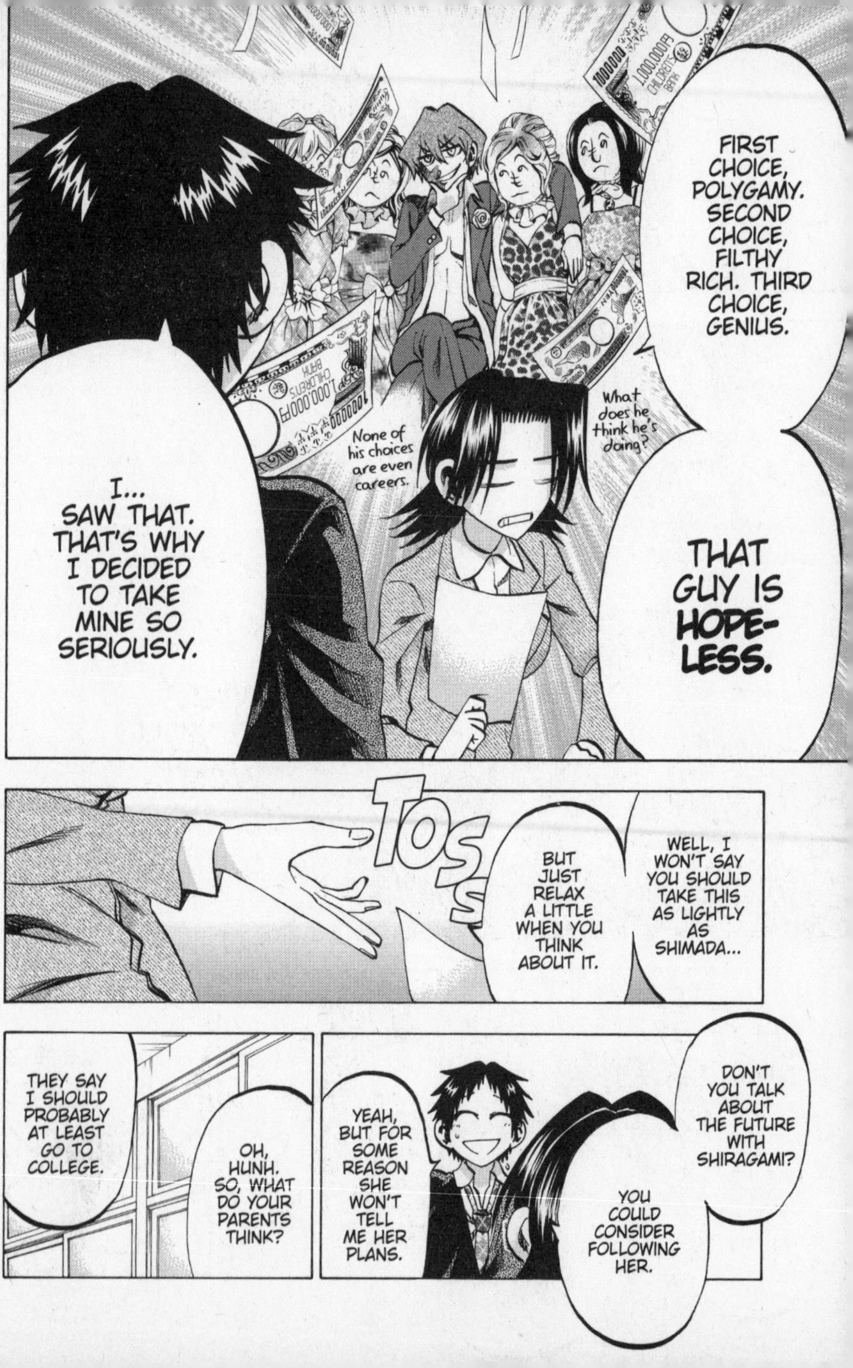
FIRST CHOICE, POLYGAMY. SECOND CHOICE, FILTHY RICH. THIRD CHOICE, GENIUS.
THAT GUY IS **HOPE-LESS.**
What does he think he's doing?
None of his choices are even careers.
I... SAW THAT. THAT'S WHY I DECIDED TO TAKE MINE SO SERIOUSLY.
WELL, I WON'T SAY YOU SHOULD TAKE THIS AS LIGHTLY AS SHIMADA...
BUT JUST RELAX A LITTLE WHEN YOU THINK ABOUT IT.
TOSS
DON'T YOU TALK ABOUT THE FUTURE WITH SHIRAGAMI?
YOU COULD CONSIDER FOLLOWING HER.
YEAH, BUT FOR SOME REASON SHE WON'T TELL ME HER PLANS.
OH, HUNH. SO, WHAT DO YOUR PARENTS THINK?
THEY SAY I SHOULD PROBABLY AT LEAST GO TO COLLEGE.

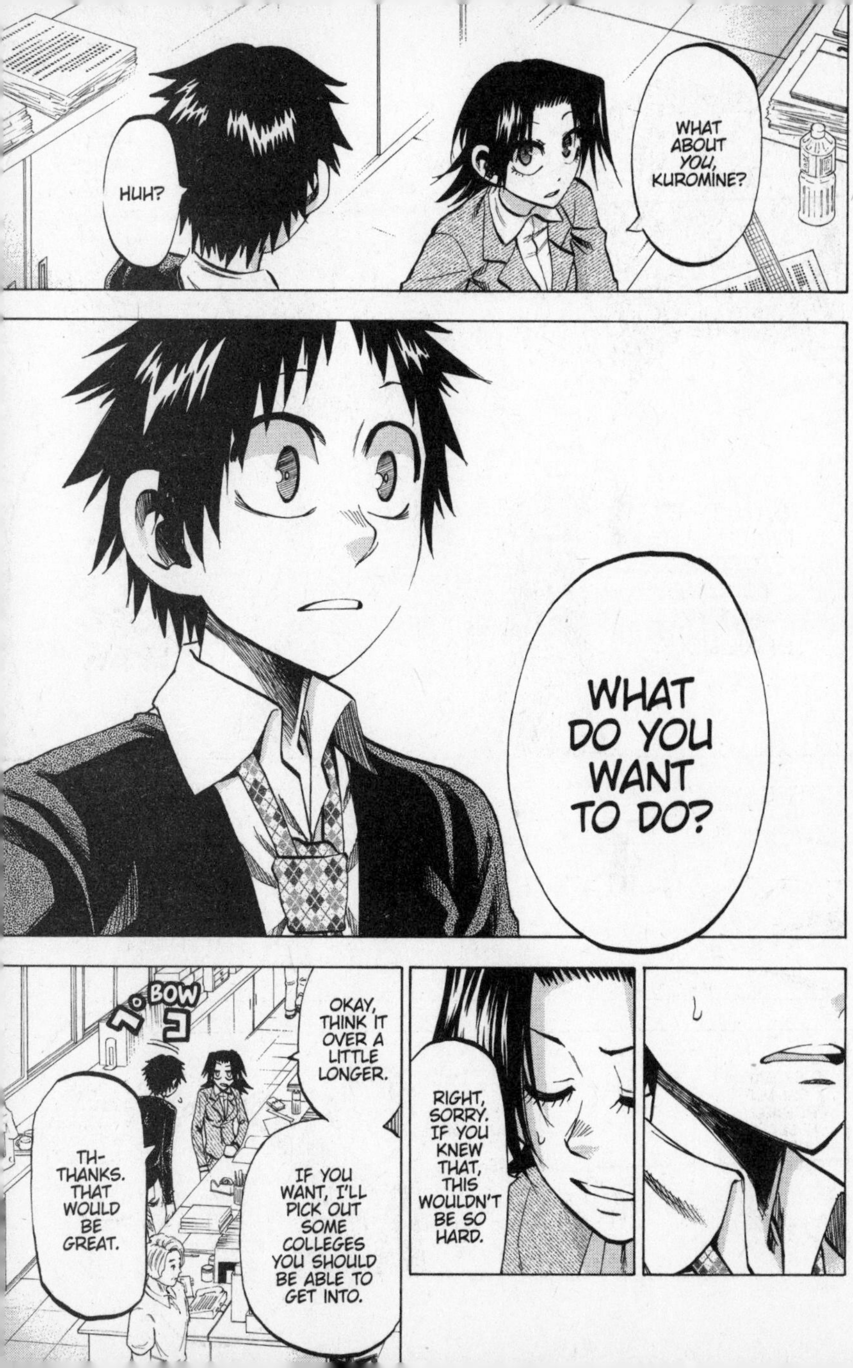

WHAT ABOUT YOU, KUROMINE?
HUH?
WHAT DO YOU WANT TO DO?
RIGHT, SORRY. IF YOU KNEW THAT, THIS WOULDN'T BE SO HARD.
OKAY, THINK IT OVER A LITTLE LONGER.
BOW
IF YOU WANT, I'LL PICK OUT SOME COLLEGES YOU SHOULD BE ABLE TO GET INTO.
TH-THANKS. THAT WOULD BE GREAT.

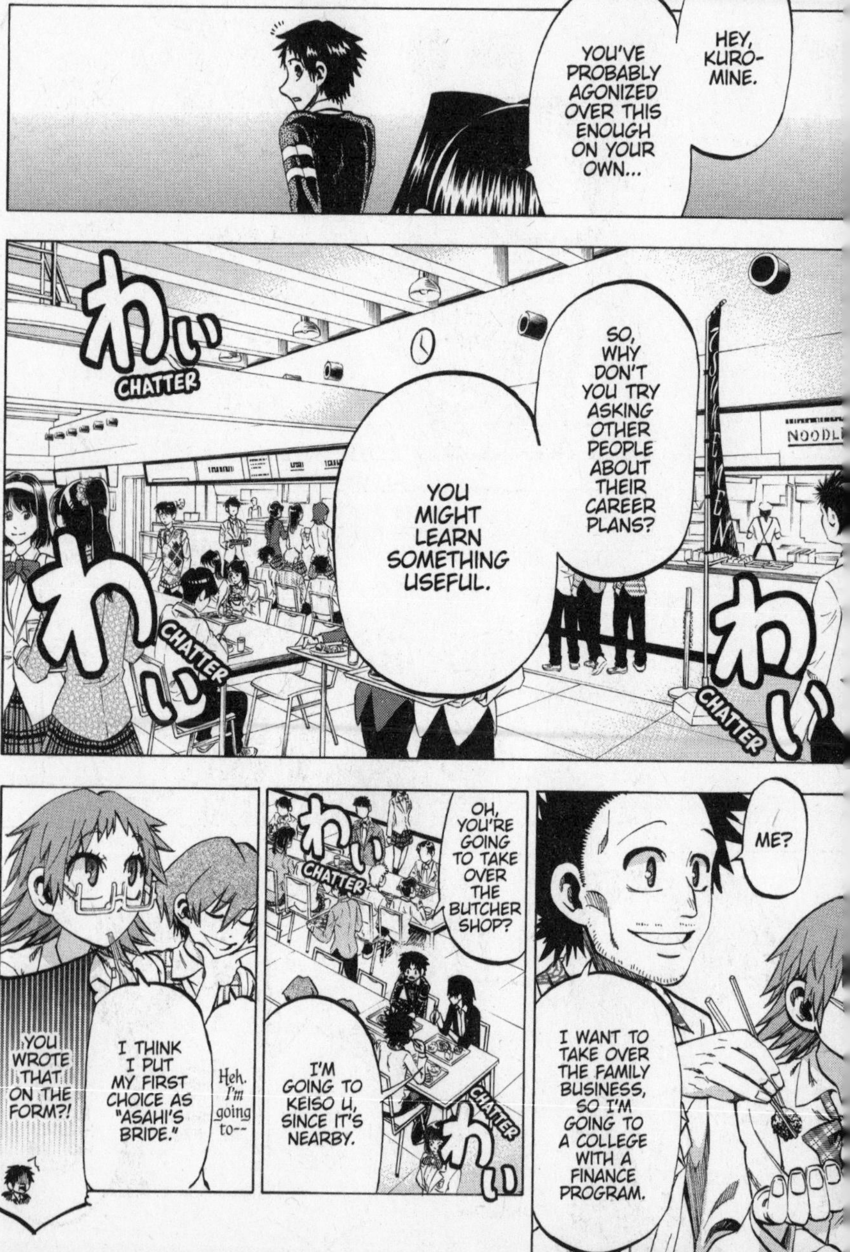
HEY, KURO-MINE.
YOU'VE PROBABLY AGONIZED OVER THIS ENOUGH ON YOUR OWN...
わい
CHATTER
SO, WHY DON'T YOU TRY ASKING OTHER PEOPLE ABOUT THEIR CAREER PLANS?
NOODL
YOU MIGHT LEARN SOMETHING USEFUL.
わい
CHATTER
わい
CHATTER
ME?
I WANT TO TAKE OVER THE FAMILY BUSINESS, SO I'M GOING TO A COLLEGE WITH A FINANCE PROGRAM.
OH, YOU'RE GOING TO TAKE OVER THE BUTCHER SHOP?
わい
CHATTER
I'M GOING TO KEISO U, SINCE IT'S NEARBY.
わい
CHATTER
Heh. I'm going to--
I THINK I PUT MY FIRST CHOICE AS "ASAHI'S BRIDE."
YOU WROTE THAT ON THE FORM?!

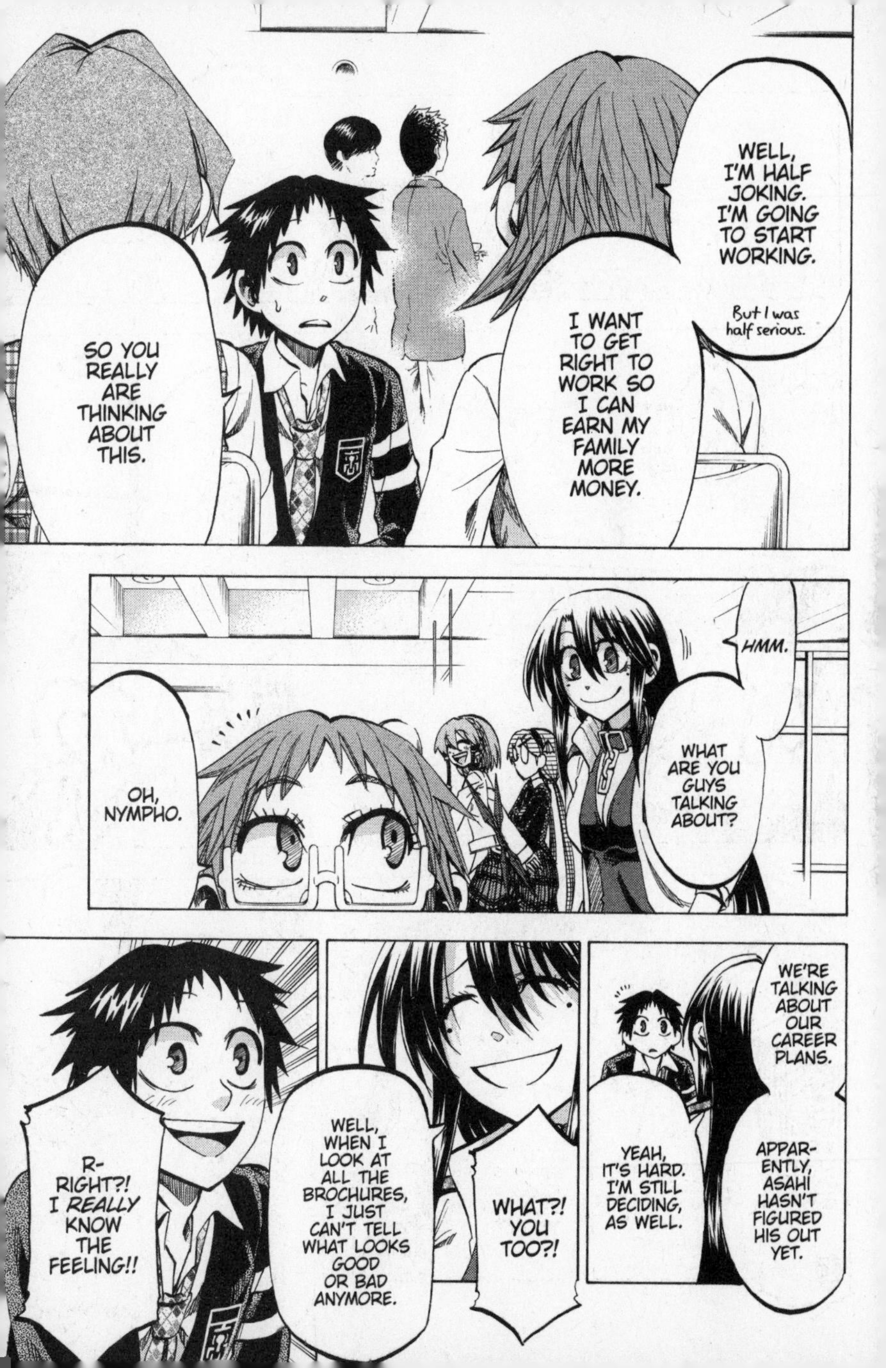
WELL, I'M HALF JOKING. I'M GOING TO START WORKING.
But I was half serious.
I WANT TO GET RIGHT TO WORK SO I CAN EARN MY FAMILY MORE MONEY.
SO YOU REALLY ARE THINKING ABOUT THIS.
HMM.
WHAT ARE YOU GUYS TALKING ABOUT?
OH, NYMPHO.
WE'RE TALKING ABOUT OUR CAREER PLANS.
APPAR-ENTLY, ASAHI HASN'T FIGURED HIS OUT YET.
YEAH, IT'S HARD. I'M STILL DECIDING, AS WELL.
WHAT?! YOU TOO?!
WELL, WHEN I LOOK AT ALL THE BROCHURES, I JUST CAN'T TELL WHAT LOOKS GOOD OR BAD ANYMORE.
R-RIGHT?! I *REALLY* KNOW THE FEELING!!

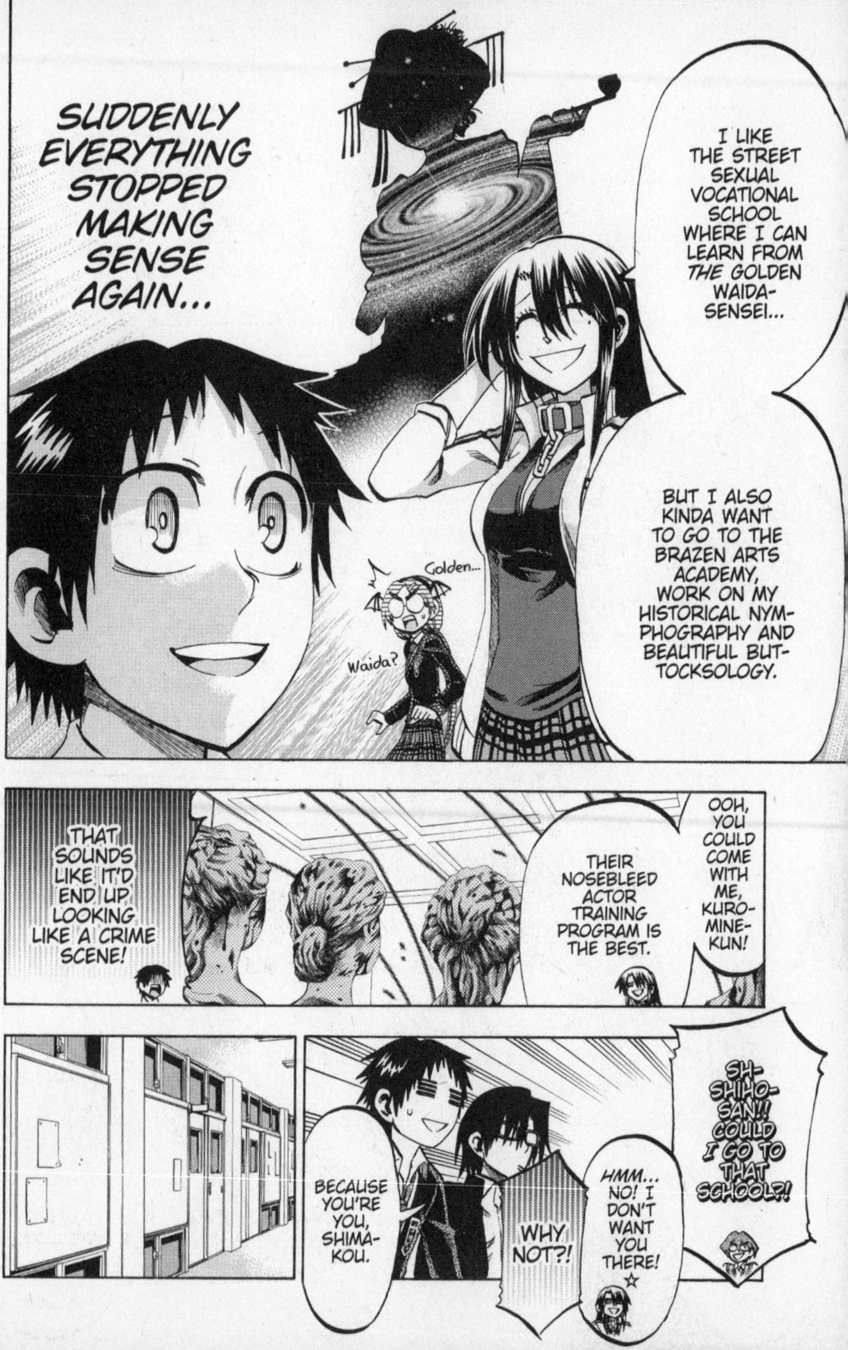
I LIKE THE STREET SEXUAL VOCATIONAL SCHOOL WHERE I CAN LEARN FROM *THE* GOLDEN WAIDA-SENSEI...
BUT I ALSO KINDA WANT TO GO TO THE BRAZEN ARTS ACADEMY, WORK ON MY HISTORICAL NYMPHOGRAPHY AND BEAUTIFUL BUTTOCKSOLOGY.
Golden...
Waida?
SUDDENLY EVERYTHING STOPPED MAKING SENSE AGAIN...
OOH, YOU COULD COME WITH ME, KUROMINE-KUN!
THEIR NOSEBLEED ACTOR TRAINING PROGRAM IS THE BEST.
THAT SOUNDS LIKE IT'D END UP LOOKING LIKE A CRIME SCENE!
SH-SHIHO-SAN!! COULD I GO TO THAT SCHOOL?!
HMM... NO! I DON'T WANT YOU THERE! ☆
WHY NOT?!
BECAUSE YOU'RE YOU, SHIMAKOU.

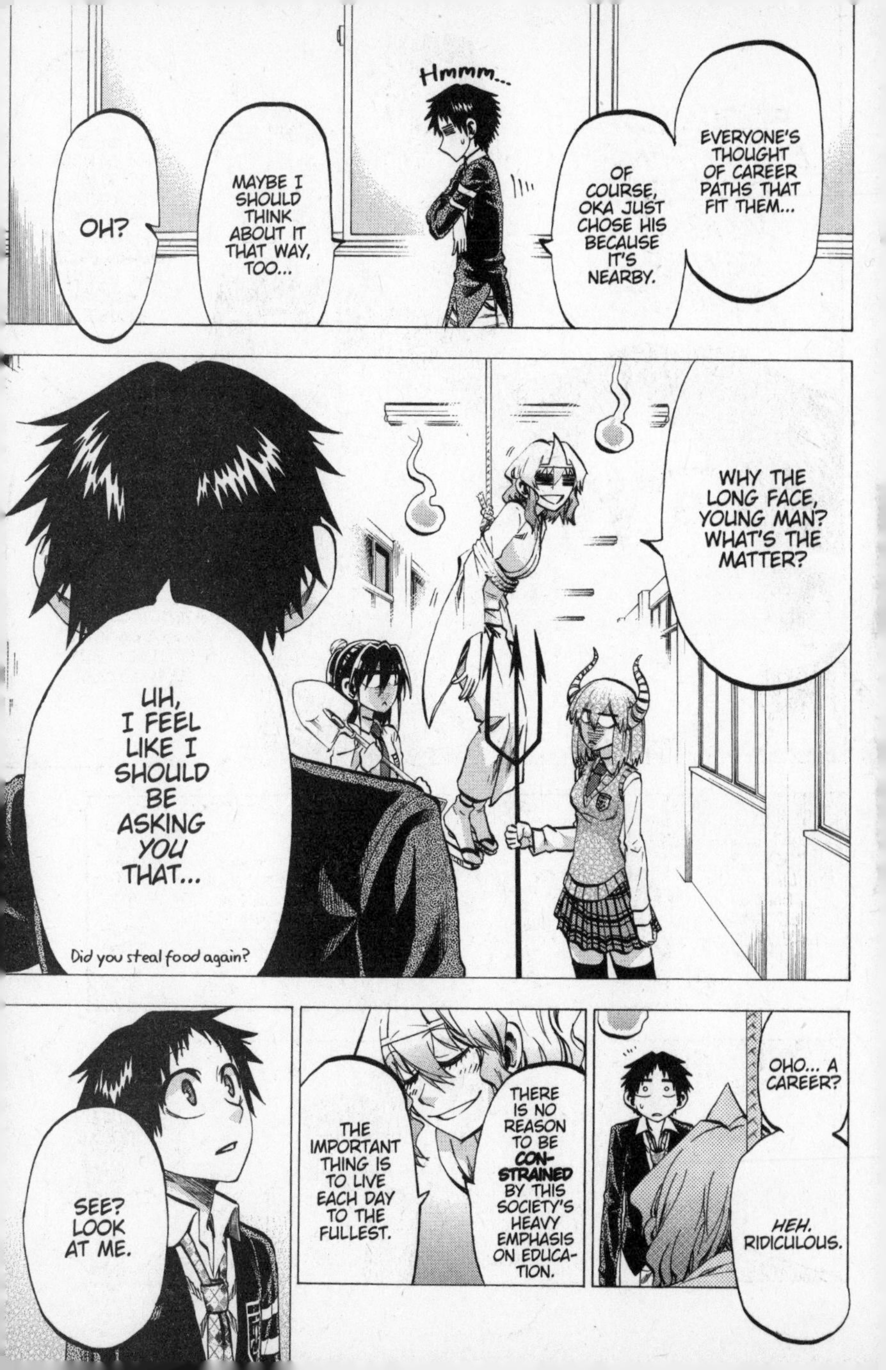
EVERYONE'S THOUGHT OF CAREER PATHS THAT FIT THEM...
OF COURSE, OKA JUST CHOSE HIS BECAUSE IT'S NEARBY.
Hmmm...
MAYBE I SHOULD THINK ABOUT IT THAT WAY, TOO...
OH?
WHY THE LONG FACE, YOUNG MAN? WHAT'S THE MATTER?
UH, I FEEL LIKE I SHOULD BE ASKING *YOU* THAT...
Did you steal food again?
OHO... A CAREER?
HEH. RIDICULOUS.
THERE IS NO REASON TO BE **CON-STRAINED** BY THIS SOCIETY'S HEAVY EMPHASIS ON EDUCA-TION.
THE IMPORTANT THING IS TO LIVE EACH DAY TO THE FULLEST.
SEE? LOOK AT ME.

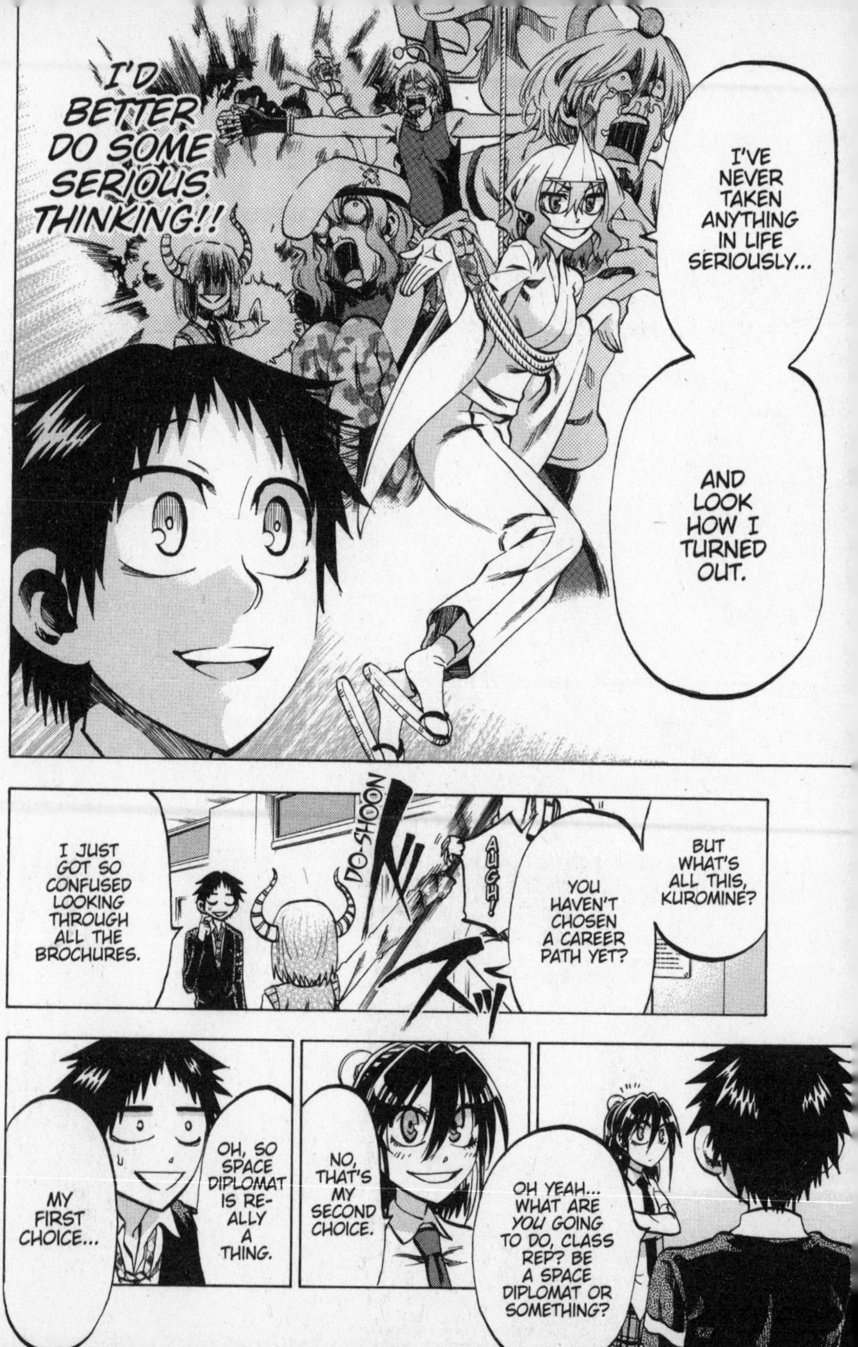

I'VE NEVER TAKEN ANYTHING IN LIFE SERIOUSLY...
AND LOOK HOW I TURNED OUT.
I'D BETTER DO SOME SERIOUS THINKING!!
BUT WHAT'S ALL THIS, KUROMINE?
YOU HAVEN'T CHOSEN A CAREER PATH YET?
AUGH!
DO-SHOON
I JUST GOT SO CONFUSED LOOKING THROUGH ALL THE BROCHURES.
OH YEAH... WHAT ARE YOU GOING TO DO, CLASS REP? BE A SPACE DIPLOMAT OR SOMETHING?
NO, THAT'S MY SECOND CHOICE.
OH, SO SPACE DIPLOMAT IS RE-ALLY A THING.
MY FIRST CHOICE...

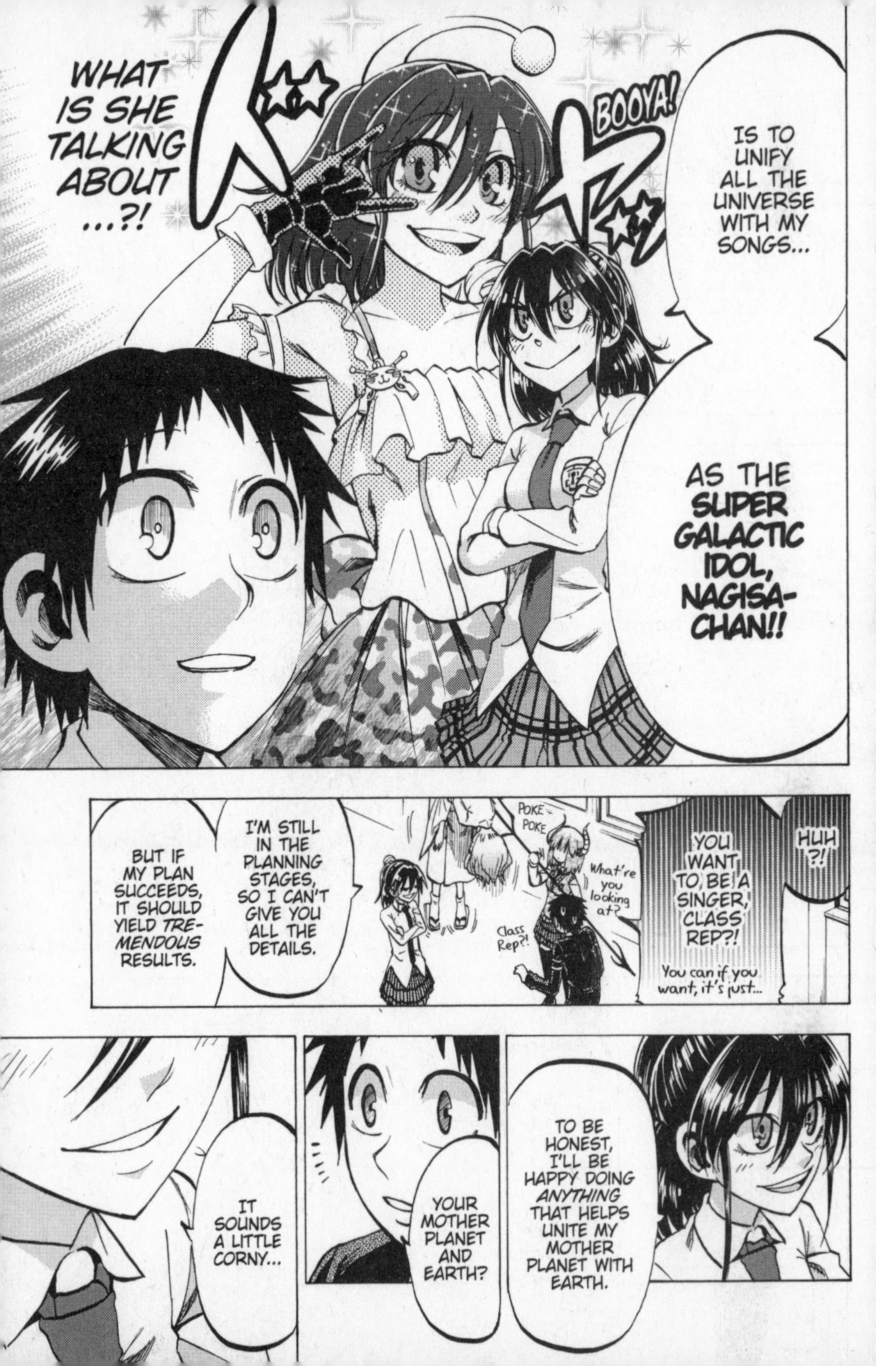
IS TO UNIFY ALL THE UNIVERSE WITH MY SONGS...
AS THE SUPER GALACTIC IDOL, NAGISA-CHAN!!
BOOYA!
WHAT IS SHE TALKING ABOUT ...?!
HUH ?!
YOU WANT TO BE A SINGER, CLASS REP?!
You can if you want, it's just...
POKE POKE
What're you looking at?
Class Rep?!
I'M STILL IN THE PLANNING STAGES, SO I CAN'T GIVE YOU ALL THE DETAILS.
BUT IF MY PLAN SUCCEEDS, IT SHOULD YIELD TREMENDOUS RESULTS.
TO BE HONEST, I'LL BE HAPPY DOING ANYTHING THAT HELPS UNITE MY MOTHER PLANET WITH EARTH.
YOUR MOTHER PLANET AND EARTH?
IT SOUNDS A LITTLE CORNY...

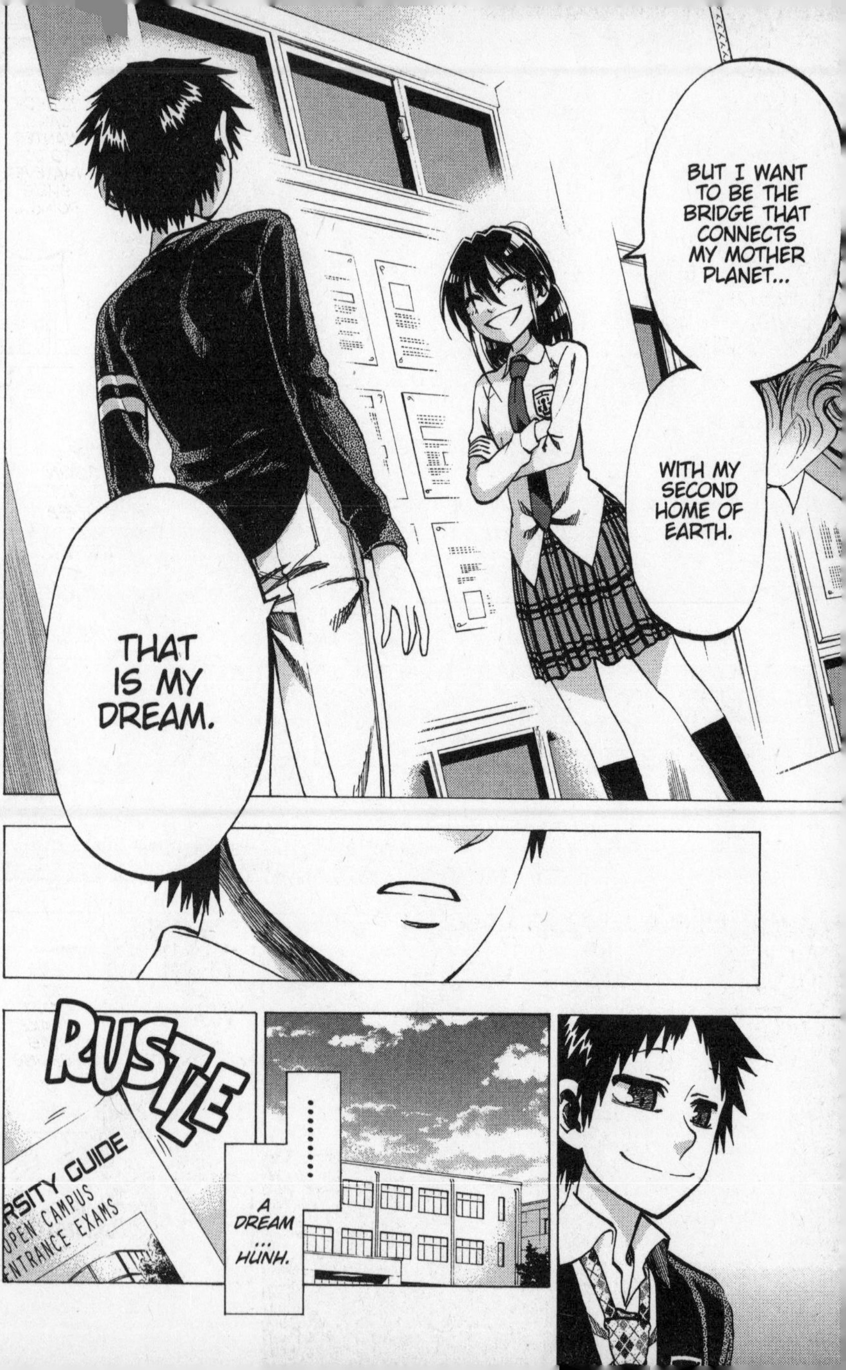
BUT I WANT TO BE THE BRIDGE THAT CONNECTS MY MOTHER PLANET...
WITH MY SECOND HOME OF EARTH.
THAT IS MY DREAM.
....
A DREAM ... HÜNH.
RUSTLE
RSITY GUIDE
OPEN CAMPUS
NTRANCE EXAMS

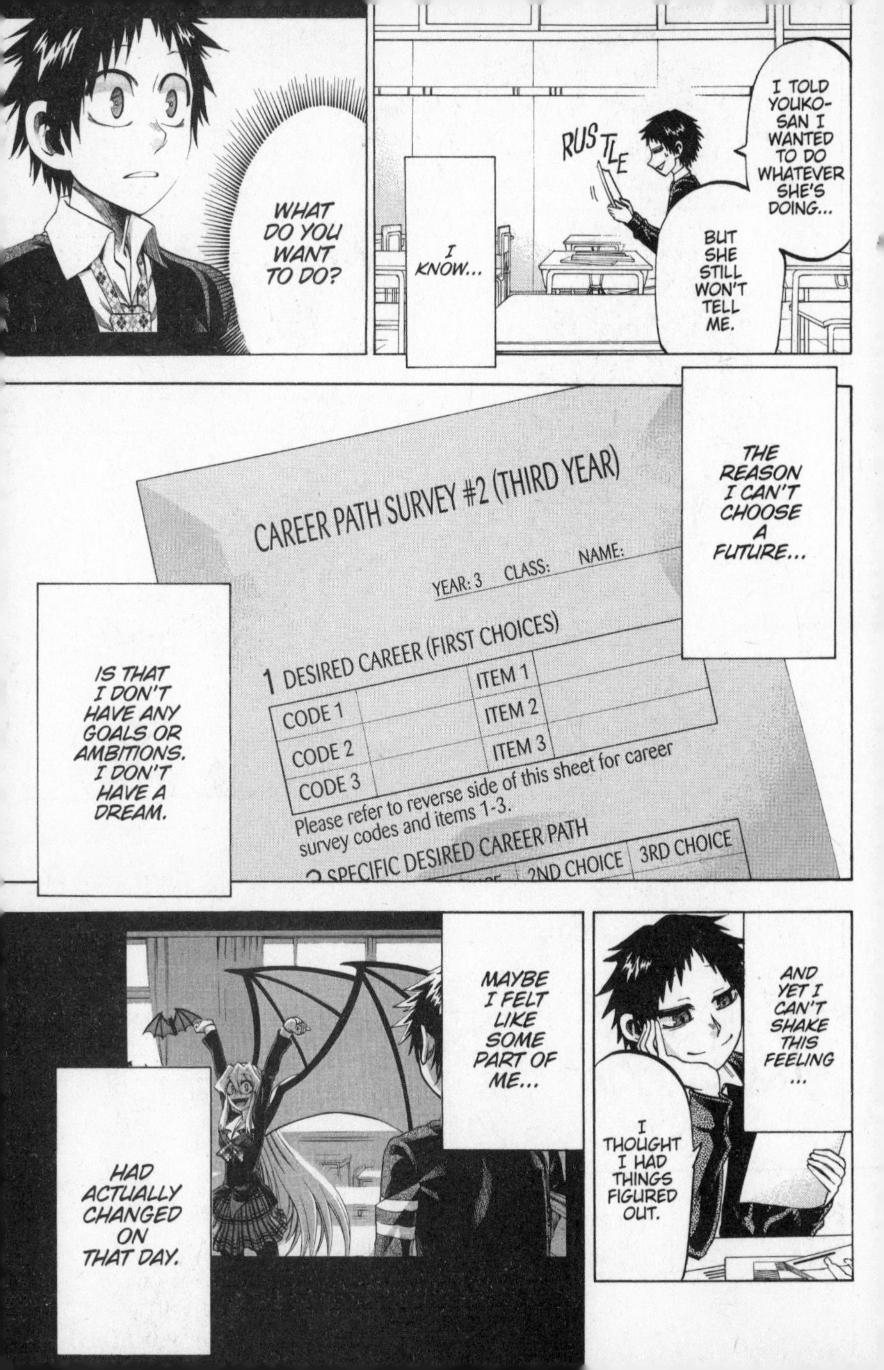
I TOLD YOUKO-SAN I WANTED TO DO WHATEVER SHE'S DOING...
RUSTLE
BUT SHE STILL WON'T TELL ME.
I KNOW...
WHAT DO YOU WANT TO DO?
THE REASON I CAN'T CHOOSE A FUTURE...
CAREER PATH SURVEY #2 (THIRD YEAR)
YEAR: 3 CLASS: NAME:
1 DESIRED CAREER (FIRST CHOICES)
CODE 1
CODE 2
CODE 3
ITEM 1
ITEM 2
ITEM 3
Please refer to reverse side of this sheet for career survey codes and items 1-3.
2 SPECIFIC DESIRED CAREER PATH
2ND CHOICE
3RD CHOICE
IS THAT I DON'T HAVE ANY GOALS OR AMBITIONS. I DON'T HAVE A DREAM.
AND YET I CAN'T SHAKE THIS FEELING...
I THOUGHT I HAD THINGS FIGURED OUT.
MAYBE I FELT LIKE SOME PART OF ME...
HAD ACTUALLY CHANGED ON THAT DAY.

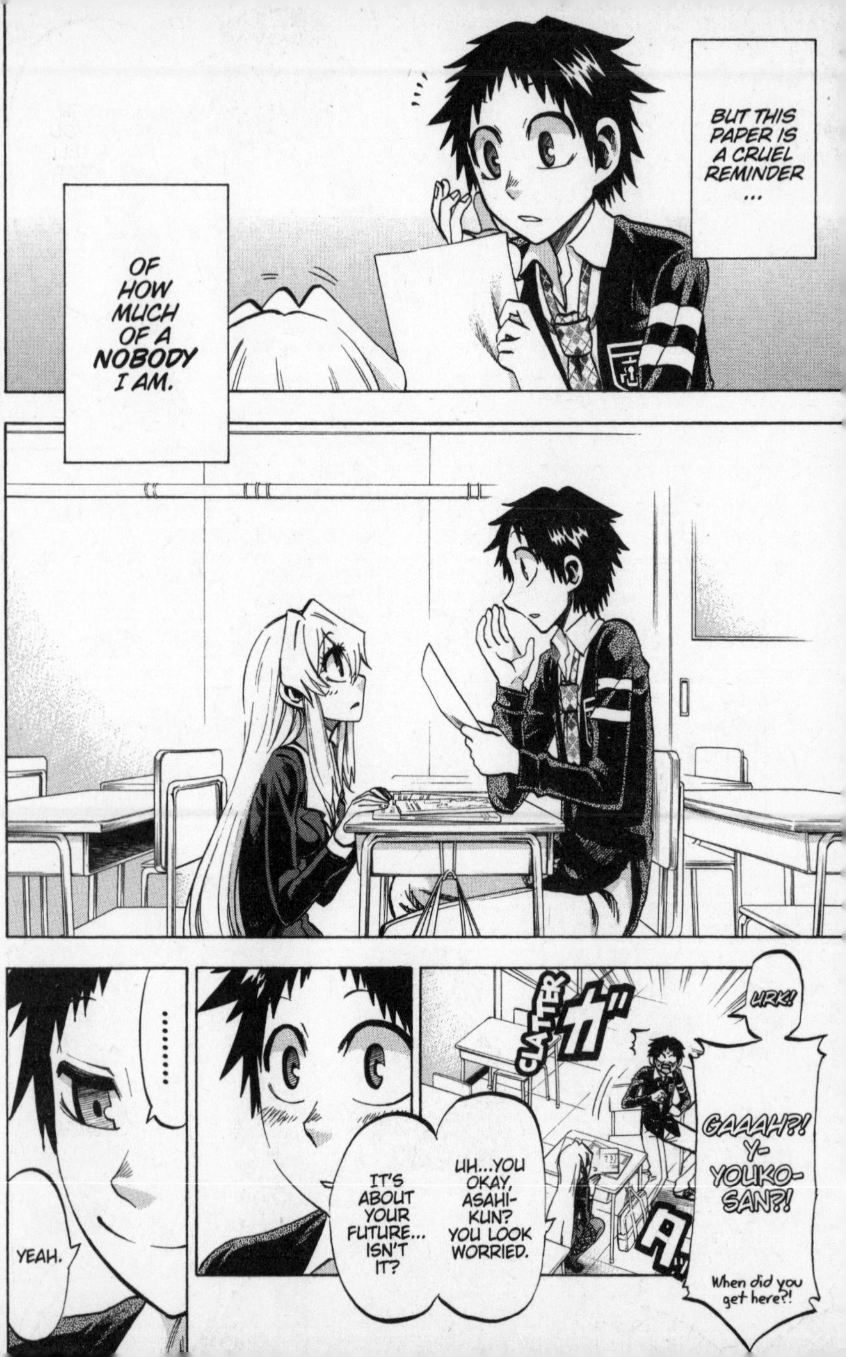

BUT THIS PAPER IS A CRUEL REMINDER ...
OF HOW MUCH OF A NOBODY I AM.
URK!
CLATTER
GAAAH?! Y-YOUKO-SAN?!
When did you get here?!
UH...YOU OKAY, ASAHI-KUN? YOU LOOK WORRIED.
IT'S ABOUT YOUR FUTURE... ISN'T IT?
......
YEAH.

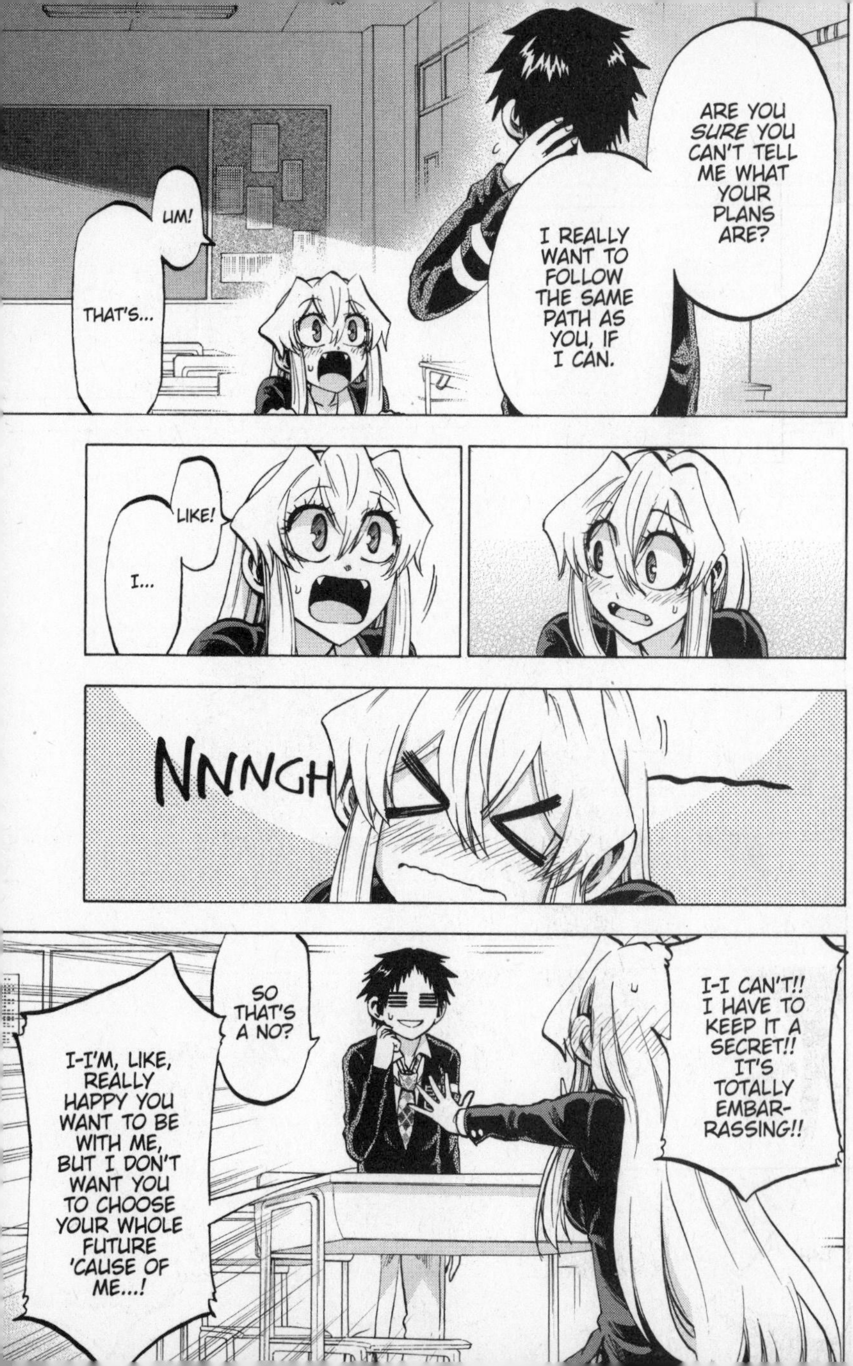
ARE YOU SURE YOU CAN'T TELL ME WHAT YOUR PLANS ARE?
I REALLY WANT TO FOLLOW THE SAME PATH AS YOU, IF I CAN.
UM!
THAT'S...
LIKE!
I...
NNNGH
I-I CAN'T!! I HAVE TO KEEP IT A SECRET!! IT'S TOTALLY EMBAR-RASSING!!
SO THAT'S A NO?
I-I'M, LIKE, REALLY HAPPY YOU WANT TO BE WITH ME, BUT I DON'T WANT YOU TO CHOOSE YOUR WHOLE FUTURE 'CAUSE OF ME...!

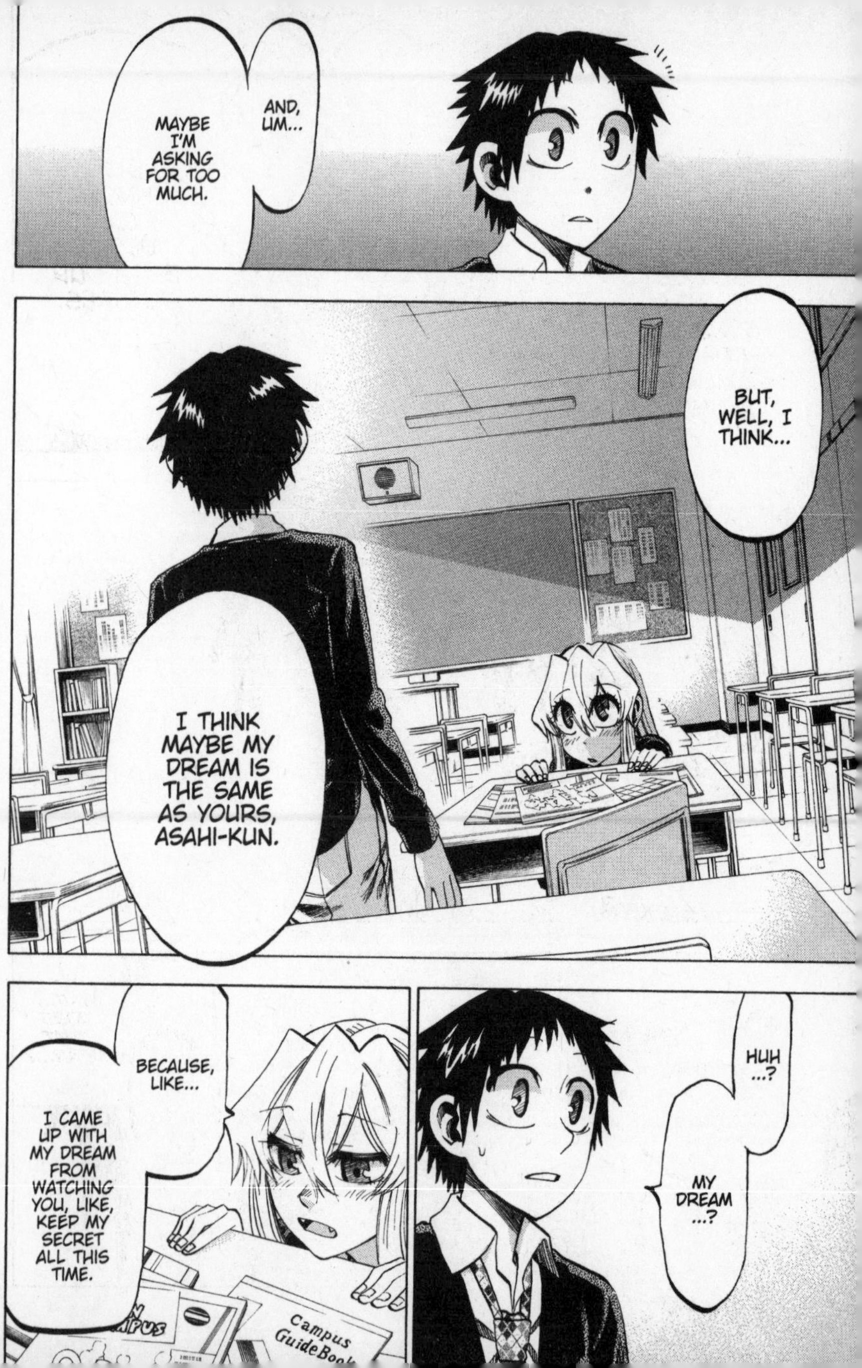
AND, UM...
MAYBE I'M ASKING FOR TOO MUCH.
BUT, WELL, I THINK...
I THINK MAYBE MY DREAM IS THE SAME AS YOURS, ASAHI-KUN.
HUH ...?
MY DREAM ...?
BECAUSE, LIKE...
I CAME UP WITH MY DREAM FROM WATCHING YOU, LIKE, KEEP MY SECRET ALL THIS TIME.
Campus GuideBook

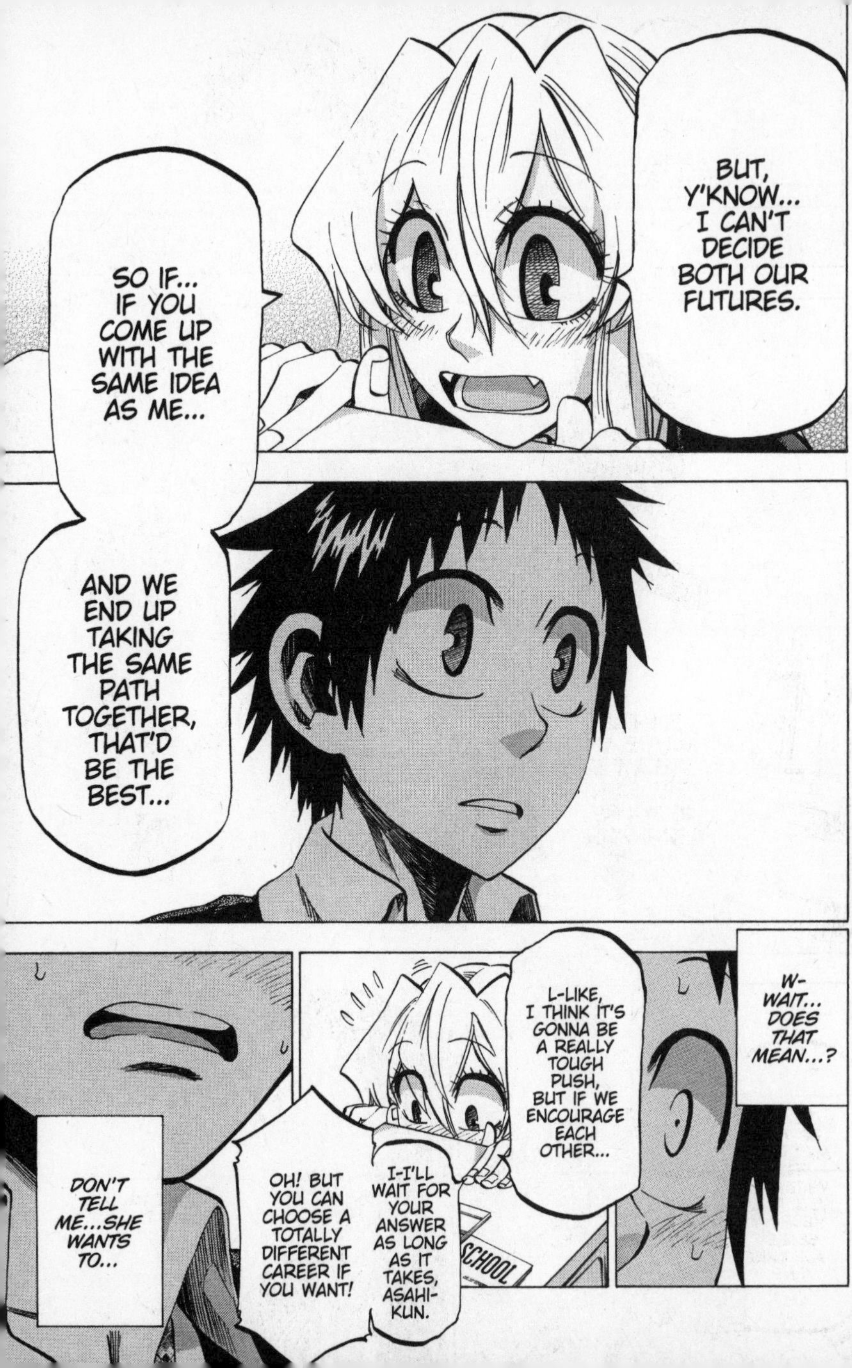
BUT, Y'KNOW... I CAN'T DECIDE BOTH OUR FUTURES.
SO IF... IF YOU COME UP WITH THE SAME IDEA AS ME...
AND WE END UP TAKING THE SAME PATH TOGETHER, THAT'D BE THE BEST...
W-WAIT... DOES THAT MEAN...?
L-LIKE, I THINK IT'S GONNA BE A REALLY TOUGH PUSH, BUT IF WE ENCOURAGE EACH OTHER...
I-I'LL WAIT FOR YOUR ANSWER AS LONG AS IT TAKES, ASAHI-KUN.
SCHOOL
OH! BUT YOU CAN CHOOSE A TOTALLY DIFFERENT CAREER IF YOU WANT!
DON'T TELL ME...SHE WANTS TO...

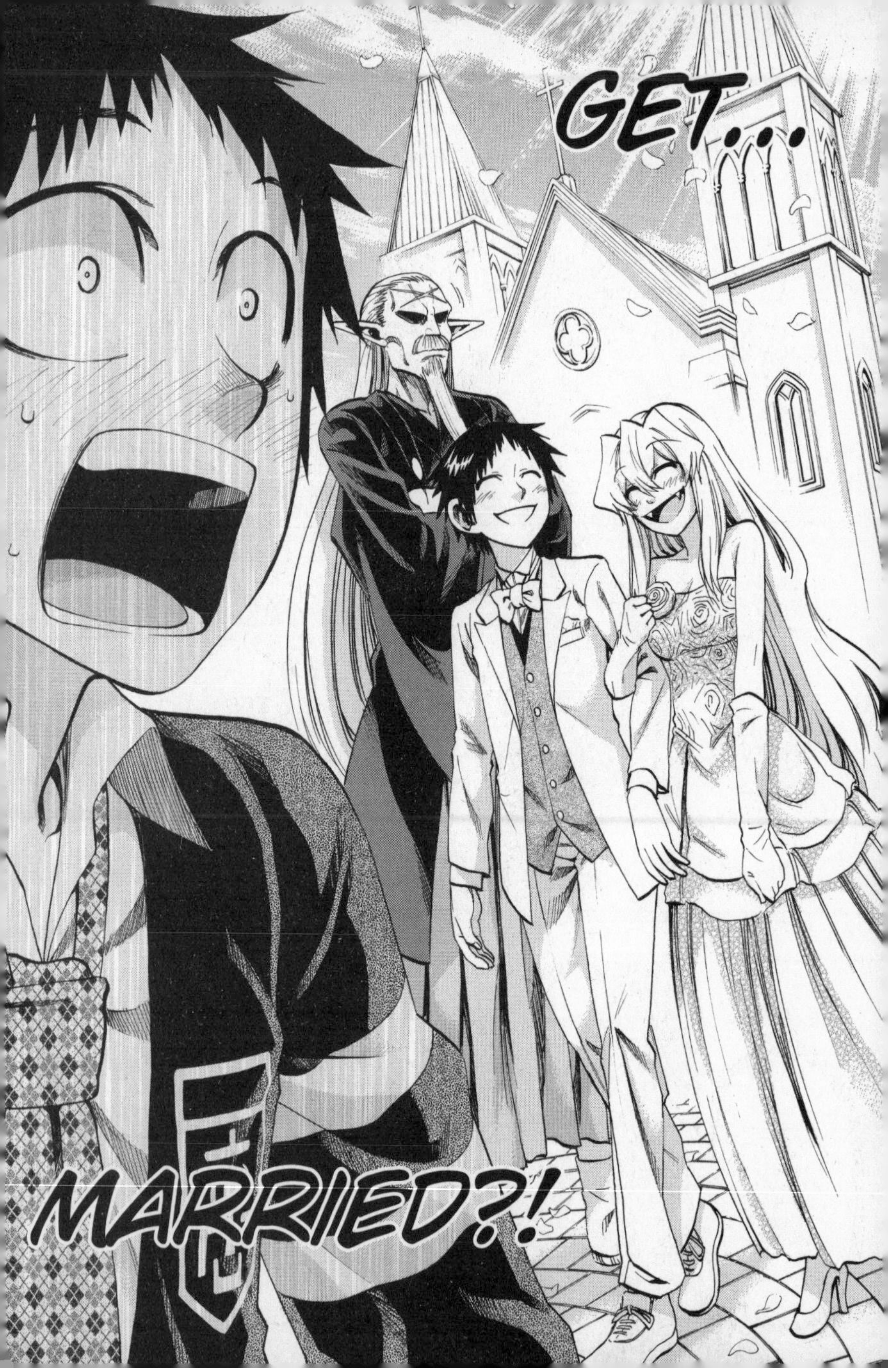
GET...
MARRIED?!

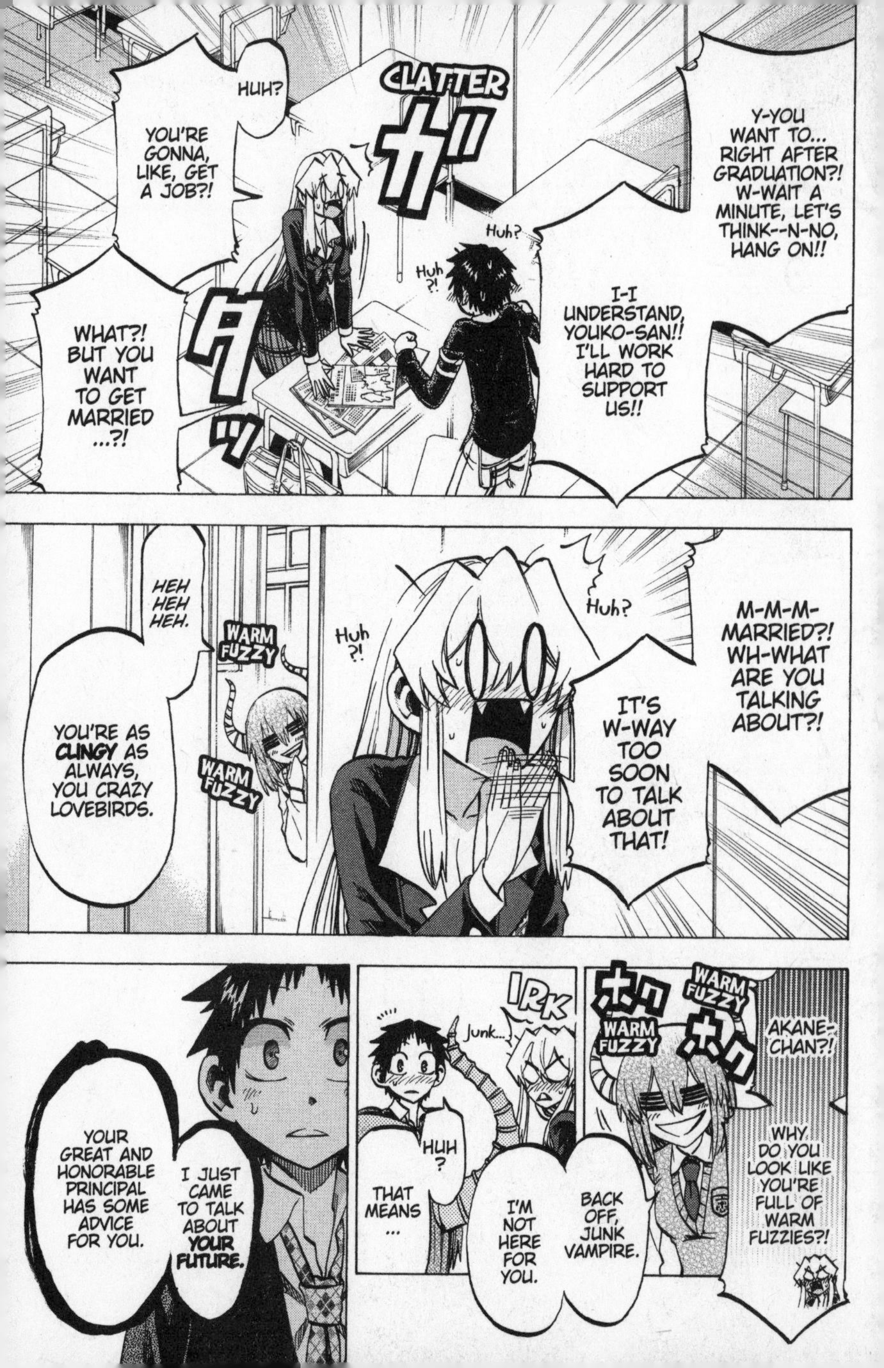

Y-YOU WANT TO... RIGHT AFTER GRADUATION?! W-WAIT A MINUTE, LET'S THINK--N-NO, HANG ON!!
CLATTER
Huh?
HUH?
YOU'RE GONNA, LIKE, GET A JOB?!
Huh ?!
I-I UNDERSTAND, YOUKO-SAN!! I'LL WORK HARD TO SUPPORT US!!
WHAT?! BUT YOU WANT TO GET MARRIED ...?!
M-M-M-MARRIED?! WH-WHAT ARE YOU TALKING ABOUT?!
Huh?
IT'S W-WAY TOO SOON TO TALK ABOUT THAT!
Huh ?!
HEH HEH HEH.
WARM FUZZY
WARM FUZZY
YOU'RE AS **CLINGY** AS ALWAYS, YOU CRAZY LOVEBIRDS.
AKANE-CHAN?!
WARM FUZZY
WARM FUZZY
WHY DO YOU LOOK LIKE YOU'RE FULL OF WARM FUZZIES?!
IRK
Junk...
BACK OFF, JUNK VAMPIRE.
I'M NOT HERE FOR YOU.
HUH ?
THAT MEANS ...
I JUST CAME TO TALK ABOUT **YOUR FUTURE.**
YOUR GREAT AND HONORABLE PRINCIPAL HAS SOME ADVICE FOR YOU.

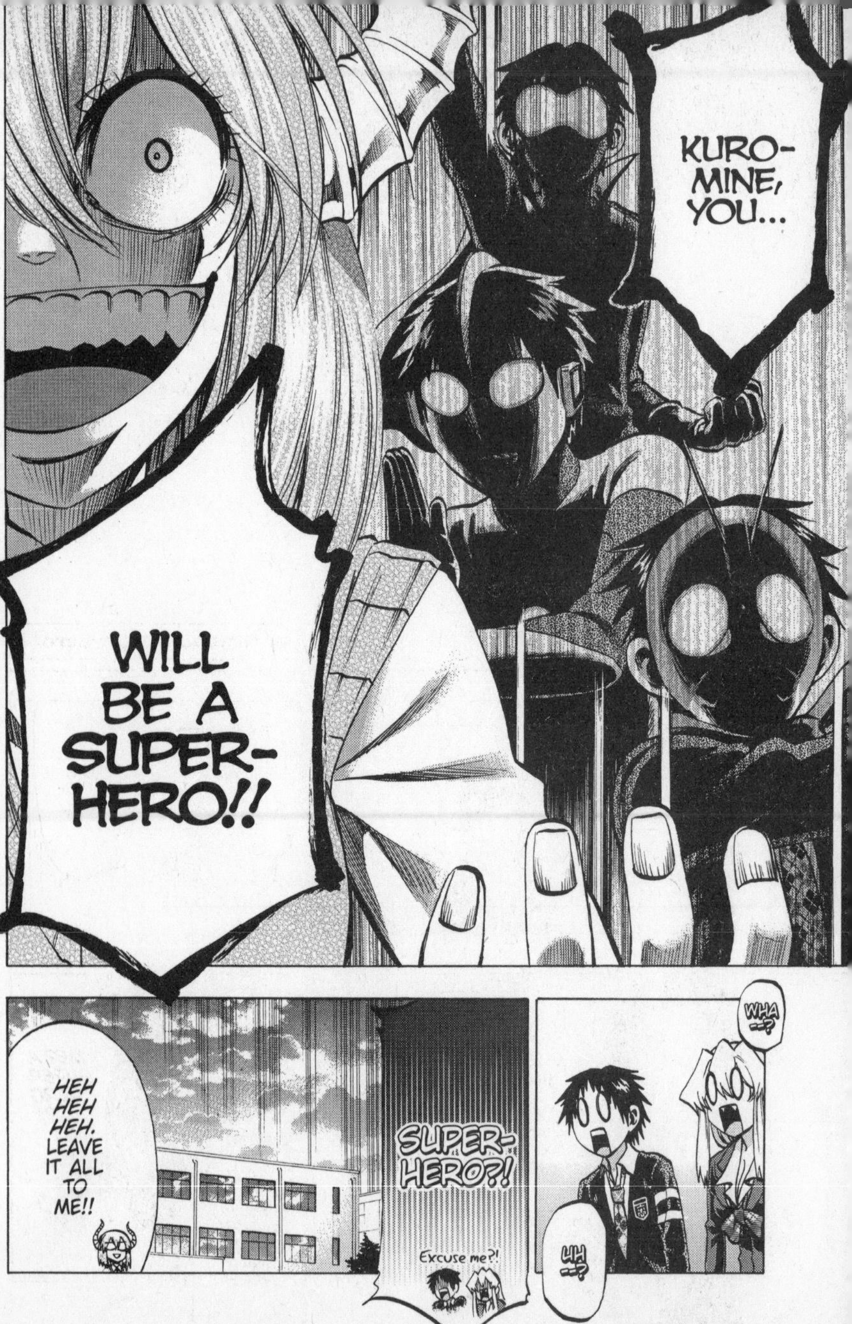
KURO-MINE, YOU...
WILL BE A SUPER-HERO!!
WHA--?
UH--?
SUPER-HERO?!
Excuse me?!
HEH HEH HEH. LEAVE IT ALL TO ME!!

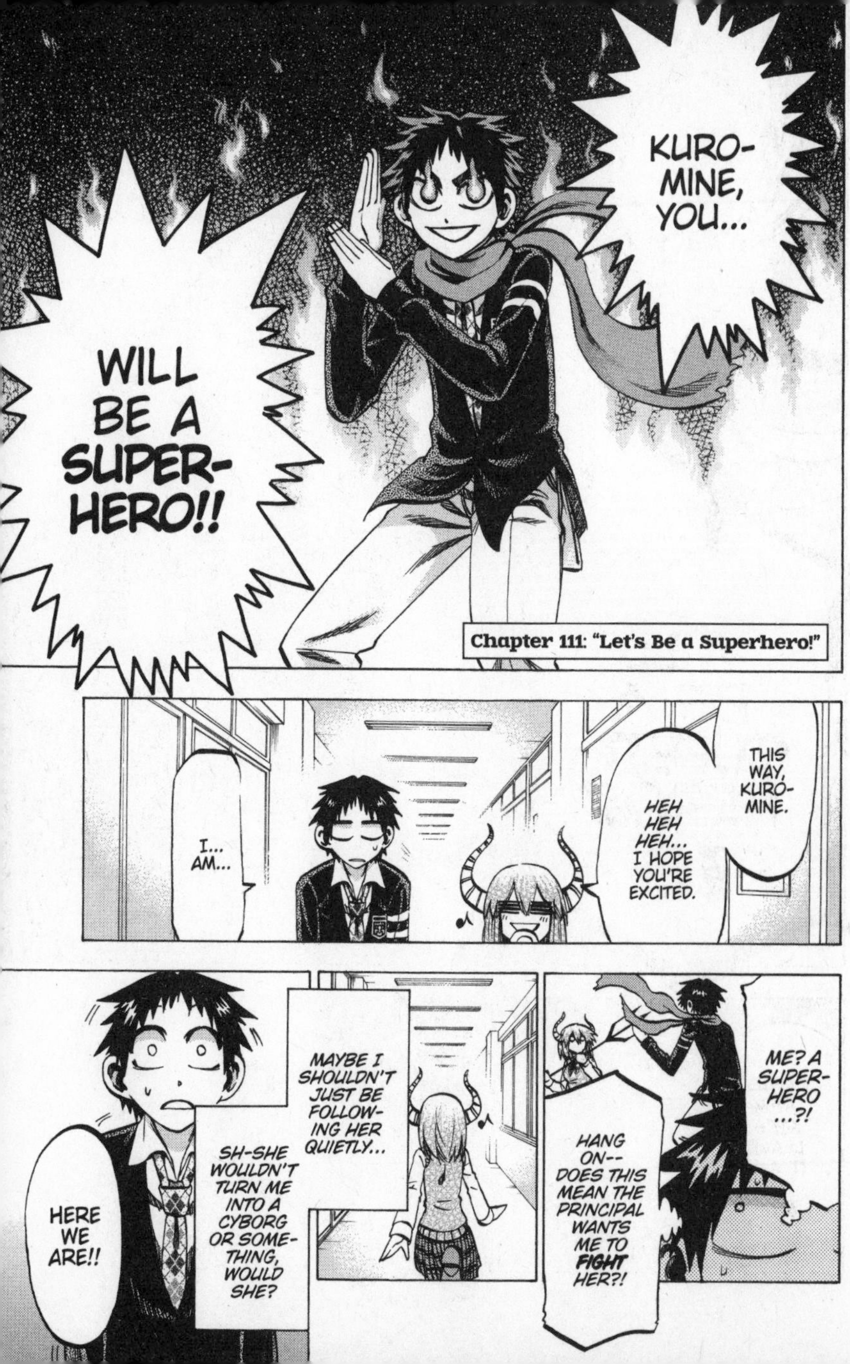
KURO-MINE, YOU...
WILL BE A SUPER-HERO!!
Chapter 111: "Let's Be a Superhero!"
THIS WAY, KURO-MINE.
HEH HEH HEH... I HOPE YOU'RE EXCITED.
I... AM...
ME? A SUPER-HERO ...?!
HANG ON-- DOES THIS MEAN THE PRINCIPAL WANTS ME TO FIGHT HER?!
MAYBE I SHOULDN'T JUST BE FOLLOWING HER QUIETLY...
SH-SHE WOULDN'T TURN ME INTO A CYBORG OR SOME-THING, WOULD SHE?
HERE WE ARE!!

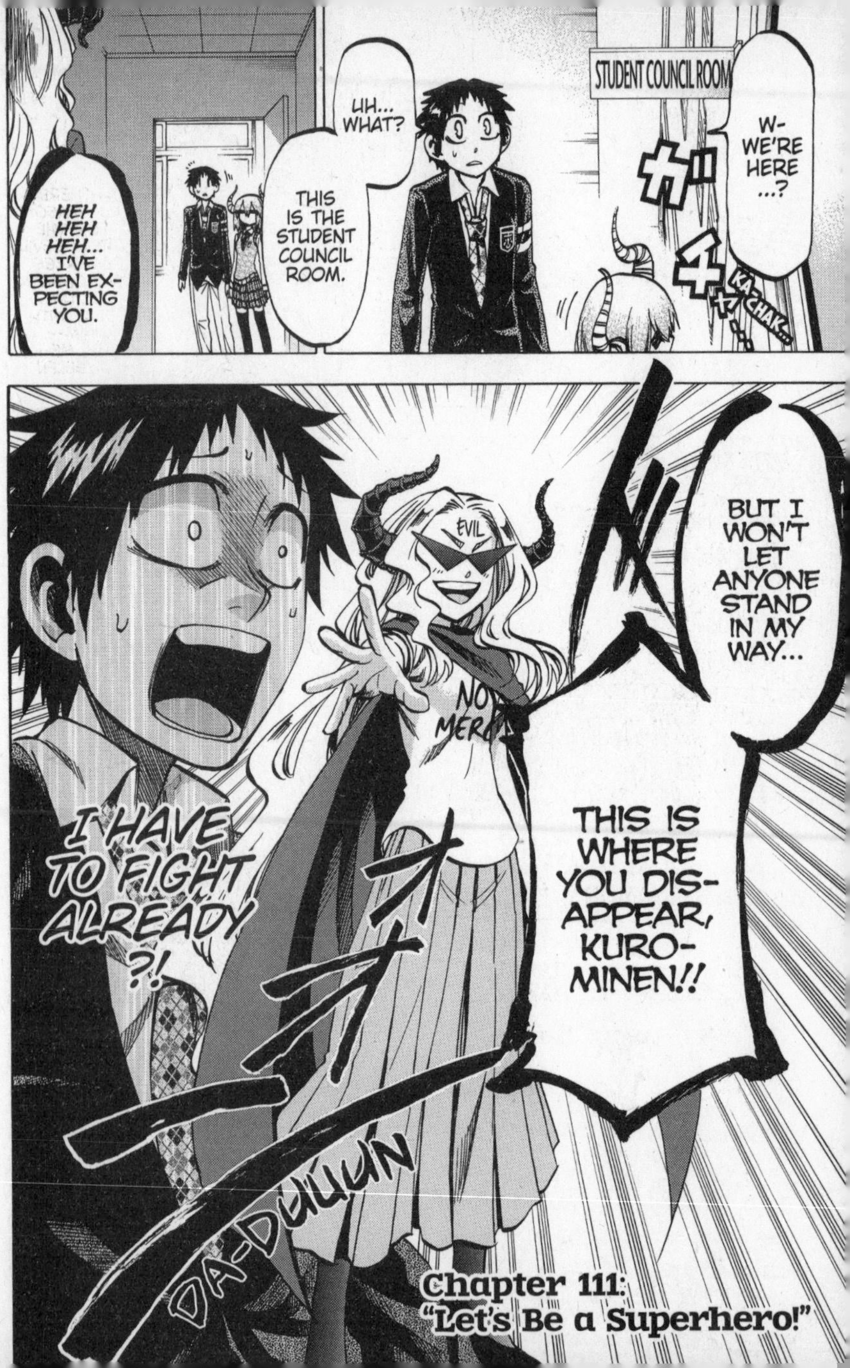
STUDENT COUNCIL ROOM
W-WE'RE HERE...?
KA-CHAK...
UH... WHAT?
THIS IS THE STUDENT COUNCIL ROOM.
HEH HEH HEH... I'VE BEEN EXPECTING YOU.
BUT I WON'T LET ANYONE STAND IN MY WAY...
THIS IS WHERE YOU DISAPPEAR, KUROMINEN!!
EVIL
I HAVE TO FIGHT ALREADY?!
DA-DUUUN
Chapter 111: "Let's Be a Superhero!"

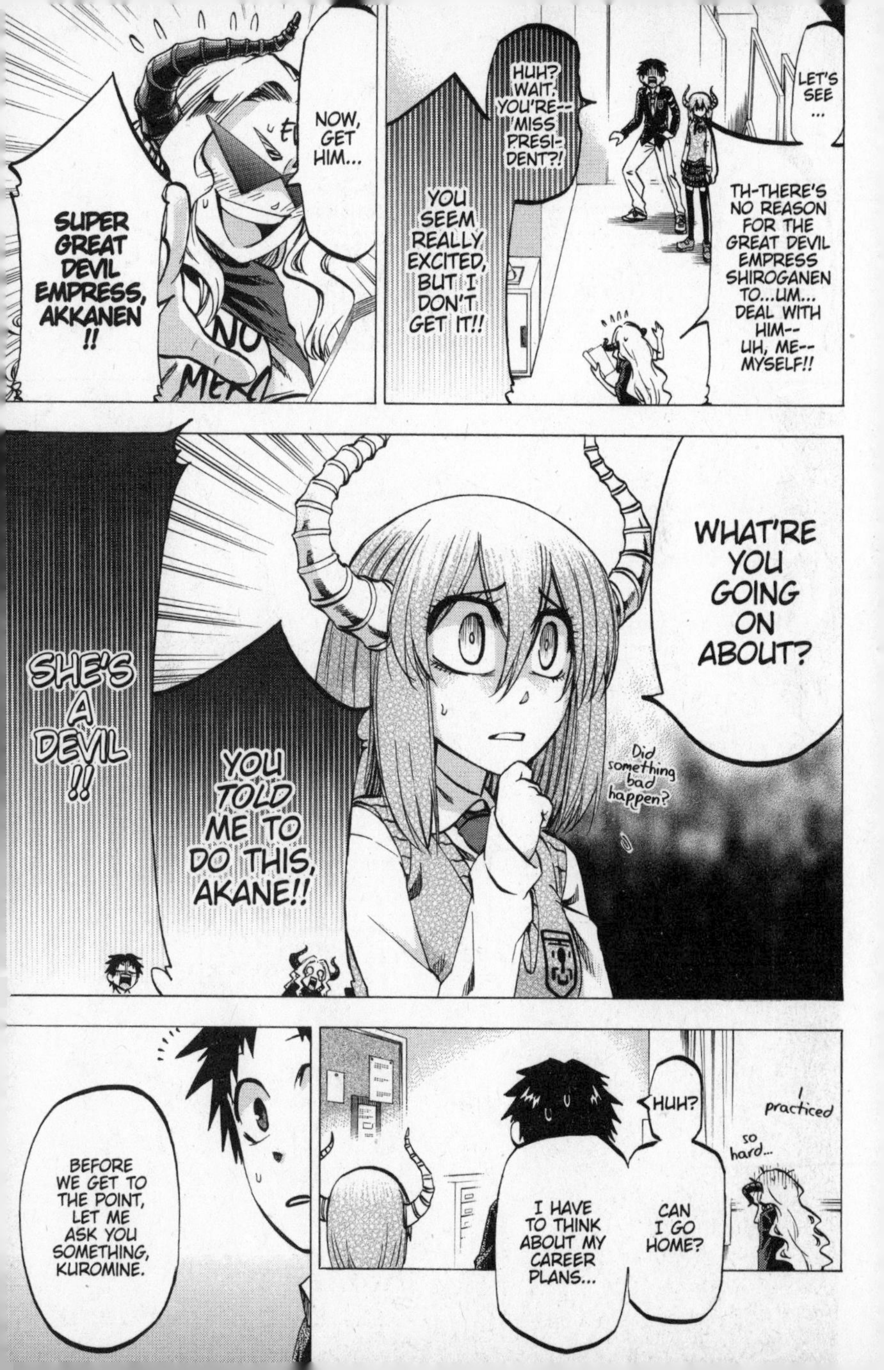
LET'S SEE ...
TH-THERE'S NO REASON FOR THE GREAT DEVIL EMPRESS SHIROGANEN TO...UM... DEAL WITH HIM-- UH, ME-- MYSELF!!
HUH? WAIT. YOU'RE-- MISS PRESIDENT?!
YOU SEEM REALLY EXCITED, BUT I DON'T GET IT!!
NOW, GET HIM...
SUPER GREAT DEVIL EMPRESS, AKKANEN!!
WHAT'RE YOU GOING ON ABOUT?
Did something bad happen?
YOU TOLD ME TO DO THIS, AKANE!!
SHE'S A DEVIL!!
HUH?
I practiced so hard...
CAN I GO HOME?
I HAVE TO THINK ABOUT MY CAREER PLANS...
BEFORE WE GET TO THE POINT, LET ME ASK YOU SOMETHING, KUROMINE.

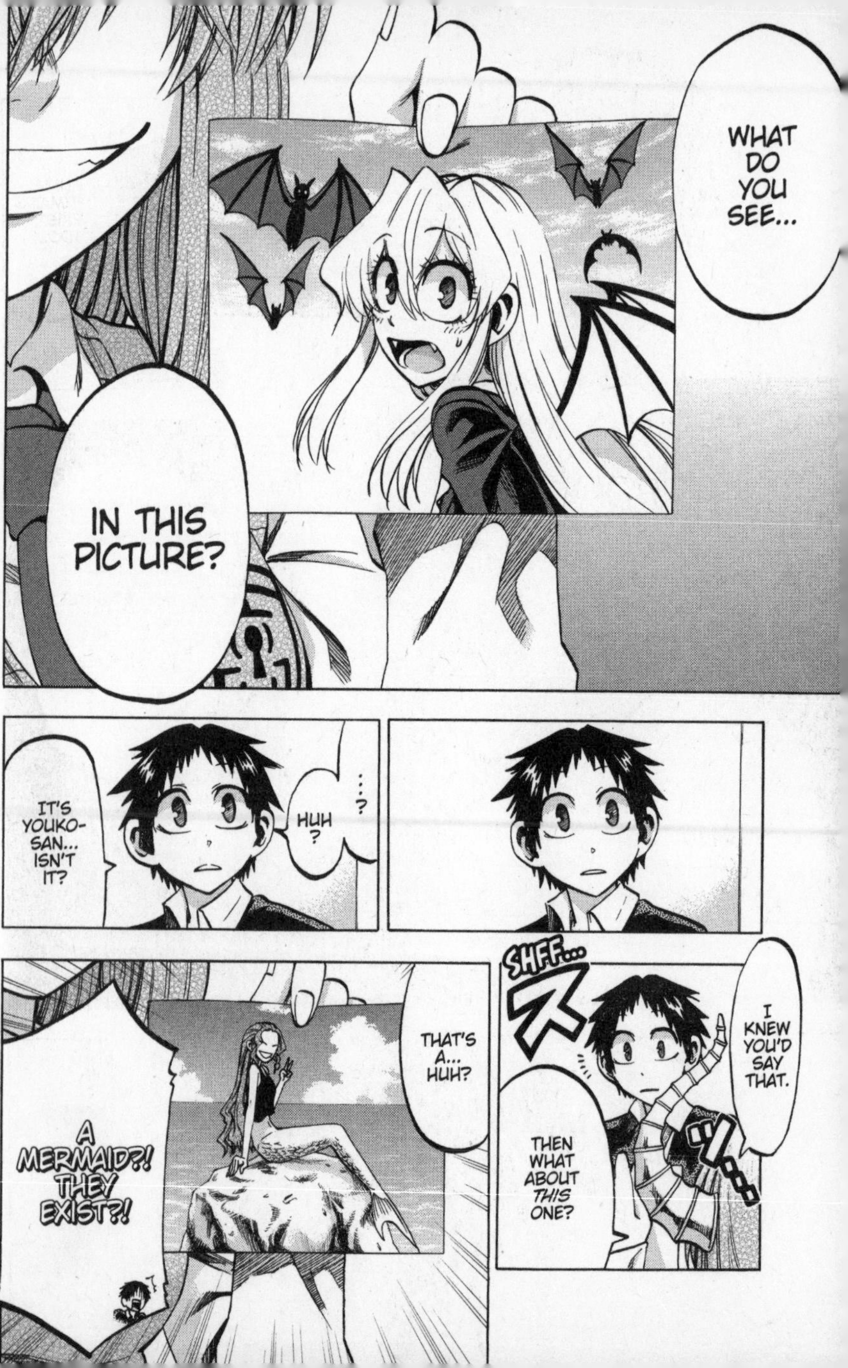
WHAT DO YOU SEE...
IN THIS PICTURE?
...?
HUH?
IT'S YOUKO-SAN... ISN'T IT?
I KNEW YOU'D SAY THAT.
SHFF...
ス
THEN WHAT ABOUT *THIS* ONE?
THAT'S A... HUH?
A MERMAID?! THEY EXIST?!

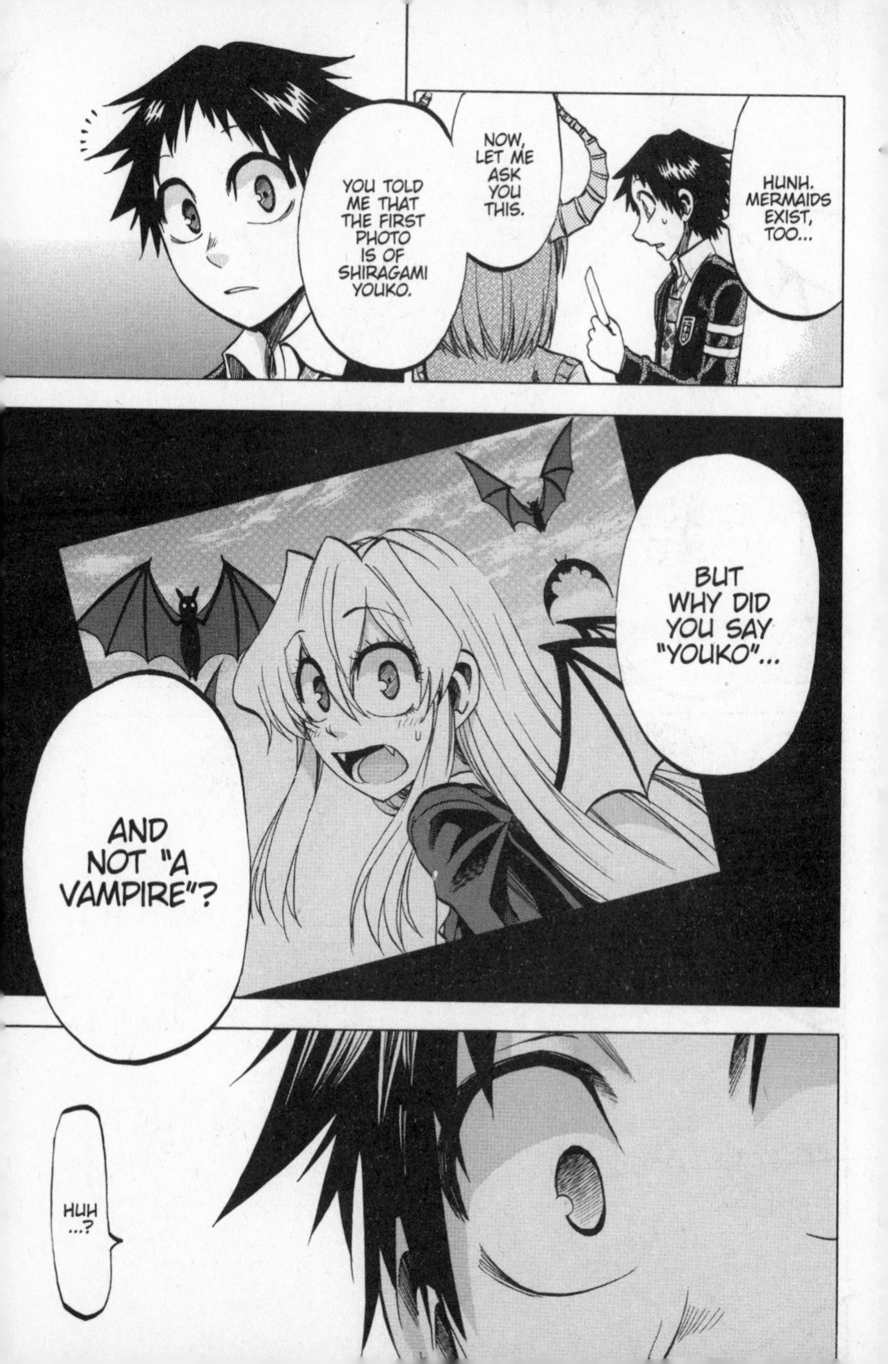
HUNH. MERMAIDS EXIST, TOO...
NOW, LET ME ASK YOU THIS.
YOU TOLD ME THAT THE FIRST PHOTO IS OF SHIRAGAMI YOUKO.
BUT WHY DID YOU SAY "YOUKO"...
AND NOT "A VAMPIRE"?
HUH ...?

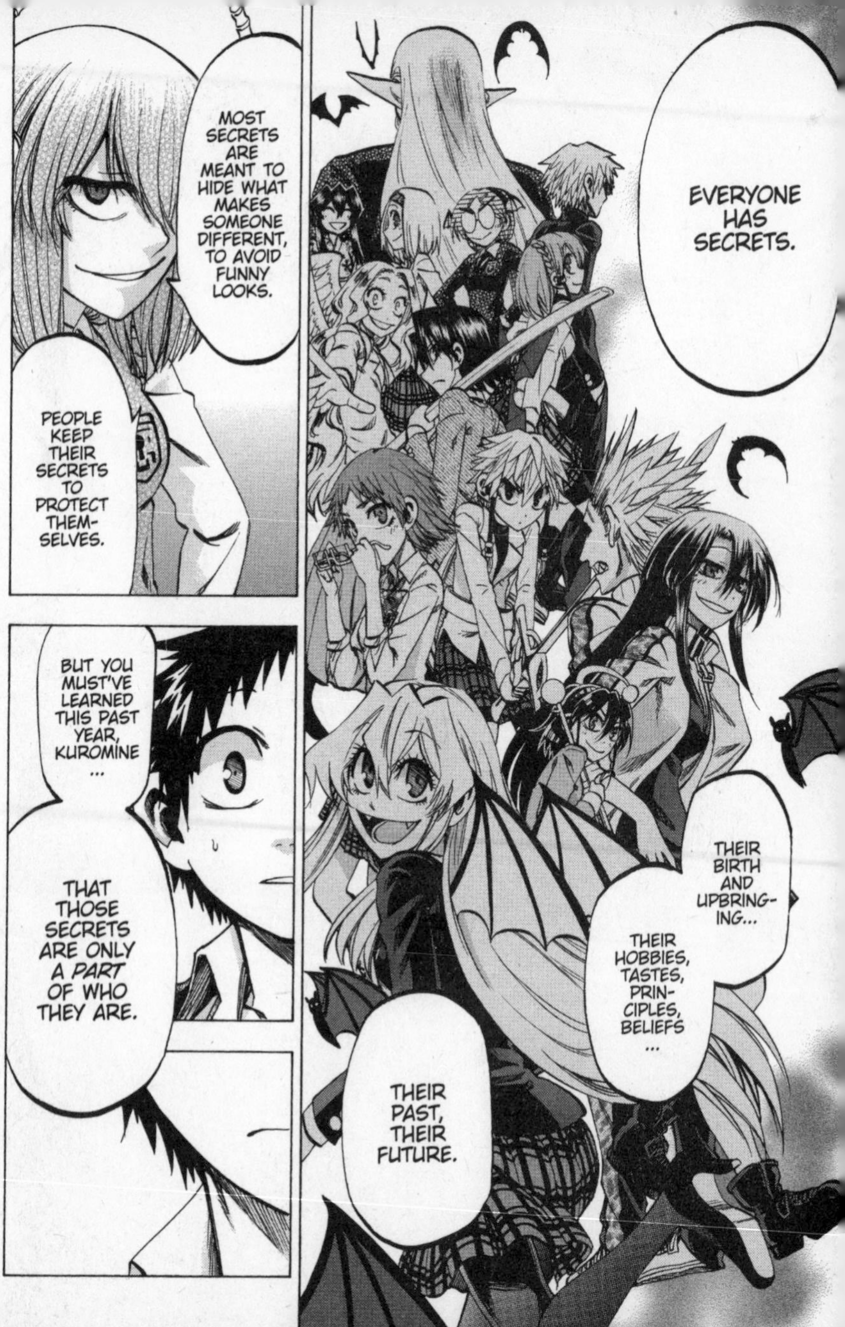
EVERYONE HAS SECRETS.
THEIR BIRTH AND UPBRINGING...
THEIR HOBBIES, TASTES, PRINCIPLES, BELIEFS...
THEIR PAST, THEIR FUTURE.
MOST SECRETS ARE MEANT TO HIDE WHAT MAKES SOMEONE DIFFERENT, TO AVOID FUNNY LOOKS.
PEOPLE KEEP THEIR SECRETS TO PROTECT THEMSELVES.
BUT YOU MUST'VE LEARNED THIS PAST YEAR, KUROMINE...
THAT THOSE SECRETS ARE ONLY A *PART* OF WHO THEY ARE.

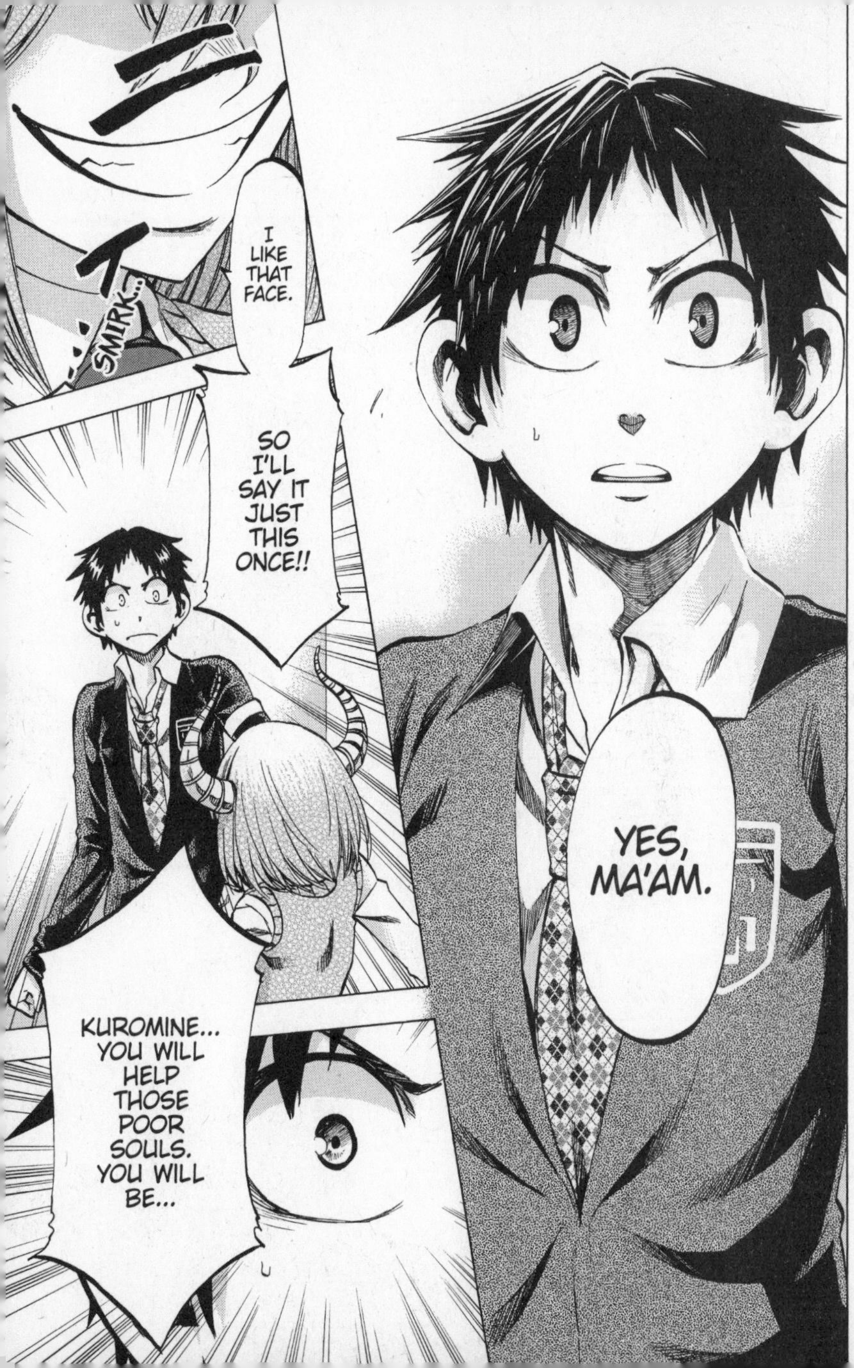
YES, MA'AM.
I LIKE THAT FACE.
SMIRK...
SO I'LL SAY IT JUST THIS ONCE!!
KUROMINE... YOU WILL HELP THOSE POOR SOULS. YOU WILL BE...

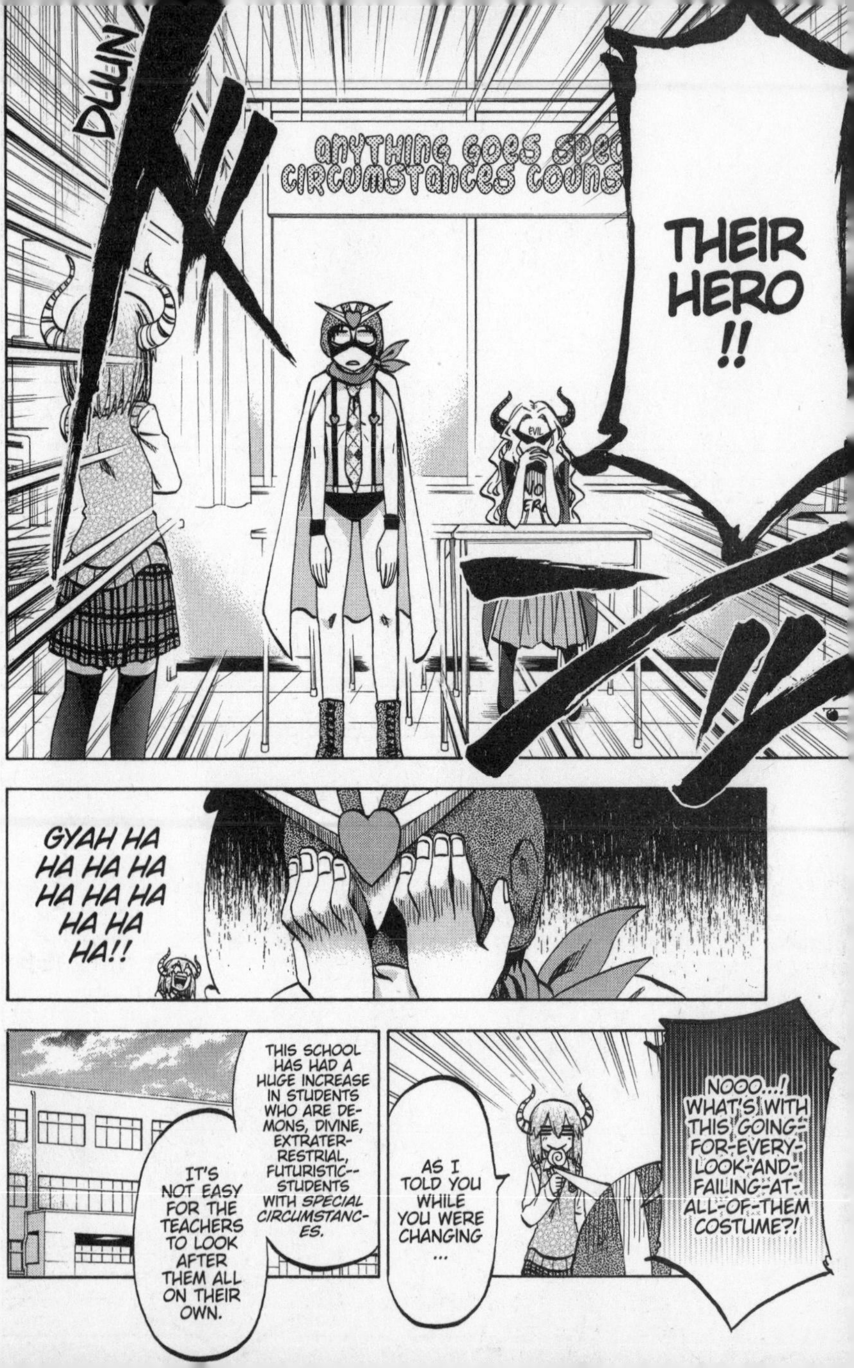
THEIR HERO !!
ANYTHING GOES SPEC
CIRCUMSTANCES COUNS
EVIL
DUUN
GYAH HA HA HA HA HA HA HA HA HA HA HA!!
NOOO...! WHAT'S WITH THIS GOING-FOR-EVERY-LOOK-AND-FAILING-AT-ALL-OF-THEM COSTUME?!
AS I TOLD YOU WHILE YOU WERE CHANGING ...
THIS SCHOOL HAS HAD A HUGE INCREASE IN STUDENTS WHO ARE DEMONS, DIVINE, EXTRATERRESTRIAL, FUTURISTIC-- STUDENTS WITH *SPECIAL CIRCUMSTANCES.*
IT'S NOT EASY FOR THE TEACHERS TO LOOK AFTER THEM ALL ON THEIR OWN.

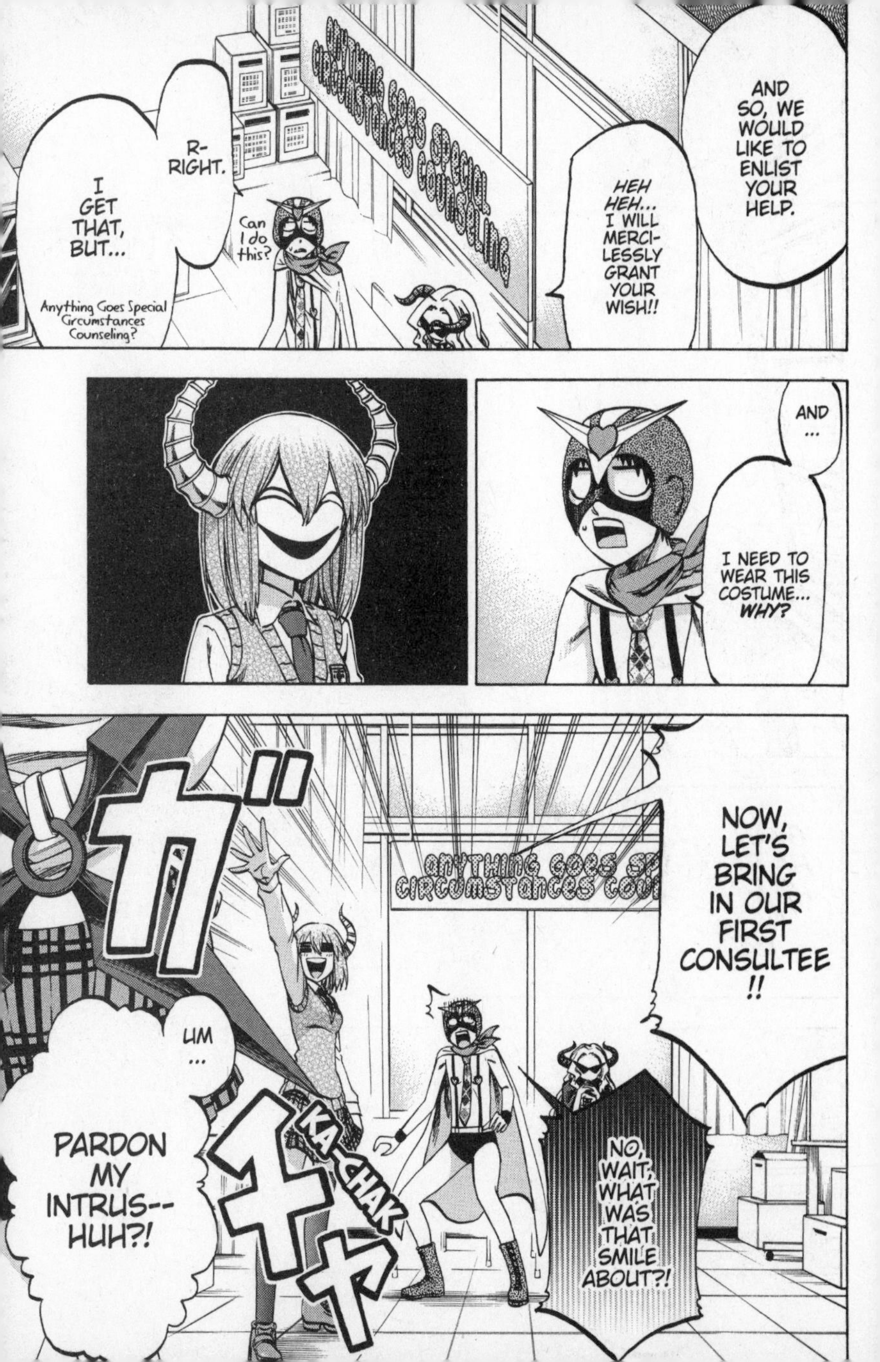
AND SO, WE WOULD LIKE TO ENLIST YOUR HELP.
HEH HEH... I WILL MERCILESSLY GRANT YOUR WISH!!
ANYTHING GOES SPECIAL CIRCUMSTANCES COUNSELING
R-RIGHT.
Can I do this?
I GET THAT, BUT...
Anything Goes Special Circumstances Counseling?
AND ...
I NEED TO WEAR THIS COSTUME... WHY?
NOW, LET'S BRING IN OUR FIRST CONSULTEE !!
ANYTHING GOES SP
CIRCUMSTANCES COU
NO, WAIT, WHAT WAS THAT SMILE ABOUT?!
KA-CHAK
UM ...
PARDON MY INTRUS-- HUH?!

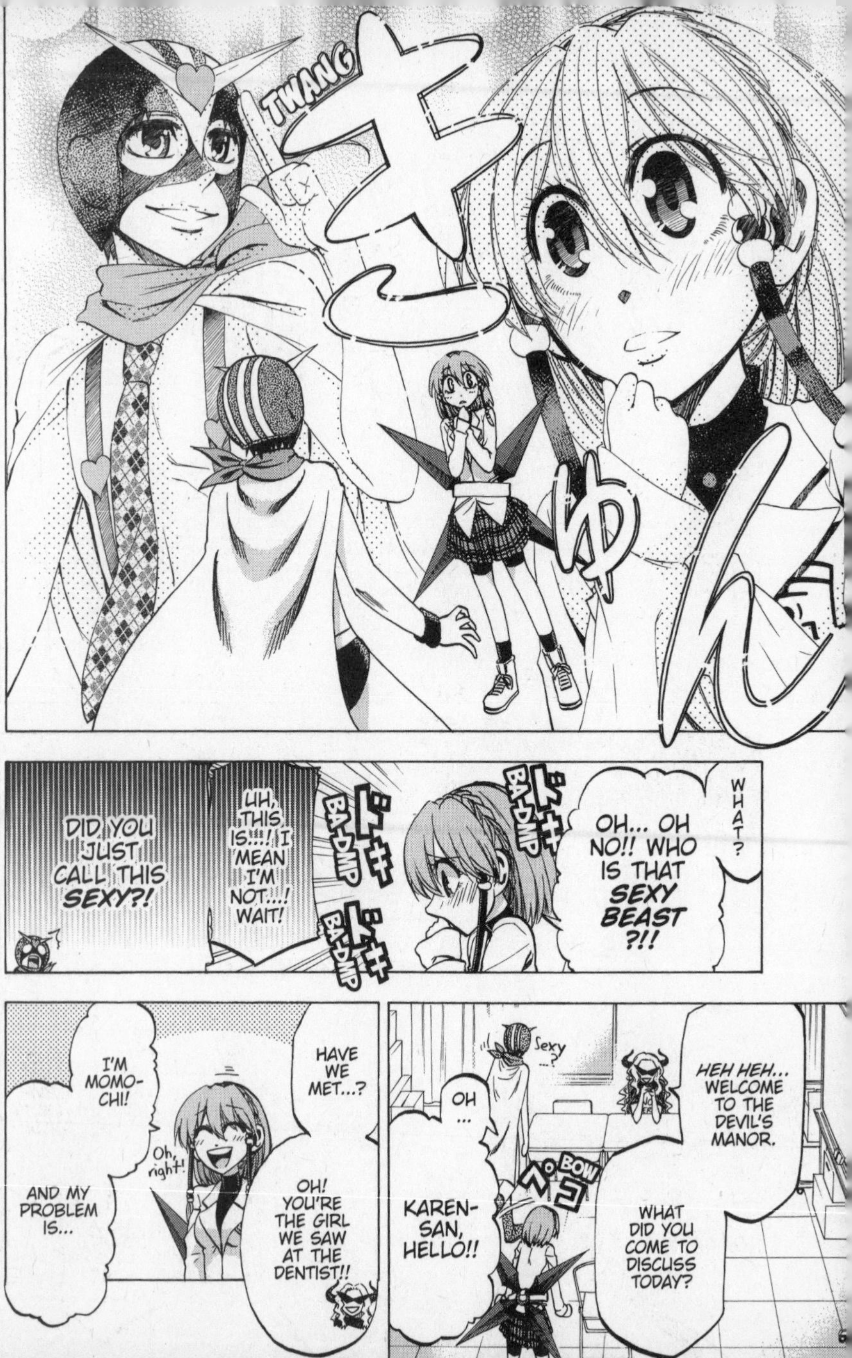
TWANG
WHAT?
OH... OH NO!! WHO IS THAT SEXY BEAST?!!
BA-DMP
BA-DMP
BA-DMP
UH, THIS IS...! I MEAN I'M NOT...! WAIT!
DID YOU JUST CALL THIS SEXY?!
HEH HEH... WELCOME TO THE DEVIL'S MANOR.
Sexy...?
OH...
WHAT DID YOU COME TO DISCUSS TODAY?
BOW
KAREN-SAN, HELLO!!
HAVE WE MET...?
I'M MOMOCHI!
OH! YOU'RE THE GIRL WE SAW AT THE DENTIST!!
Oh, right!
AND MY PROBLEM IS...

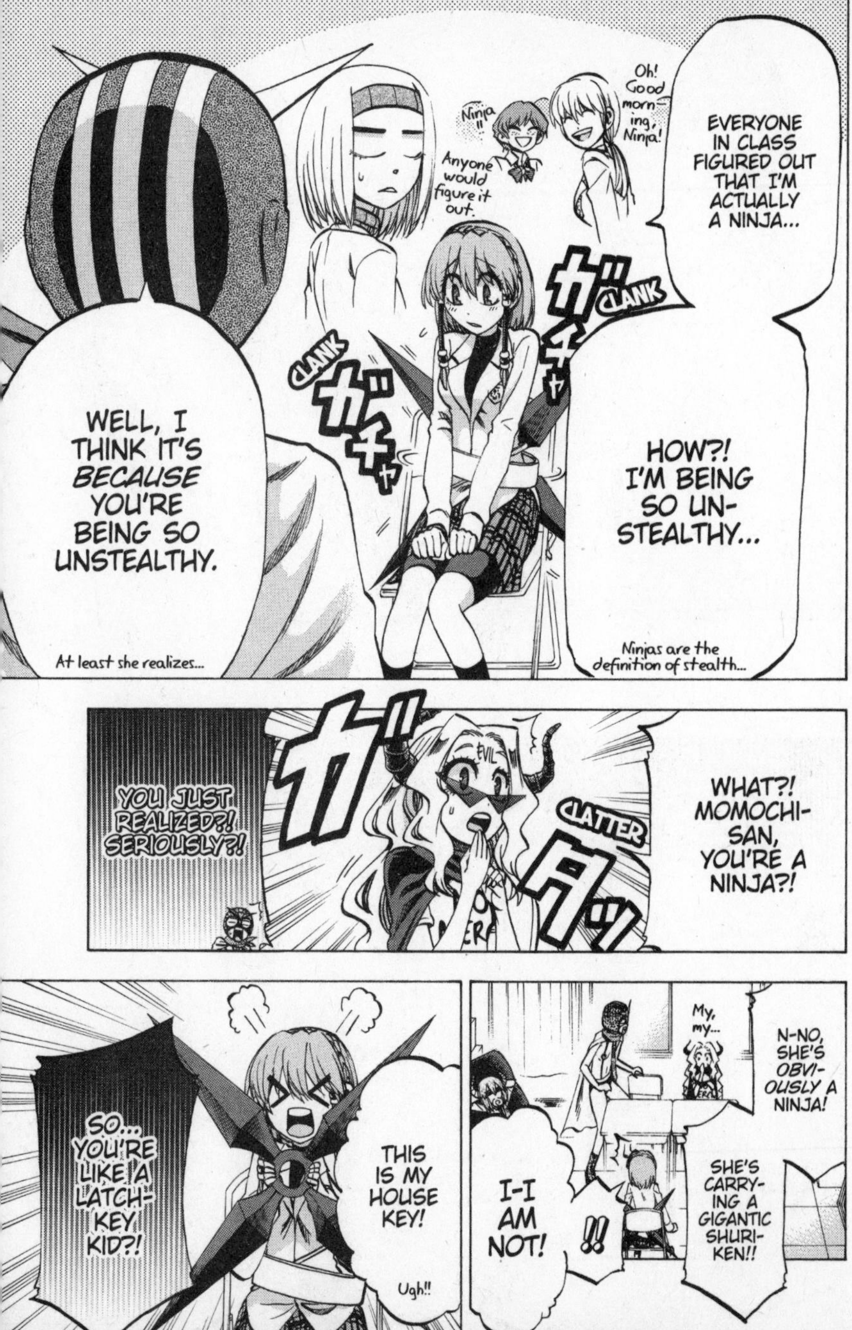
EVERYONE IN CLASS FIGURED OUT THAT I'M ACTUALLY A NINJA...
Oh! Good morn-ing, Ninja!
Ninja!!
Anyone would figure it out.
CLANK
CLANK
HOW?! I'M BEING SO UN-STEALTHY...
Ninjas are the definition of stealth...
WELL, I THINK IT'S *BECAUSE* YOU'RE BEING SO UNSTEALTHY.
At least she realizes...
WHAT?! MOMOCHI-SAN, YOU'RE A NINJA?!
CLATTER
EVIL
YOU JUST REALIZED?! SERIOUSLY?!
N-NO, SHE'S OBVI-OUSLY A NINJA!
My, my...
SHE'S CARRY-ING A GIGANTIC SHURI-KEN!!
!!
I-I AM NOT!
THIS IS MY HOUSE KEY!
Ugh!!
SO... YOU'RE LIKE A LATCH-KEY KID?!

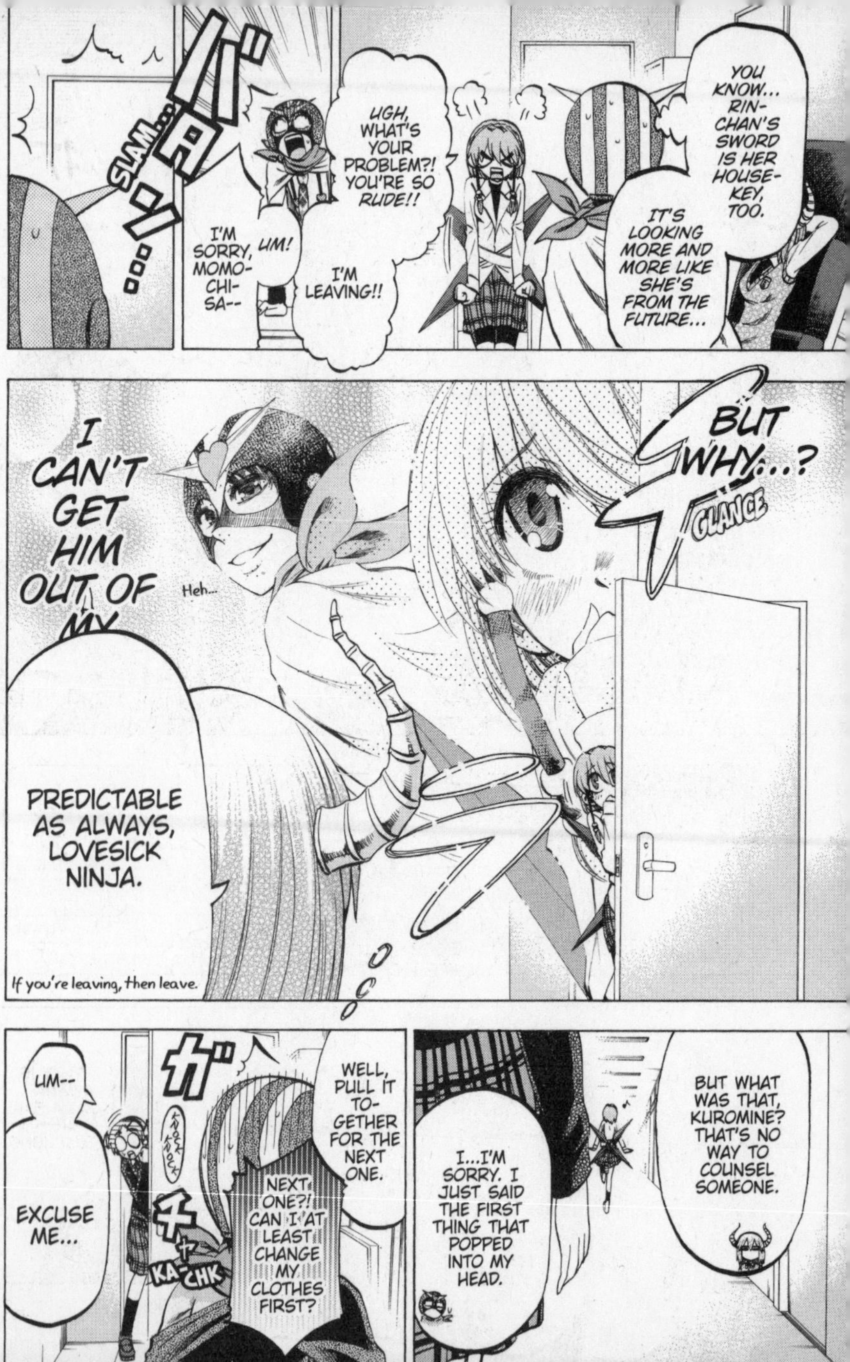
YOU KNOW... RIN-CHAN'S SWORD IS HER HOUSE-KEY, TOO.
IT'S LOOKING MORE AND MORE LIKE SHE'S FROM THE FUTURE...
UGH, WHAT'S YOUR PROBLEM?! YOU'RE SO RUDE!!
I'M LEAVING!!
UM!
I'M SORRY, MOMO-CHI-SA--
SLAM...!
BUT WHY...?
GLANCE
I CAN'T GET HIM OUT OF MY
Heh...
PREDICTABLE AS ALWAYS, LOVESICK NINJA.
If you're leaving, then leave.
BUT WHAT WAS THAT, KUROMINE? THAT'S NO WAY TO COUNSEL SOMEONE.
I...I'M SORRY. I JUST SAID THE FIRST THING THAT POPPED INTO MY HEAD.
WELL, PULL IT TO-GETHER FOR THE NEXT ONE.
NEXT ONE?! CAN I AT LEAST CHANGE MY CLOTHES FIRST?
KA-CHK
KNOCK KNOCK
UM--
EXCUSE ME...

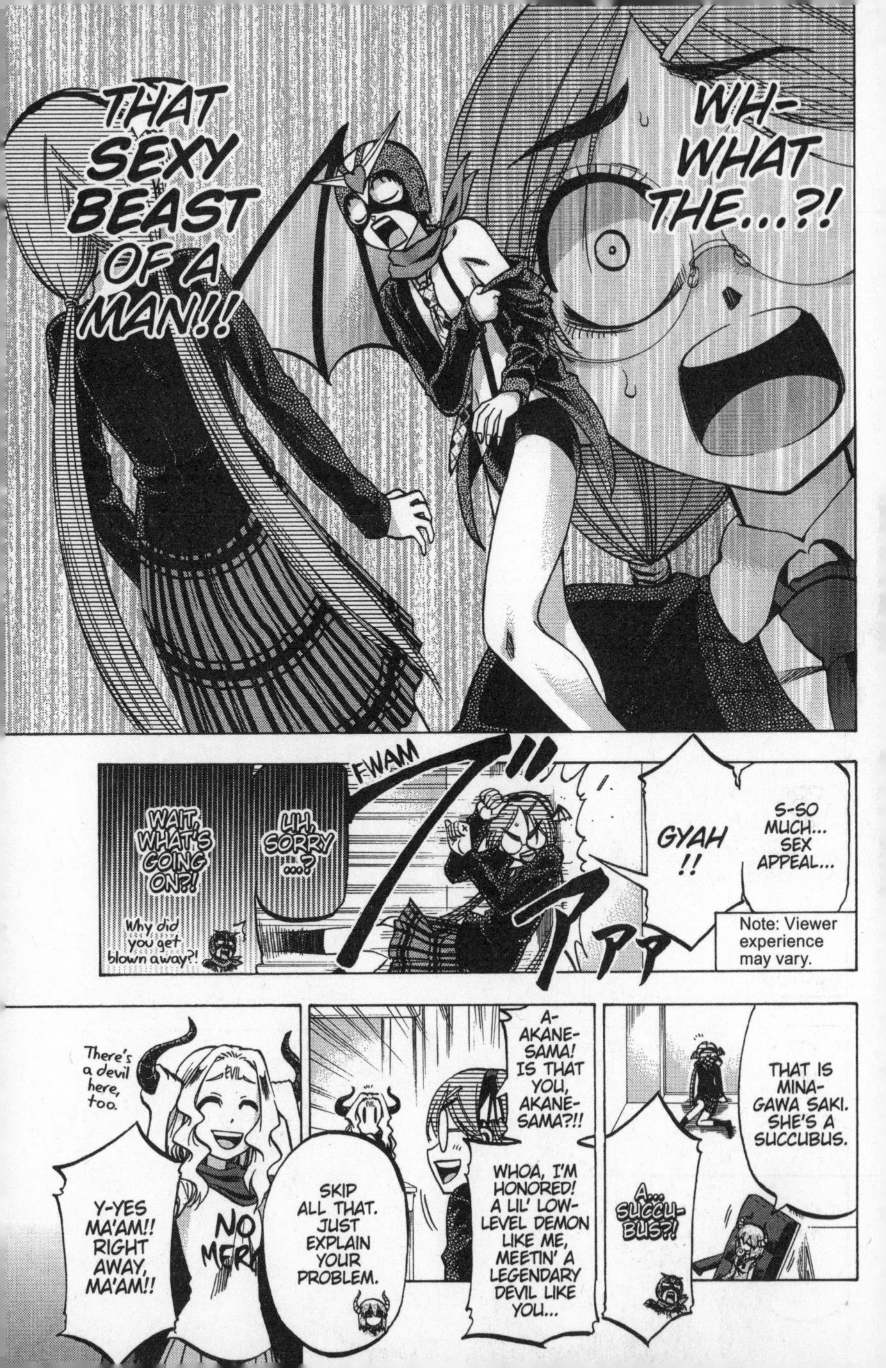
WH-WHAT THE...?!
THAT SEXY BEAST OF A MAN!!
S-SO MUCH... SEX APPEAL...
Note: Viewer experience may vary.
GYAH!!
FWAM
UH, SORRY...?
WAIT, WHAT'S GOING ON?!
Why did you get blown away?!
THAT IS MINA-GAWA SAKI. SHE'S A SUCCUBUS.
A... SUCCU-BUS?!
A-AKANE-SAMA! IS THAT YOU, AKANE-SAMA?!!
WHOA, I'M HONORED! A LIL' LOW-LEVEL DEMON LIKE ME, MEETIN' A LEGENDARY DEVIL LIKE YOU...
SKIP ALL THAT. JUST EXPLAIN YOUR PROBLEM.
Y-YES MA'AM!! RIGHT AWAY, MA'AM!!
There's a devil here, too.
EVIL

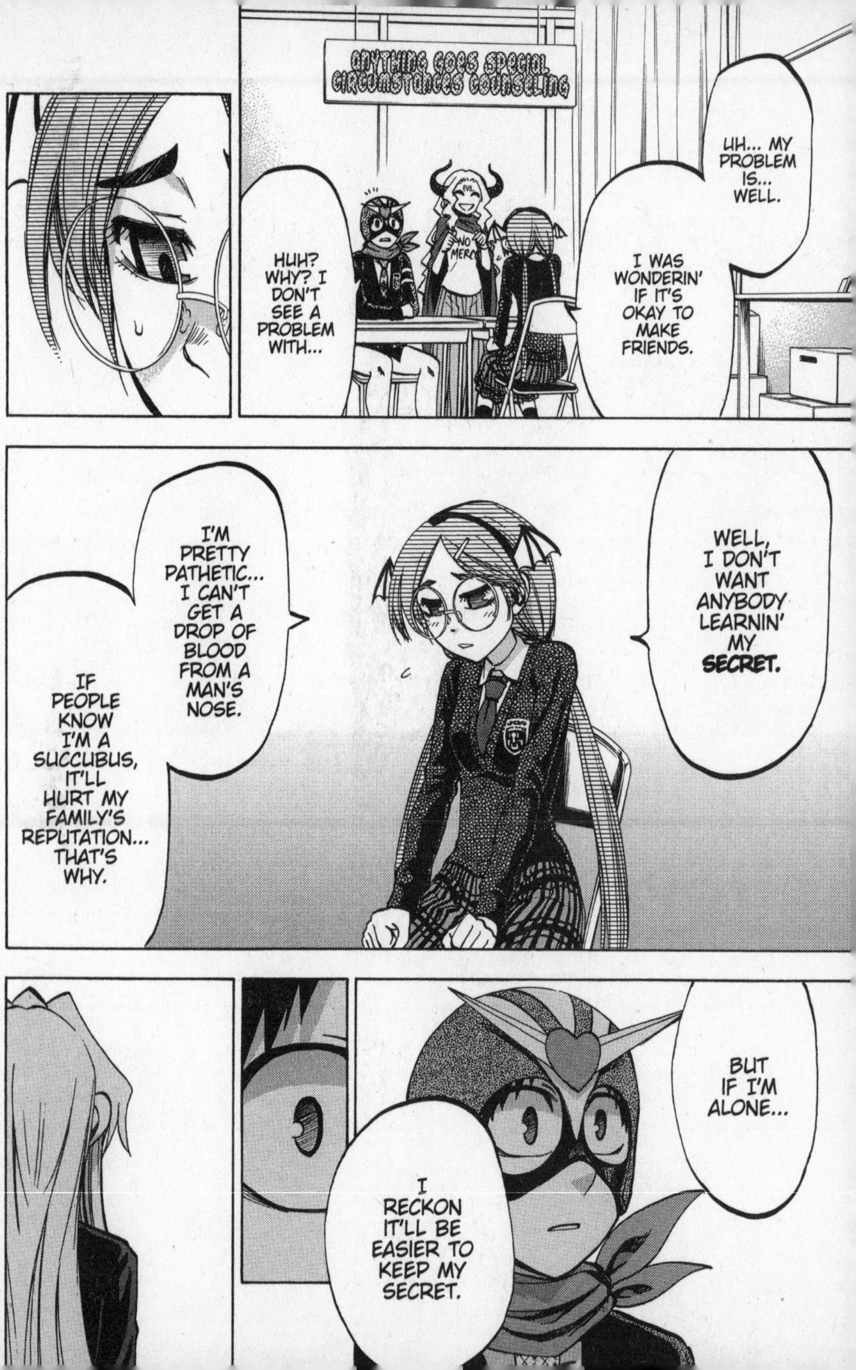
ANYTHING GOES SPECIAL CIRCUMSTANCES COUNSELING
UH... MY PROBLEM IS... WELL.
I WAS WONDERIN' IF IT'S OKAY TO MAKE FRIENDS.
HUH? WHY? I DON'T SEE A PROBLEM WITH...
WELL, I DON'T WANT ANYBODY LEARNIN' MY **SECRET.**
I'M PRETTY PATHETIC... I CAN'T GET A DROP OF BLOOD FROM A MAN'S NOSE.
IF PEOPLE KNOW I'M A SUCCUBUS, IT'LL HURT MY FAMILY'S REPUTATION... THAT'S WHY.
BUT IF I'M ALONE...
I RECKON IT'LL BE EASIER TO KEEP MY SECRET.

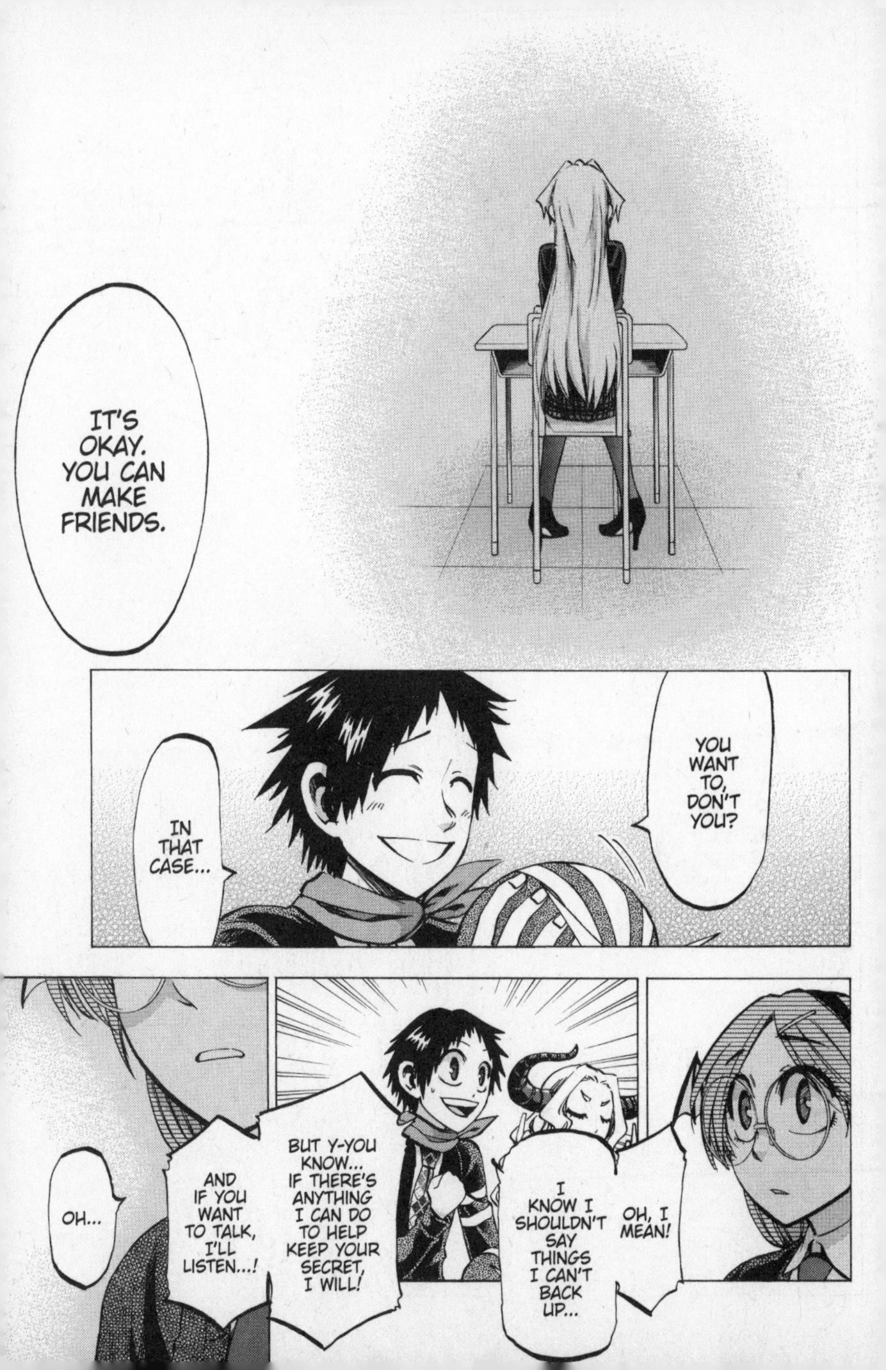
IT'S OKAY. YOU CAN MAKE FRIENDS.
YOU WANT TO, DON'T YOU?
IN THAT CASE...
OH, I MEAN!
I KNOW I SHOULDN'T SAY THINGS I CAN'T BACK UP...
BUT Y-YOU KNOW... IF THERE'S ANYTHING I CAN DO TO HELP KEEP YOUR SECRET, I WILL!
AND IF YOU WANT TO TALK, I'LL LISTEN...!
OH...

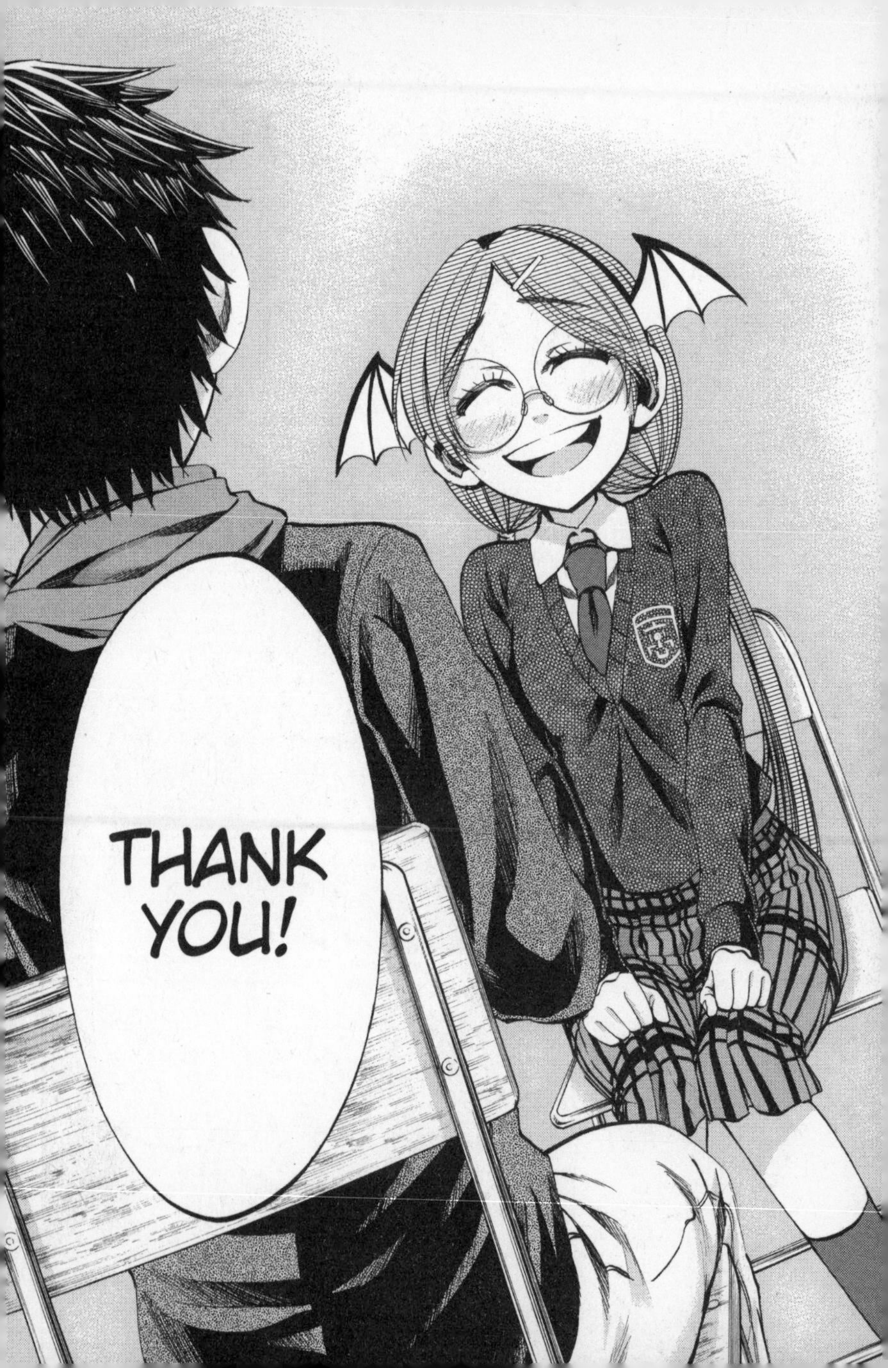
THANK YOU!

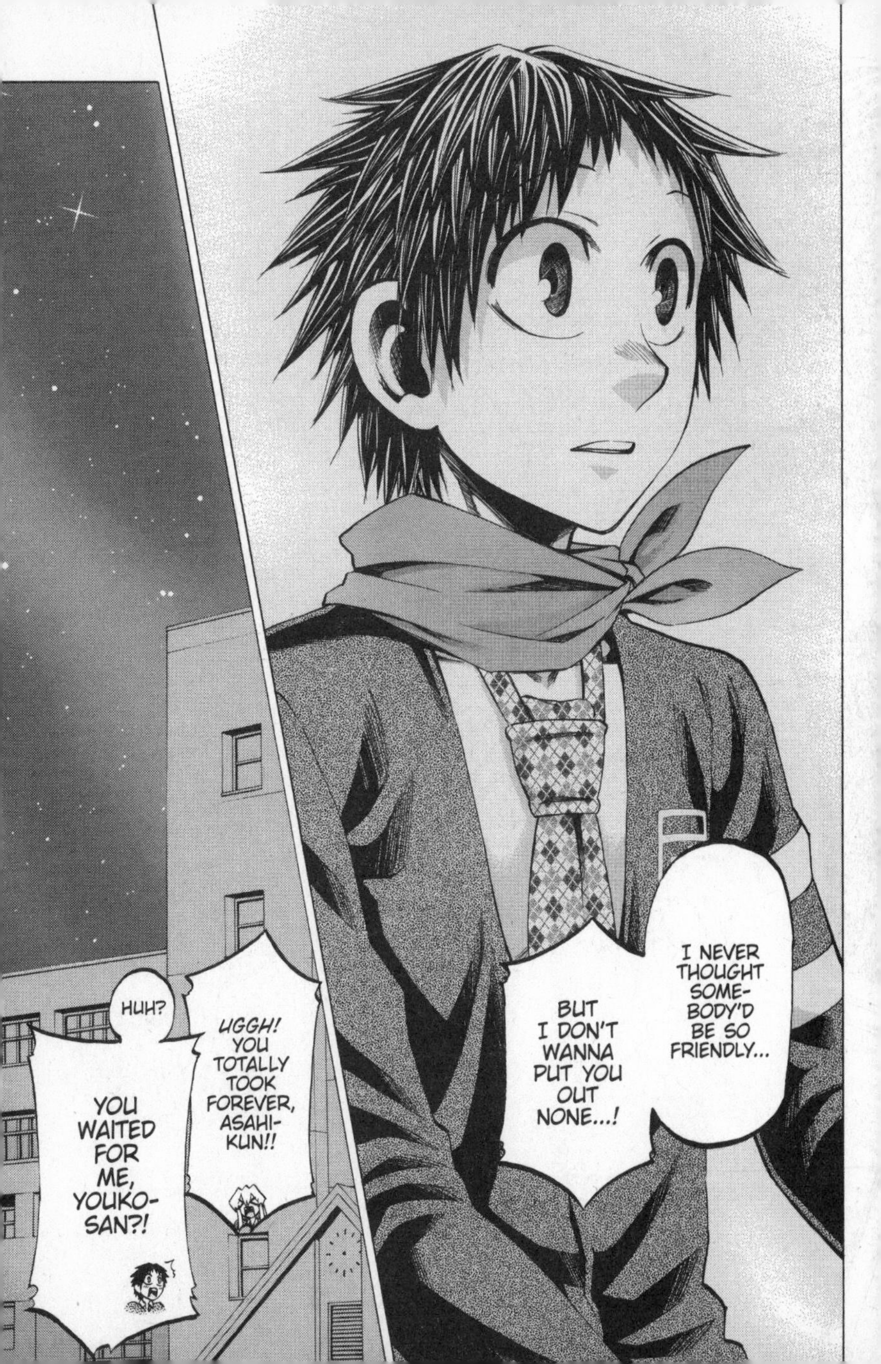
I NEVER THOUGHT SOME-BODY'D BE SO FRIENDLY...
BUT I DON'T WANNA PUT YOU OUT NONE...!
UGGH! YOU TOTALLY TOOK FOREVER, ASAHI-KUN!!
HUH?
YOU WAITED FOR ME, YOUKO-SAN?!

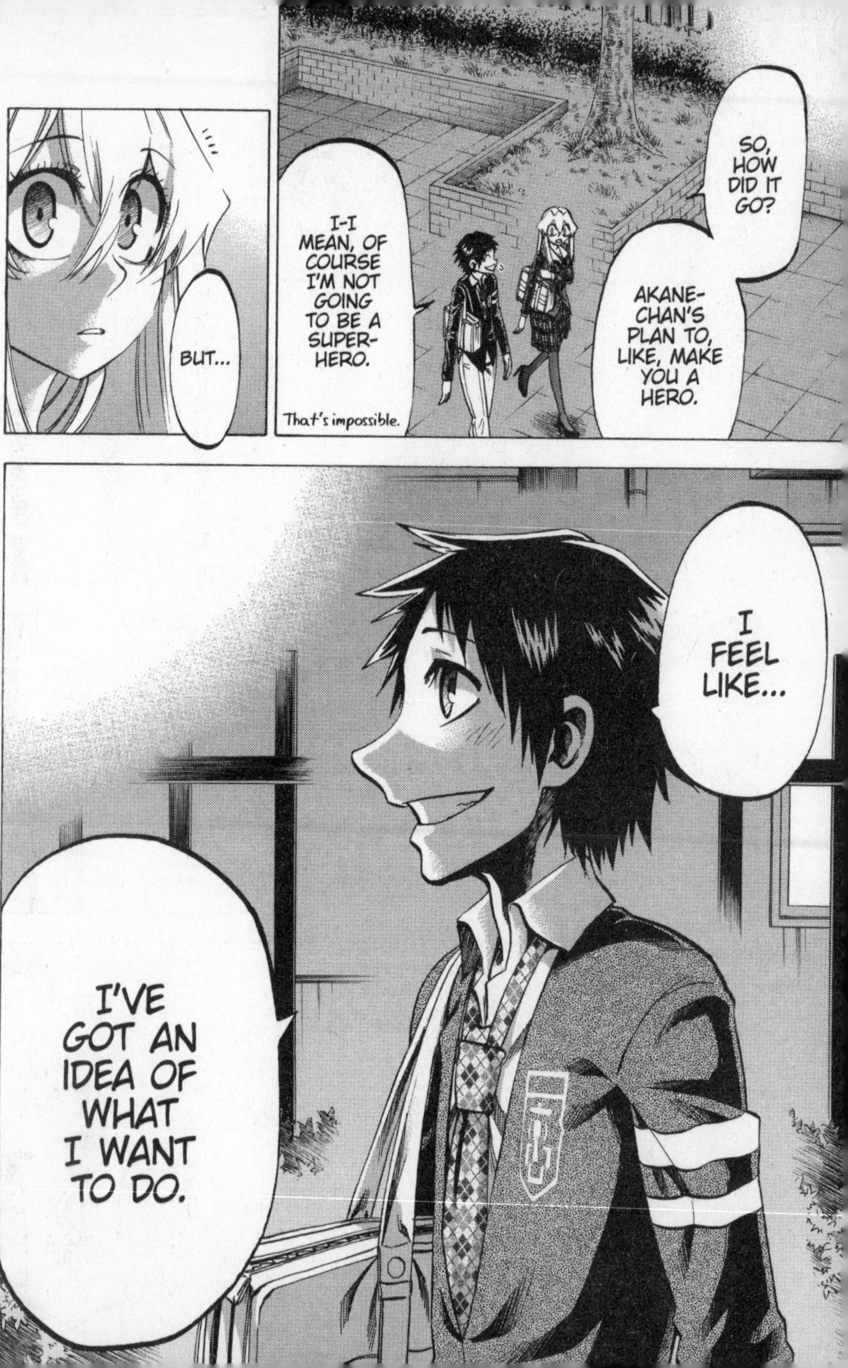
SO, HOW DID IT GO?
AKANE-CHAN'S PLAN TO, LIKE, MAKE YOU A HERO.
I-I MEAN, OF COURSE I'M NOT GOING TO BE A SUPER-HERO.
That's impossible.
BUT...
I FEEL LIKE...
I'VE GOT AN IDEA OF WHAT I WANT TO DO.

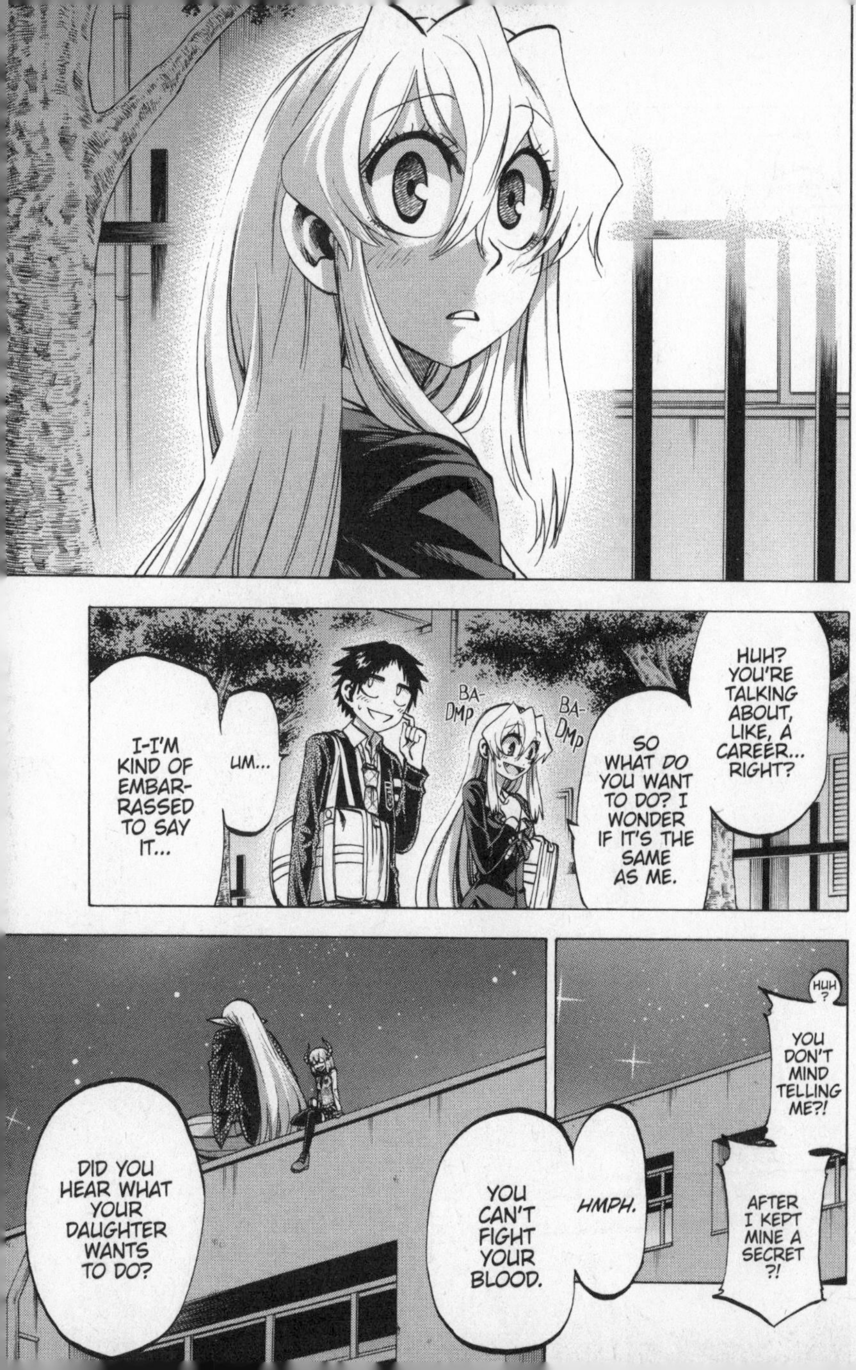
HUH? YOU'RE TALKING ABOUT, LIKE, A CAREER... RIGHT?
SO WHAT DO YOU WANT TO DO? I WONDER IF IT'S THE SAME AS ME.
BA-DMP
BA-DMP
UM...
I-I'M KIND OF EMBARRASSED TO SAY IT...
HUH?
YOU DON'T MIND TELLING ME?!
AFTER I KEPT MINE A SECRET?!
DID YOU HEAR WHAT YOUR DAUGHTER WANTS TO DO?
HMPH.
YOU CAN'T FIGHT YOUR BLOOD.

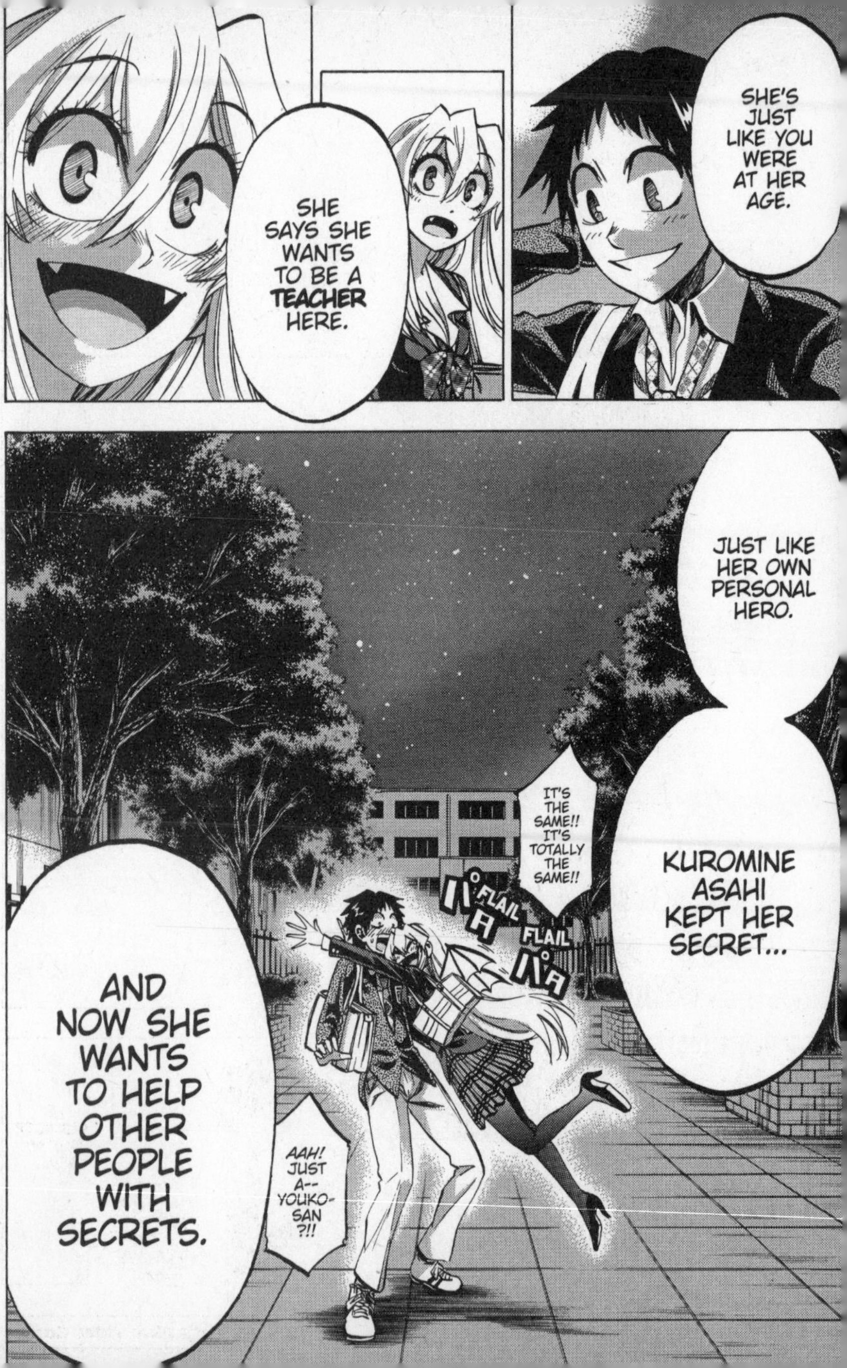
SHE'S JUST LIKE YOU WERE AT HER AGE.
SHE SAYS SHE WANTS TO BE A **TEACHER** HERE.
JUST LIKE HER OWN PERSONAL HERO.
KUROMINE ASAHI KEPT HER SECRET...
IT'S THE SAME!! IT'S TOTALLY THE SAME!!
パ FLAIL
パ FLAIL
AND NOW SHE WANTS TO HELP OTHER PEOPLE WITH SECRETS.
AAH! JUST A-- YOUKO-SAN?!!

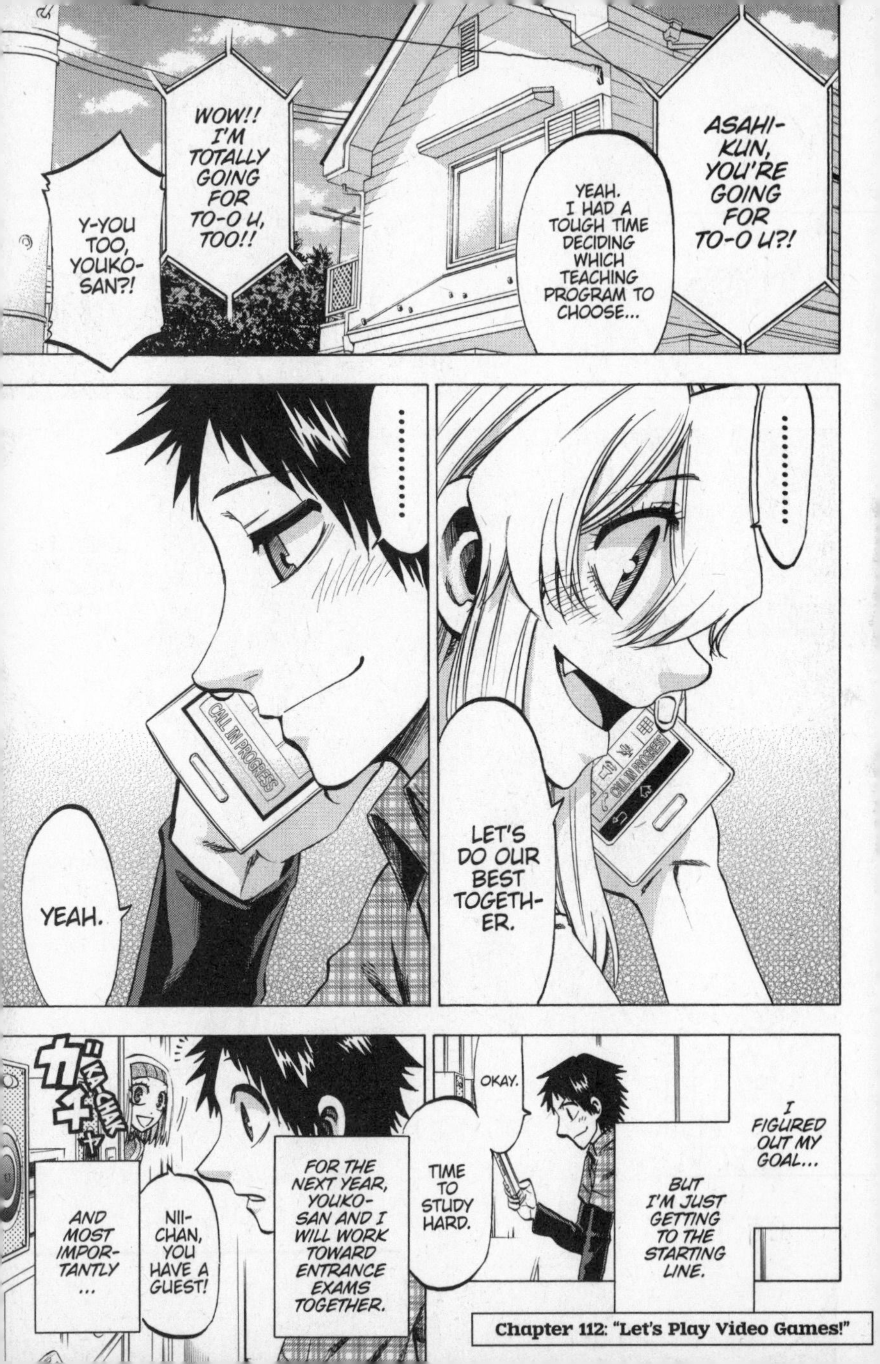
ASAHI-KUN, YOU'RE GOING FOR TO-O U?!
YEAH. I HAD A TOUGH TIME DECIDING WHICH TEACHING PROGRAM TO CHOOSE...
WOW!! I'M TOTALLY GOING FOR TO-O U, TOO!!
Y-YOU TOO, YOUKO-SAN?!
......
CALL IN PROGRESS
LET'S DO OUR BEST TOGETH-ER.
......
CALL IN PROGRESS
YEAH.
I FIGURED OUT MY GOAL...
BUT I'M JUST GETTING TO THE STARTING LINE.
OKAY.
TIME TO STUDY HARD.
FOR THE NEXT YEAR, YOUKO-SAN AND I WILL WORK TOWARD ENTRANCE EXAMS TOGETHER.
KA-CHAK
NII-CHAN, YOU HAVE A GUEST!
AND MOST IMPOR-TANTLY ...
Chapter 112: "Let's Play Video Games!"

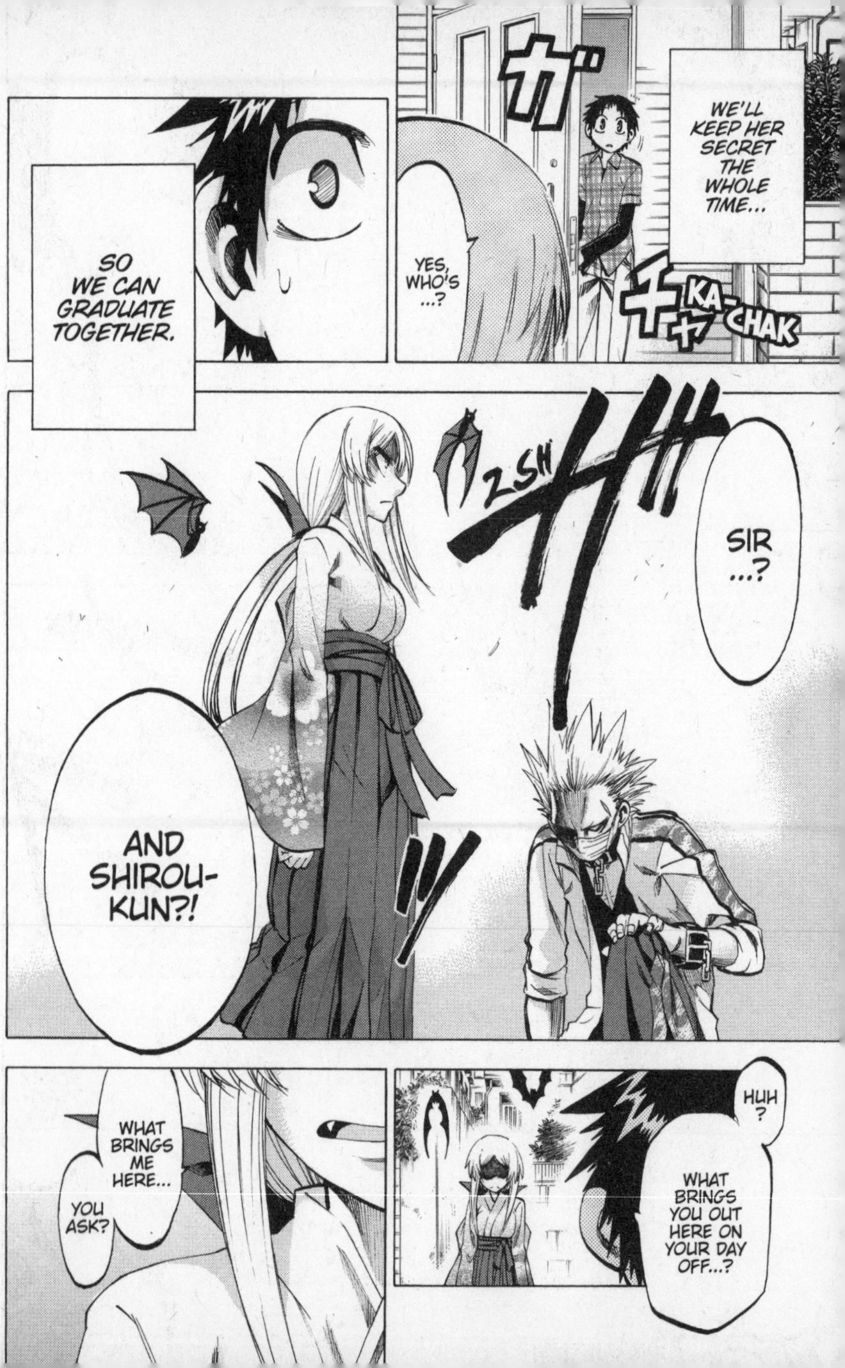
WE'LL KEEP HER SECRET THE WHOLE TIME...
ガ
YES, WHO'S ...?
チャ
KA-CHAK
SO WE CAN GRADUATE TOGETHER.
SIR ...?
ZSH
AND SHIROU-KUN?!
HUH?
WHAT BRINGS YOU OUT HERE ON YOUR DAY OFF...?
WHAT BRINGS ME HERE...
YOU ASK?

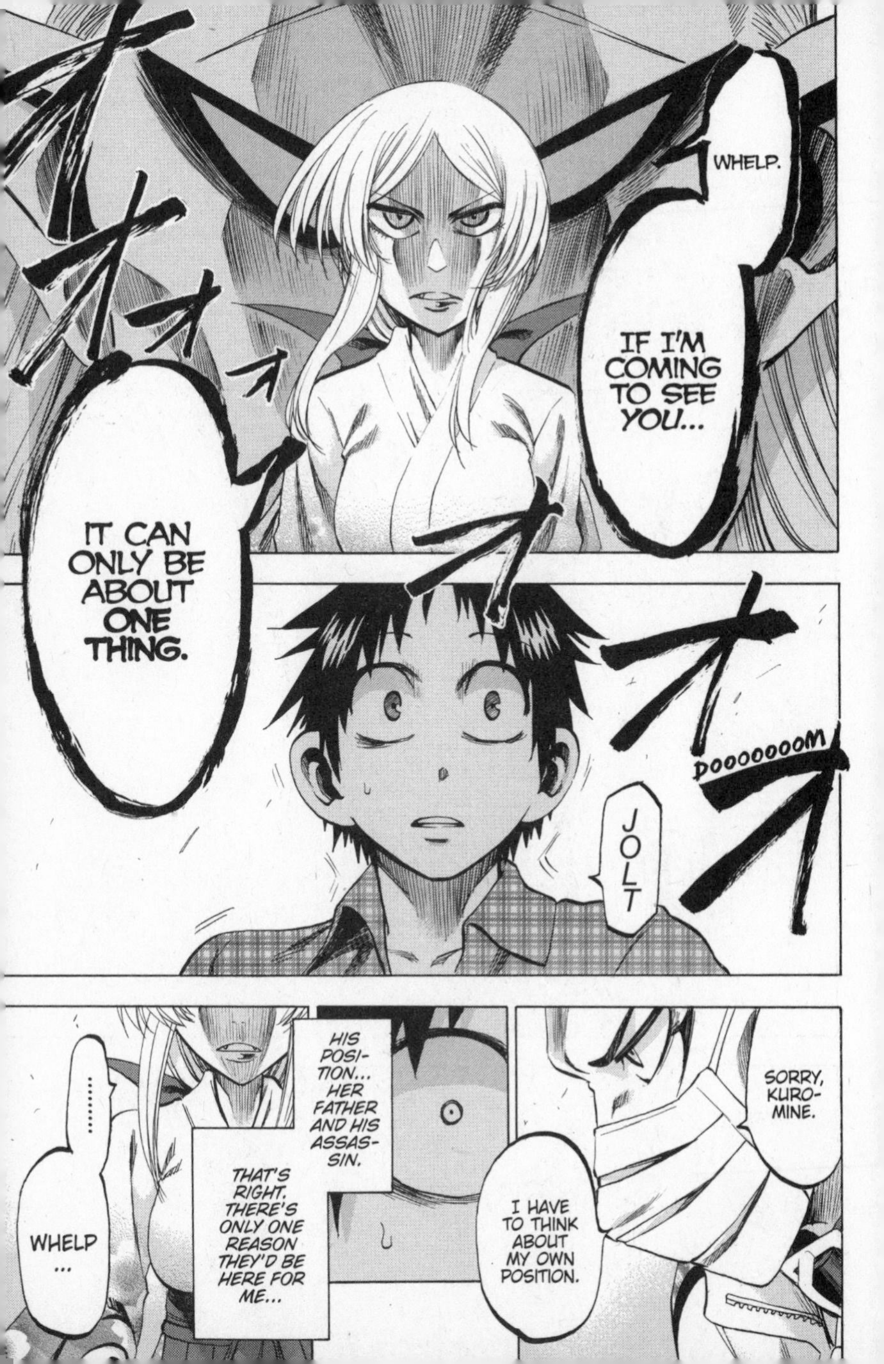
WHELP.
IF I'M COMING TO SEE YOU...
IT CAN ONLY BE ABOUT ONE THING.
DOOOOOOOM
JOLT
SORRY, KURO-MINE.
I HAVE TO THINK ABOUT MY OWN POSITION.
HIS POSI-TION... HER FATHER AND HIS ASSAS-SIN.
THAT'S RIGHT. THERE'S ONLY ONE REASON THEY'D BE HERE FOR ME...
....
WHELP ...

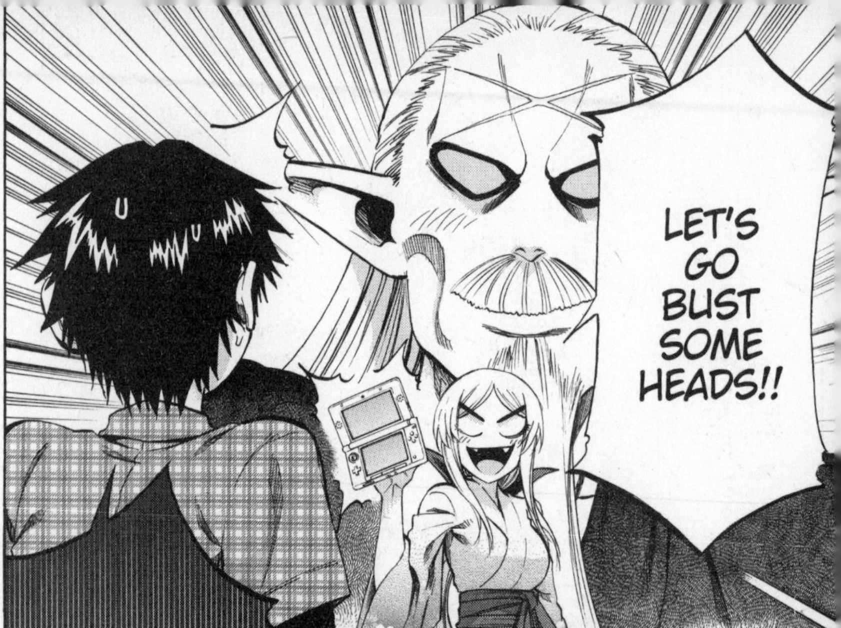
LET'S GO BUST SOME HEADS!!
Y-YOU WANT ME TO PLAY A GAME?!

Chapter 112: "Let's Play Video Games!"

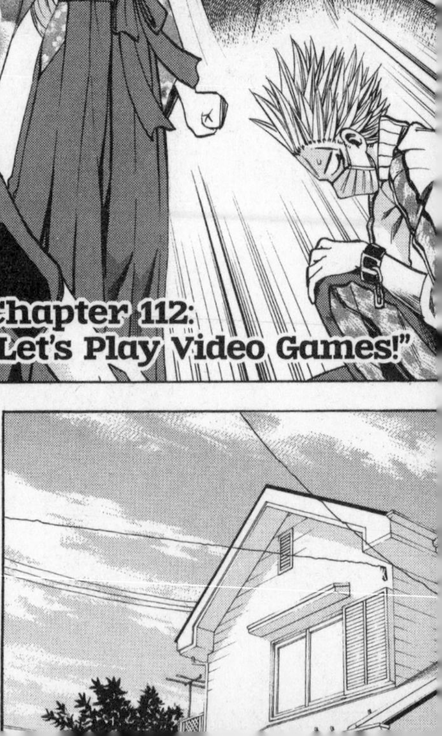

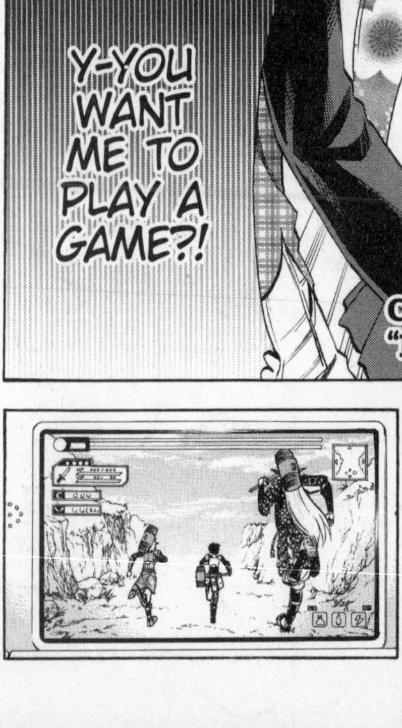

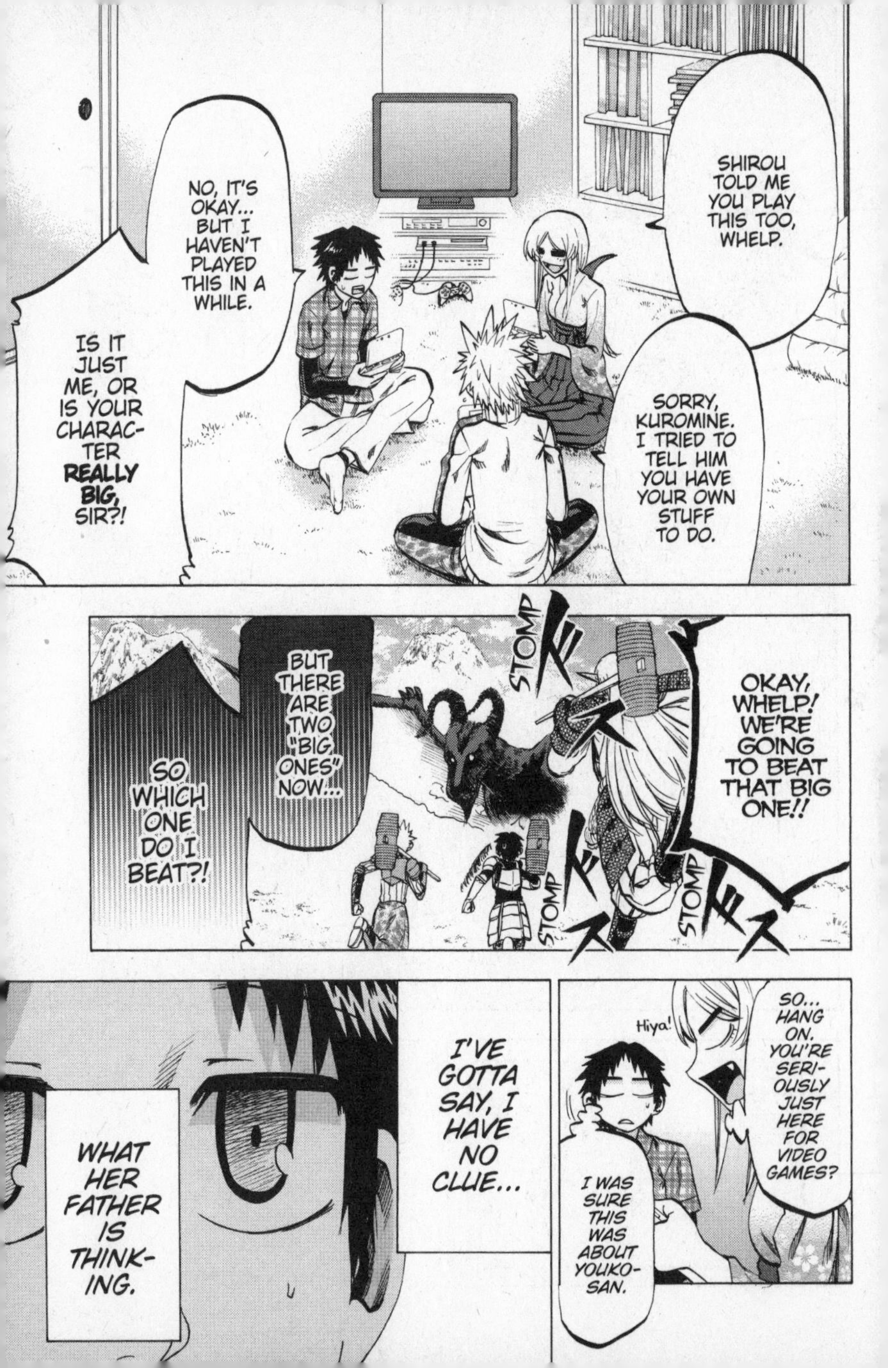
SHIROU TOLD ME YOU PLAY THIS TOO, WHELP.
SORRY, KUROMINE. I TRIED TO TELL HIM YOU HAVE YOUR OWN STUFF TO DO.
NO, IT'S OKAY... BUT I HAVEN'T PLAYED THIS IN A WHILE.
IS IT JUST ME, OR IS YOUR CHARACTER **REALLY BIG,** SIR?!
OKAY, WHELP! WE'RE GOING TO BEAT THAT BIG ONE!!
STOMP
STOMP
STOMP
BUT THERE ARE TWO "BIG ONES" NOW...
SO WHICH ONE DO I BEAT?!
SO... HANG ON. YOU'RE SERIOUSLY JUST HERE FOR VIDEO GAMES?
Hiya!
I WAS SURE THIS WAS ABOUT YOUKO-SAN.
I'VE GOTTA SAY, I HAVE NO CLUE...
WHAT HER FATHER IS THINKING.

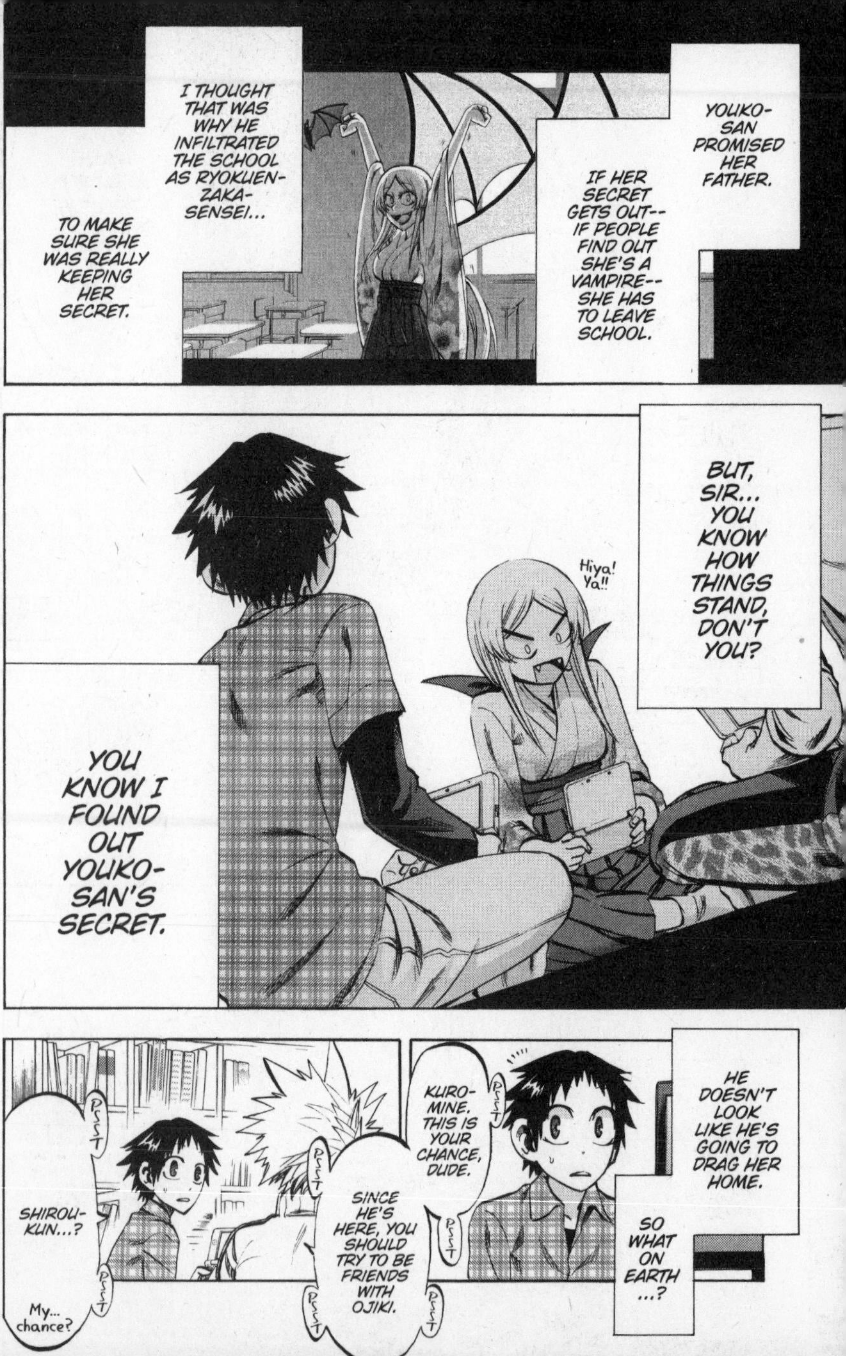
YOUKO-SAN PROMISED HER FATHER.
IF HER SECRET GETS OUT--IF PEOPLE FIND OUT SHE'S A VAMPIRE--SHE HAS TO LEAVE SCHOOL.
I THOUGHT THAT WAS WHY HE INFILTRATED THE SCHOOL AS RYOKUEN-ZAKA-SENSEI...
TO MAKE SURE SHE WAS REALLY KEEPING HER SECRET.
BUT, SIR... YOU KNOW HOW THINGS STAND, DON'T YOU?
Hiya! Ya!!
YOU KNOW I FOUND OUT YOUKO-SAN'S SECRET.
HE DOESN'T LOOK LIKE HE'S GOING TO DRAG HER HOME.
SO WHAT ON EARTH...?
PSST
KURO-MINE. THIS IS YOUR CHANCE, DUDE.
PSST
PSST
SINCE HE'S HERE, YOU SHOULD TRY TO BE FRIENDS WITH OJIKI.
PSST
PSST
PSST
SHIROU-KUN...?
PSST
My... chance?

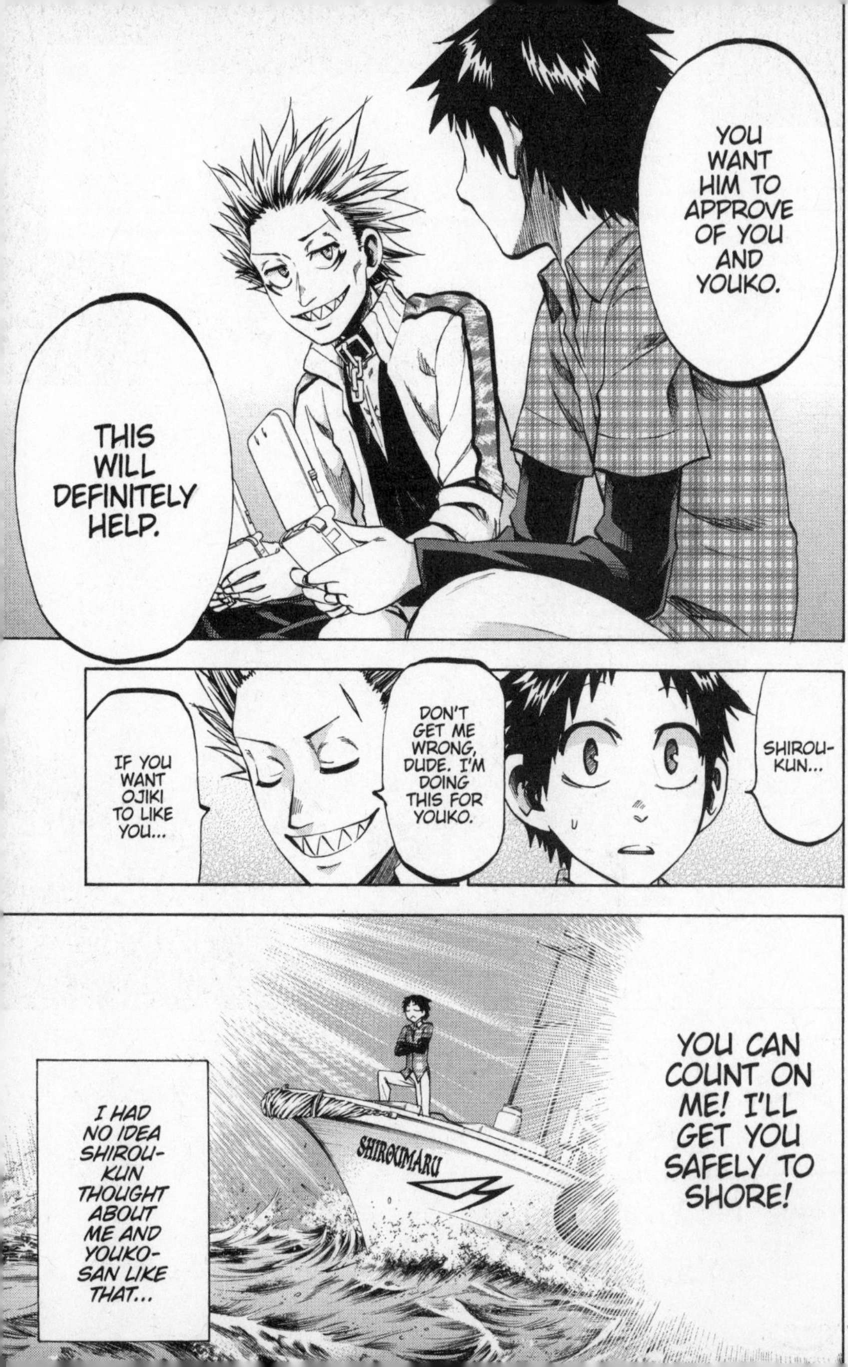
YOU WANT HIM TO APPROVE OF YOU AND YOUKO.
THIS WILL DEFINITELY HELP.
SHIROU-KUN...
DON'T GET ME WRONG, DUDE. I'M DOING THIS FOR YOUKO.
IF YOU WANT OJIKI TO LIKE YOU...
YOU CAN COUNT ON ME! I'LL GET YOU SAFELY TO SHORE!
SHIROUMARU
I HAD NO IDEA SHIROU-KUN THOUGHT ABOUT ME AND YOUKO-SAN LIKE THAT...

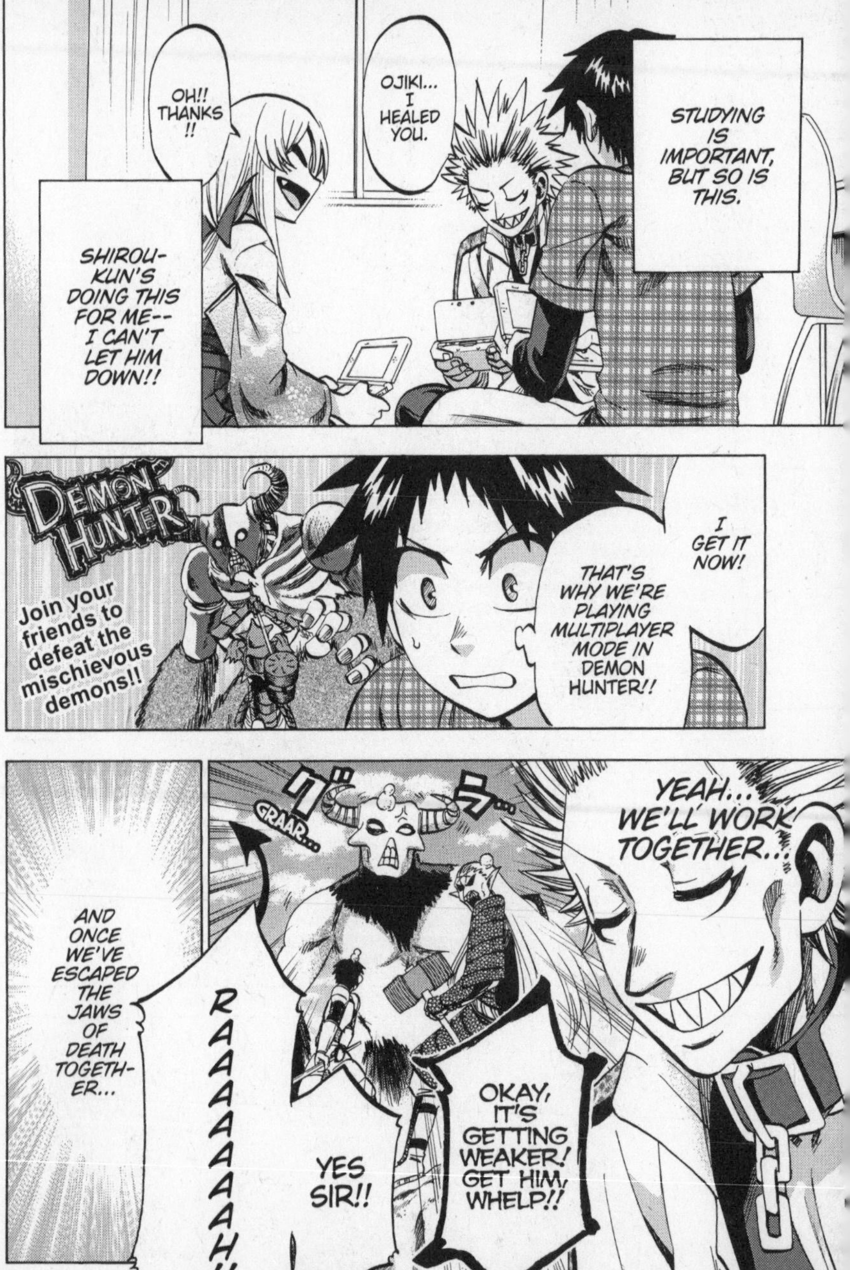
STUDYING IS IMPORTANT, BUT SO IS THIS.
OJIKI... I HEALED YOU.
OH!! THANKS!!
SHIROU-KUN'S DOING THIS FOR ME-- I CAN'T LET HIM DOWN!!
I GET IT NOW!
THAT'S WHY WE'RE PLAYING MULTIPLAYER MODE IN DEMON HUNTER!!
DEMON HUNTER
Join your friends to defeat the mischievous demons!!
YEAH... WE'LL WORK TOGETHER...
GRAAR...
OKAY, IT'S GETTING WEAKER! GET HIM, WHELP!!
YES SIR!!
RAAAAAAAAH!!
AND ONCE WE'VE ESCAPED THE JAWS OF DEATH TOGETH-ER...

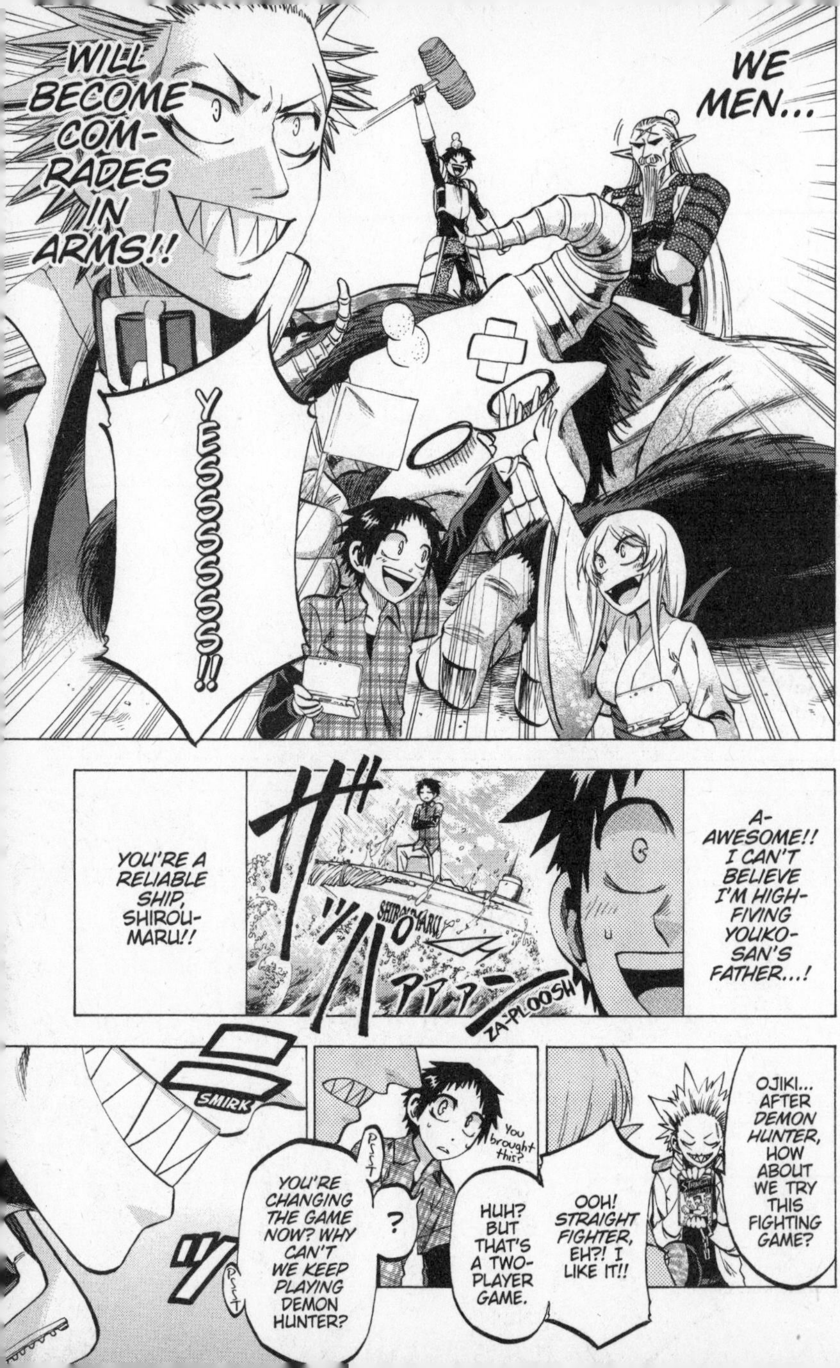
WE MEN...
WILL BECOME COM-RADES IN ARMS!!
YESSSSSSS!!
A-AWESOME!! I CAN'T BELIEVE I'M HIGH-FIVING YOUKO-SAN'S FATHER...!
SHIROUMARU
ZA-PLOOSH
YOU'RE A RELIABLE SHIP, SHIROU-MARU!!
OJIKI... AFTER DEMON HUNTER, HOW ABOUT WE TRY THIS FIGHTING GAME?
OOH! STRAIGHT FIGHTER, EH?! I LIKE IT!!
You brought this?
HUH? BUT THAT'S A TWO-PLAYER GAME.
PSST
?
YOU'RE CHANGING THE GAME NOW? WHY CAN'T WE KEEP PLAYING DEMON HUNTER?
PSST
SMIRK

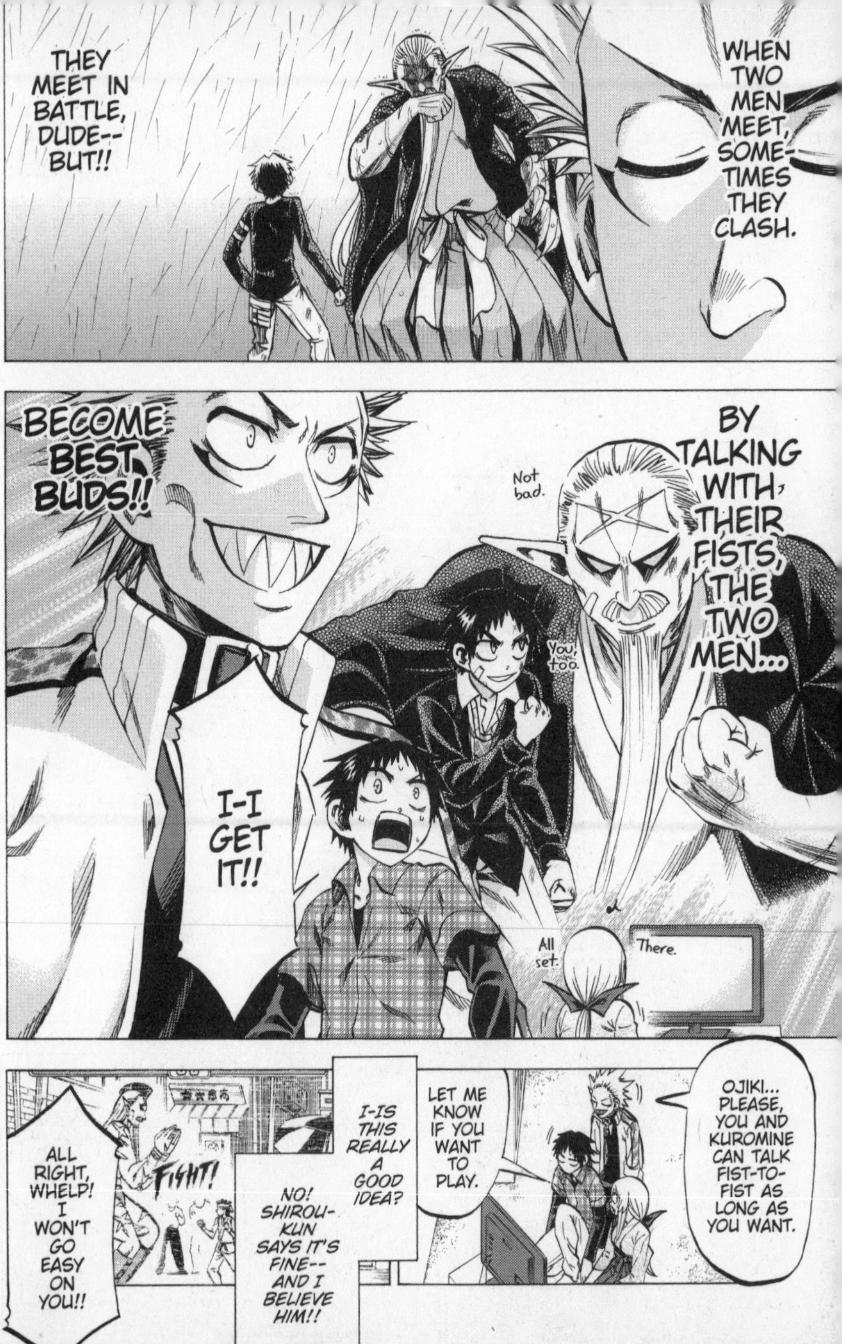
WHEN TWO MEN MEET, SOMETIMES THEY CLASH.
THEY MEET IN BATTLE, DUDE--BUT!!
BY TALKING WITH THEIR FISTS, THE TWO MEN...
Not bad.
BECOME BEST BUDS!!
You, too.
I-I GET IT!!
There.
All set.
OJIKI... PLEASE, YOU AND KUROMINE CAN TALK FIST-TO-FIST AS LONG AS YOU WANT.
LET ME KNOW IF YOU WANT TO PLAY.
I-IS THIS REALLY A GOOD IDEA?
NO! SHIROU-KUN SAYS IT'S FINE--AND I BELIEVE HIM!!
FIGHT!
ALL RIGHT, WHELP! I WON'T GO EASY ON YOU!!

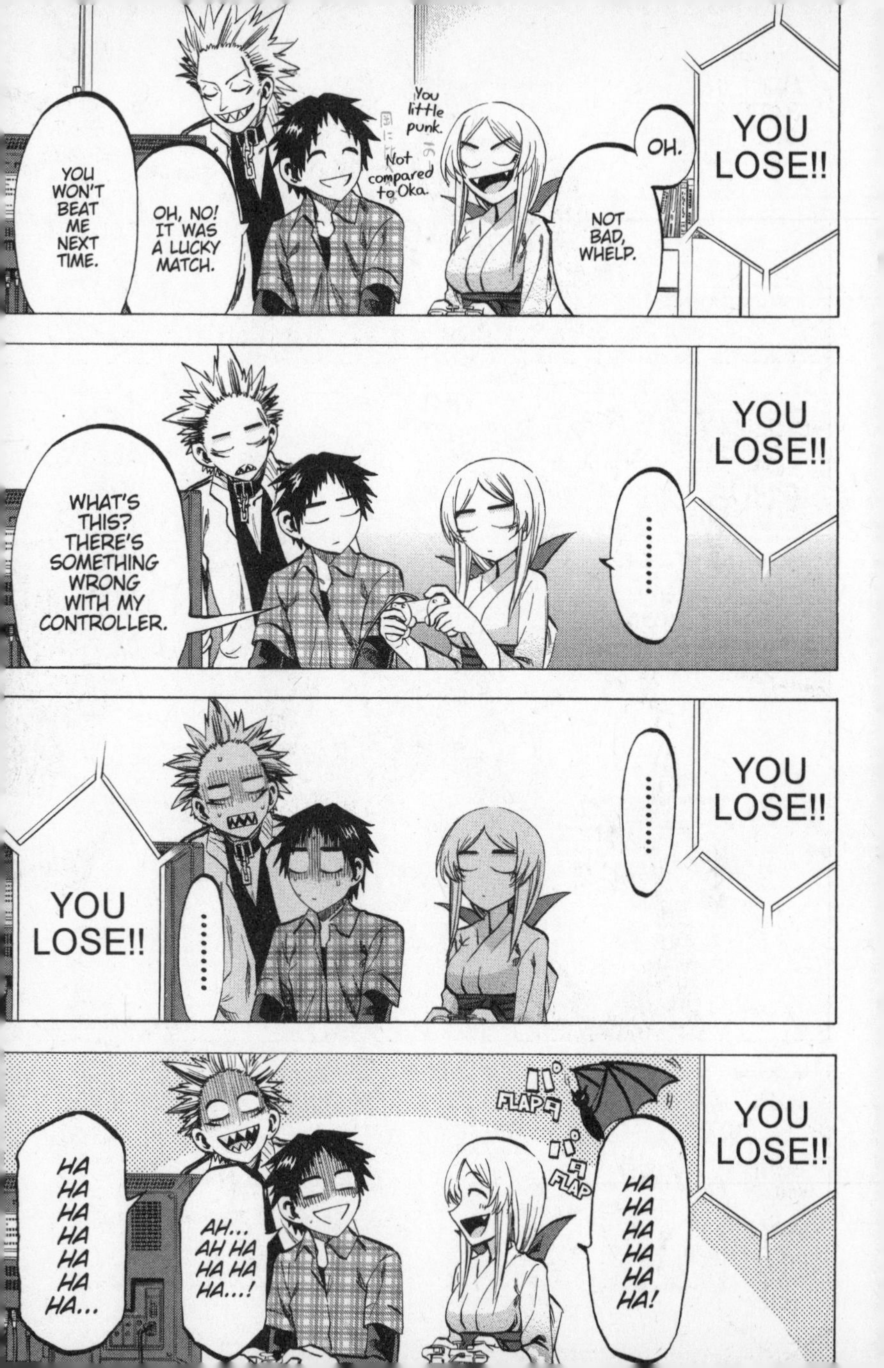
YOU LOSE!!
OH.
NOT BAD, WHELP.
You little punk.
Not compared to Oka.
OH, NO! IT WAS A LUCKY MATCH.
YOU WON'T BEAT ME NEXT TIME.
YOU LOSE!!
....
WHAT'S THIS? THERE'S SOMETHING WRONG WITH MY CONTROLLER.
YOU LOSE!!
....
......
YOU LOSE!!
YOU LOSE!!
FLAP
FLAP
HA HA HA HA HA HA!
AH... AH HA HA HA HA...!
HA HA HA HA HA HA HA...

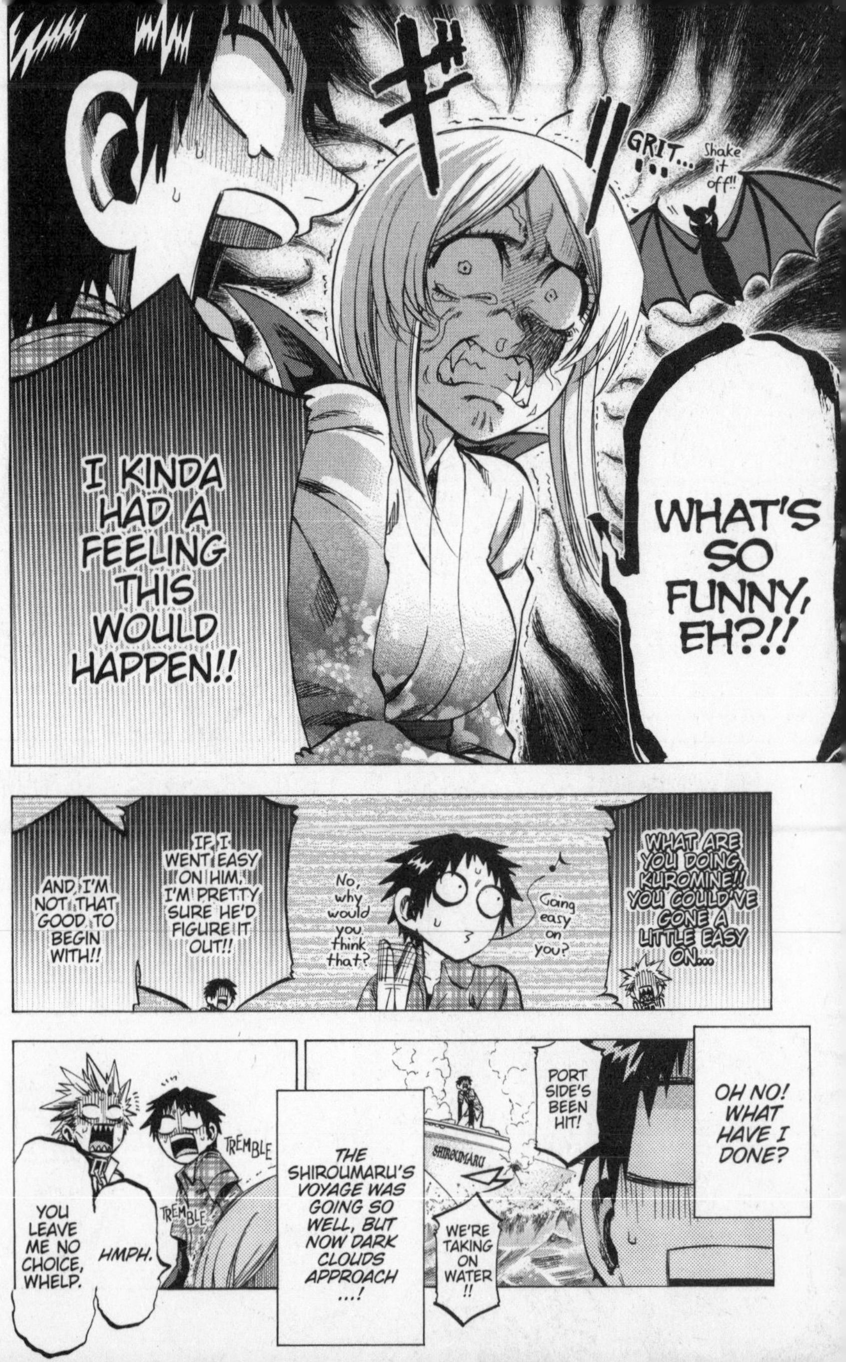
GRIT...
Shake it off!!
WHAT'S SO FUNNY, EH?!!
I KINDA HAD A FEELING THIS WOULD HAPPEN!!
WHAT ARE YOU DOING, KUROMINE!! YOU COULD'VE GONE A LITTLE EASY ON...
Going easy on you?
No, why would you think that?
IF I WENT EASY ON HIM, I'M PRETTY SURE HE'D FIGURE IT OUT!!
AND I'M NOT THAT GOOD TO BEGIN WITH!!
OH NO! WHAT HAVE I DONE?
PORT SIDE'S BEEN HIT!
SHIROUMARU
WE'RE TAKING ON WATER!!
THE SHIROUMARU'S VOYAGE WAS GOING SO WELL, BUT NOW DARK CLOUDS APPROACH...!
TREMBLE
TREMBLE
HMPH.
YOU LEAVE ME NO CHOICE, WHELP.

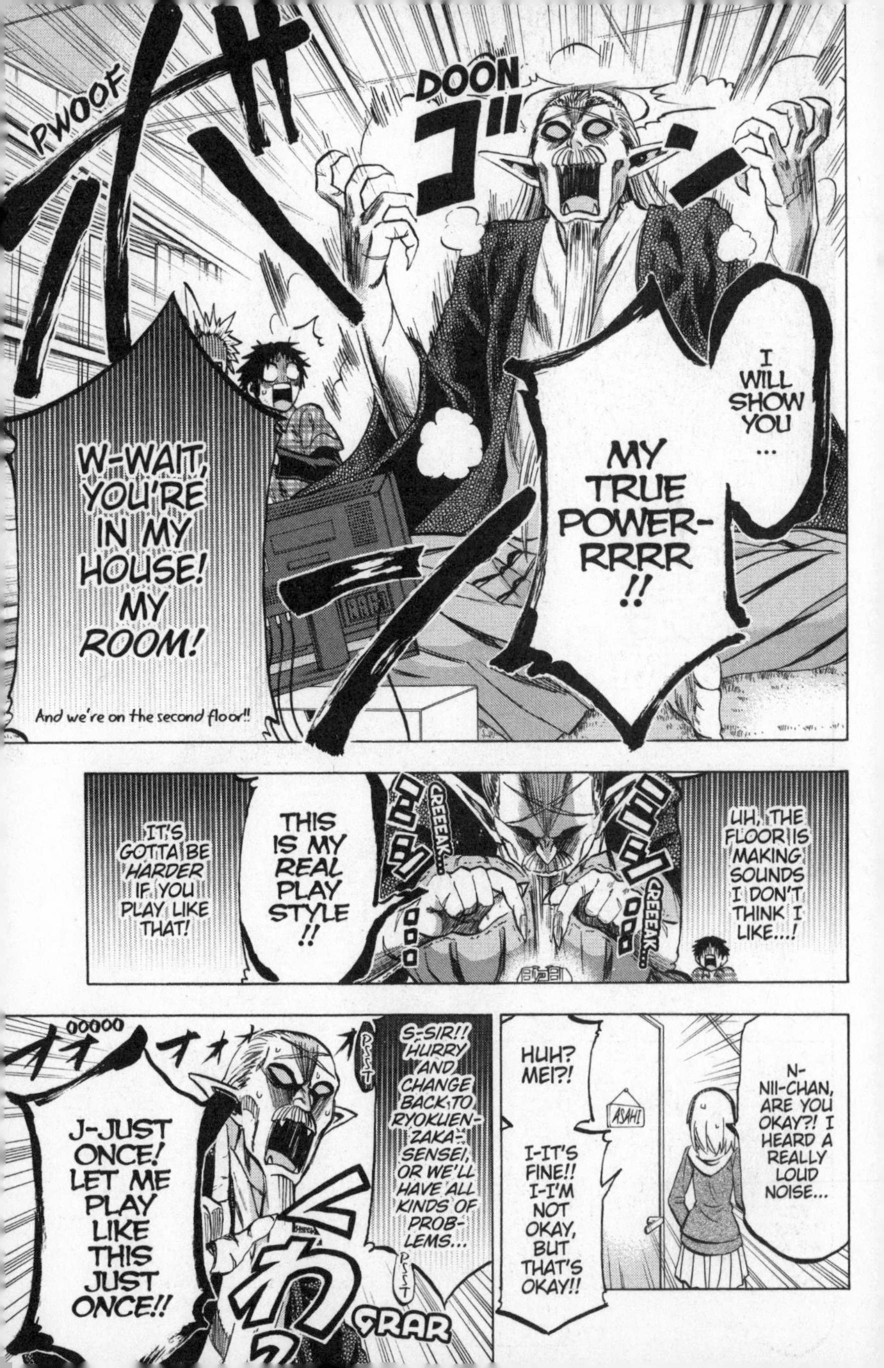
DOON
PWOOF
I WILL SHOW YOU ...
MY TRUE POWER-RRRR !!
W-WAIT, YOU'RE IN MY HOUSE! MY ROOM!
And we're on the second floor!!
UH, THE FLOOR IS MAKING SOUNDS I DON'T THINK I LIKE...!
CREEEAK...
CREEEAK...
THIS IS MY REAL PLAY STYLE !!
IT'S GOTTA BE HARDER IF YOU PLAY LIKE THAT!
N-NII-CHAN, ARE YOU OKAY?! I HEARD A REALLY LOUD NOISE...
ASAHI
HUH? MEI?!
I-IT'S FINE!! I-I'M NOT OKAY, BUT THAT'S OKAY!!
S-SIR!! HURRY AND CHANGE BACK TO RYOKUEN-ZAKA-SENSEI, OR WE'LL HAVE ALL KINDS OF PROB-LEMS...
PSST
PSST
OOOOO
J-JUST ONCE! LET ME PLAY LIKE THIS JUST ONCE!!
GRAR

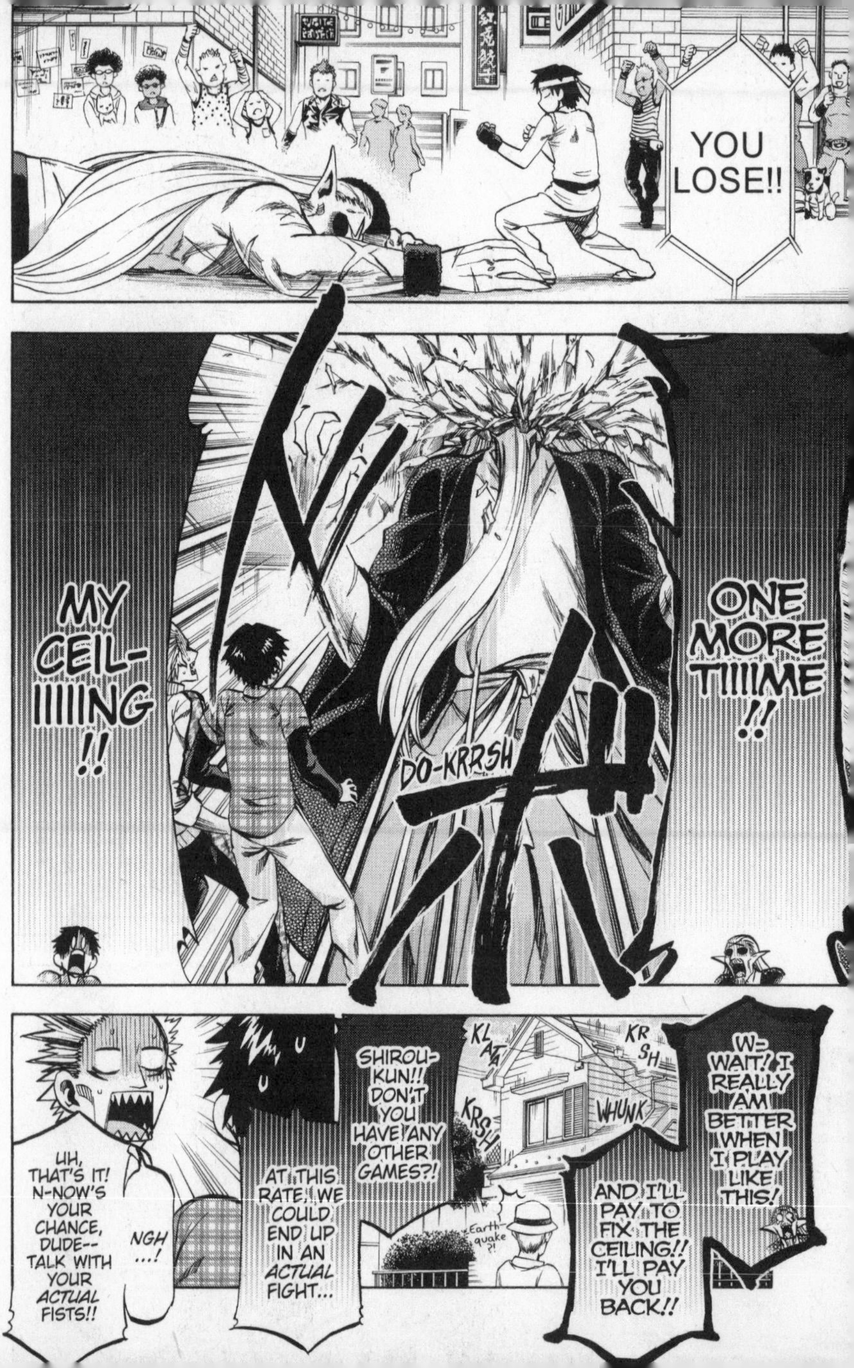
YOU LOSE!!
ONE MORE TIIIIME!!
DO-KRRSH
MY CEIL-IIIIING!!
W-WAIT! I REALLY AM BETTER WHEN I PLAY LIKE THIS!
AND I'LL PAY TO FIX THE CEILING!! I'LL PAY YOU BACK!!
KR SH
WHUNK
KRSH
KLATA
Earth-quake?!
SHIROU-KUN!! DON'T YOU HAVE ANY OTHER GAMES?!
AT THIS RATE, WE COULD END UP IN AN ACTUAL FIGHT...
NGH...!
UH, THAT'S IT! N-NOW'S YOUR CHANCE, DUDE--TALK WITH YOUR ACTUAL FISTS!!

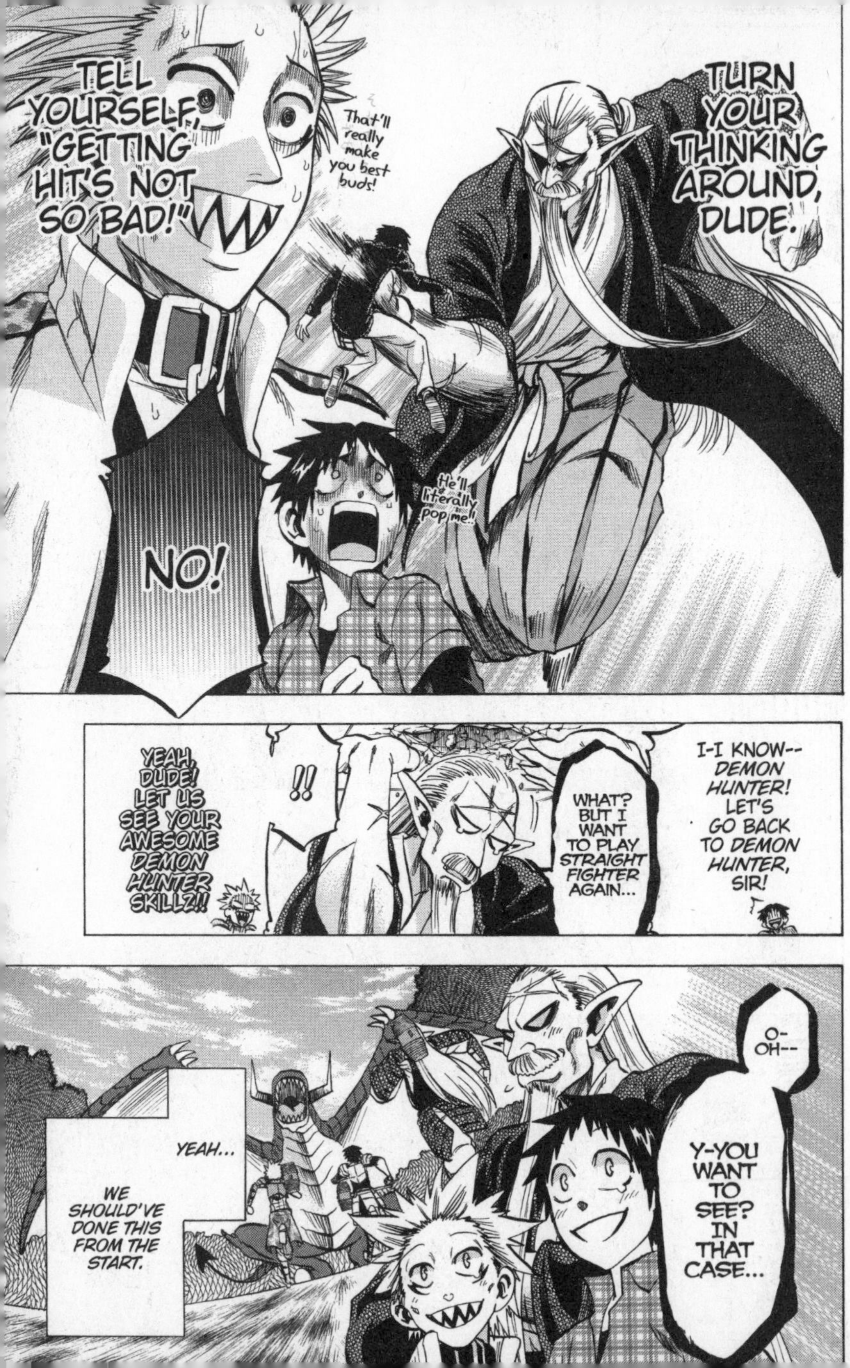
TURN YOUR THINKING AROUND, DUDE.
That'll really make you best buds!
TELL YOURSELF, "GETTING HIT'S NOT SO BAD!"
He'll literally pop me!!
NO!
I-I KNOW-- DEMON HUNTER! LET'S GO BACK TO DEMON HUNTER, SIR!
WHAT? BUT I WANT TO PLAY STRAIGHT FIGHTER AGAIN...
!!
YEAH, DUDE! LET US SEE YOUR AWESOME DEMON HUNTER SKILLZ!!
O-OH--
Y-YOU WANT TO SEE? IN THAT CASE...
YEAH...
WE SHOULD'VE DONE THIS FROM THE START.

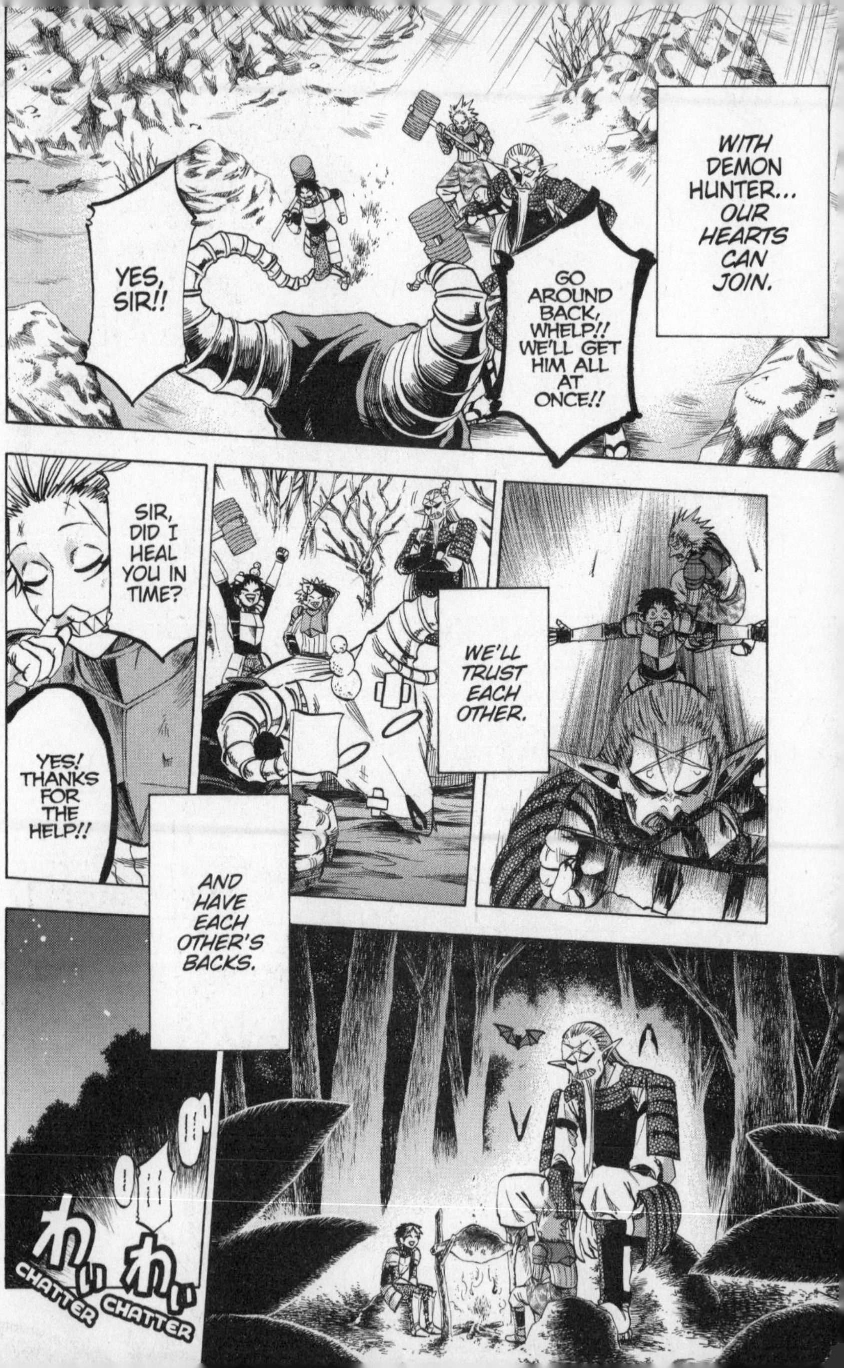
WITH DEMON HUNTER... OUR HEARTS CAN JOIN.
GO AROUND BACK, WHELP!! WE'LL GET HIM ALL AT ONCE!!
YES, SIR!!
WE'LL TRUST EACH OTHER.
SIR, DID I HEAL YOU IN TIME?
YES! THANKS FOR THE HELP!!
AND HAVE EACH OTHER'S BACKS.
わいわい
CHATTER CHATTER

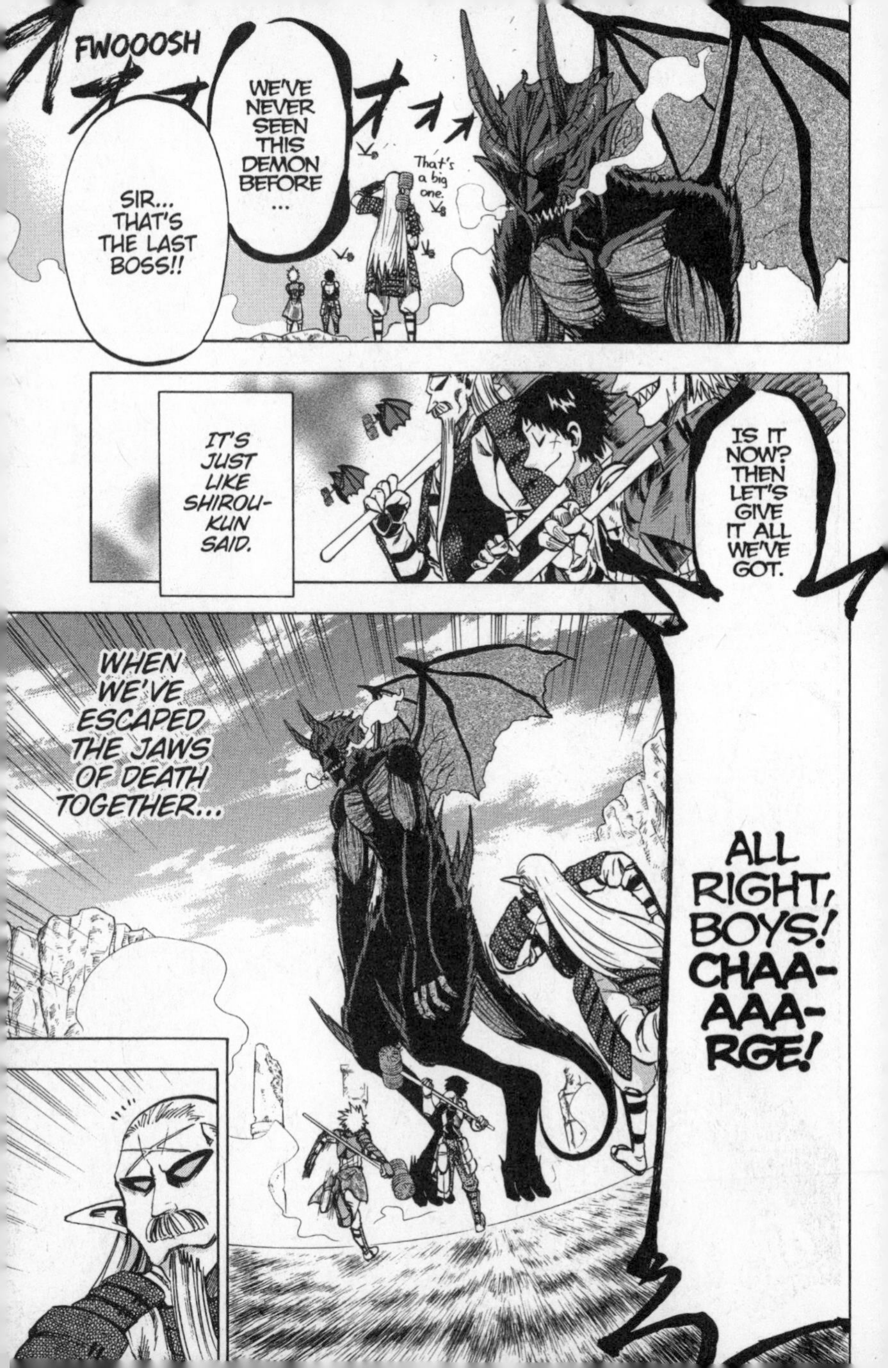
That's a big one.
WE'VE NEVER SEEN THIS DEMON BEFORE...
FWOOOSH
SIR... THAT'S THE LAST BOSS!!
IS IT NOW? THEN LET'S GIVE IT ALL WE'VE GOT.
IT'S JUST LIKE SHIROU-KUN SAID.
ALL RIGHT, BOYS! CHAAAAAARGE!
WHEN WE'VE ESCAPED THE JAWS OF DEATH TOGETHER...

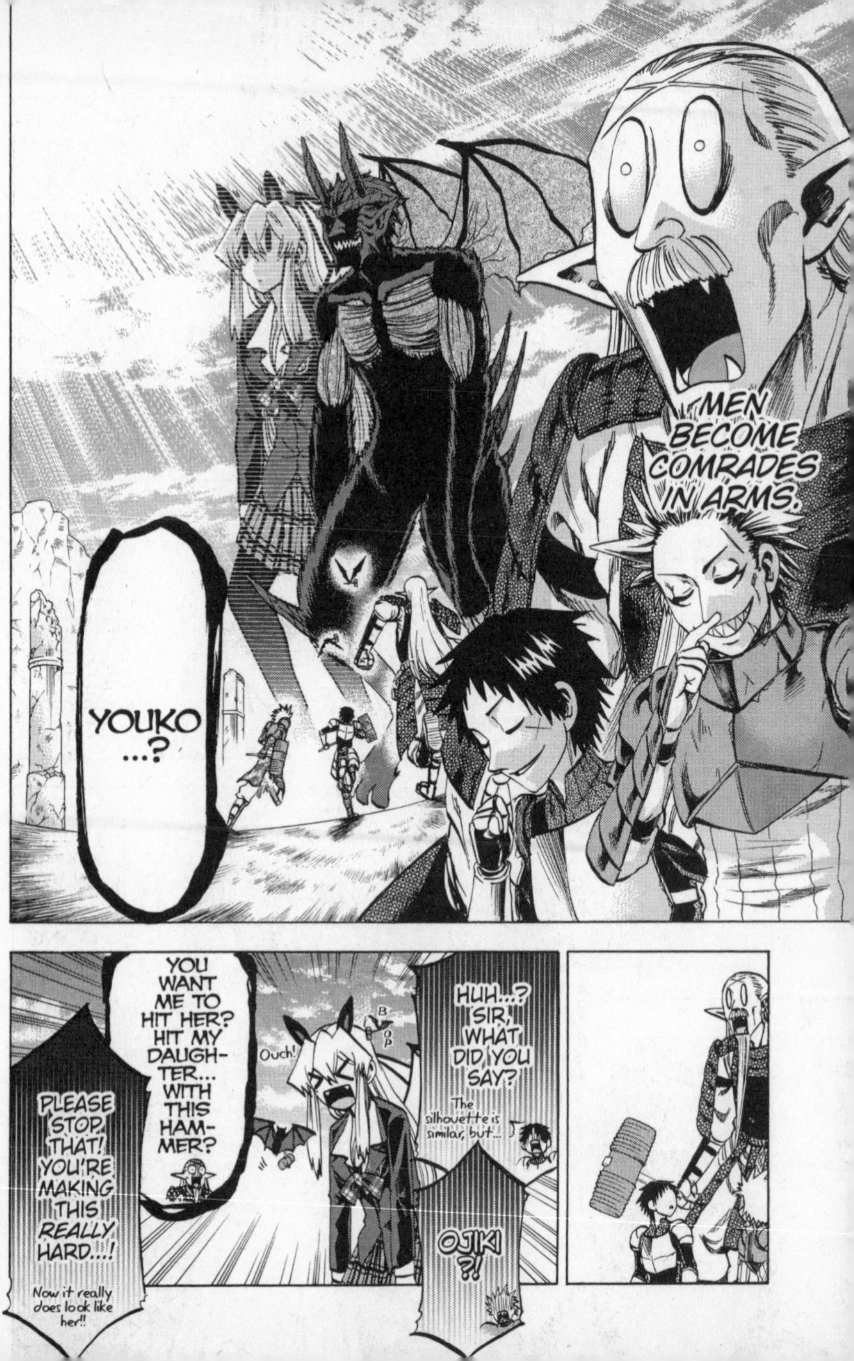
MEN BECOME COMRADES IN ARMS.
YOUKO ...?
HUH...? SIR, WHAT DID YOU SAY?
The silhouette is similar, but...
OJIKI ?!
YOU WANT ME TO HIT HER? HIT MY DAUGHTER... WITH THIS HAMMER?
BOP
Ouch!
PLEASE STOP THAT! YOU'RE MAKING THIS REALLY HARD...!
Now it really does look like her!!

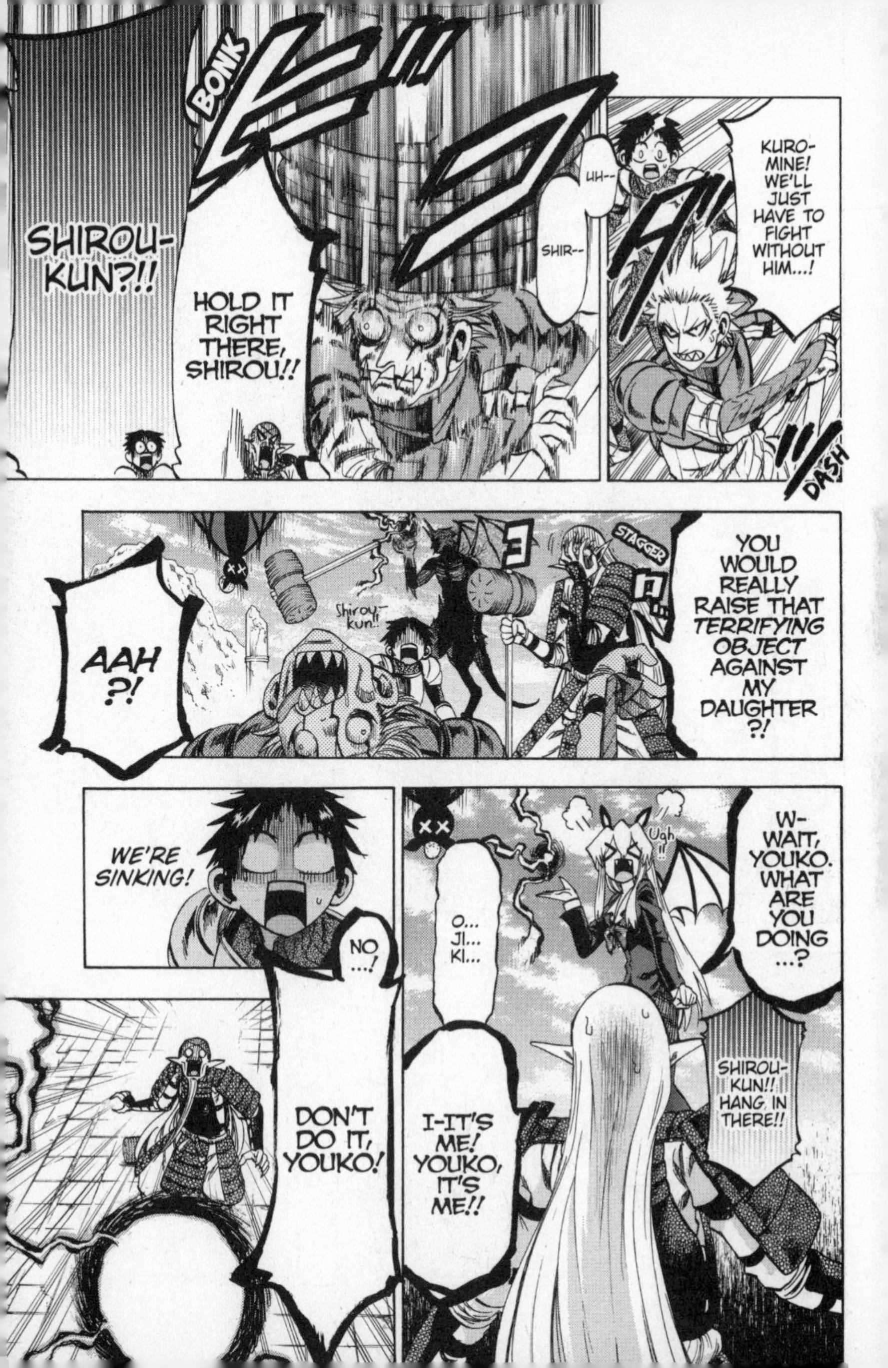
KURO-MINE! WE'LL JUST HAVE TO FIGHT WITHOUT HIM...!
UH--
SHIR--
DASH
BONK
SHIROU-KUN?!!
HOLD IT RIGHT THERE, SHIROU!!
STAGGER
YOU WOULD REALLY RAISE THAT TERRIFYING OBJECT AGAINST MY DAUGHTER?!
Shirou-kun!!
AAH?!
W-WAIT, YOUKO. WHAT ARE YOU DOING...?
Ugh!!
O... JI... KI...
NO...!
WE'RE SINKING!
SHIROU-KUN!! HANG IN THERE!!
I-IT'S ME! YOUKO, IT'S ME!!
DON'T DO IT, YOUKO!

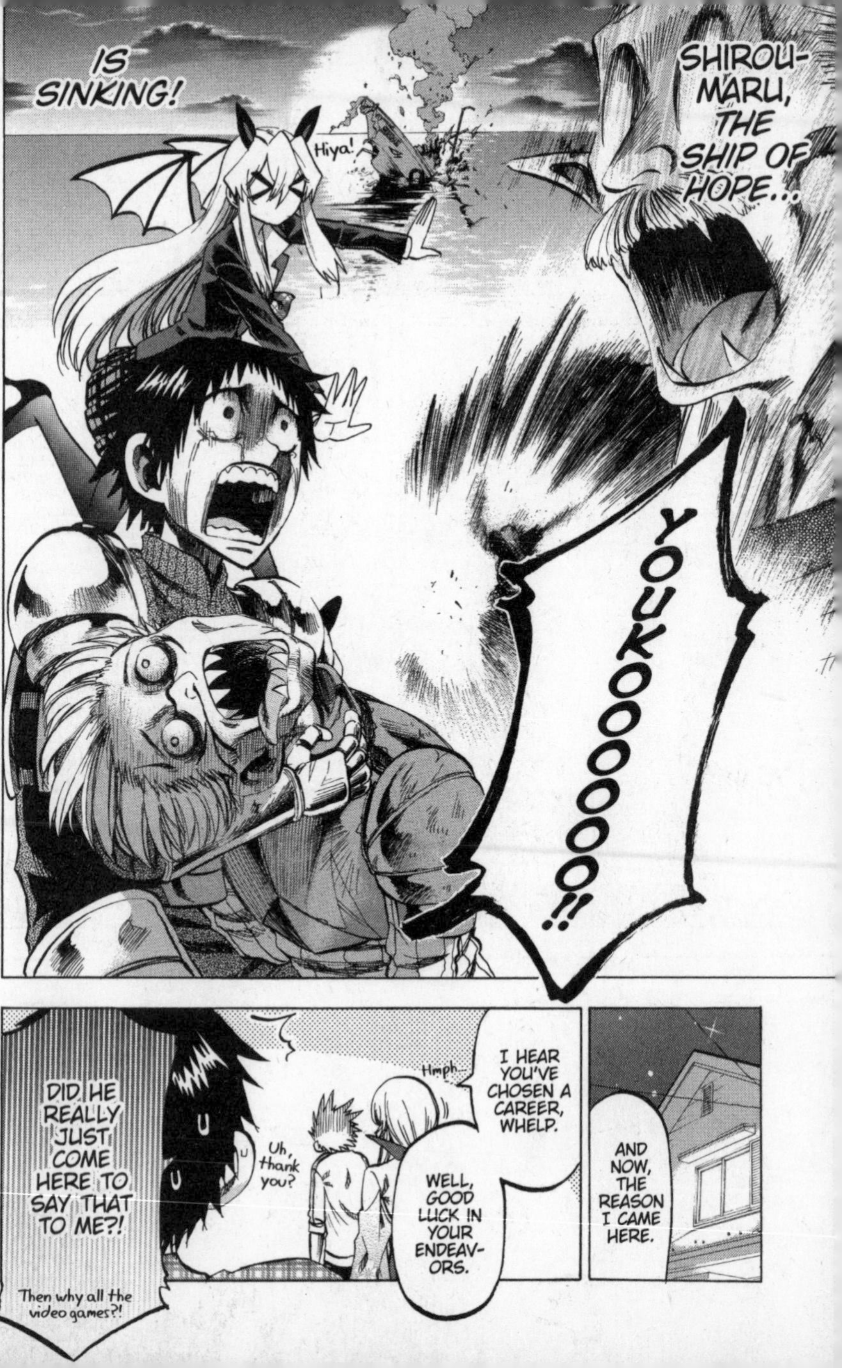
SHIROU-MARU, THE SHIP OF HOPE...
IS SINKING!
Hiya!
YOUKOOOOOOOO!!
AND NOW, THE REASON I CAME HERE.
I HEAR YOU'VE CHOSEN A CAREER, WHELP.
Hmph...
WELL, GOOD LUCK IN YOUR ENDEAVORS.
Uh, thank you?
DID HE REALLY JUST COME HERE TO SAY THAT TO ME?!
Then why all the video games?!

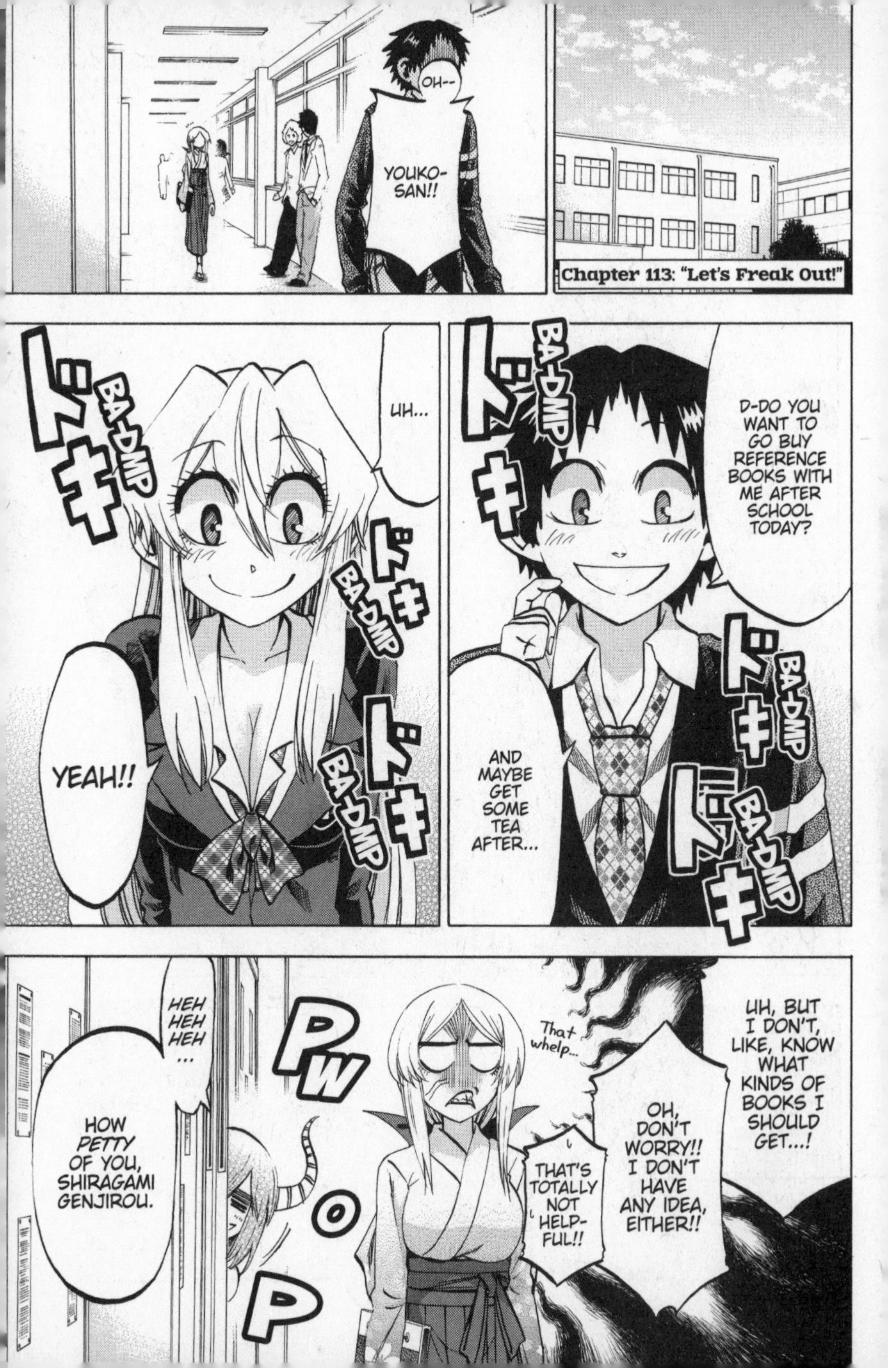
Chapter 113: "Let's Freak Out!"
OH--
YOUKO-SAN!!
ドキ
BA-DMP
D-DO YOU WANT TO GO BUY REFERENCE BOOKS WITH ME AFTER SCHOOL TODAY?
AND MAYBE GET SOME TEA AFTER...
ドキ
BA-DMP
ドキ
BA-DMP
ドキ
BA-DMP
UH...
ドキ
BA-DMP
ドキ
BA-DMP
YEAH!!
UH, BUT I DON'T, LIKE, KNOW WHAT KINDS OF BOOKS I SHOULD GET...!
OH, DON'T WORRY!! I DON'T HAVE ANY IDEA, EITHER!!
THAT'S TOTALLY NOT HELPFUL!!
That whelp...
PWOP
HEH HEH HEH...
HOW PETTY OF YOU, SHIRAGAMI GENJIROU.

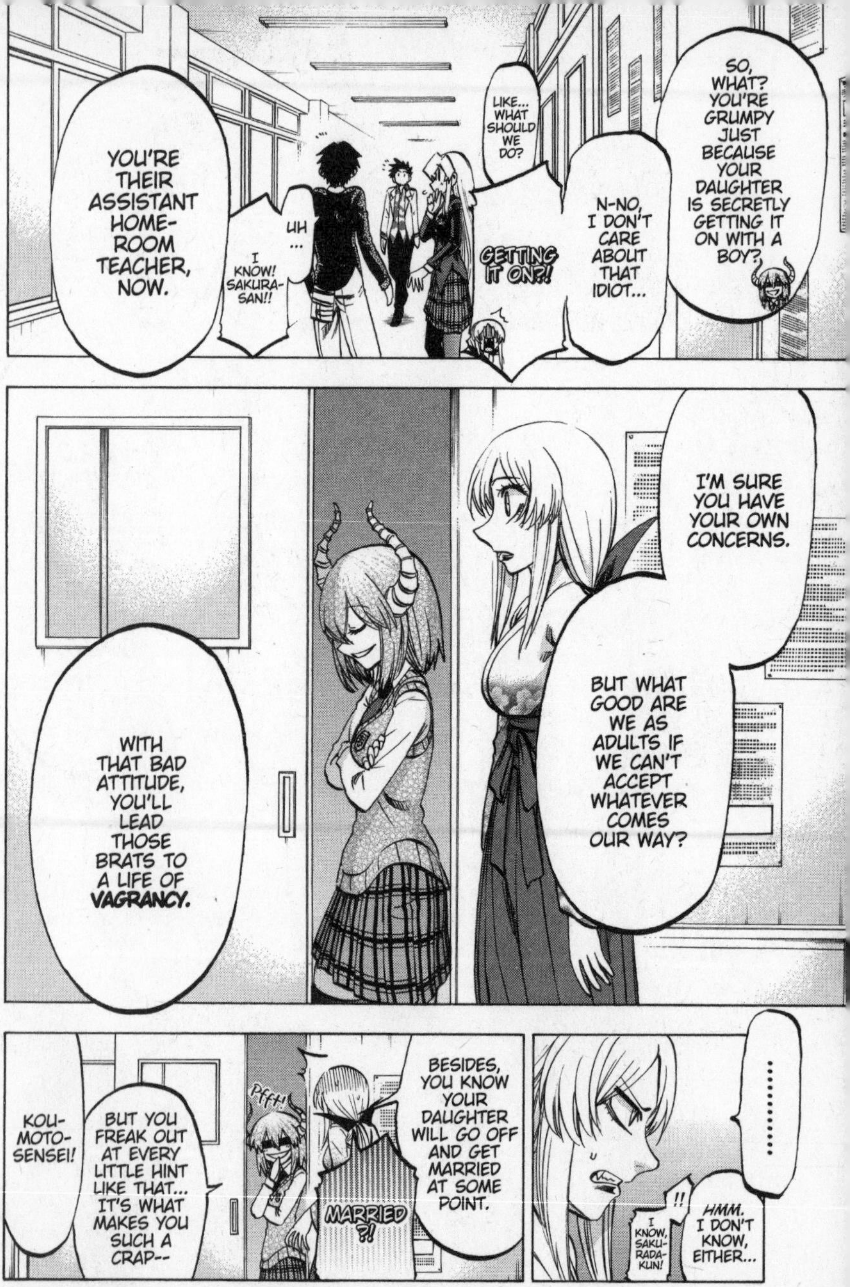
SO, WHAT? YOU'RE GRUMPY JUST BECAUSE YOUR DAUGHTER IS SECRETLY GETTING IT ON WITH A BOY?
N-NO, I DON'T CARE ABOUT THAT IDIOT...
GETTING IT ON?!
LIKE... WHAT SHOULD WE DO?
UH ...
I KNOW! SAKURA-SAN!!
YOU'RE THEIR ASSISTANT HOME-ROOM TEACHER, NOW.
I'M SURE YOU HAVE YOUR OWN CONCERNS.
BUT WHAT GOOD ARE WE AS ADULTS IF WE CAN'T ACCEPT WHATEVER COMES OUR WAY?
WITH THAT BAD ATTITUDE, YOU'LL LEAD THOSE BRATS TO A LIFE OF **VAGRANCY.**
......
HMM. I DON'T KNOW, EITHER...
!!
I KNOW, SAKURADA-KUN!
BESIDES, YOU KNOW YOUR DAUGHTER WILL GO OFF AND GET MARRIED AT SOME POINT.
MARRIED ?!
Pfft!
BUT YOU FREAK OUT AT EVERY LITTLE HINT LIKE THAT... IT'S WHAT MAKES YOU SUCH A CRAP--
KOU-MOTO-SENSEI!

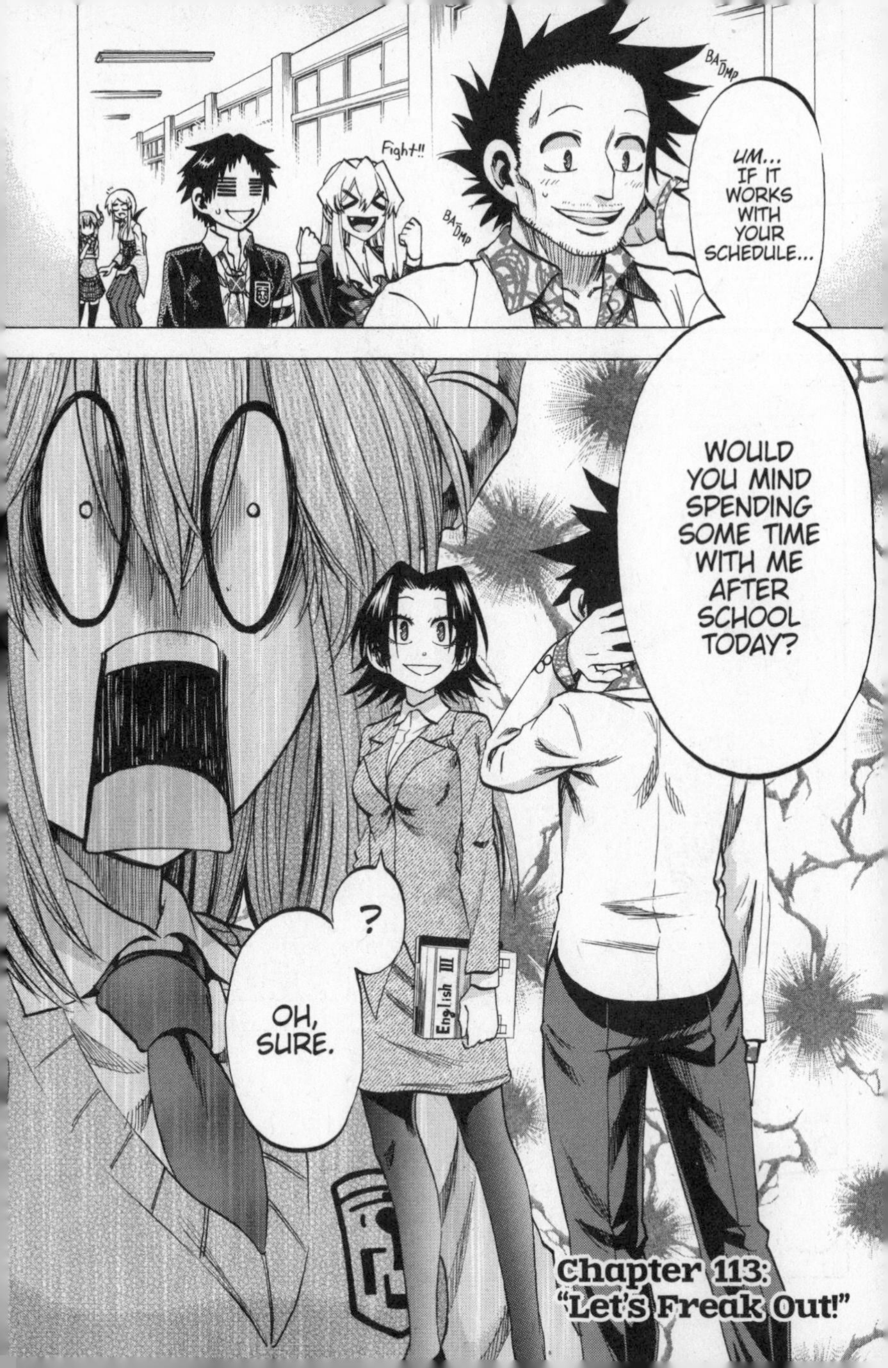
BA-DMP
UM... IF IT WORKS WITH YOUR SCHEDULE...
BA-DMP
Fight!!
WOULD YOU MIND SPENDING SOME TIME WITH ME AFTER SCHOOL TODAY?
?
OH, SURE.
English III

Chapter 113: "Let's Freak Out!"

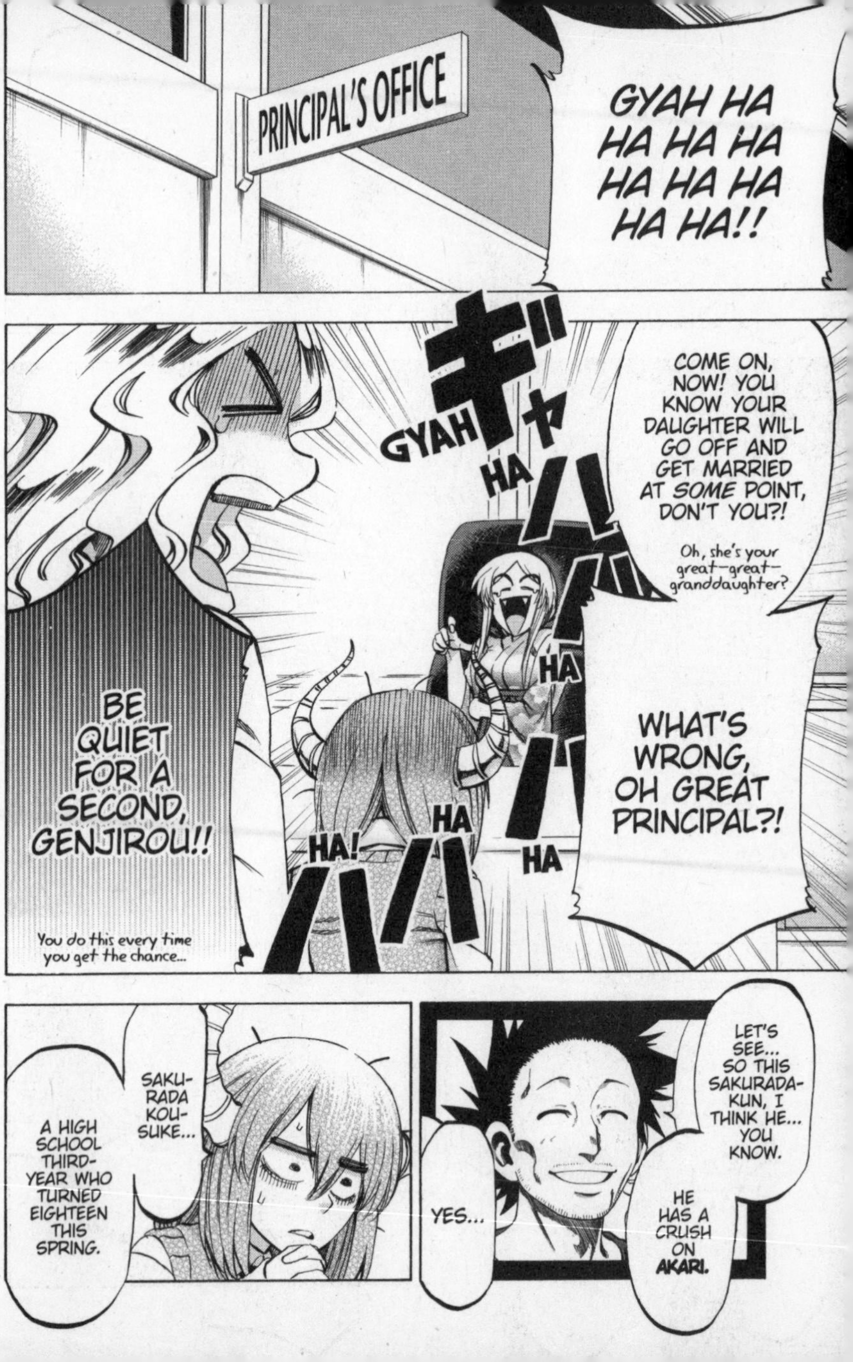
PRINCIPAL'S OFFICE
GYAH HA HA HA HA HA HA HA HA HA HA HA HA HA!!
COME ON, NOW! YOU KNOW YOUR DAUGHTER WILL GO OFF AND GET MARRIED AT *SOME* POINT, DON'T YOU?!
Oh, she's your great-great-granddaughter?
GYAH HA HA HA HA HA HA!
WHAT'S WRONG, OH GREAT PRINCIPAL?!
BE QUIET FOR A SECOND, GENJIROU!!
You do this every time you get the chance...
LET'S SEE... SO THIS SAKURADA-KUN, I THINK HE... YOU KNOW.
HE HAS A CRUSH ON **AKARI.**
YES...
SAKURADA KOUSUKE...
A HIGH SCHOOL THIRD-YEAR WHO TURNED EIGHTEEN THIS SPRING.

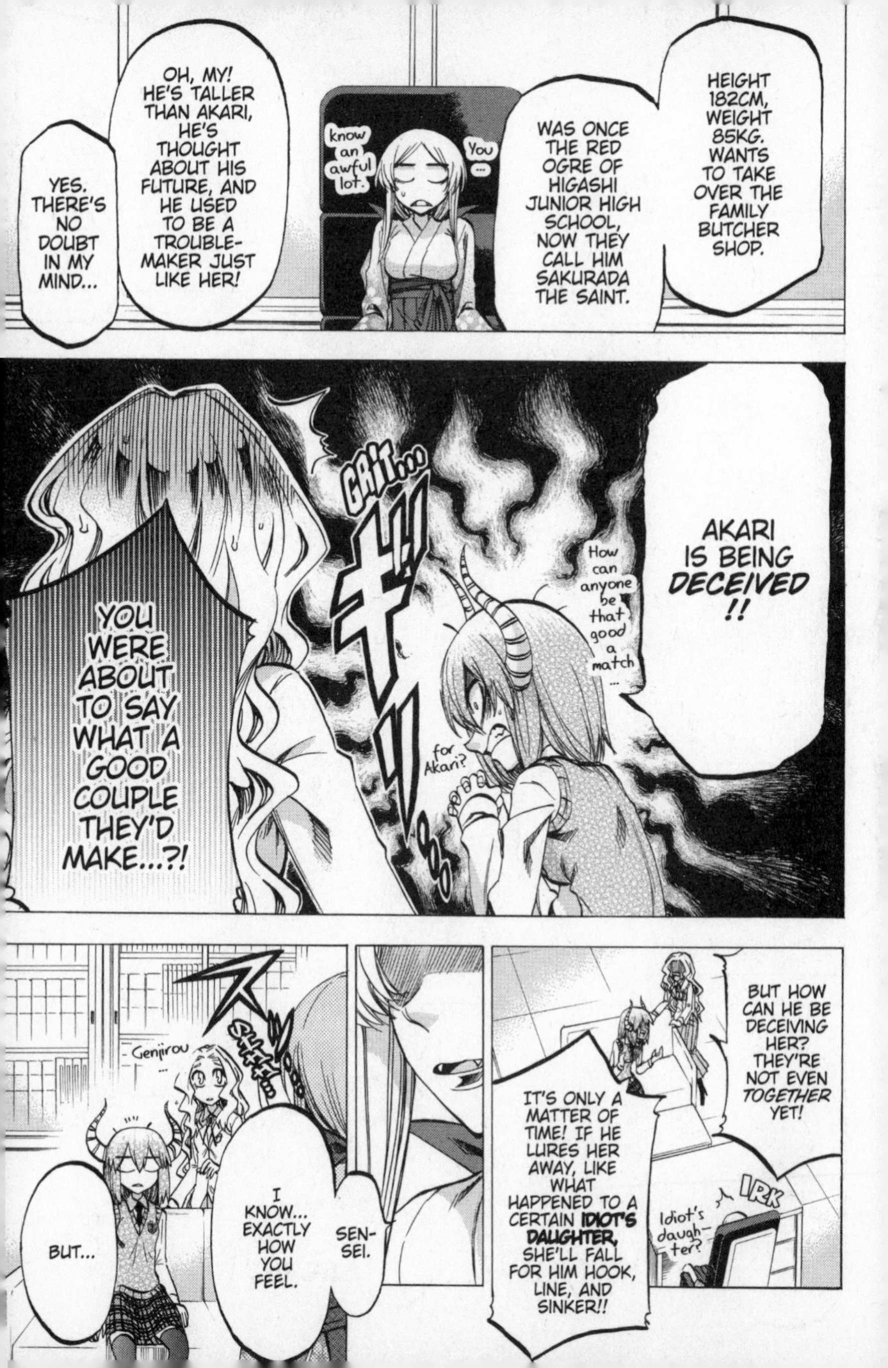
HEIGHT 182CM, WEIGHT 85KG. WANTS TO TAKE OVER THE FAMILY BUTCHER SHOP.
WAS ONCE THE RED OGRE OF HIGASHI JUNIOR HIGH SCHOOL, NOW THEY CALL HIM SAKURADA THE SAINT.
You ...
know an awful lot.
OH, MY! HE'S TALLER THAN AKARI, HE'S THOUGHT ABOUT HIS FUTURE, AND HE USED TO BE A TROUBLE-MAKER JUST LIKE HER!
YES. THERE'S NO DOUBT IN MY MIND...
AKARI IS BEING DECEIVED !!
How can anyone be that good a match ...
for Akari?
GRIT...
YOU WERE ABOUT TO SAY WHAT A GOOD COUPLE THEY'D MAKE...?!
BUT HOW CAN HE BE DECEIVING HER? THEY'RE NOT EVEN TOGETHER YET!
IT'S ONLY A MATTER OF TIME! IF HE LURES HER AWAY, LIKE WHAT HAPPENED TO A CERTAIN IDIOT'S DAUGHTER, SHE'LL FALL FOR HIM HOOK, LINE, AND SINKER!!
IRK
Idiot's daugh-ter?
SEN-SEI.
I KNOW... EXACTLY HOW YOU FEEL.
Genjirou ...
BUT...

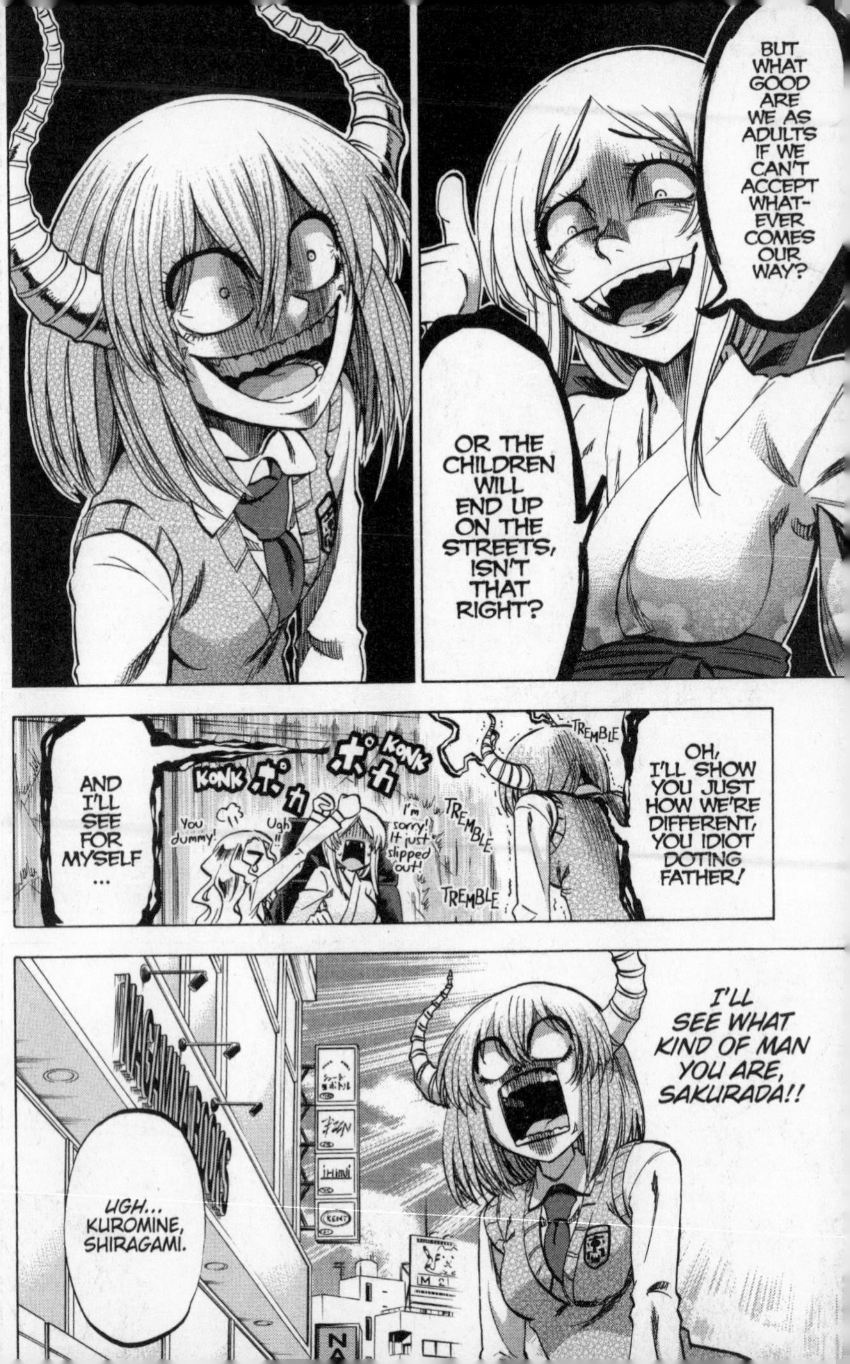
BUT WHAT GOOD ARE WE AS ADULTS IF WE CAN'T ACCEPT WHAT-EVER COMES OUR WAY?
OR THE CHILDREN WILL END UP ON THE STREETS, ISN'T THAT RIGHT?
OH, I'LL SHOW YOU JUST HOW WE'RE DIFFERENT, YOU IDIOT DOTING FATHER!
TREMBLE
TREMBLE
TREMBLE
KONK
ポカ
KONK
ポカ
I'm sorry! It just slipped out!
Ugh!!
You dummy!
AND I'LL SEE FOR MYSELF...
I'LL SEE WHAT KIND OF MAN YOU ARE, SAKURADA!!
UGH... KUROMINE, SHIRAGAMI.

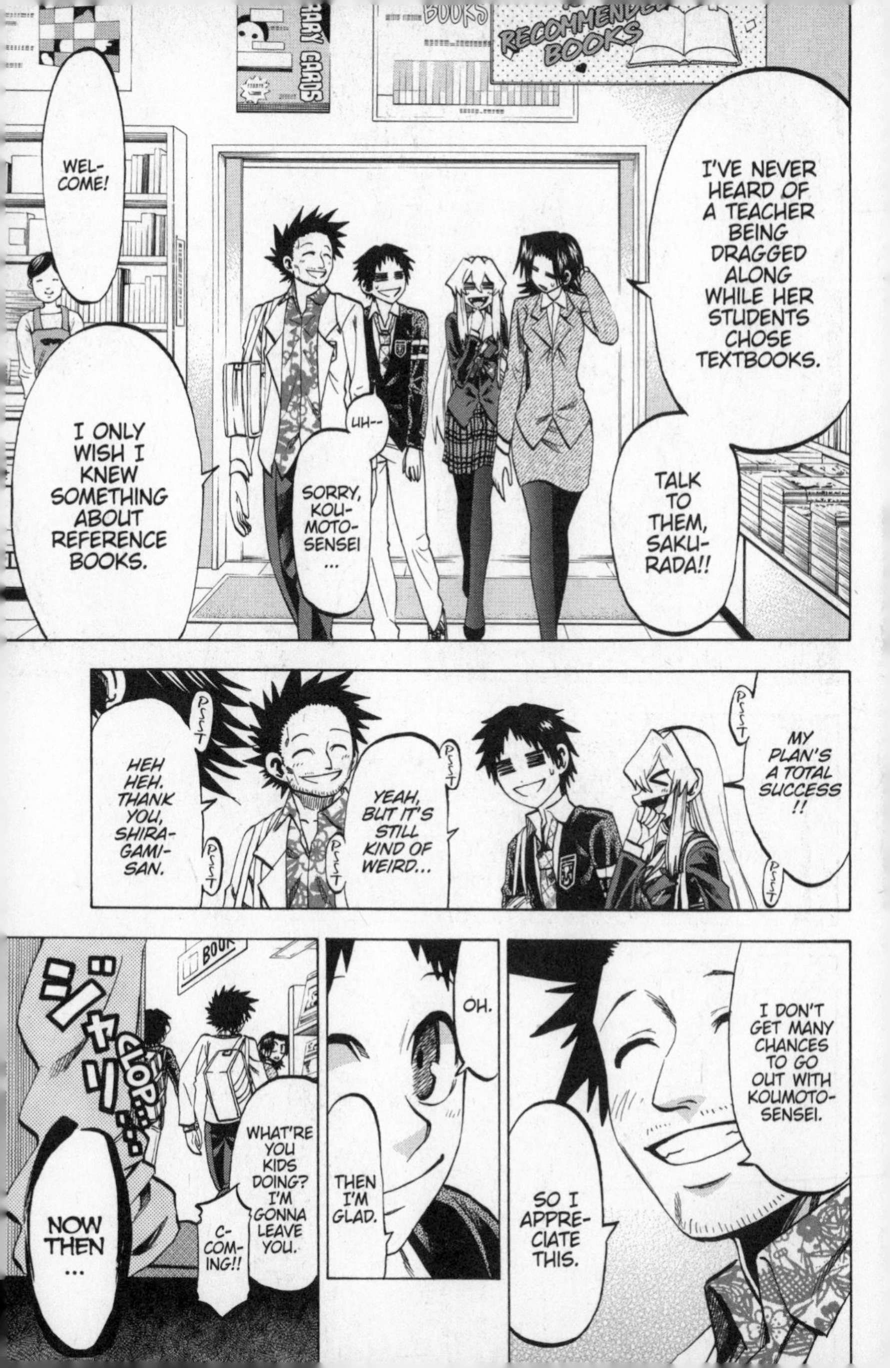
BOOKS
I'VE NEVER HEARD OF A TEACHER BEING DRAGGED ALONG WHILE HER STUDENTS CHOSE TEXTBOOKS.
TALK TO THEM, SAKURADA!!
SORRY, KOUMOTO-SENSEI...
UH--
I ONLY WISH I KNEW SOMETHING ABOUT REFERENCE BOOKS.
WELCOME!
PSST
MY PLAN'S A TOTAL SUCCESS!!
PSST
PSST
YEAH, BUT IT'S STILL KIND OF WEIRD...
PSST
PSST
HEH HEH. THANK YOU, SHIRAGAMI-SAN.
PSST
I DON'T GET MANY CHANCES TO GO OUT WITH KOUMOTO-SENSEI.
SO I APPRECIATE THIS.
OH.
THEN I'M GLAD.
WHAT'RE YOU KIDS DOING? I'M GONNA LEAVE YOU.
C-COMING!!
ジャリ…
CLOP...
NOW THEN...

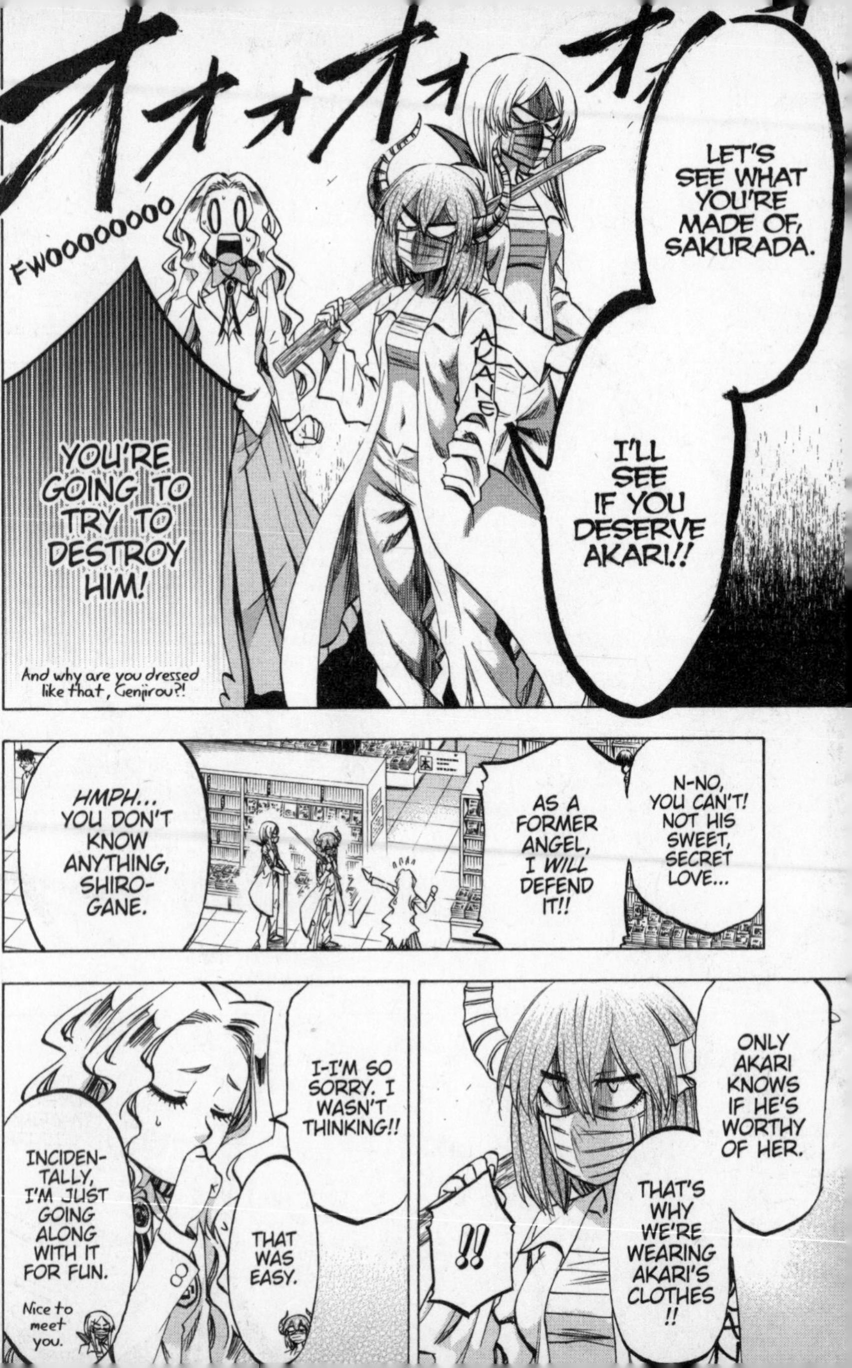

LET'S SEE WHAT YOU'RE MADE OF, SAKURADA.
I'LL SEE IF YOU DESERVE AKARI!!
オォォォォォ
AKANE
FWOOOOOOOO
YOU'RE GOING TO TRY TO DESTROY HIM!
And why are you dressed like that, Genjirou?!
N-NO, YOU CAN'T! NOT HIS SWEET, SECRET LOVE...
AS A FORMER ANGEL, I *WILL* DEFEND IT!!
HMPH... YOU DON'T KNOW ANYTHING, SHIRO-GANE.
ONLY AKARI KNOWS IF HE'S WORTHY OF HER.
THAT'S WHY WE'RE WEARING AKARI'S CLOTHES!!
!!
I-I'M SO SORRY. I WASN'T THINKING!!
INCIDEN-TALLY, I'M JUST GOING ALONG WITH IT FOR FUN.
THAT WAS EASY.
Nice to meet you.

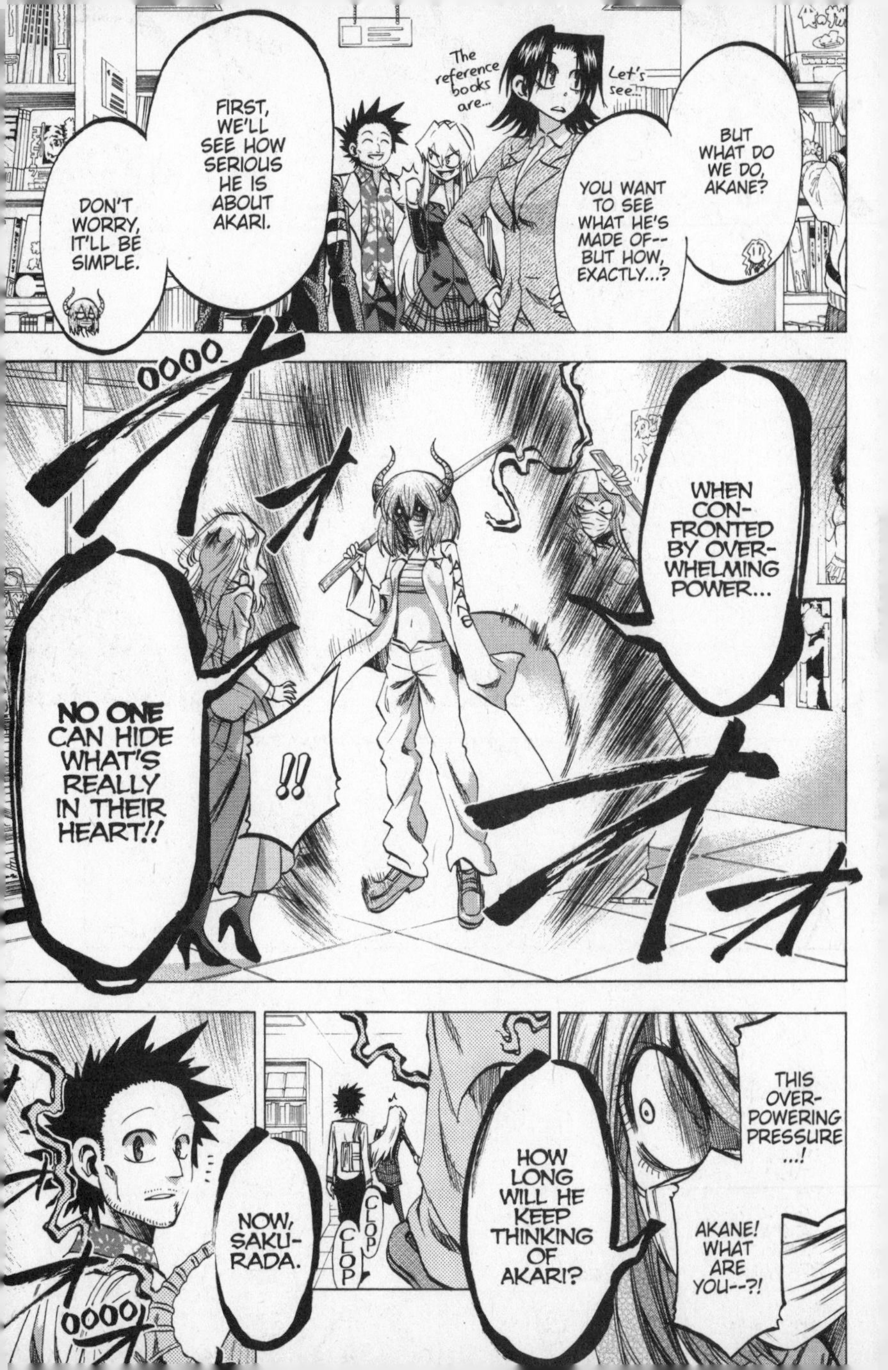
Let's see...
The reference books are...
BUT WHAT DO WE DO, AKANE?
YOU WANT TO SEE WHAT HE'S MADE OF-- BUT HOW, EXACTLY...?
FIRST, WE'LL SEE HOW SERIOUS HE IS ABOUT AKARI.
DON'T WORRY, IT'LL BE SIMPLE.
OOOO
WHEN CON-FRONTED BY OVER-WHELMING POWER...
!!
NO ONE CAN HIDE WHAT'S REALLY IN THEIR HEART!!
THIS OVER-POWERING PRESSURE ...!
AKANE! WHAT ARE YOU--?!
HOW LONG WILL HE KEEP THINKING OF AKARI?
CLOP CLOP
NOW, SAKU-RADA.
OOOO

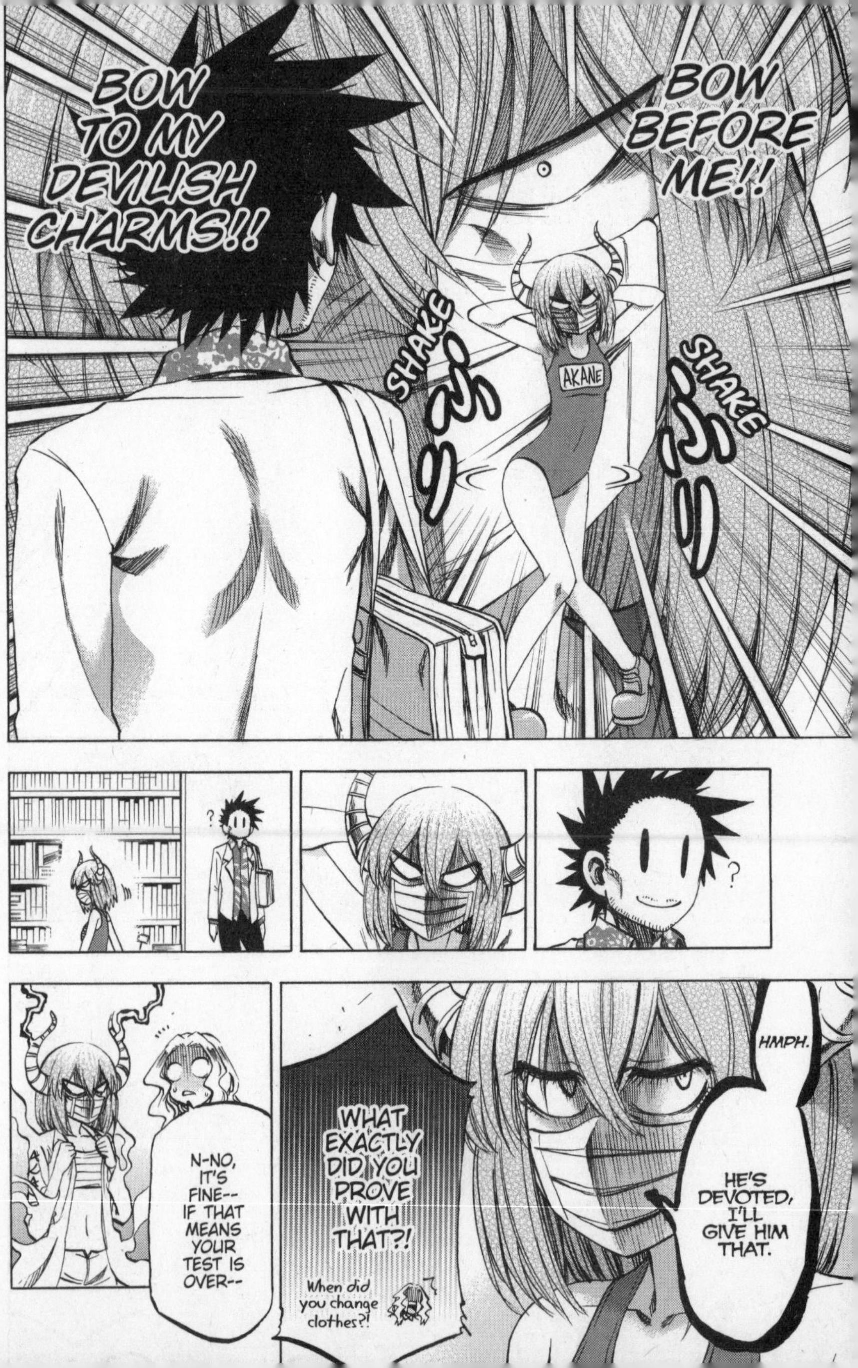

BOW BEFORE ME!!
BOW TO MY DEVILISH CHARMS!!
SHAKE
AKANE
SHAKE
?
?
HMPH.
HE'S DEVOTED, I'LL GIVE HIM THAT.
WHAT EXACTLY DID YOU PROVE WITH THAT?!
When did you change clothes?!
N-NO, IT'S FINE-- IF THAT MEANS YOUR TEST IS OVER--

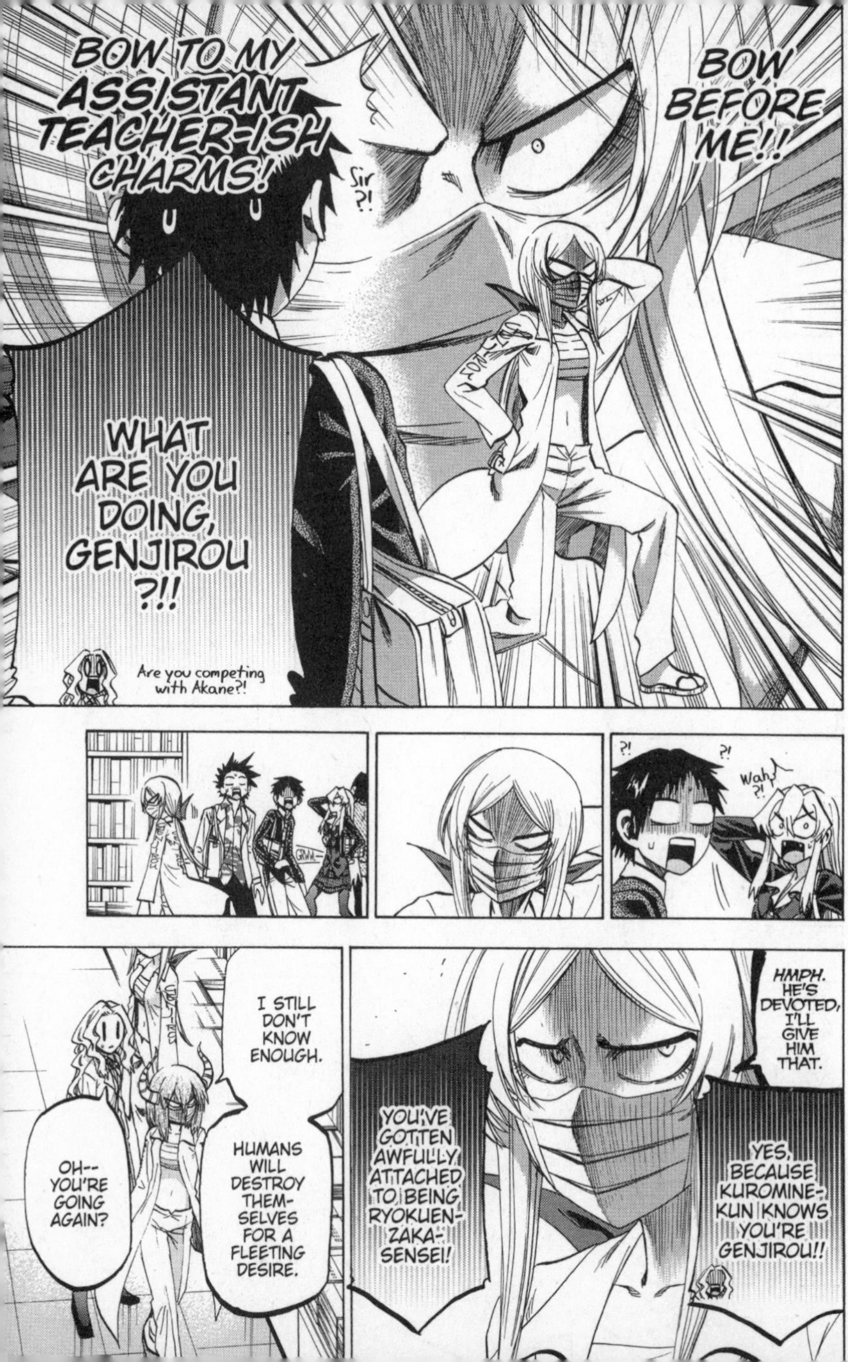
BOW BEFORE ME!!
BOW TO MY ASSISTANT TEACHER-ISH CHARMS!
Sir ?!
WHAT ARE YOU DOING, GENJIROU ?!!
Are you competing with Akane?!
?!
?!
Wah ?!
HMPH. HE'S DEVOTED, I'LL GIVE HIM THAT.
YES. BECAUSE KUROMINE-KUN KNOWS YOU'RE GENJIROU!!
YOU'VE GOTTEN AWFULLY ATTACHED TO BEING RYOKUEN-ZAKA-SENSEI!
I STILL DON'T KNOW ENOUGH.
HUMANS WILL DESTROY THEM-SELVES FOR A FLEETING DESIRE.
OH-- YOU'RE GOING AGAIN?

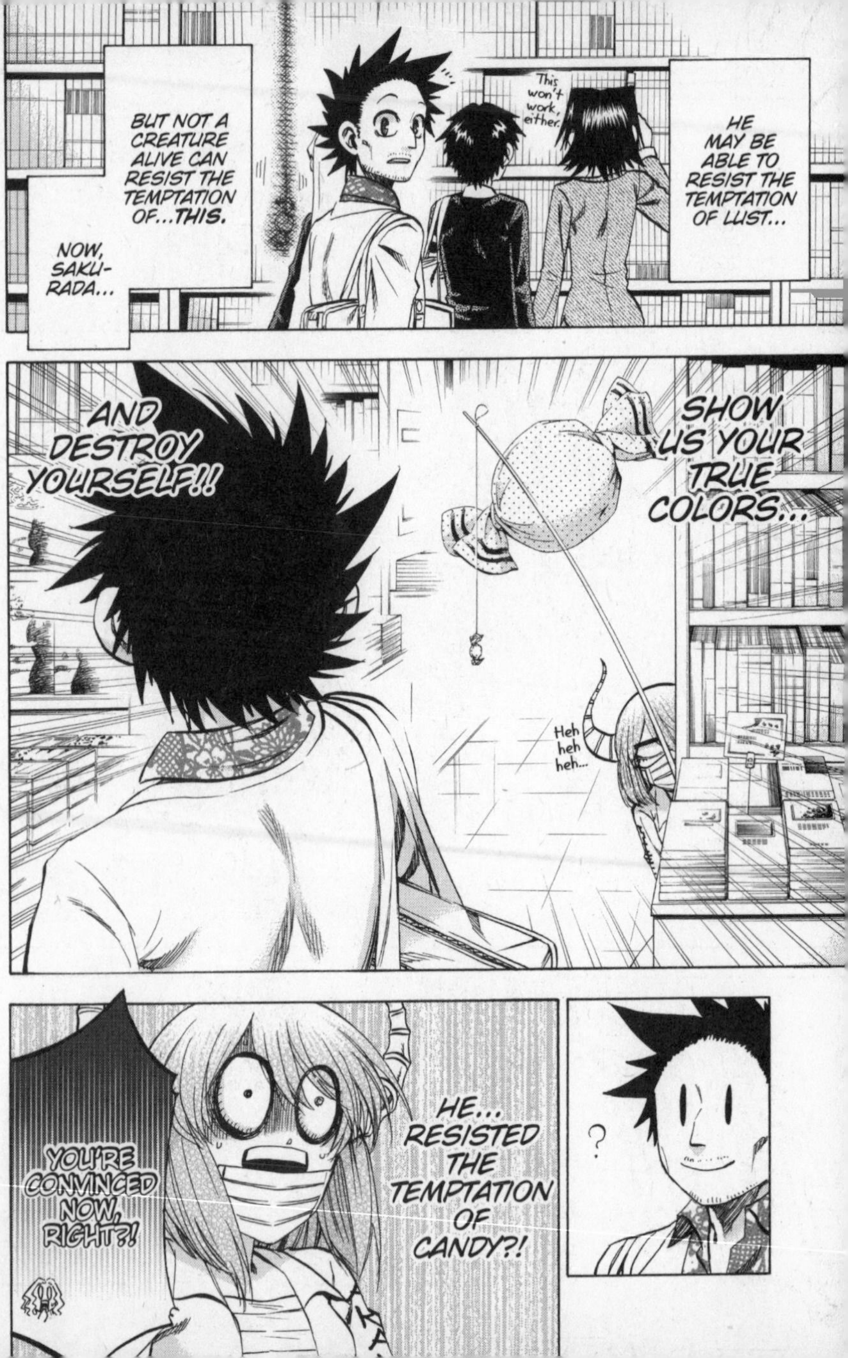
HE MAY BE ABLE TO RESIST THE TEMPTATION OF LUST...
This won't work, either.
BUT NOT A CREATURE ALIVE CAN RESIST THE TEMPTATION OF...THIS.
NOW, SAKURADA...
SHOW US YOUR TRUE COLORS...
Heh heh heh...
AND DESTROY YOURSELF!!
?
HE... RESISTED THE TEMPTATION OF CANDY?!
YOU'RE CONVINCED NOW, RIGHT?!

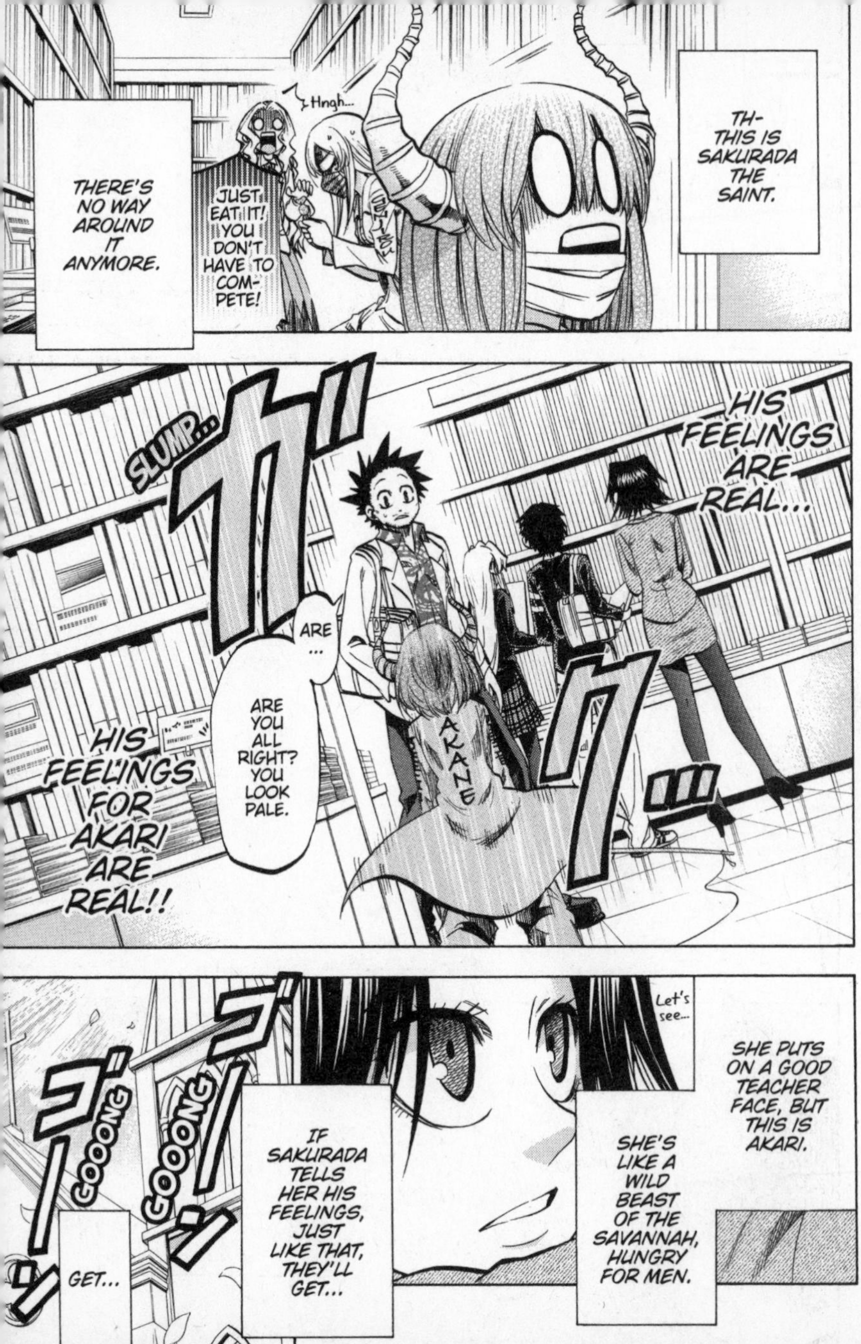

TH-
THIS IS SAKURADA THE SAINT.
Hngh...
JUST EAT IT! YOU DON'T HAVE TO COMPETE!
THERE'S NO WAY AROUND IT ANYMORE.
HIS FEELINGS ARE REAL...
SLUMP...
ARE...
ARE YOU ALL RIGHT? YOU LOOK PALE.
AKANE
HIS FEELINGS FOR AKARI ARE REAL!!
Let's see...
SHE PUTS ON A GOOD TEACHER FACE, BUT THIS IS AKARI.
SHE'S LIKE A WILD BEAST OF THE SAVANNAH, HUNGRY FOR MEN.
IF SAKURADA TELLS HER HIS FEELINGS, JUST LIKE THAT, THEY'LL GET...
GOOONG
GOOONG
GET...

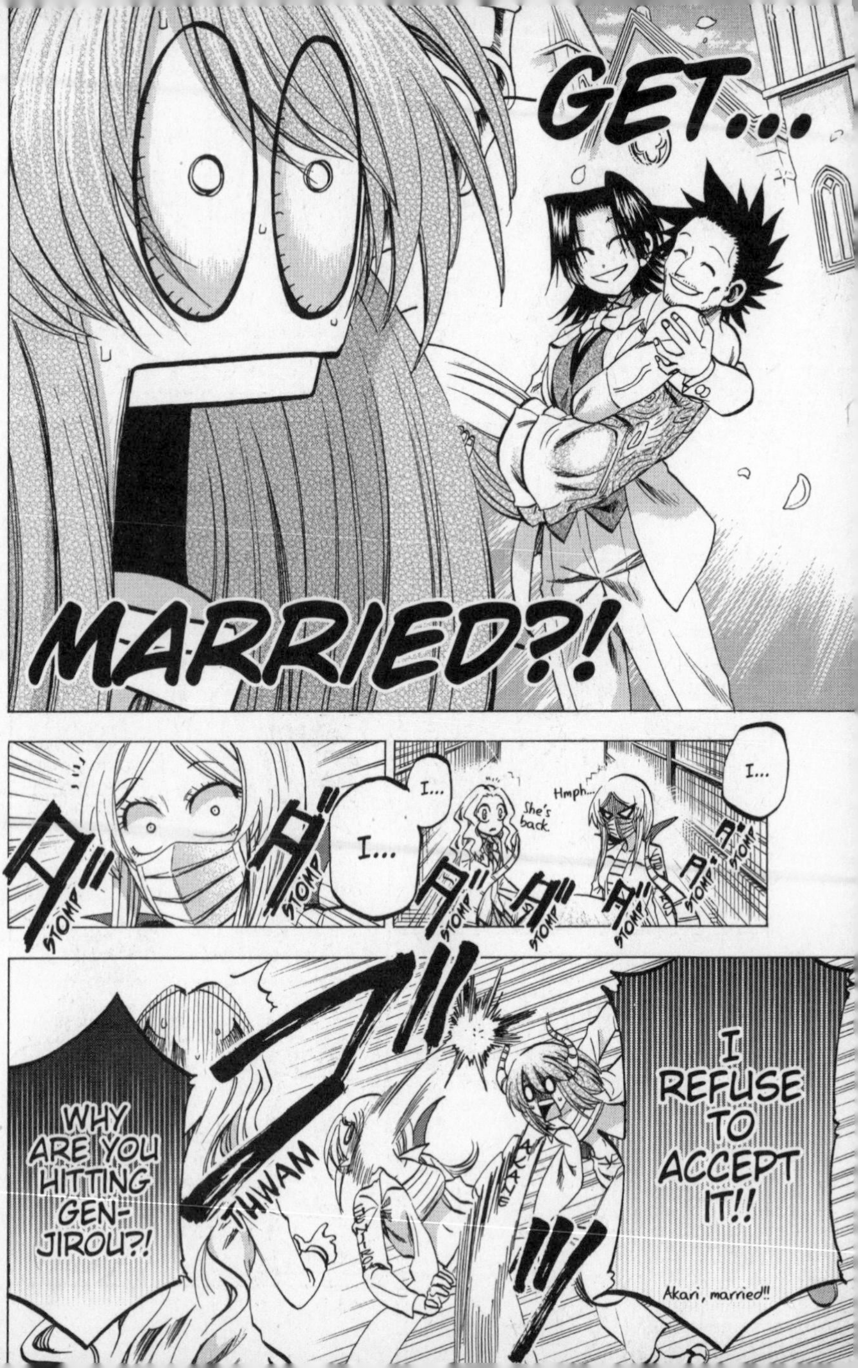
GET...
MARRIED?!
I...
Hmph...
She's back.
I...
STOMP STOMP STOMP STOMP STOMP STOMP
I...
STOMP STOMP
I REFUSE TO ACCEPT IT!!
Akari, married!!
THWAM
WHY ARE YOU HITTING GEN-JIROU?!

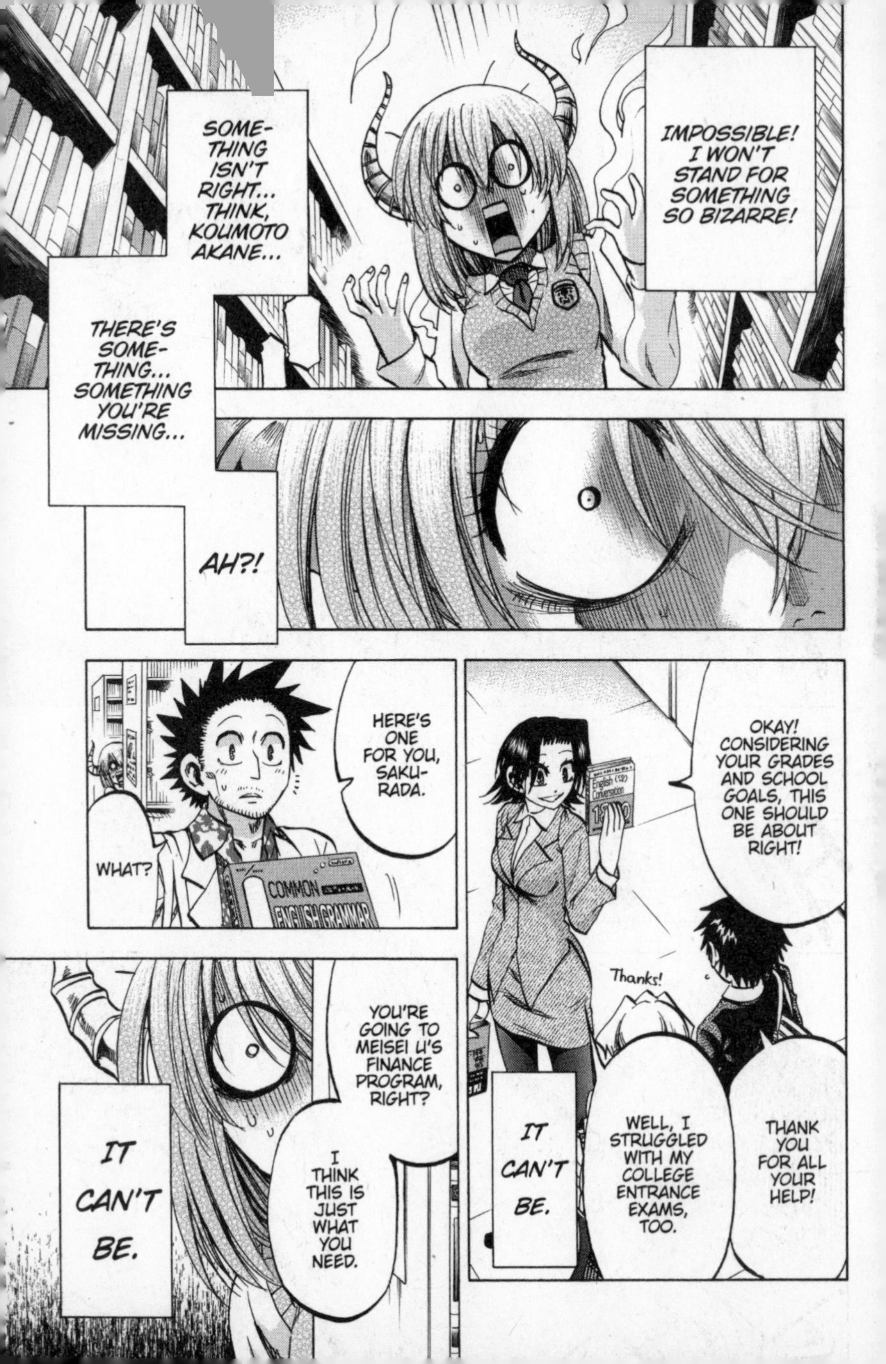
IMPOSSIBLE! I WON'T STAND FOR SOMETHING SO BIZARRE!
SOME-THING ISN'T RIGHT... THINK, KOUMOTO AKANE...
THERE'S SOME-THING... SOMETHING YOU'RE MISSING...
AH?!
OKAY! CONSIDERING YOUR GRADES AND SCHOOL GOALS, THIS ONE SHOULD BE ABOUT RIGHT!
English Conversation
Thanks!
THANK YOU FOR ALL YOUR HELP!
WELL, I STRUGGLED WITH MY COLLEGE ENTRANCE EXAMS, TOO.
IT CAN'T BE.
HERE'S ONE FOR YOU, SAKU-RADA.
WHAT?
COMMON ENGLISH GRAMMAR
YOU'RE GOING TO MEISEI U'S FINANCE PROGRAM, RIGHT?
I THINK THIS IS JUST WHAT YOU NEED.
IT CAN'T BE.

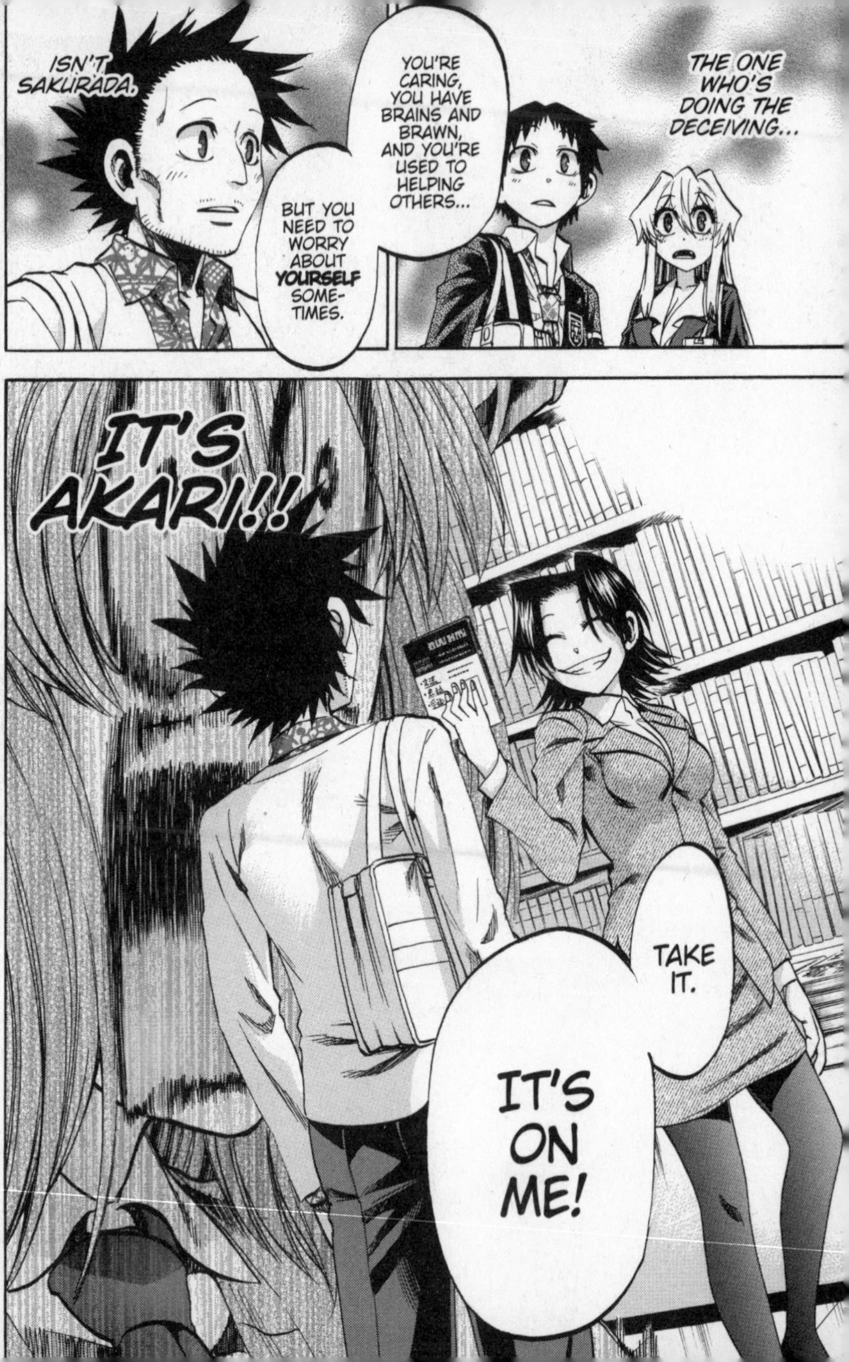
THE ONE WHO'S DOING THE DECEIVING...
YOU'RE CARING, YOU HAVE BRAINS AND BRAWN, AND YOU'RE USED TO HELPING OTHERS...
BUT YOU NEED TO WORRY ABOUT YOURSELF SOME-TIMES.
ISN'T SAKURADA.
IT'S AKARI!!
TAKE IT.
IT'S ON ME!

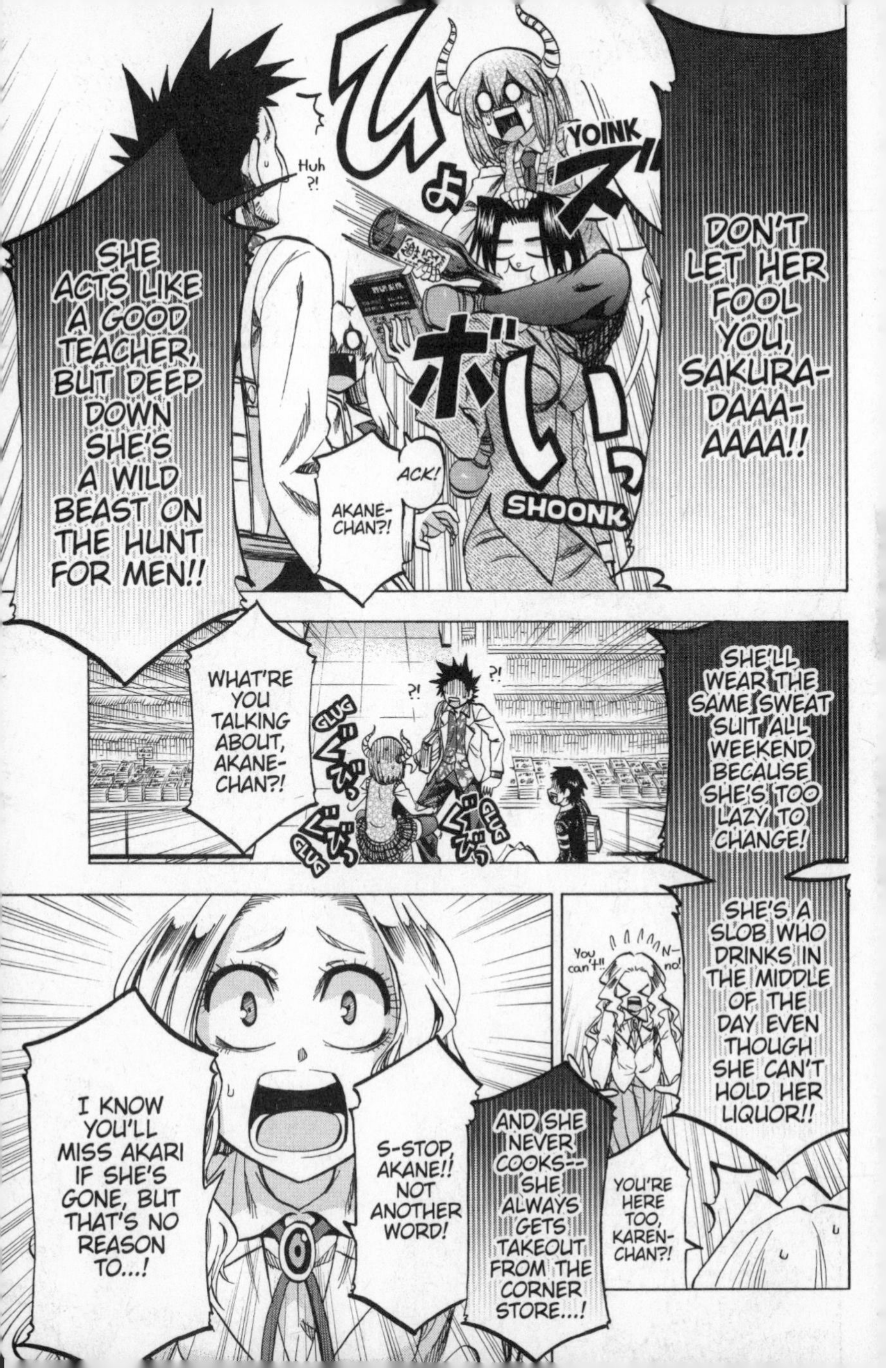
DON'T LET HER FOOL YOU, SAKURA-DAAAAAAA!!
YOINK
Huh ?!
ACK!
AKANE-CHAN?!
SHOONK
SHE ACTS LIKE A GOOD TEACHER, BUT DEEP DOWN SHE'S A WILD BEAST ON THE HUNT FOR MEN!!
SHE'LL WEAR THE SAME SWEAT SUIT ALL WEEKEND BECAUSE SHE'S TOO LAZY TO CHANGE!
?!
?!
GLUG
GLUG
GLUG
GLUG
WHAT'RE YOU TALKING ABOUT, AKANE-CHAN?!
SHE'S A SLOB WHO DRINKS IN THE MIDDLE OF THE DAY EVEN THOUGH SHE CAN'T HOLD HER LIQUOR!!
N-no!
You can't!!
YOU'RE HERE TOO, KAREN-CHAN?!
AND SHE NEVER COOKS--SHE ALWAYS GETS TAKEOUT FROM THE CORNER STORE...!
S-STOP, AKANE!! NOT ANOTHER WORD!
I KNOW YOU'LL MISS AKARI IF SHE'S GONE, BUT THAT'S NO REASON TO...!

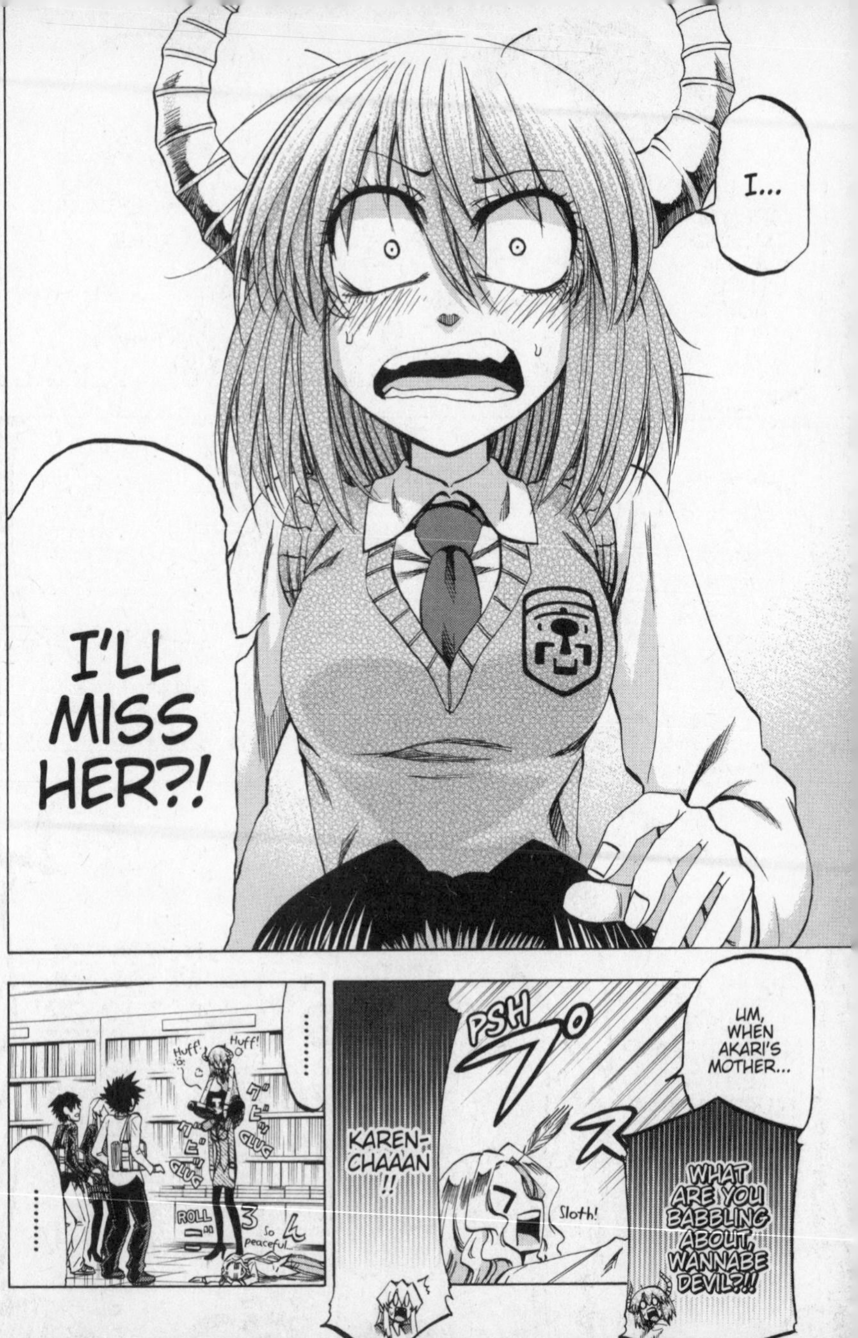
I...
I'LL MISS HER?!
UM, WHEN AKARI'S MOTHER...
PSH
WHAT ARE YOU BABBLING ABOUT, WANNABE DEVIL?!!
KAREN-CHAAAN!!
Sloth!
......
Huff! Huff!
GLUG
GLUG
ROLL
So peaceful...
......

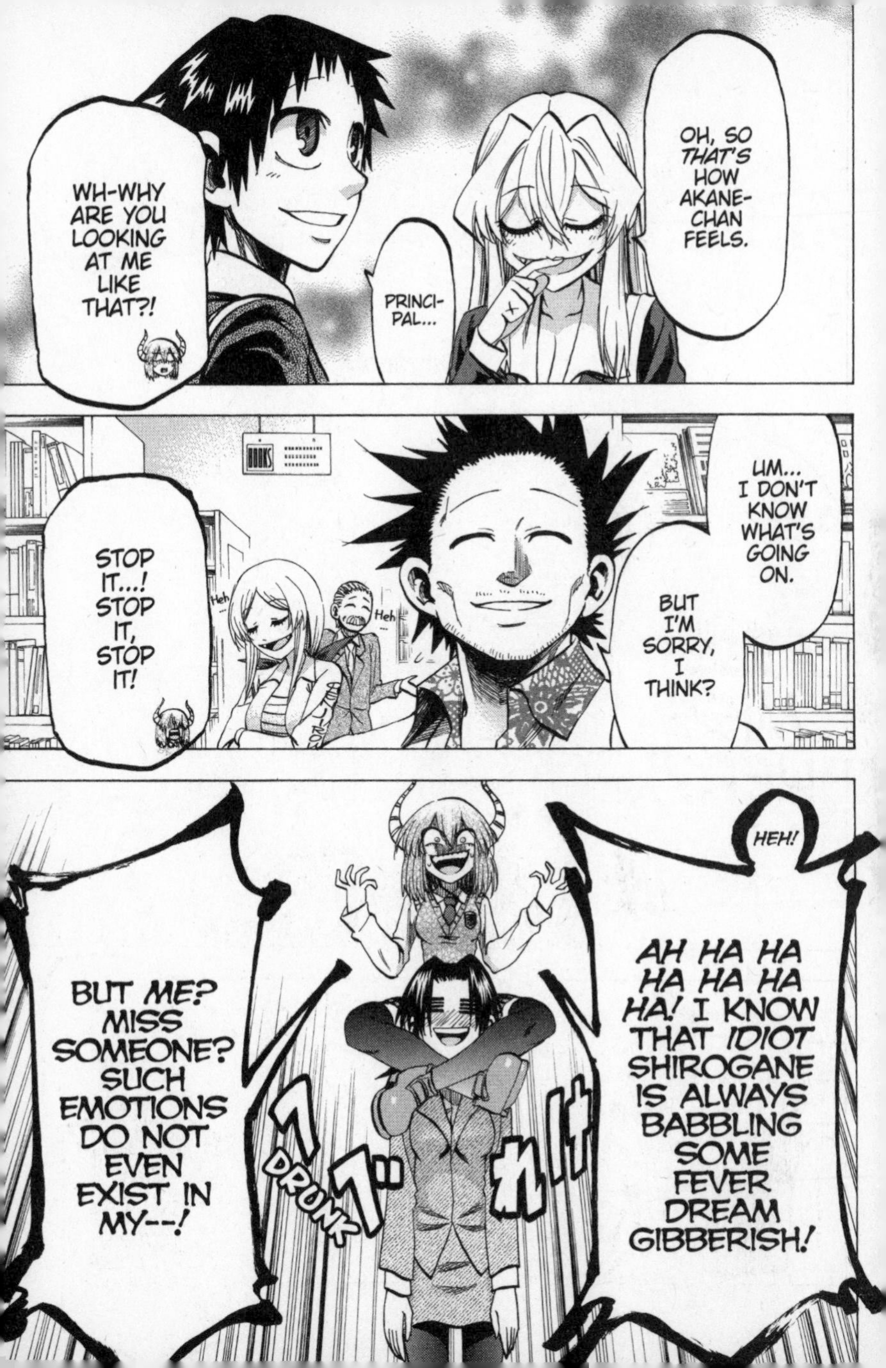
OH, SO THAT'S HOW AKANE-CHAN FEELS.
PRINCIPAL...
WH-WHY ARE YOU LOOKING AT ME LIKE THAT?!
UM... I DON'T KNOW WHAT'S GOING ON.
BUT I'M SORRY, I THINK?
Heh
Heh
STOP IT...! STOP IT, STOP IT!
HEH!
AH HA HA HA HA HA HA! I KNOW THAT IDIOT SHIROGANE IS ALWAYS BABBLING SOME FEVER DREAM GIBBERISH!
DRUNK
BUT ME? MISS SOMEONE? SUCH EMOTIONS DO NOT EVEN EXIST IN MY--!

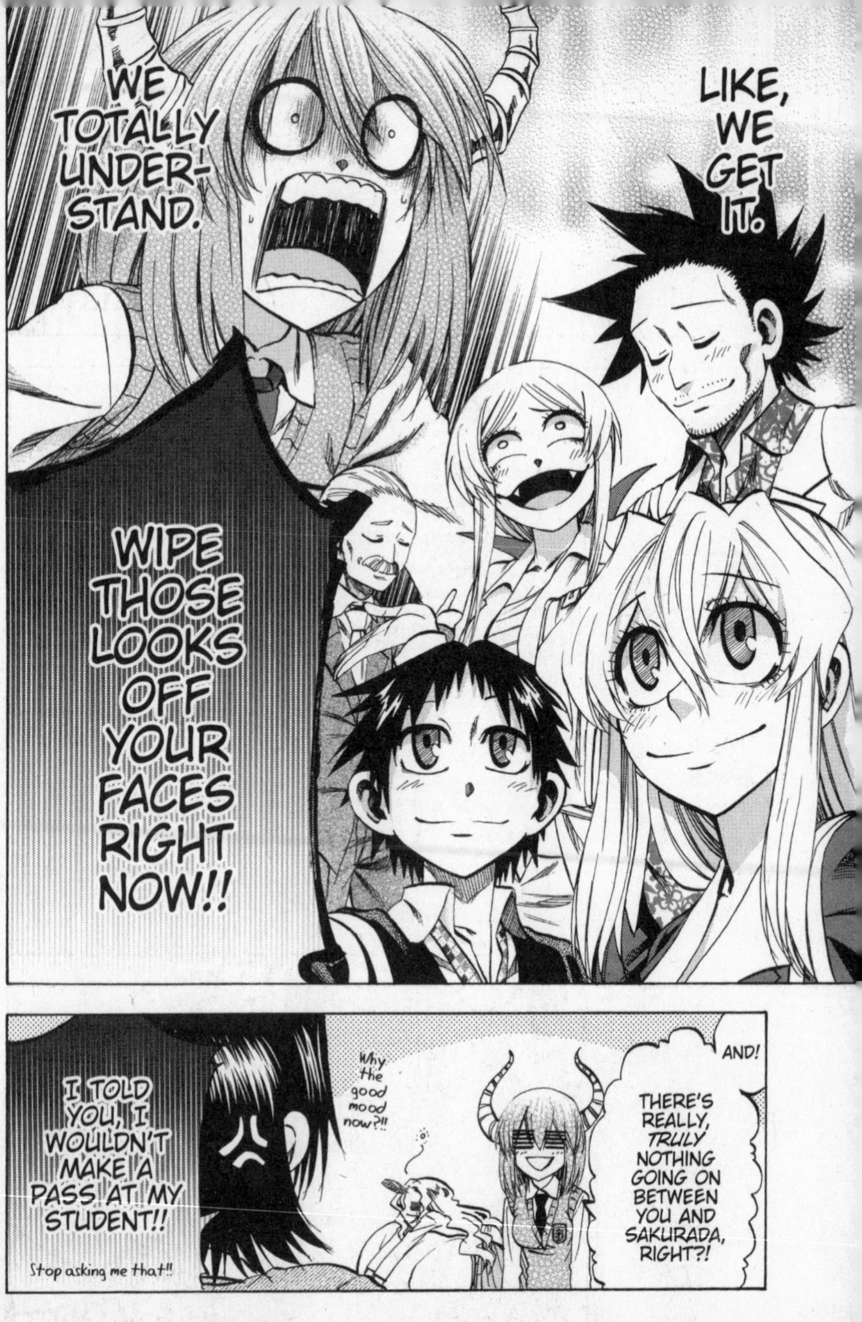
LIKE, WE GET IT.
WE TOTALLY UNDER-STAND.
WIPE THOSE LOOKS OFF YOUR FACES RIGHT NOW!!
AND!
THERE'S REALLY, *TRULY* NOTHING GOING ON BETWEEN YOU AND SAKURADA, RIGHT?!
Why the good mood now?!!
I TOLD YOU, I WOULDN'T MAKE A PASS AT MY STUDENT!!
Stop asking me that!!

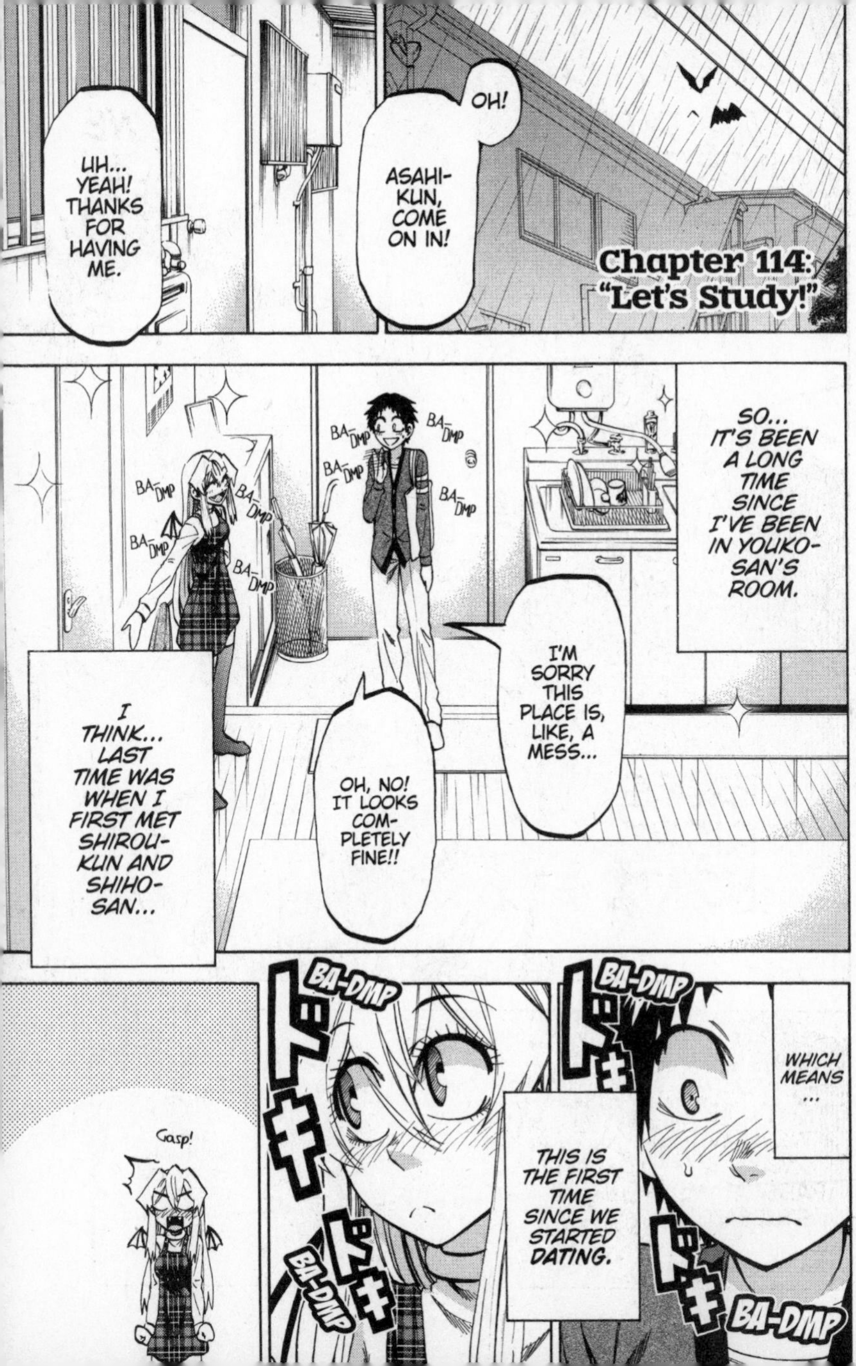
Chapter 114: "Let's Study!"
OH!
ASAHI-KUN, COME ON IN!
UH... YEAH! THANKS FOR HAVING ME.
SO... IT'S BEEN A LONG TIME SINCE I'VE BEEN IN YOUKO-SAN'S ROOM.
BA-DMP
BA-DMP
BA-DMP
BA-DMP
BA-DMP
BA-DMP
BA-DMP
I'M SORRY THIS PLACE IS, LIKE, A MESS...
OH, NO! IT LOOKS COMPLETELY FINE!!
I THINK... LAST TIME WAS WHEN I FIRST MET SHIROU-KUN AND SHIHO-SAN...
WHICH MEANS...
BA-DMP
BA-DMP
THIS IS THE FIRST TIME SINCE WE STARTED DATING.
BA-DMP
BA-DMP
Gasp!

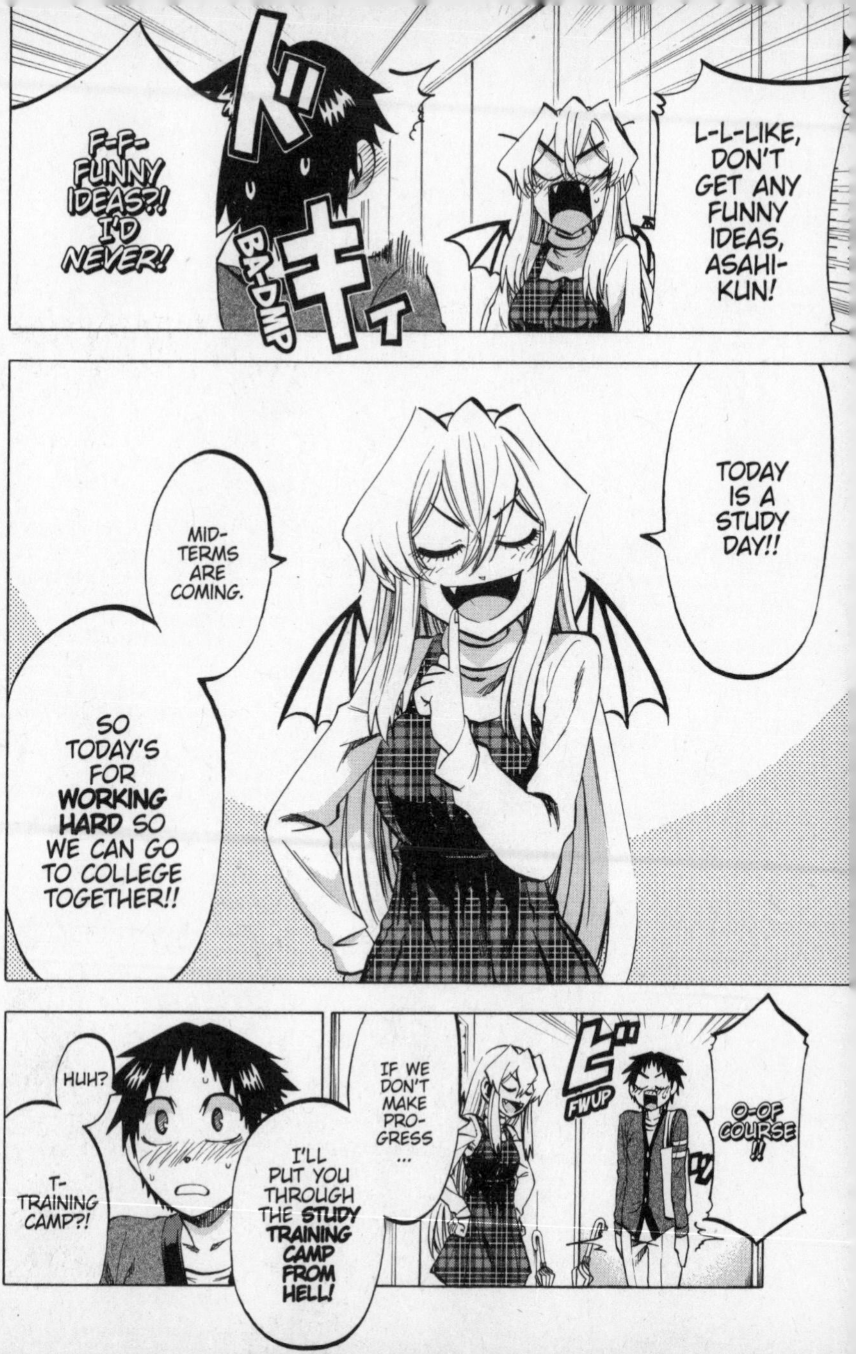
L-L-LIKE, DON'T GET ANY FUNNY IDEAS, ASAHI-KUN!
F-F-FUNNY IDEAS?! I'D NEVER!
BA-DMP
TODAY IS A STUDY DAY!!
MID-TERMS ARE COMING.
SO TODAY'S FOR WORKING HARD SO WE CAN GO TO COLLEGE TOGETHER!!
O-OF COURSE!!
FWUP
IF WE DON'T MAKE PRO-GRESS...
I'LL PUT YOU THROUGH THE STUDY TRAINING CAMP FROM HELL!
HUH?
T-TRAINING CAMP?!

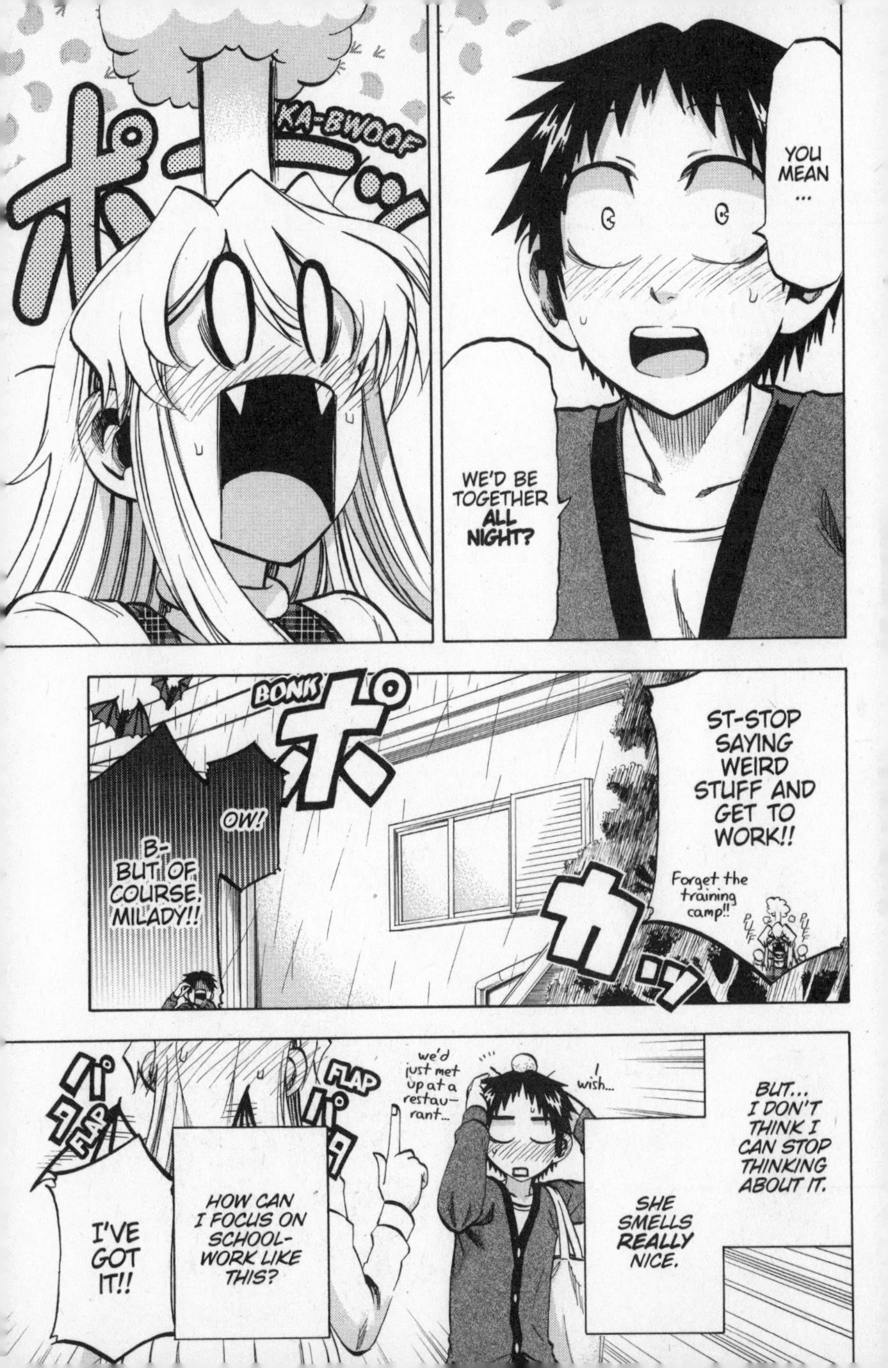
YOU MEAN ...
WE'D BE TOGETHER ALL NIGHT?
KA-BWOOF
ST-STOP SAYING WEIRD STUFF AND GET TO WORK!!
Forget the training camp!!
PUFF
PUFF
BONK
OW!
B-BUT OF COURSE, MILADY!!
BUT... I DON'T THINK I CAN STOP THINKING ABOUT IT.
I wish...
SHE SMELLS REALLY NICE.
we'd just met up at a restau-rant...
FLAP
FLAP
HOW CAN I FOCUS ON SCHOOL-WORK LIKE THIS?
I'VE GOT IT!!

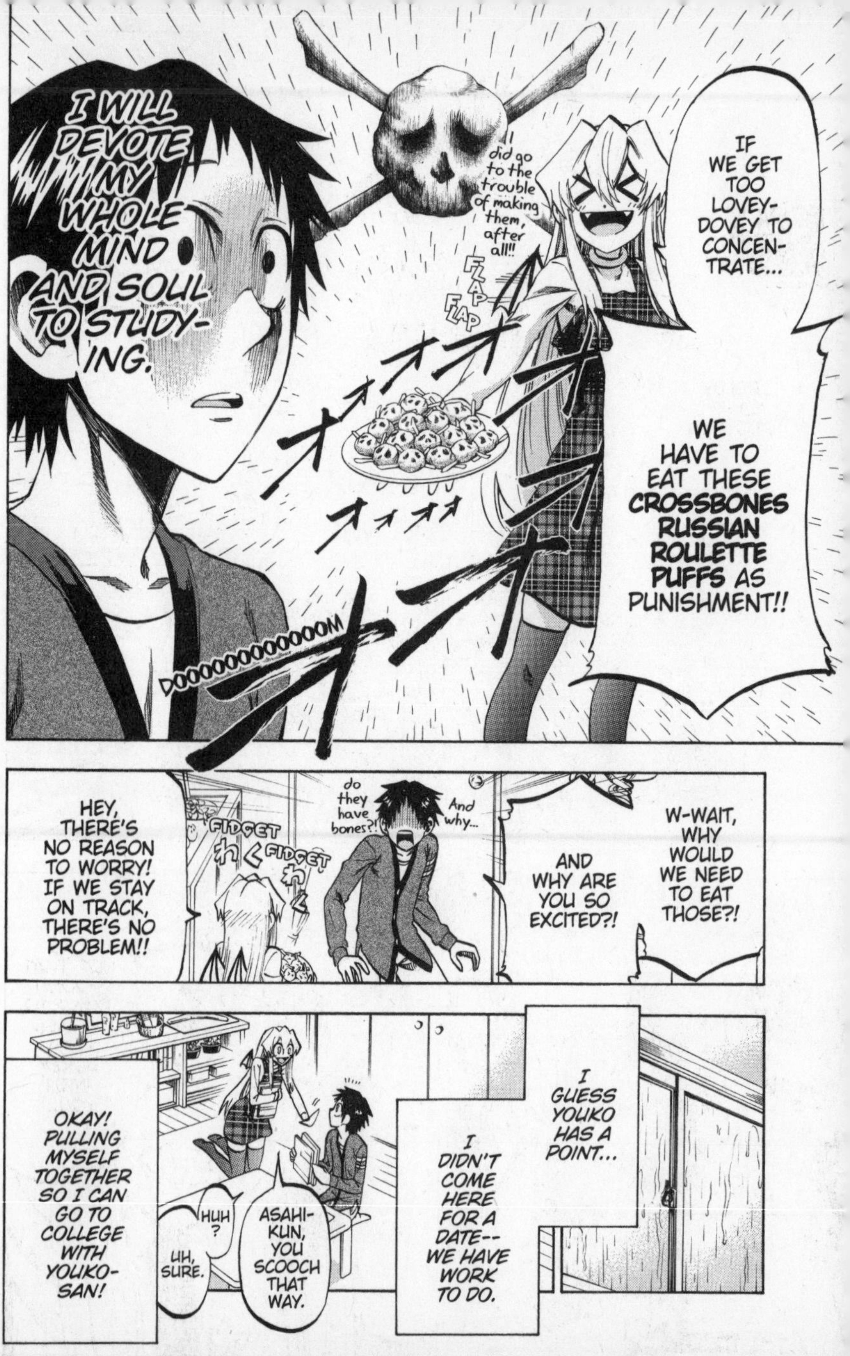
IF WE GET TOO LOVEY-DOVEY TO CONCENTRATE...
WE HAVE TO EAT THESE **CROSSBONES RUSSIAN ROULETTE PUFFS** AS PUNISHMENT!!
I did go to the trouble of making them, after all!!
FLAP
FLAP
DOOOOOOOOOOOOM
I WILL DEVOTE MY WHOLE MIND AND SOUL TO STUDYING.
W-WAIT, WHY WOULD WE NEED TO EAT THOSE?!
AND WHY ARE YOU SO EXCITED?!
And why...
do they have bones?!
FIDGET わく
FIDGET わく
HEY, THERE'S NO REASON TO WORRY! IF WE STAY ON TRACK, THERE'S NO PROBLEM!!
I GUESS YOUKO HAS A POINT...
I DIDN'T COME HERE FOR A DATE-- WE HAVE WORK TO DO.
ASAHI-KUN, YOU SCOOCH THAT WAY.
HUH?
UH, SURE.
OKAY! PULLING MYSELF TOGETHER SO I CAN GO TO COLLEGE WITH YOUKO-SAN!

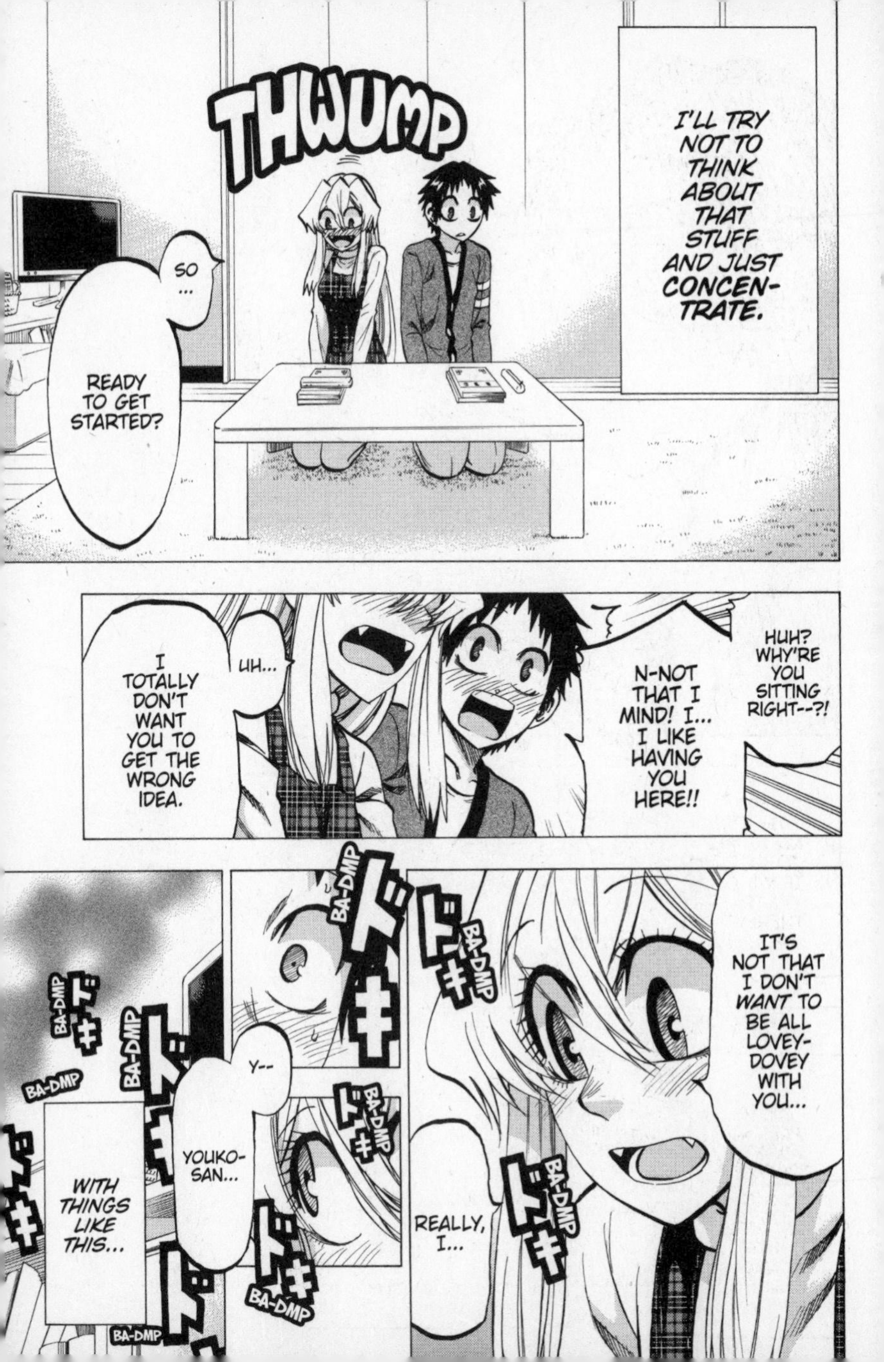
I'LL TRY NOT TO THINK ABOUT THAT STUFF AND JUST CONCENTRATE.
THWUMP
SO ...
READY TO GET STARTED?
HUH? WHY'RE YOU SITTING RIGHT--?!
N-NOT THAT I MIND! I... I LIKE HAVING YOU HERE!!
UH...
I TOTALLY DON'T WANT YOU TO GET THE WRONG IDEA.
IT'S NOT THAT I DON'T WANT TO BE ALL LOVEY-DOVEY WITH YOU...
BA-DMP
BA-DMP
REALLY, I...
BA-DMP
BA-DMP
Y--
YOUKO-SAN...
BA-DMP
BA-DMP
BA-DMP
BA-DMP
WITH THINGS LIKE THIS...
BA-DMP

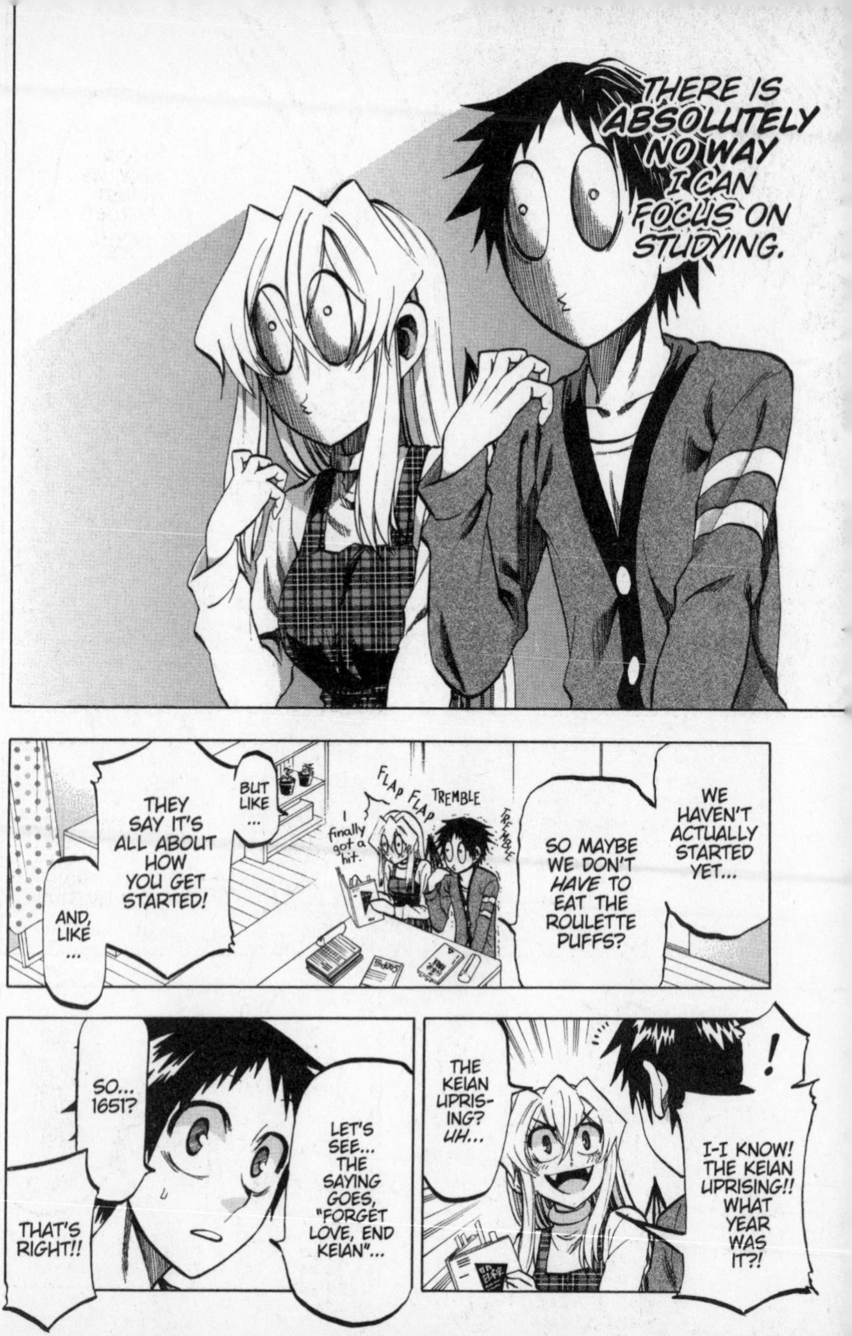
THERE IS ABSOLUTELY NO WAY I CAN FOCUS ON STUDYING.
WE HAVEN'T ACTUALLY STARTED YET...
SO MAYBE WE DON'T *HAVE* TO EAT THE ROULETTE PUFFS?
TREMBLE
TREMBLE
FLAP FLAP
I finally got a hit.
BUT LIKE...
THEY SAY IT'S ALL ABOUT HOW YOU GET STARTED!
AND, LIKE...
!
I-I KNOW! THE KEIAN UPRISING!! WHAT YEAR WAS IT?!
THE KEIAN UPRISING? UH...
LET'S SEE... THE SAYING GOES, "FORGET LOVE, END KEIAN"...
SO... 1651?
THAT'S RIGHT!!

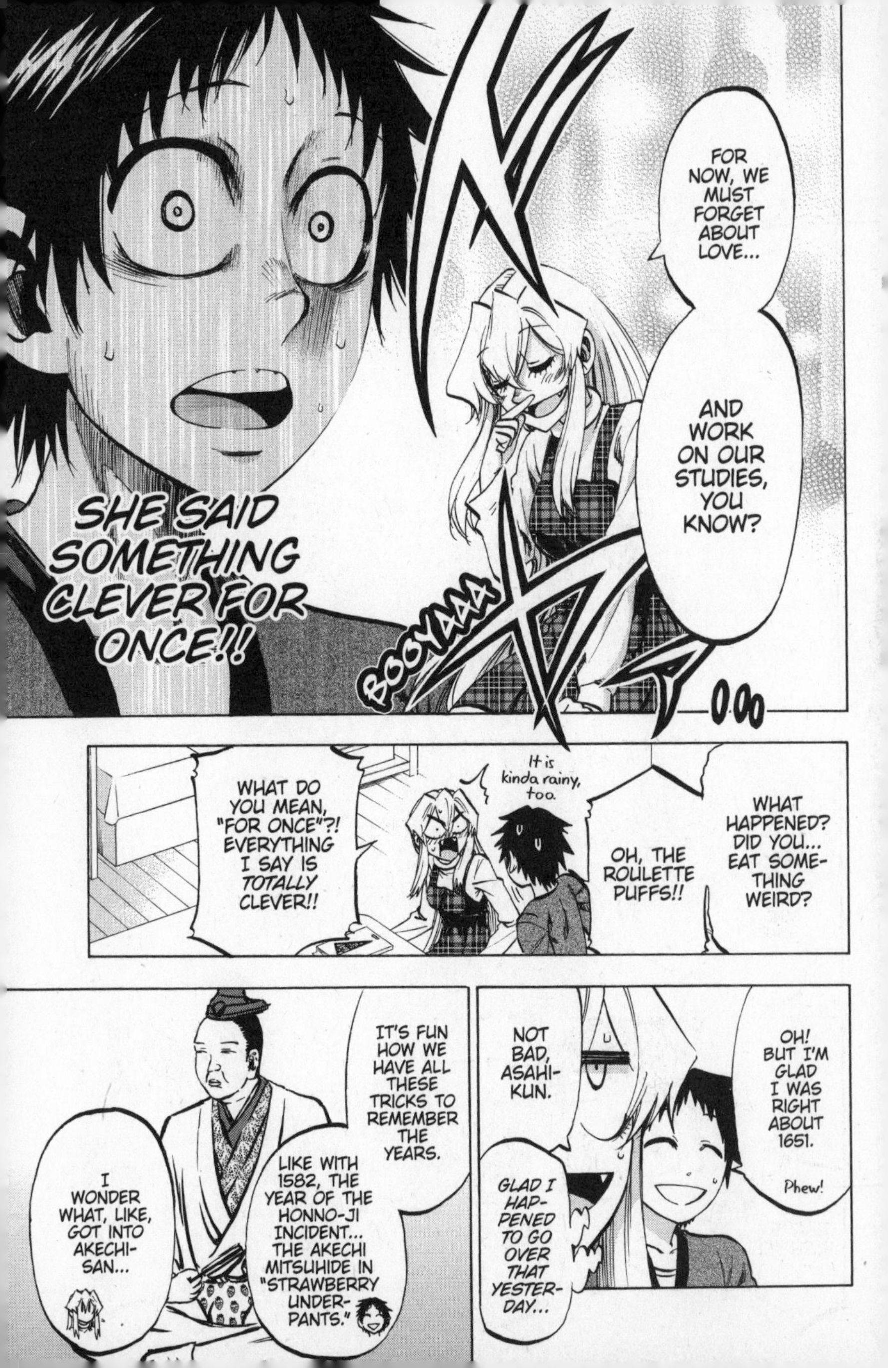
FOR NOW, WE MUST FORGET ABOUT LOVE...
AND WORK ON OUR STUDIES, YOU KNOW?
BOOYAAA
SHE SAID SOMETHING CLEVER FOR ONCE!!
WHAT HAPPENED? DID YOU... EAT SOME-THING WEIRD?
OH, THE ROULETTE PUFFS!!
It is kinda rainy, too.
WHAT DO YOU MEAN, "FOR ONCE"?! EVERYTHING I SAY IS TOTALLY CLEVER!!
OH! BUT I'M GLAD I WAS RIGHT ABOUT 1651.
Phew!
NOT BAD, ASAHI-KUN.
GLAD I HAP-PENED TO GO OVER THAT YESTER-DAY...
IT'S FUN HOW WE HAVE ALL THESE TRICKS TO REMEMBER THE YEARS.
LIKE WITH 1582, THE YEAR OF THE HONNO-JI INCIDENT... THE AKECHI MITSUHIDE IN "STRAWBERRY UNDER-PANTS."
I WONDER WHAT, LIKE, GOT INTO AKECHI-SAN...

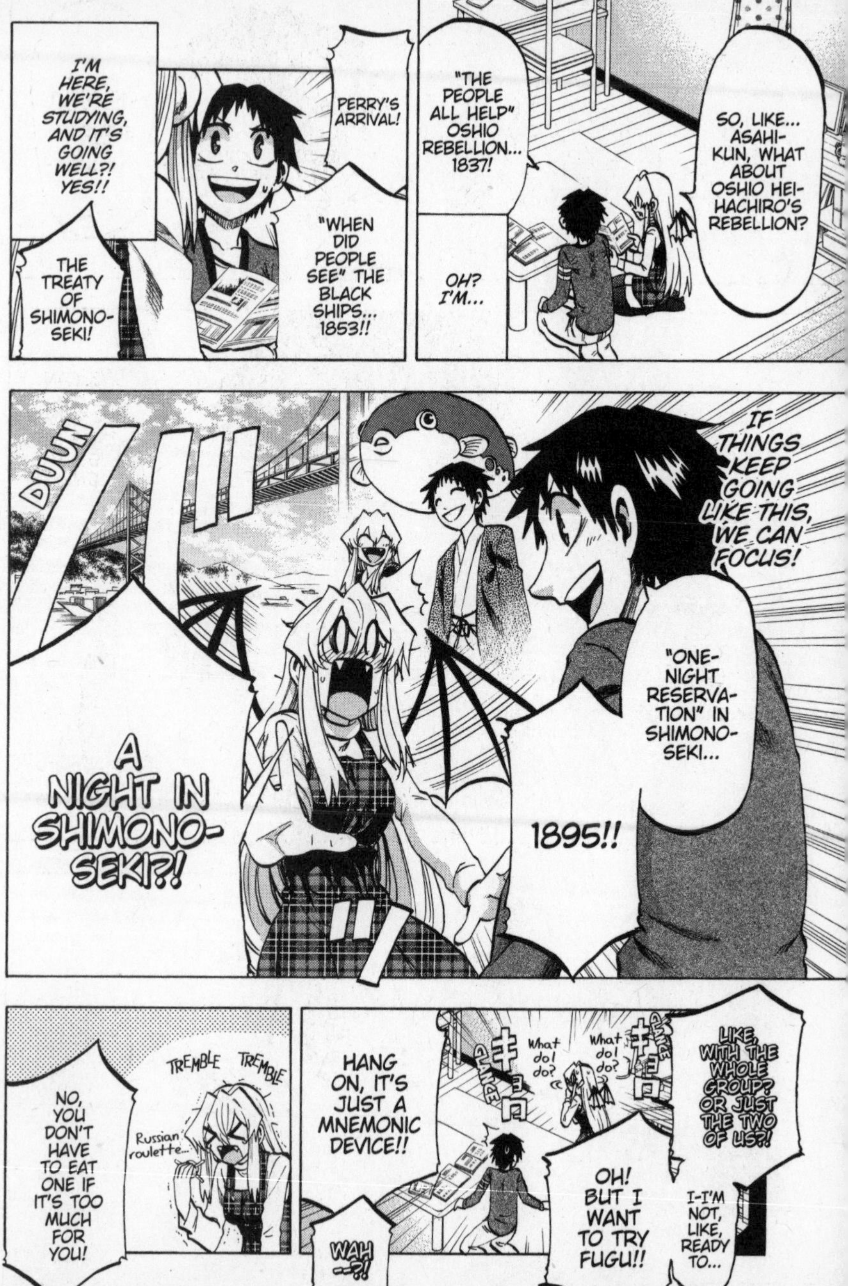

SO, LIKE... ASAHI-KUN, WHAT ABOUT OSHIO HEI-HACHIRO'S REBELLION?
OH? I'M...
"THE PEOPLE ALL HELP" OSHIO REBELLION... 1837!
PERRY'S ARRIVAL!
"WHEN DID PEOPLE SEE" THE BLACK SHIPS... 1853!!
I'M HERE, WE'RE STUDYING, AND IT'S GOING WELL?! YES!!
THE TREATY OF SHIMONOSEKI!
IF THINGS KEEP GOING LIKE THIS, WE CAN FOCUS!
"ONE-NIGHT RESERVATION" IN SHIMONOSEKI...
1895!!
DUUN
A NIGHT IN SHIMONOSEKI?!
LIKE, WITH THE WHOLE GROUP? OR JUST THE TWO OF US?!
What do I do?
What do I do?
I-I'M NOT, LIKE, READY TO...
OH! BUT I WANT TO TRY FUGU!!
HANG ON, IT'S JUST A MNEMONIC DEVICE!!
WAH--?!
TREMBLE TREMBLE
Russian roulette...
NO, YOU DON'T HAVE TO EAT ONE IF IT'S TOO MUCH FOR YOU!

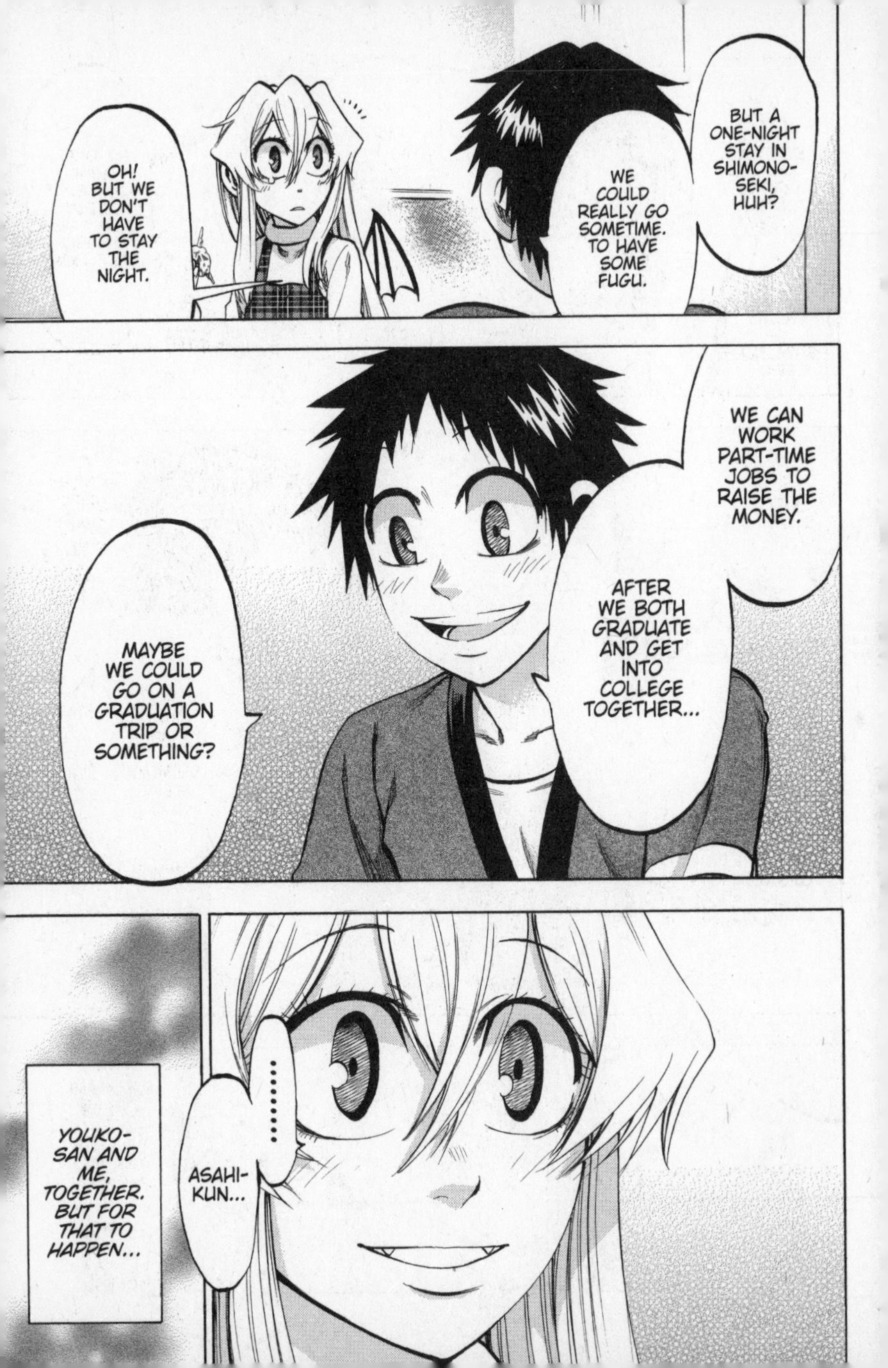
BUT A ONE-NIGHT STAY IN SHIMONOSEKI, HUH?
WE COULD REALLY GO SOMETIME. TO HAVE SOME FUGU.
OH! BUT WE DON'T HAVE TO STAY THE NIGHT.
WE CAN WORK PART-TIME JOBS TO RAISE THE MONEY.
AFTER WE BOTH GRADUATE AND GET INTO COLLEGE TOGETHER...
MAYBE WE COULD GO ON A GRADUATION TRIP OR SOMETHING?
....
ASAHI-KUN...
YOUKO-SAN AND ME, TOGETHER. BUT FOR THAT TO HAPPEN...

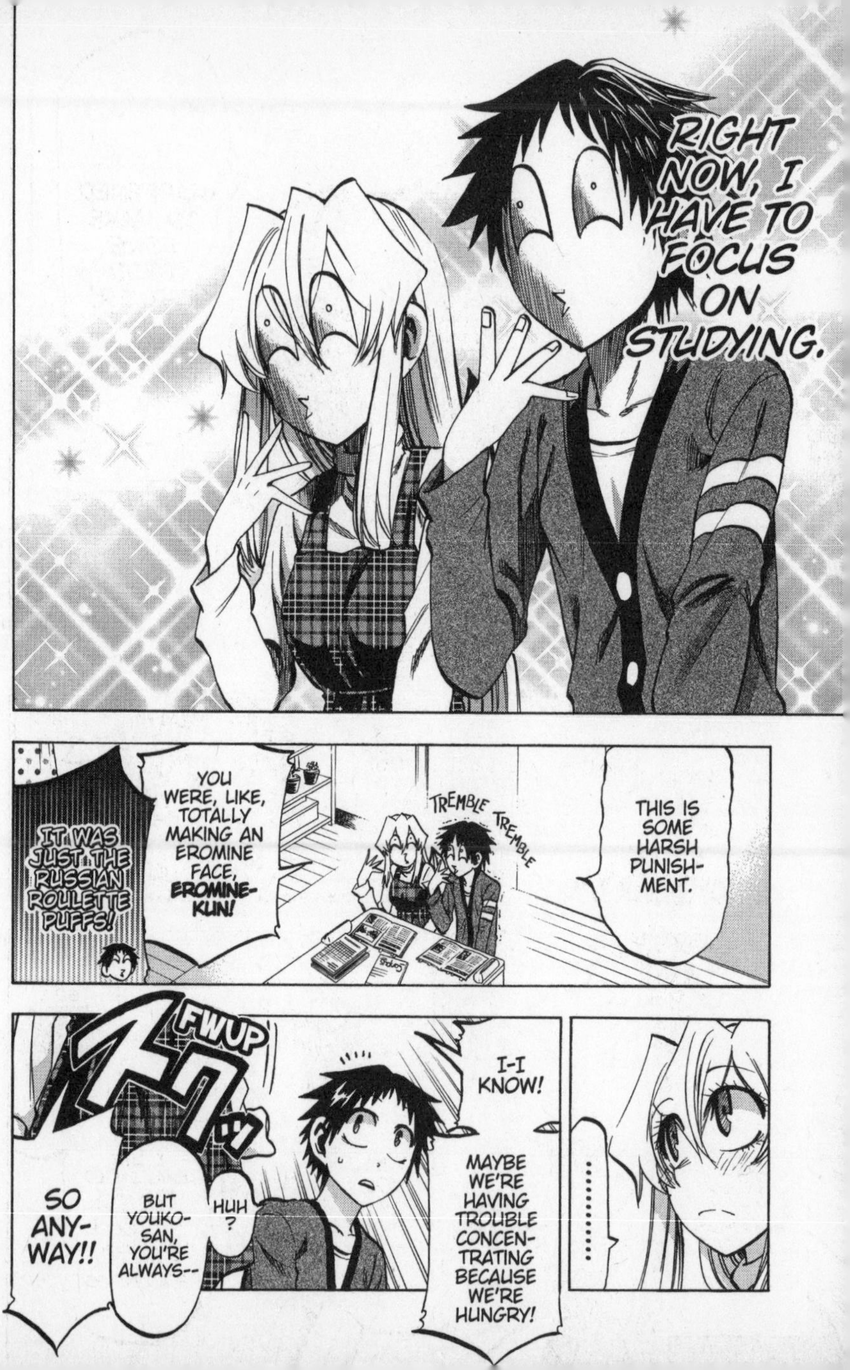
RIGHT NOW, I HAVE TO FOCUS ON STUDYING.
THIS IS SOME HARSH PUNISH-MENT.
TREMBLE TREMBLE
YOU WERE, LIKE, TOTALLY MAKING AN EROMINE FACE, **EROMINE-KUN!**
IT WAS JUST THE RUSSIAN ROULETTE PUFFS!
......
I-I KNOW!
MAYBE WE'RE HAVING TROUBLE CONCEN-TRATING BECAUSE WE'RE HUNGRY!
HUH?
BUT YOUKO-SAN, YOU'RE ALWAYS--
FWUP
SO ANY-WAY!!

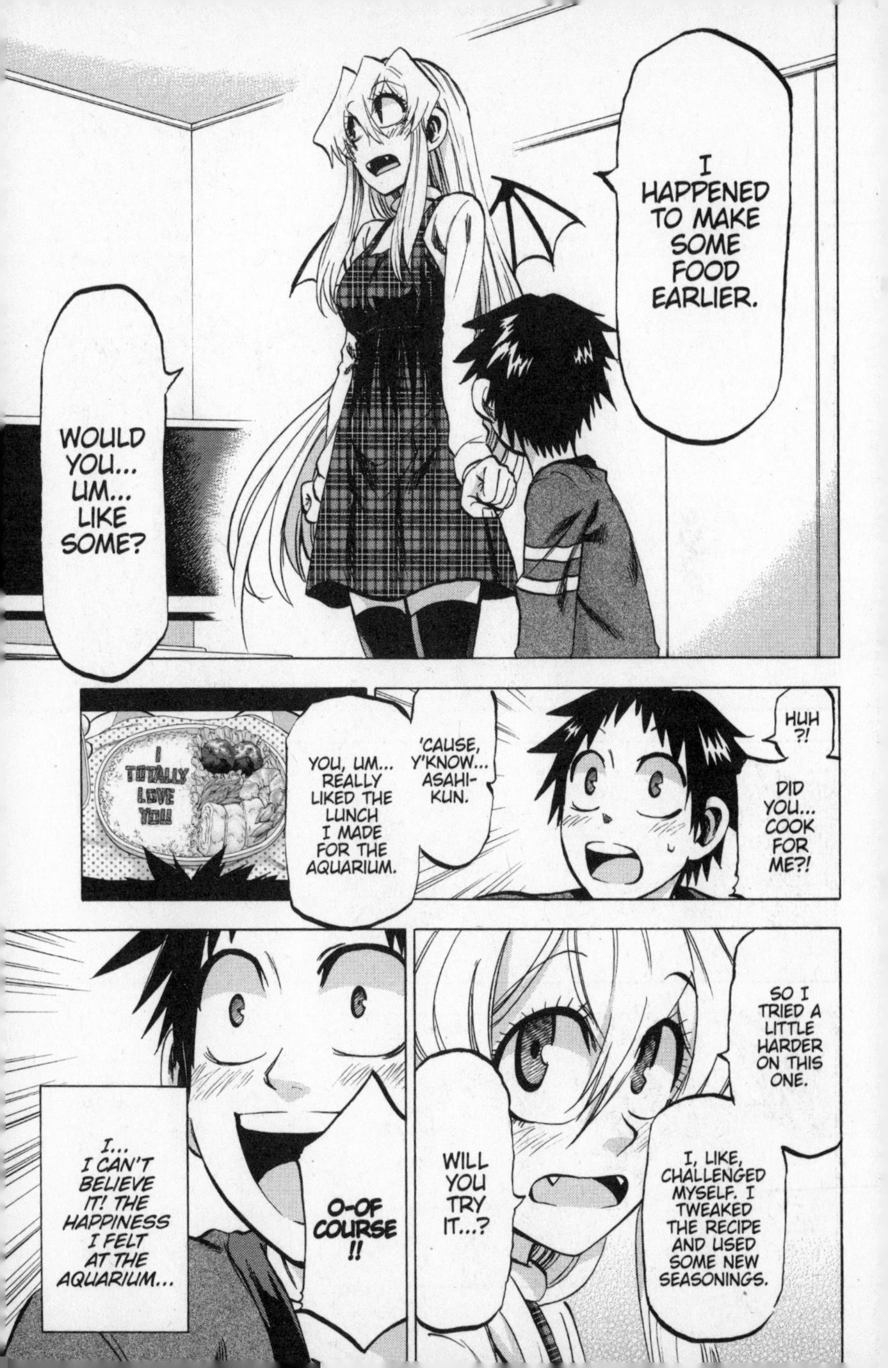
I HAPPENED TO MAKE SOME FOOD EARLIER.
WOULD YOU... UM... LIKE SOME?
HUH?!
DID YOU... COOK FOR ME?!
'CAUSE, Y'KNOW... ASAHI-KUN.
YOU, UM... REALLY LIKED THE LUNCH I MADE FOR THE AQUARIUM.
I TOTALLY LOVE YOU
SO I TRIED A LITTLE HARDER ON THIS ONE.
I, LIKE, CHALLENGED MYSELF. I TWEAKED THE RECIPE AND USED SOME NEW SEASONINGS.
WILL YOU TRY IT...?
O-OF COURSE!!
I... I CAN'T BELIEVE IT! THE HAPPINESS I FELT AT THE AQUARIUM...

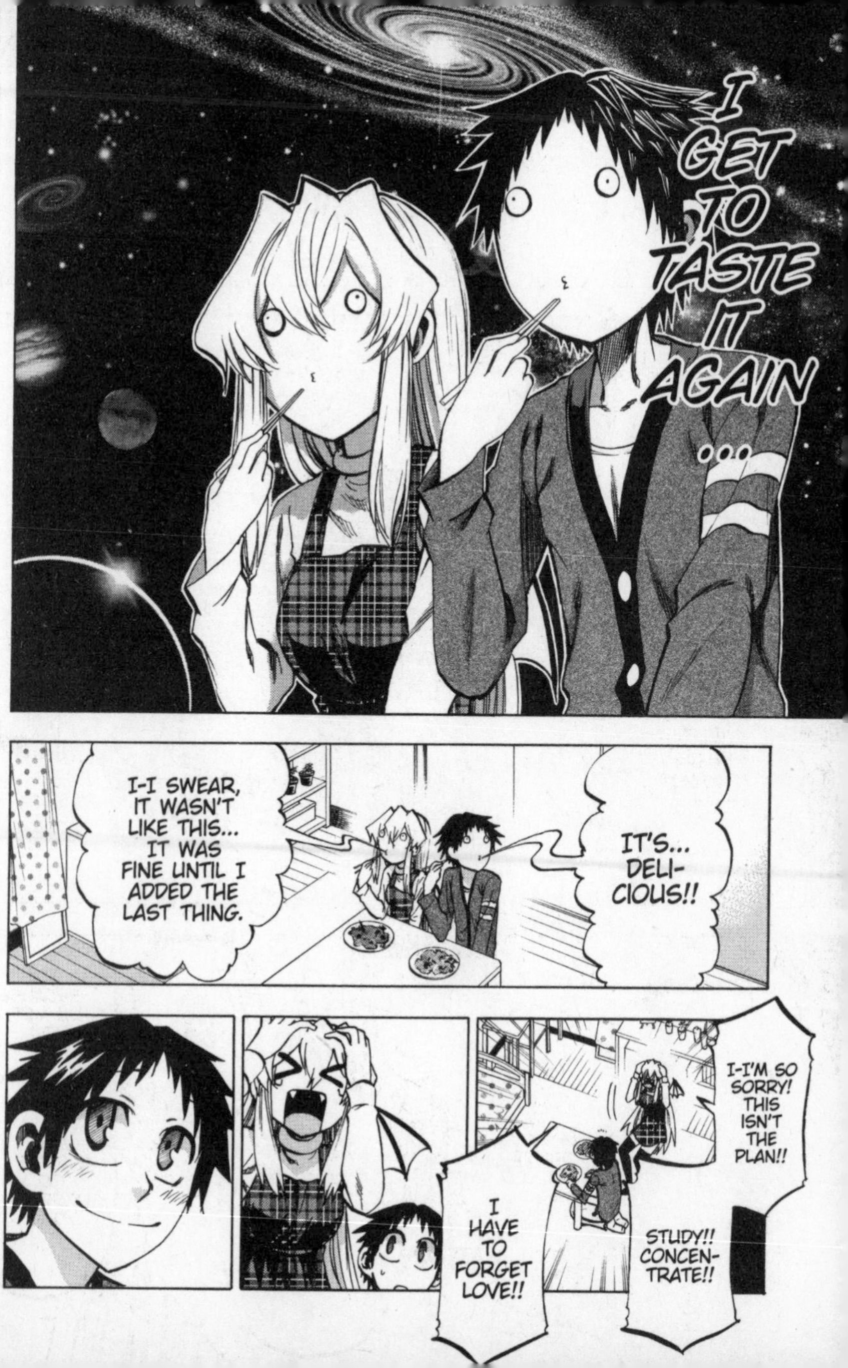
I GET TO TASTE IT AGAIN...
IT'S... DELICIOUS!!
I-I SWEAR, IT WASN'T LIKE THIS... IT WAS FINE UNTIL I ADDED THE LAST THING.
I-I'M SO SORRY! THIS ISN'T THE PLAN!!
STUDY!! CONCENTRATE!!
I HAVE TO FORGET LOVE!!

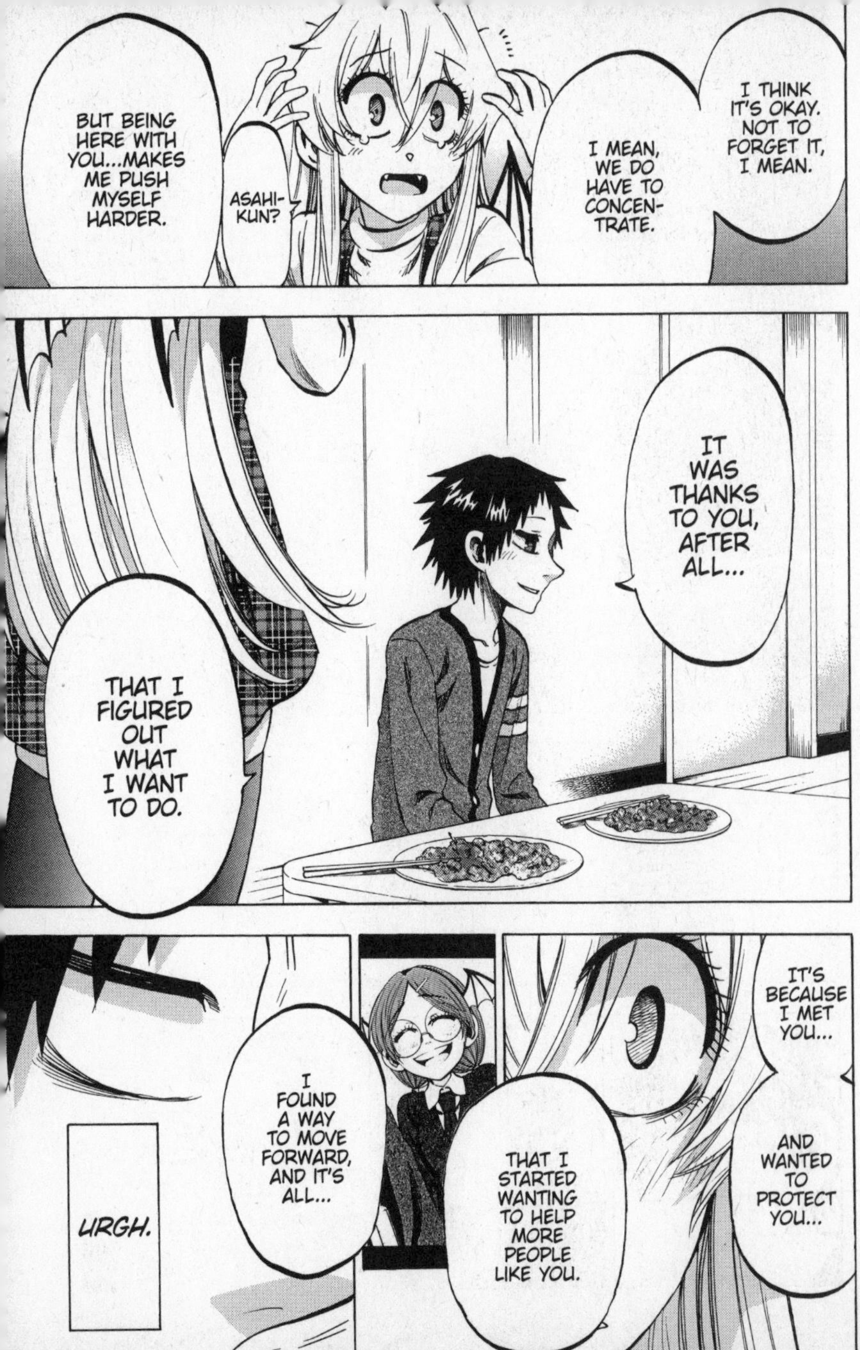
I THINK IT'S OKAY. NOT TO FORGET IT, I MEAN.
I MEAN, WE DO HAVE TO CONCENTRATE.
ASAHI-KUN?
BUT BEING HERE WITH YOU...MAKES ME PUSH MYSELF HARDER.
IT WAS THANKS TO YOU, AFTER ALL...
THAT I FIGURED OUT WHAT I WANT TO DO.
IT'S BECAUSE I MET YOU...
AND WANTED TO PROTECT YOU...
THAT I STARTED WANTING TO HELP MORE PEOPLE LIKE YOU.
I FOUND A WAY TO MOVE FORWARD, AND IT'S ALL...
URGH.

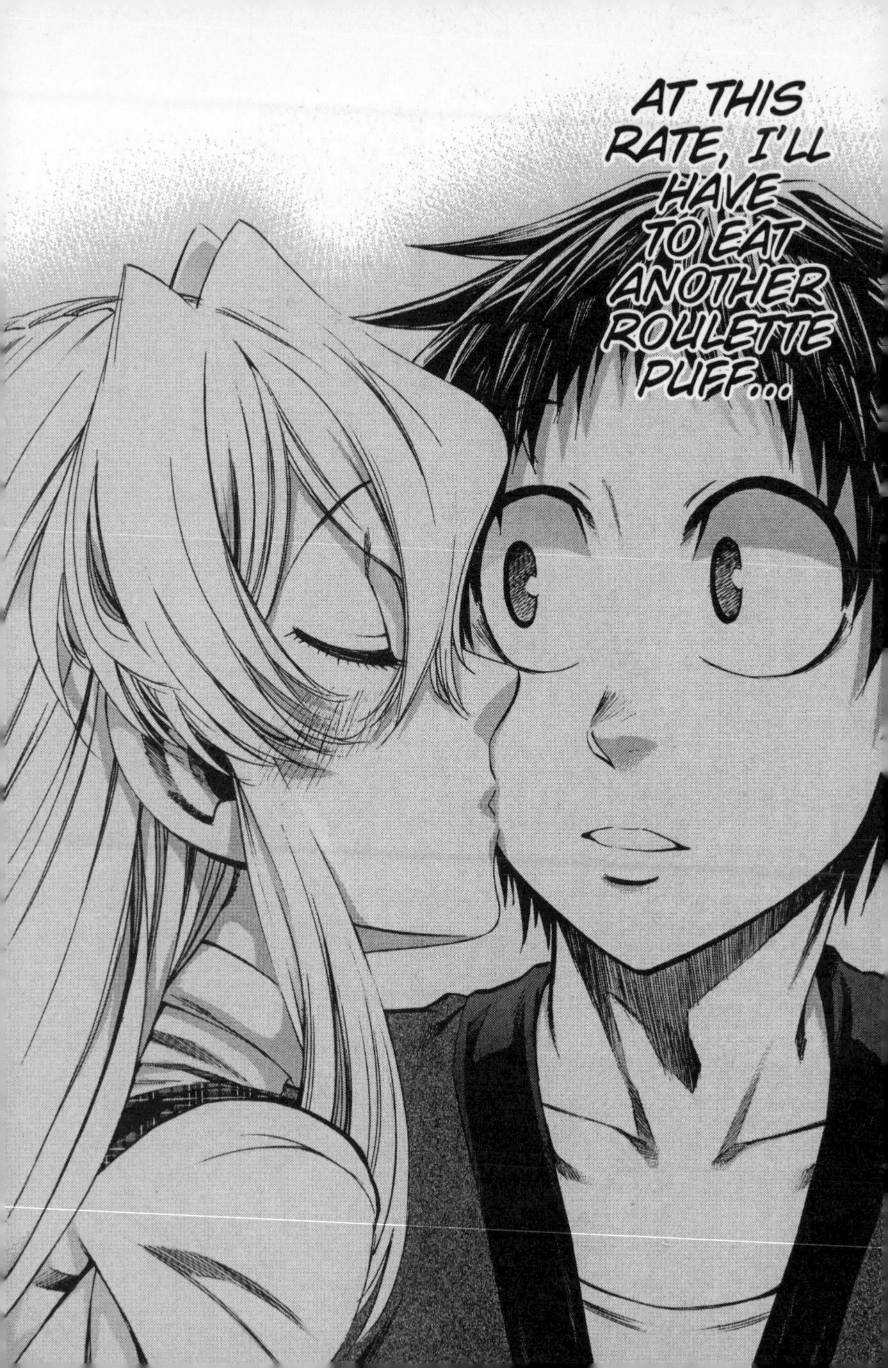
AT THIS RATE, I'LL HAVE TO EAT ANOTHER ROULETTE PUFF...

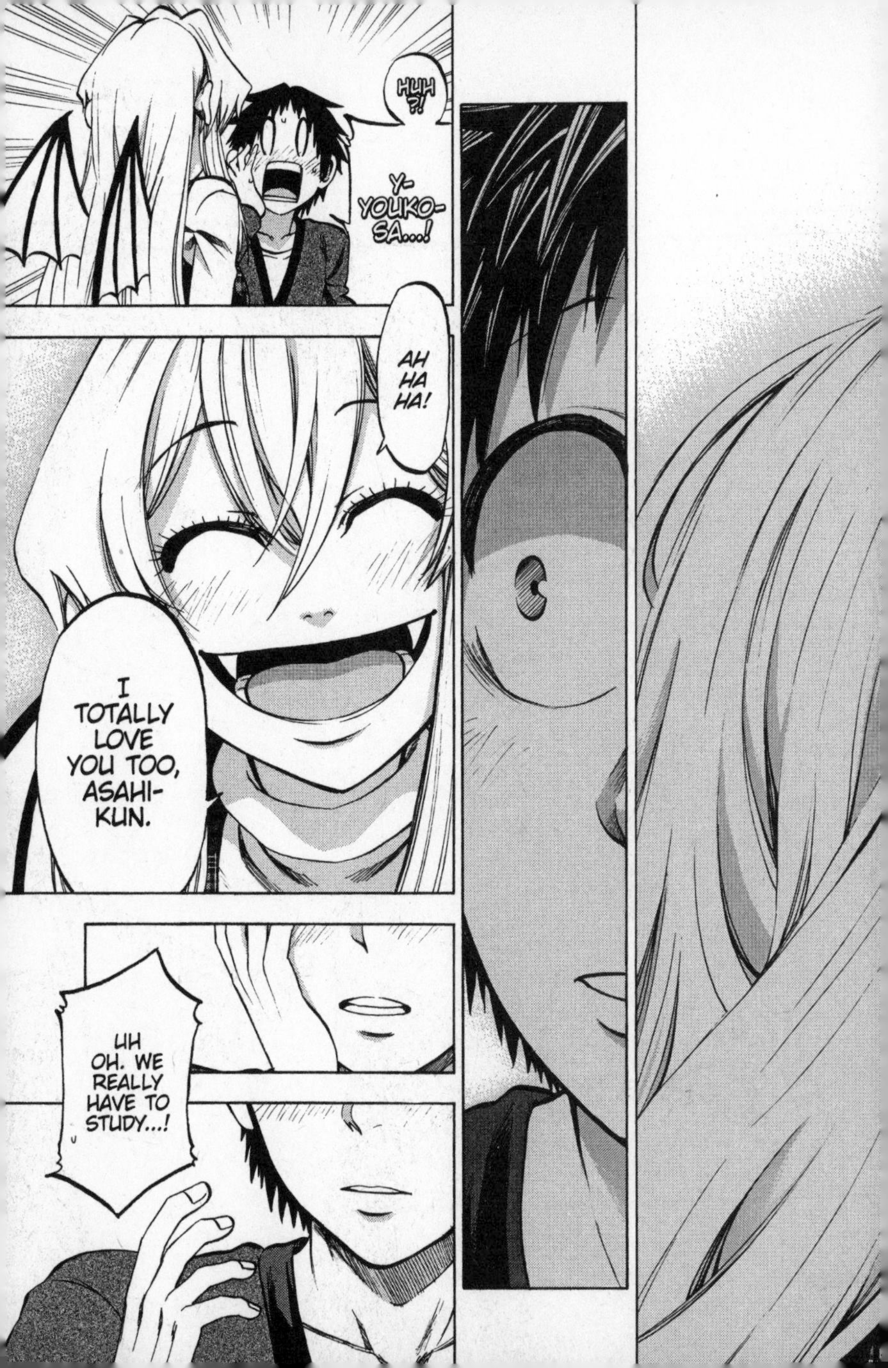
HUH?!
Y-YOUKO-SA...!
AH HA HA!
I TOTALLY LOVE YOU TOO, ASAHI-KUN.
UH OH. WE REALLY HAVE TO STUDY...!

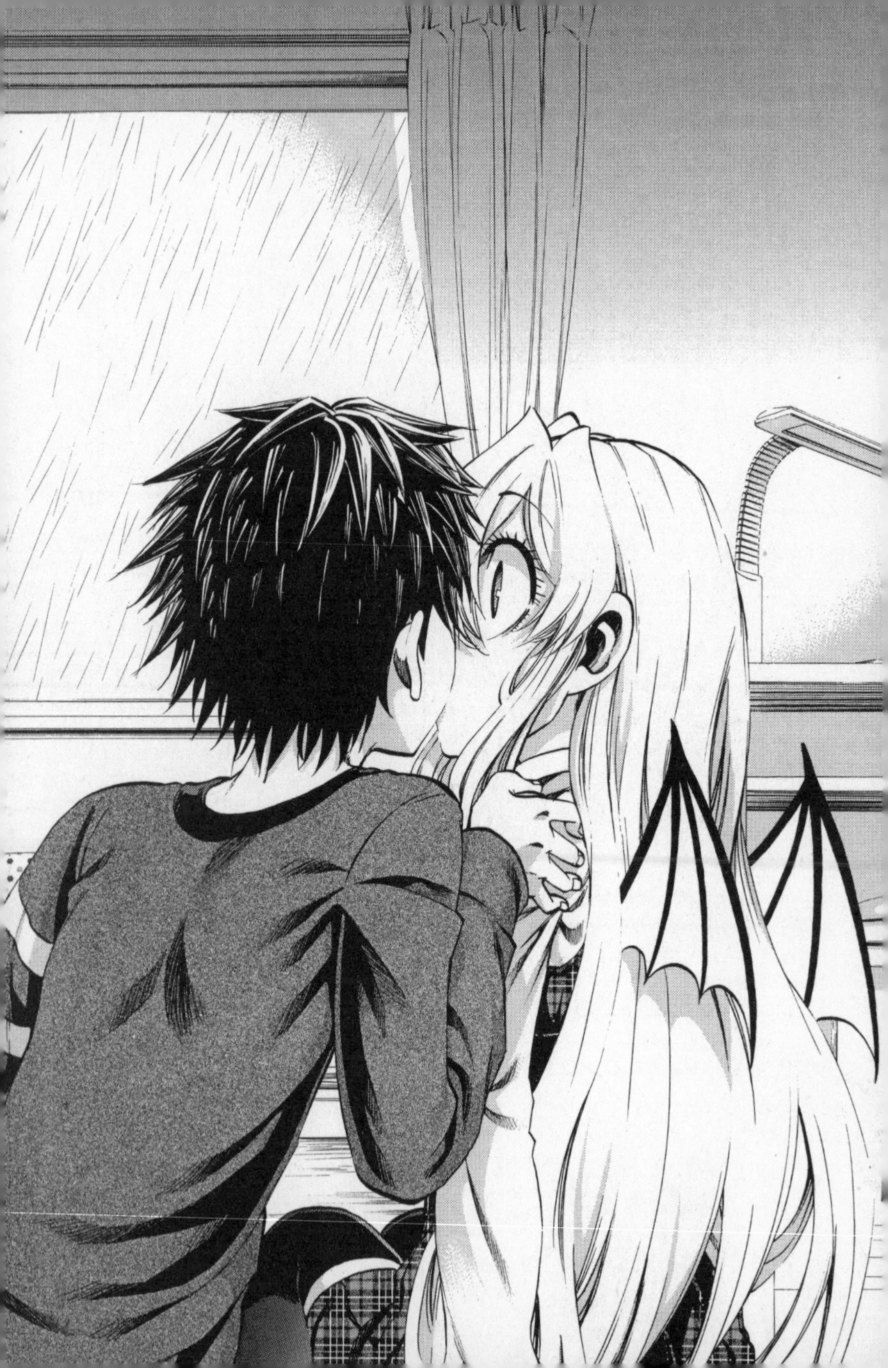

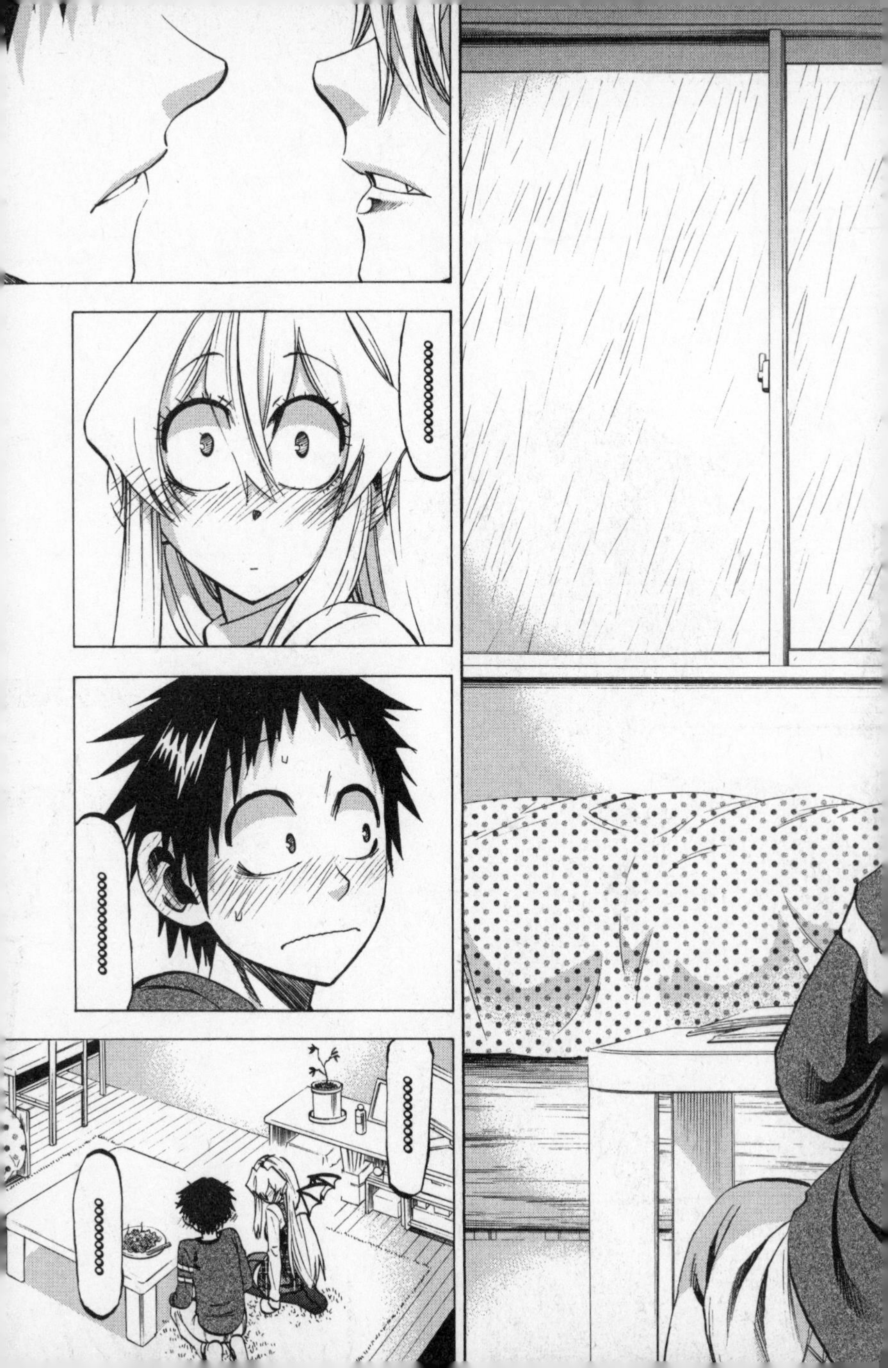
…………
…………
…………
…………

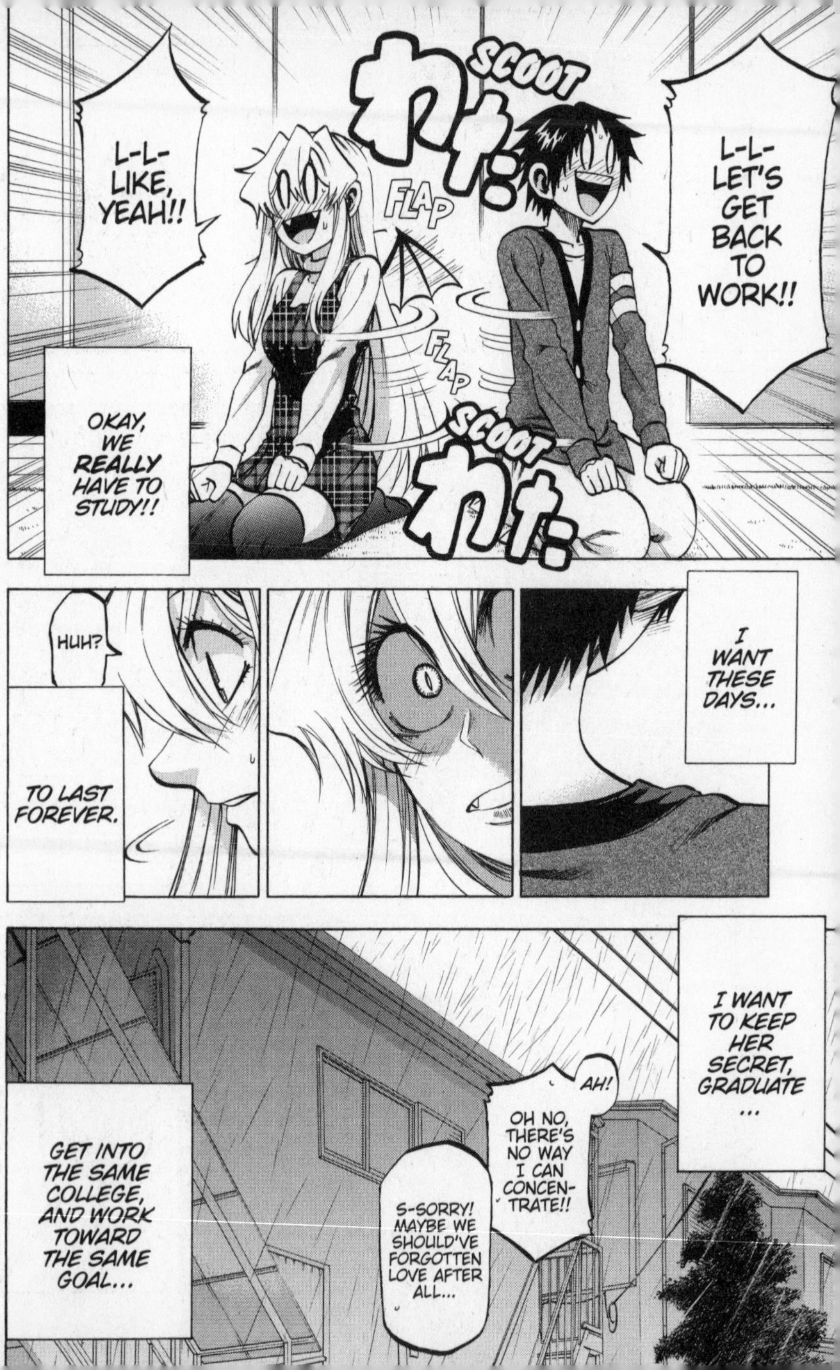
L-L-LET'S GET BACK TO WORK!!
SCOOT
FLAP
L-L-LIKE, YEAH!!
FLAP
SCOOT
OKAY, WE REALLY HAVE TO STUDY!!
I WANT THESE DAYS...
HUH?
TO LAST FOREVER.
I WANT TO KEEP HER SECRET, GRADUATE ...
AH!
OH NO, THERE'S NO WAY I CAN CONCENTRATE!!
S-SORRY! MAYBE WE SHOULD'VE FORGOTTEN LOVE AFTER ALL...
GET INTO THE SAME COLLEGE, AND WORK TOWARD THE SAME GOAL...

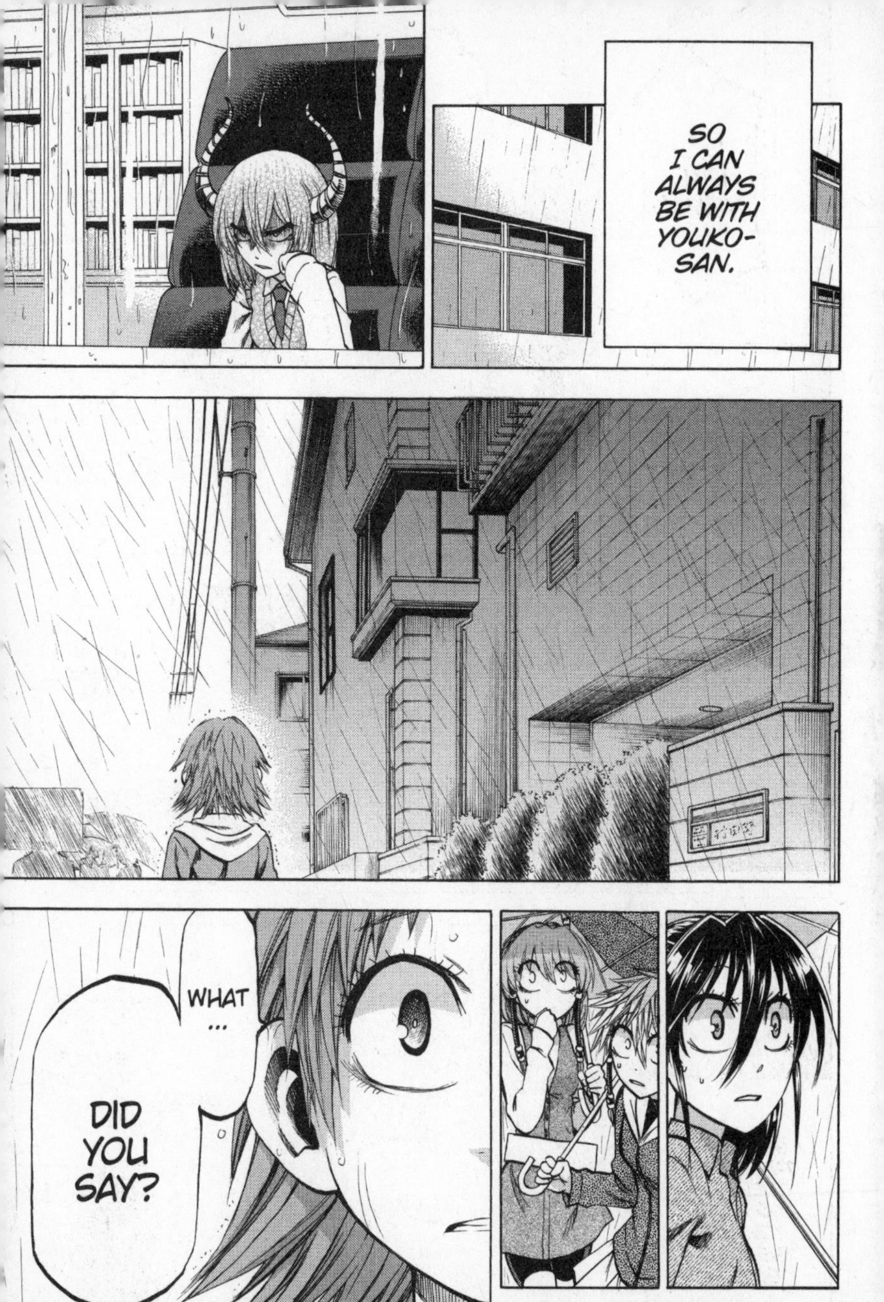
SO I CAN ALWAYS BE WITH YOUKO-SAN.
WHAT ... DID YOU SAY?

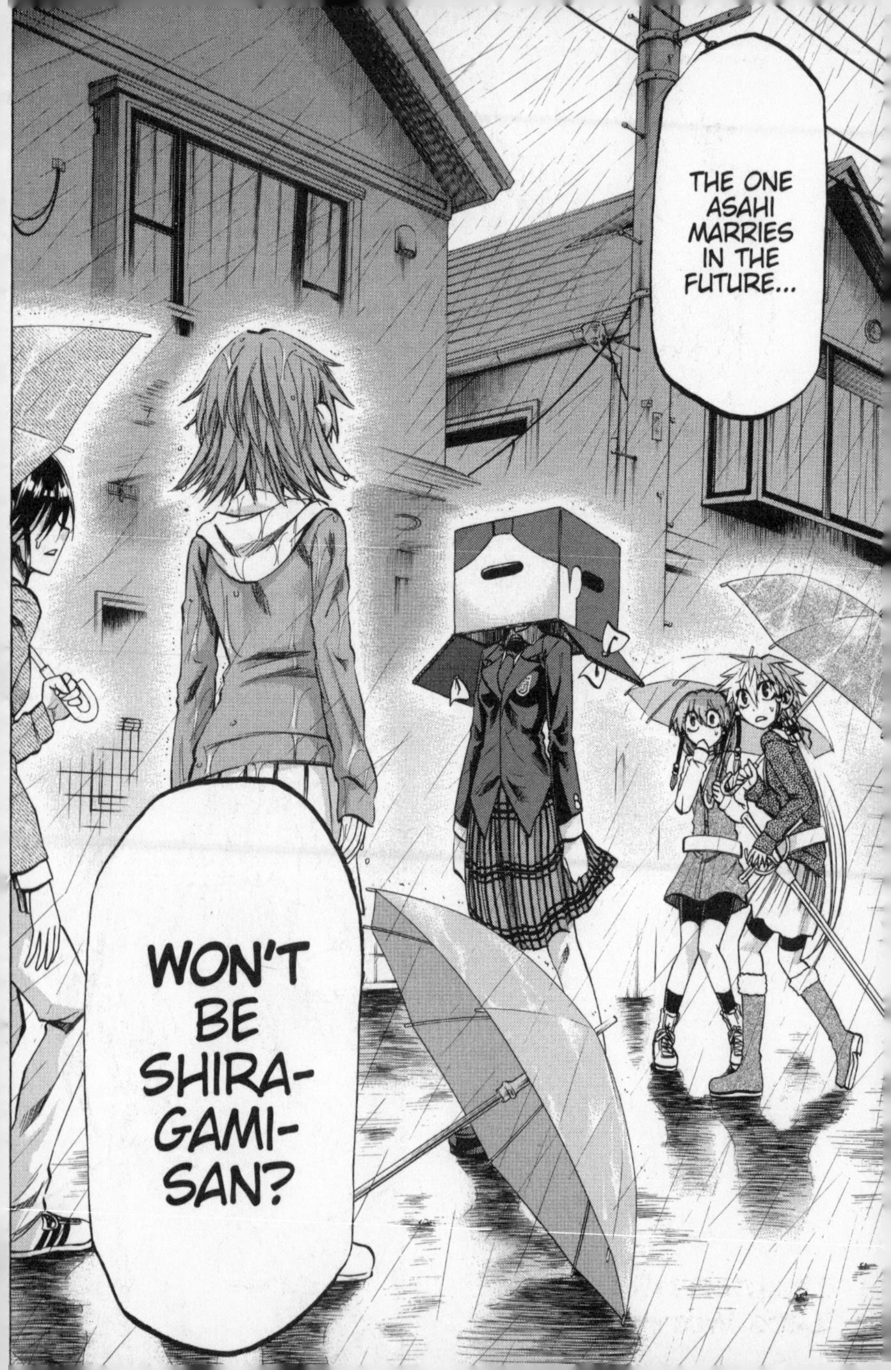
THE ONE ASAHI MARRIES IN THE FUTURE...
WON'T BE SHIRA-GAMI-SAN?

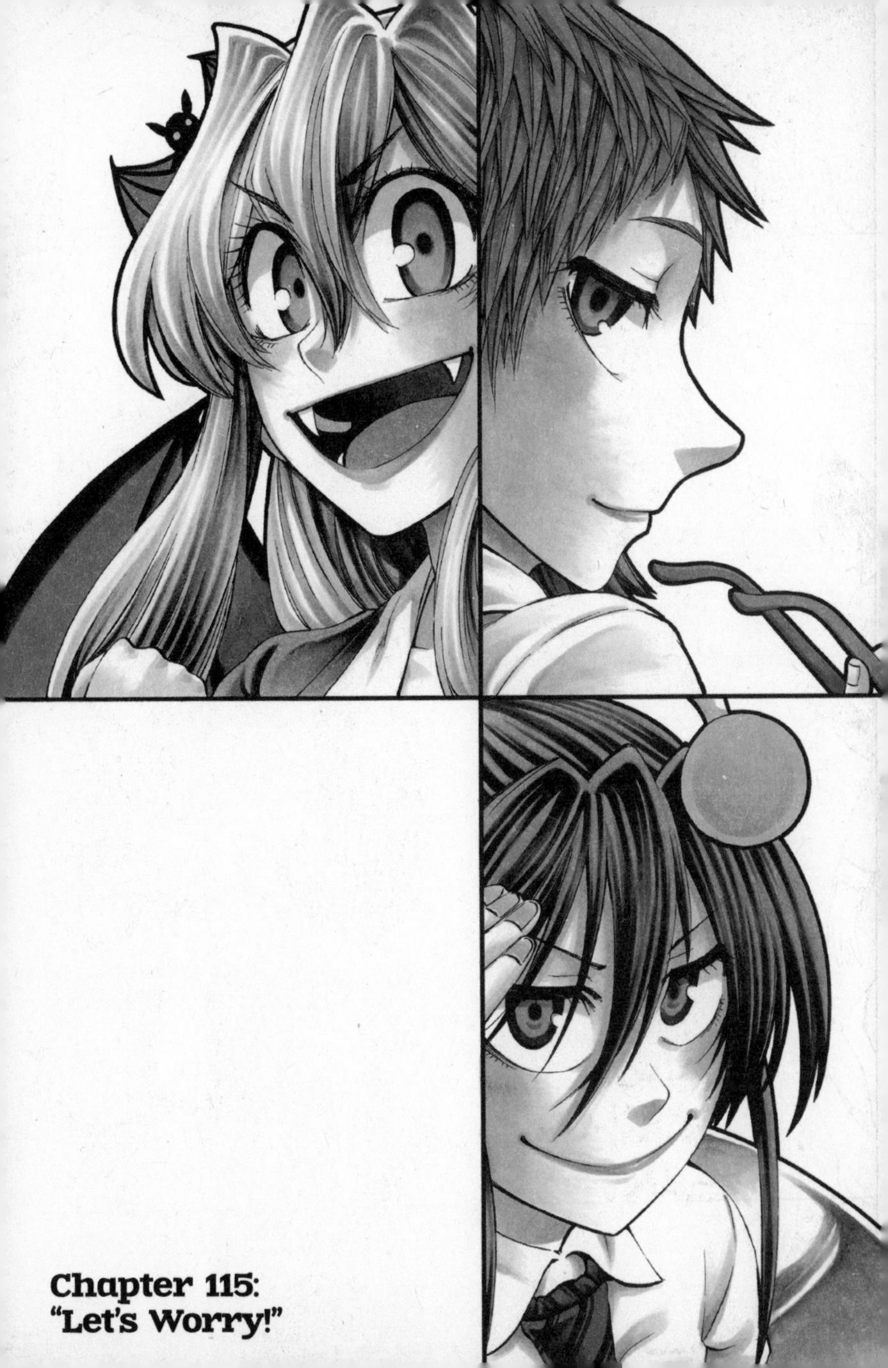
Chapter 115:
“Let’s Worry!”

TOP SECRET

My Monster Secret 13

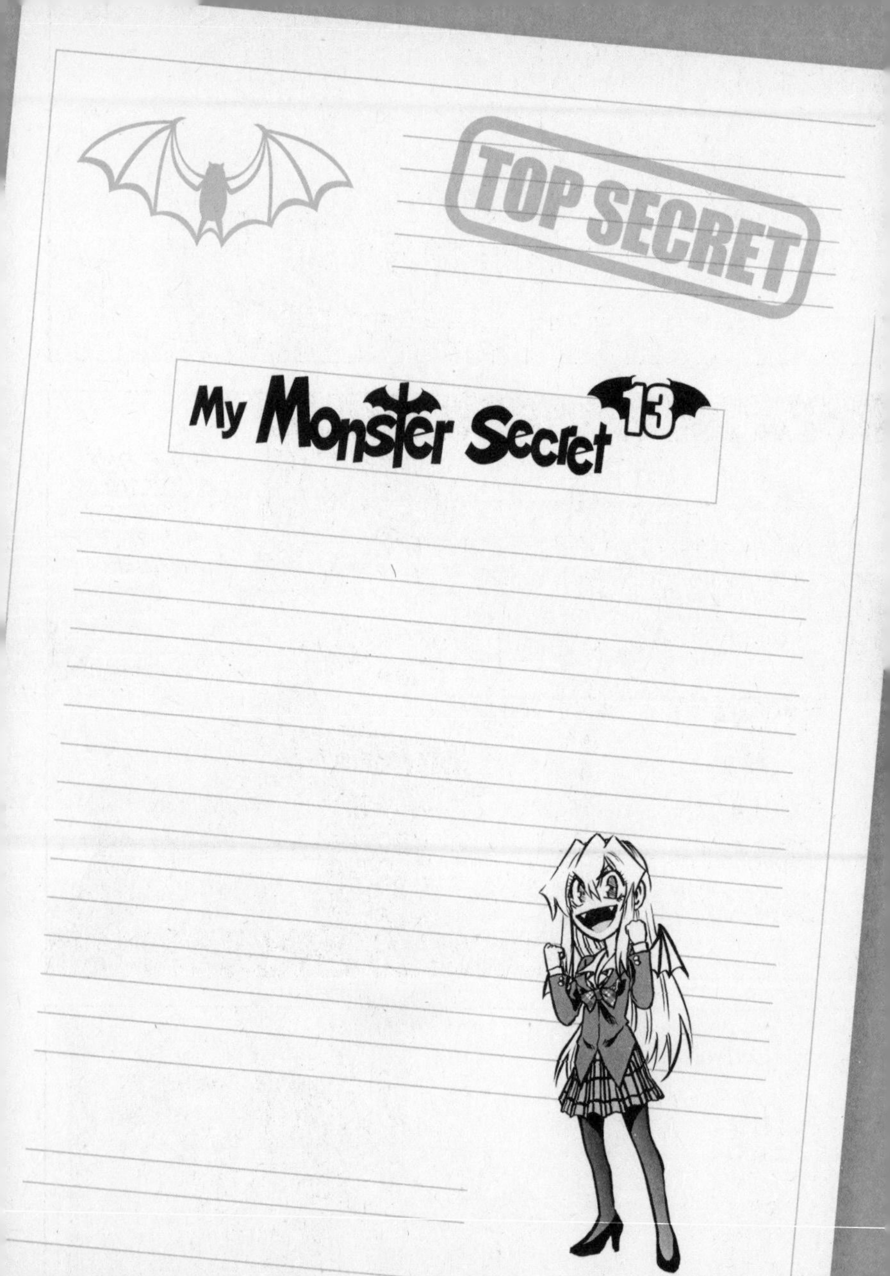

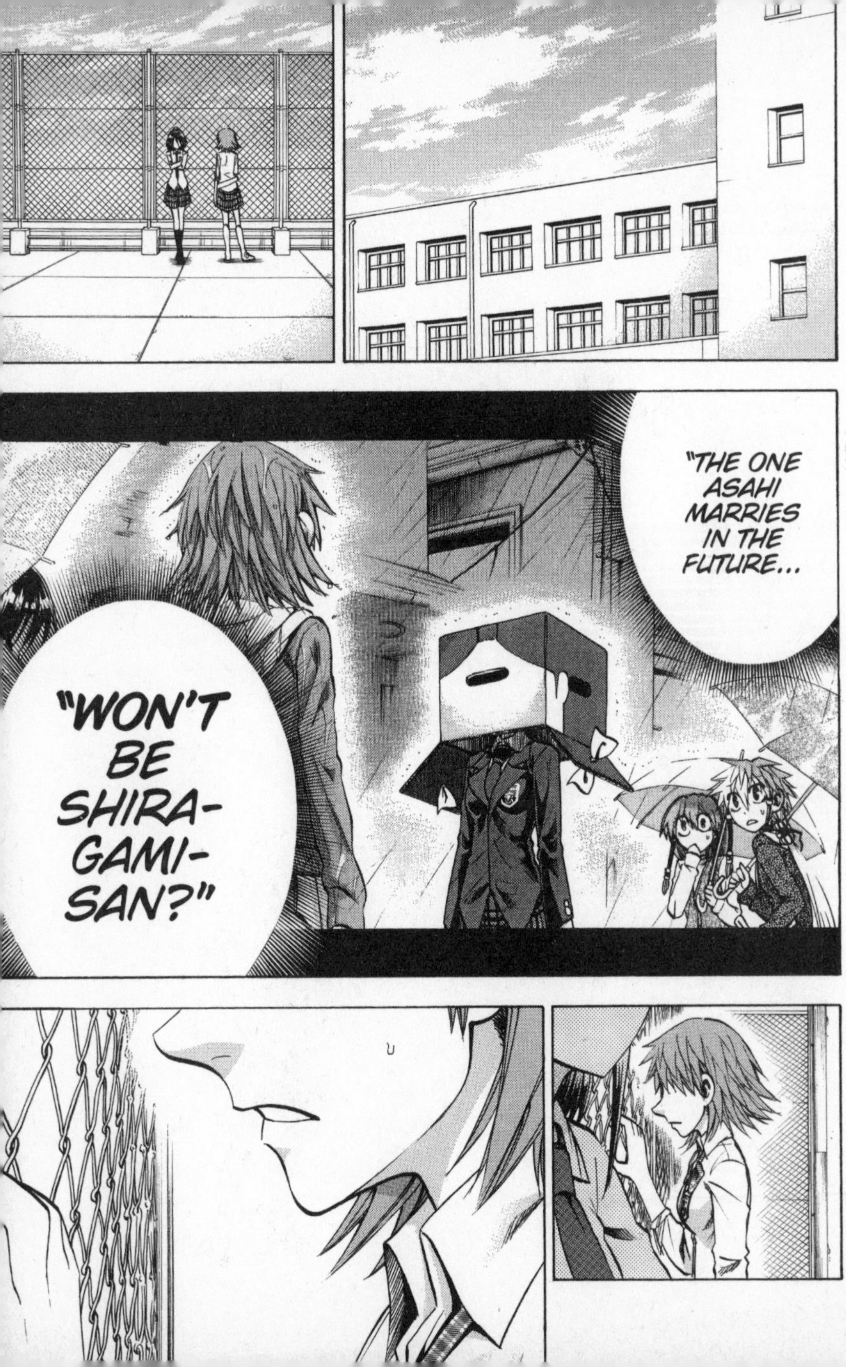
"THE ONE ASAHI MARRIES IN THE FUTURE...
"WON'T BE SHIRA-GAMI-SAN?"

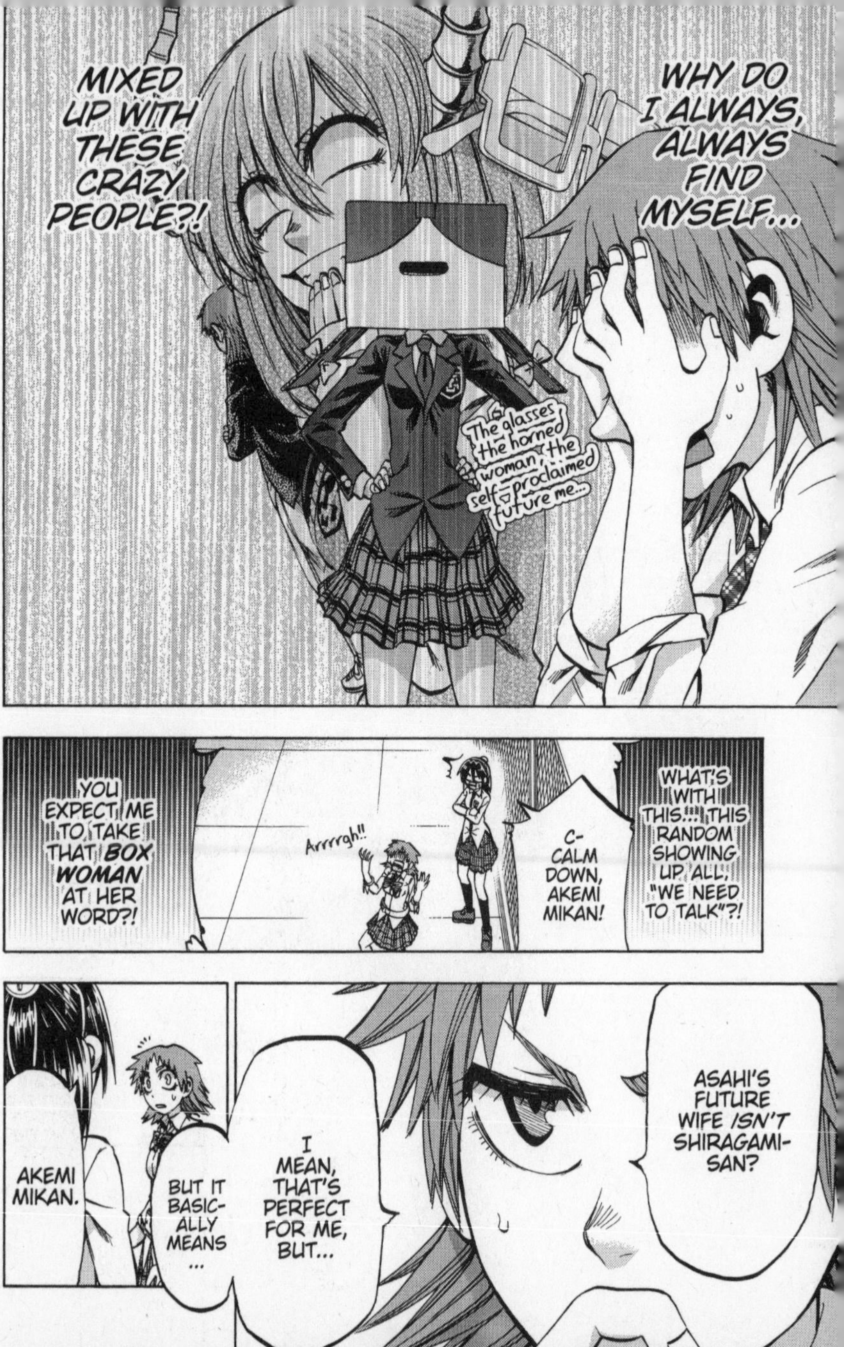
WHY DO I ALWAYS, ALWAYS FIND MYSELF...
MIXED UP WITH THESE CRAZY PEOPLE?!
The glasses, the horned woman, the self-proclaimed future me...
WHAT'S WITH THIS... THIS RANDOM SHOWING UP ALL, "WE NEED TO TALK"?!
C-CALM DOWN, AKEMI MIKAN!
...
Arrrrgh!!
YOU EXPECT ME TO TAKE THAT *BOX WOMAN* AT HER WORD?!
ASAHI'S FUTURE WIFE *ISN'T* SHIRAGAMI-SAN?
I MEAN, THAT'S PERFECT FOR ME, BUT...
BUT IT BASIC-ALLY MEANS ...
AKEMI MIKAN.

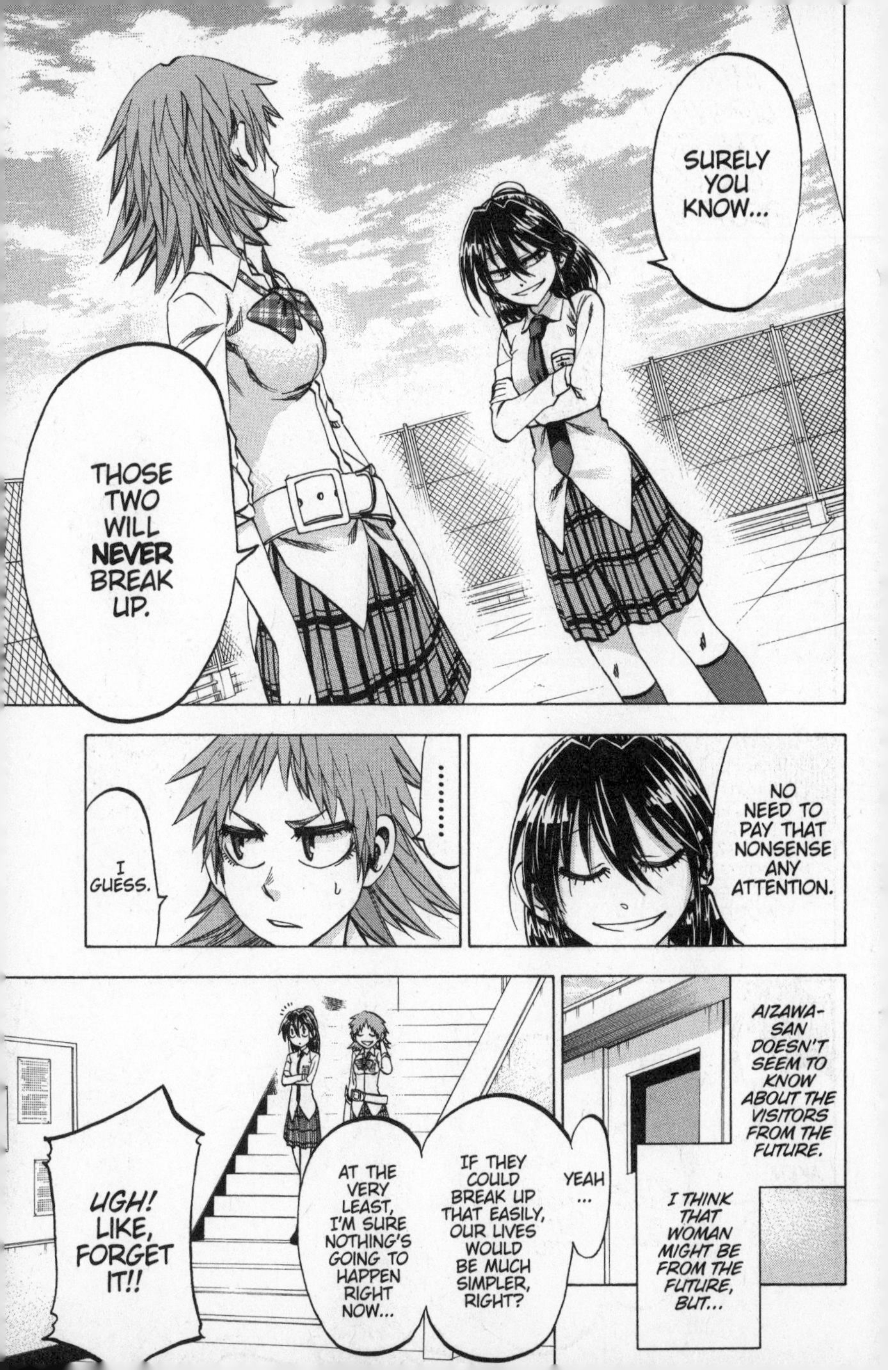

SURELY YOU KNOW...
THOSE TWO WILL **NEVER** BREAK UP.
NO NEED TO PAY THAT NONSENSE ANY ATTENTION.
......
I GUESS.
AIZAWA-SAN DOESN'T SEEM TO KNOW ABOUT THE VISITORS FROM THE FUTURE.
I THINK THAT WOMAN MIGHT BE FROM THE FUTURE, BUT...
YEAH...
IF THEY COULD BREAK UP THAT EASILY, OUR LIVES WOULD BE MUCH SIMPLER, RIGHT?
AT THE VERY LEAST, I'M SURE NOTHING'S GOING TO HAPPEN RIGHT NOW...
UGH! LIKE, FORGET IT!!

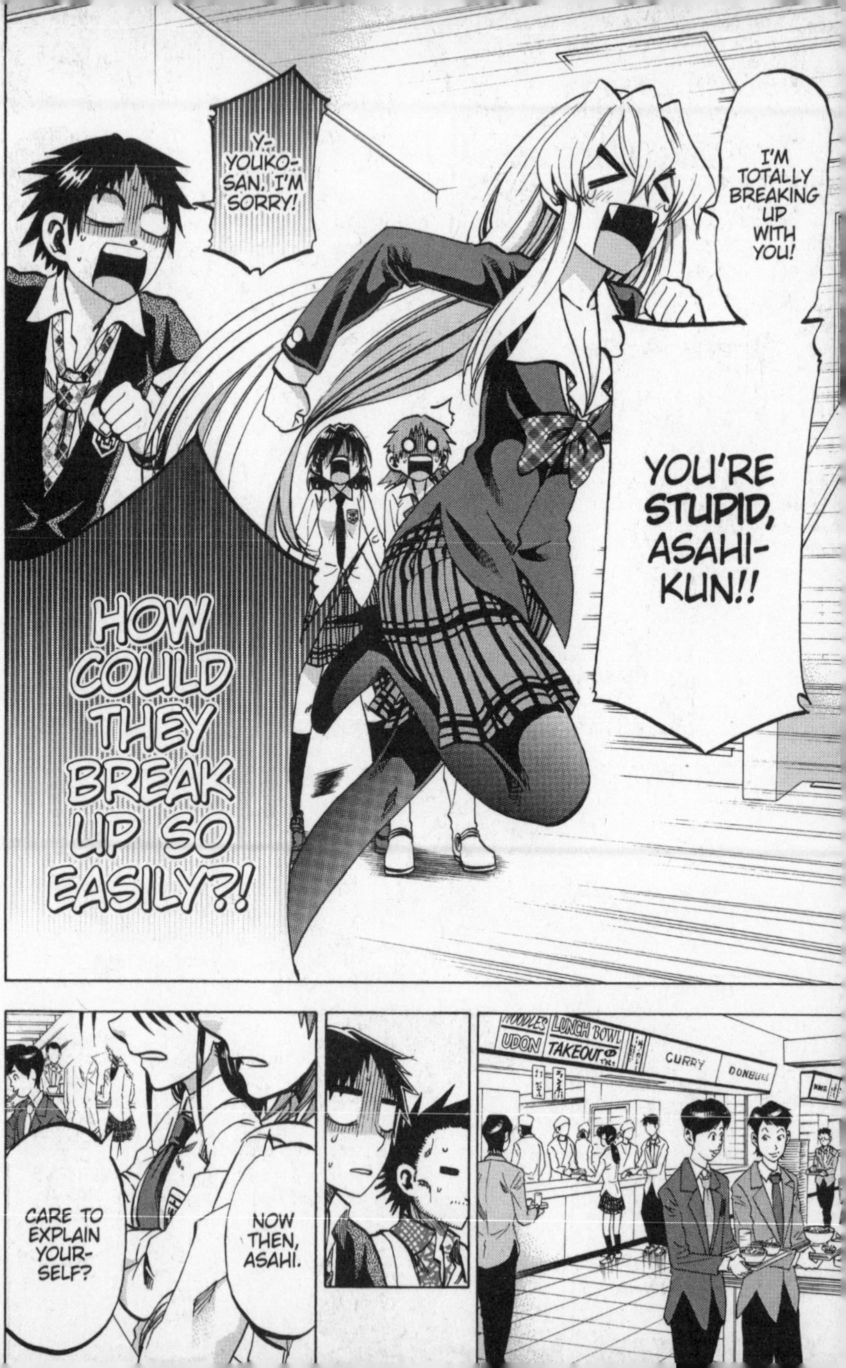
I'M TOTALLY BREAKING UP WITH YOU!
YOU'RE STUPID, ASAHI-KUN!!
Y-YOUKO-SAN, I'M SORRY!
HOW COULD THEY BREAK UP SO EASILY?!
NOODLES
UDON
LUNCH BOWL
TAKEOUT
CURRY
DONBURI
NOW THEN, ASAHI.
CARE TO EXPLAIN YOUR-SELF?

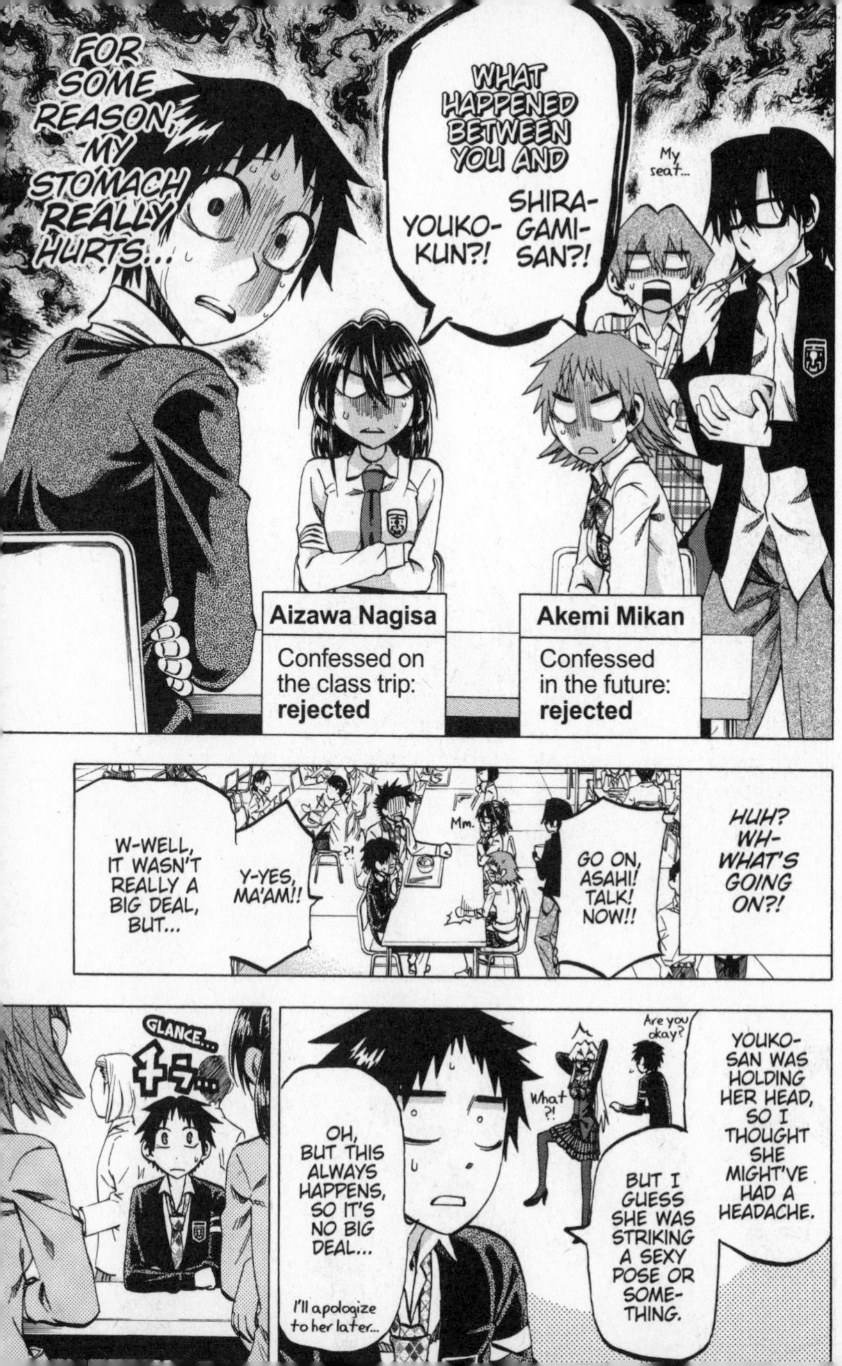
My seat...
WHAT HAPPENED BETWEEN YOU AND
SHIRA-GAMI-SAN?!
YOUKO-KUN?!
FOR SOME REASON, MY STOMACH REALLY HURTS...
Akemi Mikan
Confessed in the future: rejected
Aizawa Nagisa
Confessed on the class trip: rejected
HUH? WH-WHAT'S GOING ON?!
GO ON, ASAHI! TALK! NOW!!
Mm.
?!
Y-YES, MA'AM!!
W-WELL, IT WASN'T REALLY A BIG DEAL, BUT...
YOUKO-SAN WAS HOLDING HER HEAD, SO I THOUGHT SHE MIGHT'VE HAD A HEADACHE.
Are you okay?
What?!
BUT I GUESS SHE WAS STRIKING A SEXY POSE OR SOME-THING.
OH, BUT THIS ALWAYS HAPPENS, SO IT'S NO BIG DEAL...
I'll apologize to her later...
GLANCE...
チラ...

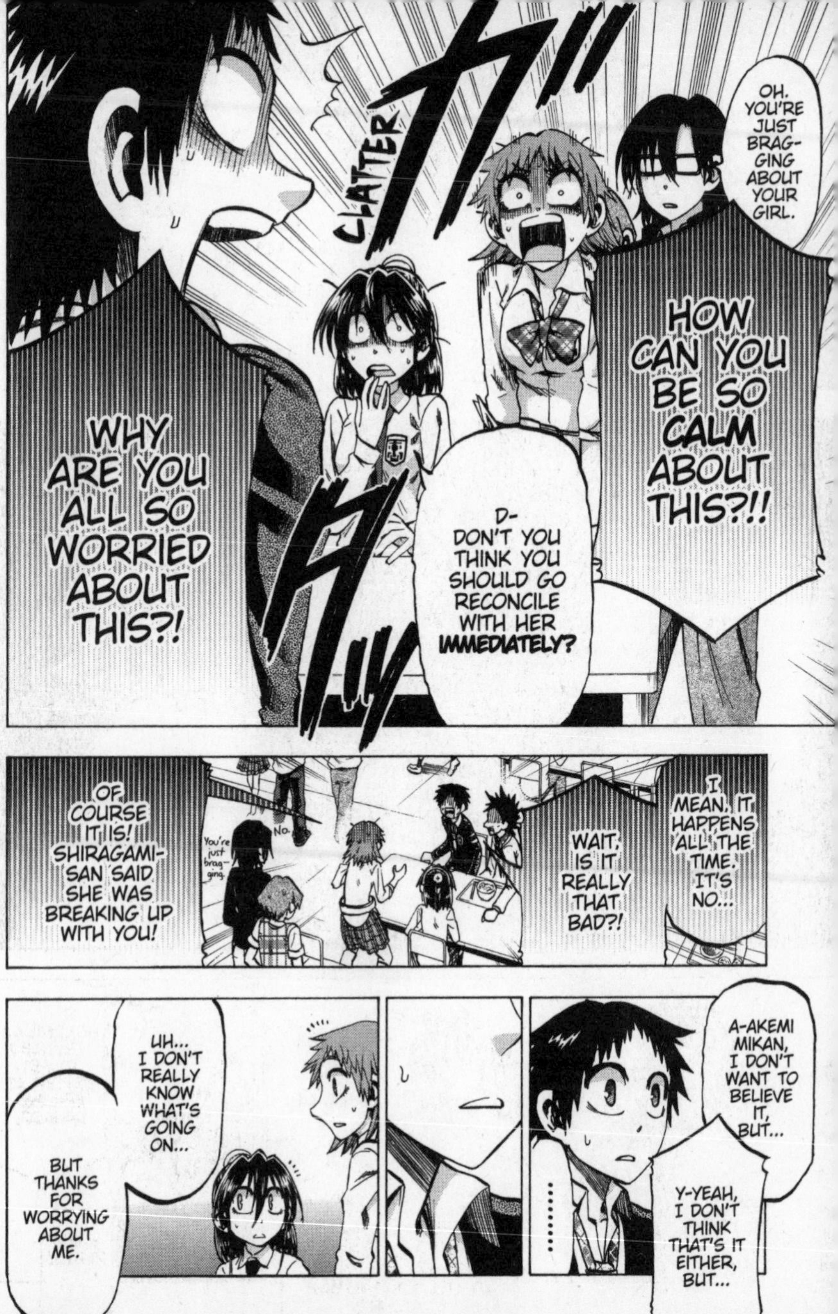
OH. YOU'RE JUST BRAG-GING ABOUT YOUR GIRL.
HOW CAN YOU BE SO CALM ABOUT THIS?!!
CLATTER
D- DON'T YOU THINK YOU SHOULD GO RECONCILE WITH HER IMMEDIATELY?
WHY ARE YOU ALL SO WORRIED ABOUT THIS?!
I MEAN, IT HAPPENS ALL THE TIME. IT'S NO...
WAIT, IS IT REALLY THAT BAD?!
No.
You're just brag-ging.
OF COURSE IT IS! SHIRAGAMI-SAN SAID SHE WAS BREAKING UP WITH YOU!
A-AKEMI MIKAN, I DON'T WANT TO BELIEVE IT, BUT...
Y-YEAH, I DON'T THINK THAT'S IT EITHER, BUT...
......
UH... I DON'T REALLY KNOW WHAT'S GOING ON...
BUT THANKS FOR WORRYING ABOUT ME.

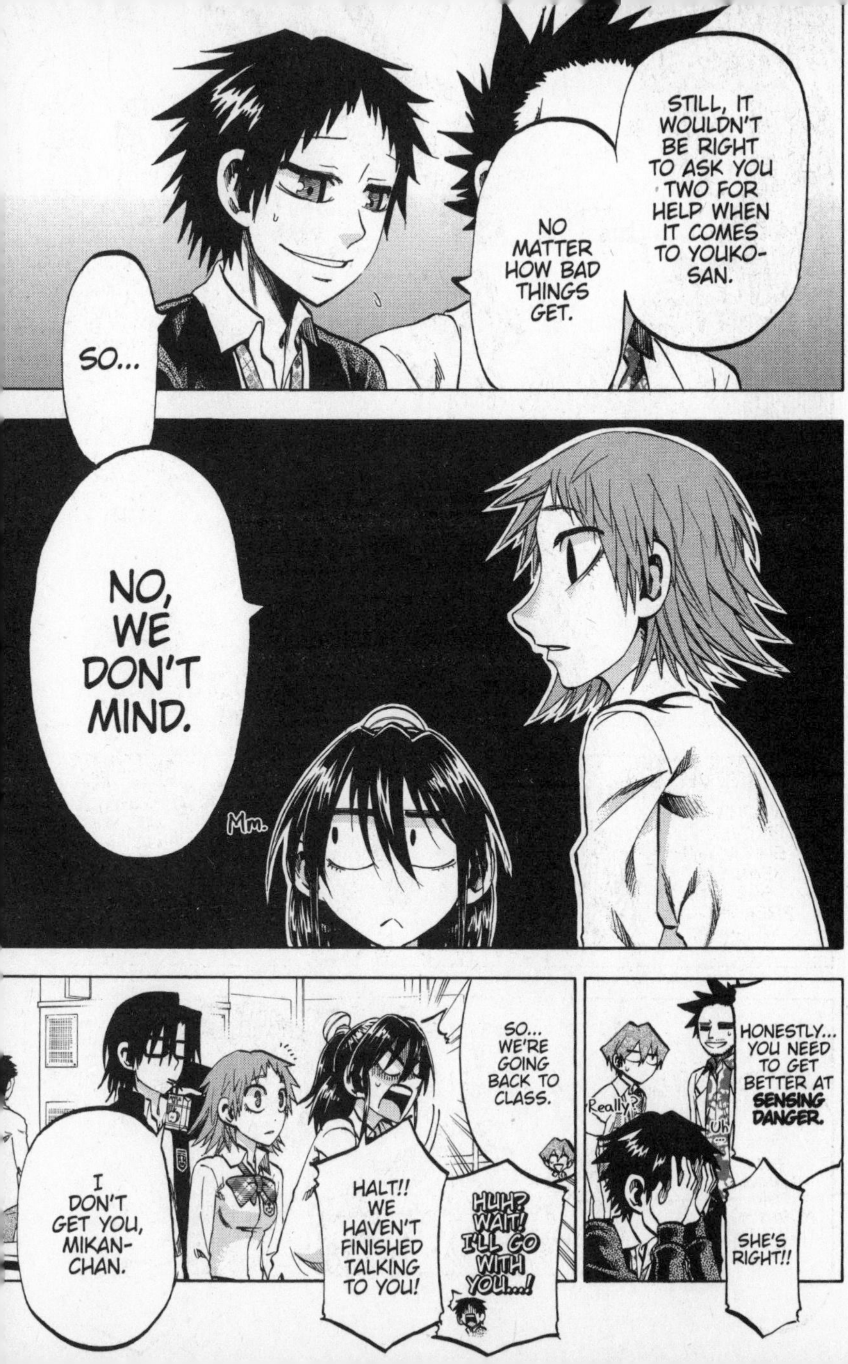
STILL, IT WOULDN'T BE RIGHT TO ASK YOU TWO FOR HELP WHEN IT COMES TO YOUKO-SAN.
NO MATTER HOW BAD THINGS GET.
SO...
NO, WE DON'T MIND.
Mm.
HONESTLY... YOU NEED TO GET BETTER AT **SENSING DANGER.**
Really?
Uh
SHE'S RIGHT!!
SO... WE'RE GOING BACK TO CLASS.
HUH? WAIT! I'LL GO WITH YOU...!
HALT!! WE HAVEN'T FINISHED TALKING TO YOU!
I DON'T GET YOU, MIKAN-CHAN.

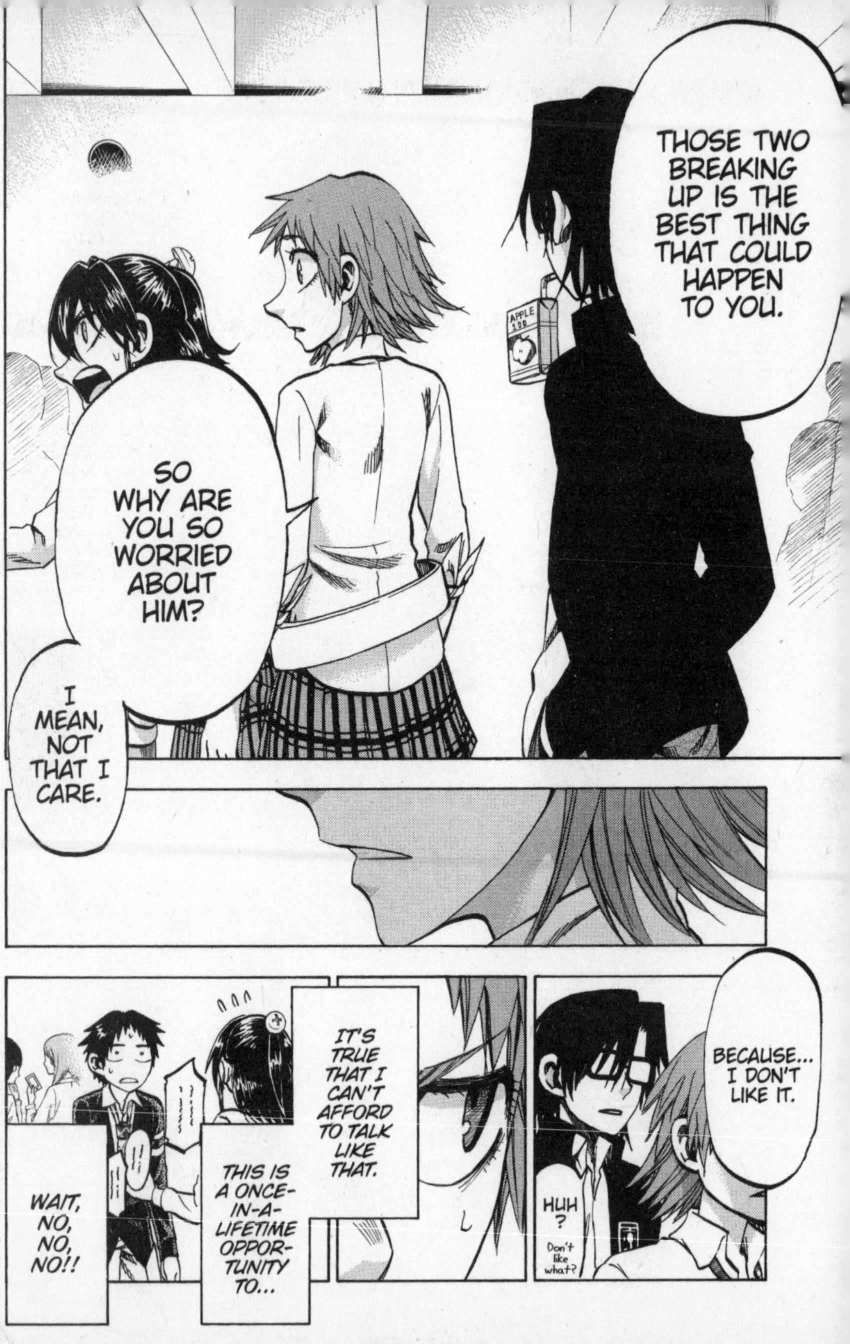
THOSE TWO BREAKING UP IS THE BEST THING THAT COULD HAPPEN TO YOU.
APPLE 100
SO WHY ARE YOU SO WORRIED ABOUT HIM?
I MEAN, NOT THAT I CARE.
BECAUSE... I DON'T LIKE IT.
HUH?
Don't like what?
IT'S TRUE THAT I CAN'T AFFORD TO TALK LIKE THAT.
THIS IS A ONCE-IN-A-LIFETIME OPPORTUNITY TO...
WAIT, NO, NO, NO!!

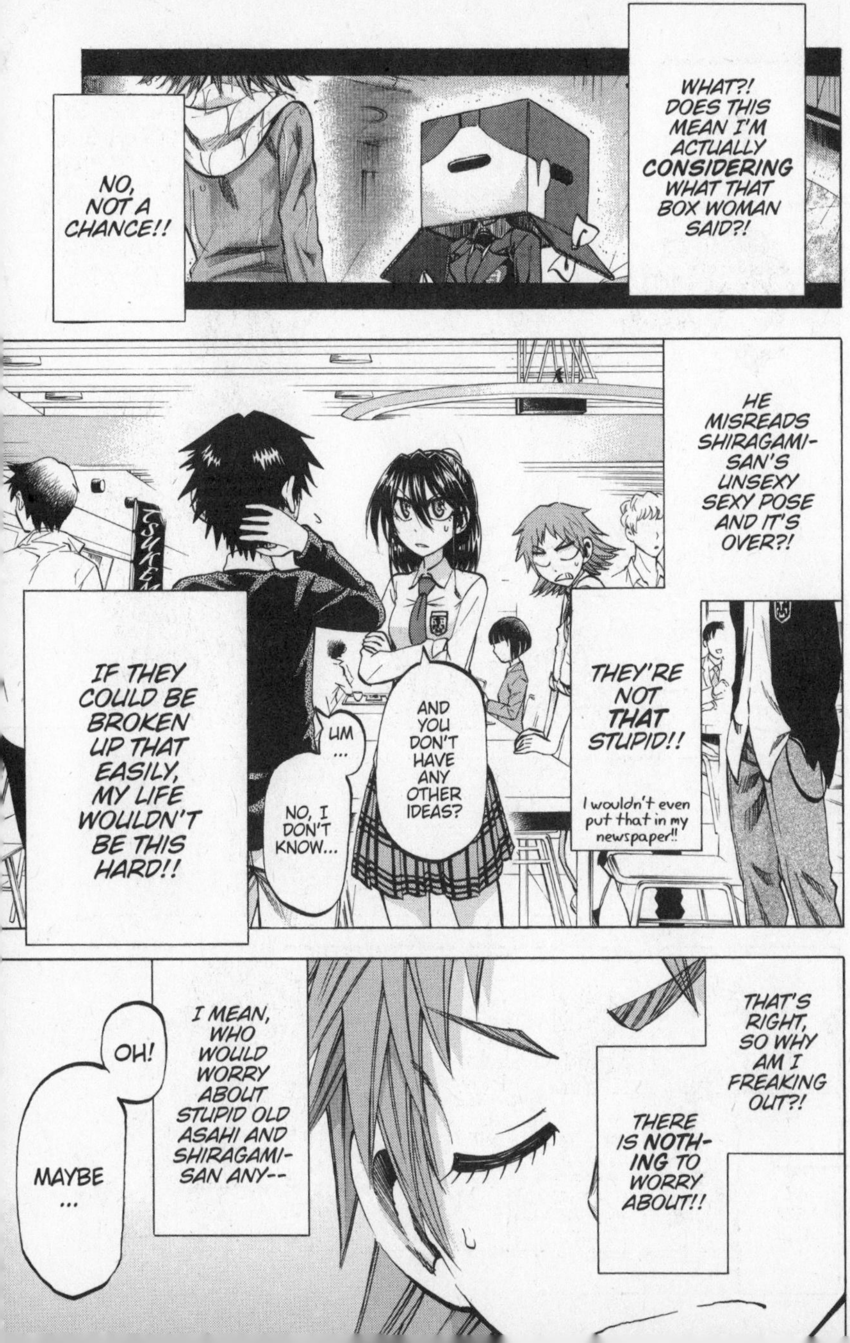

WHAT?! DOES THIS MEAN I'M ACTUALLY CONSIDERING WHAT THAT BOX WOMAN SAID?!
NO, NOT A CHANCE!!
HE MISREADS SHIRAGAMI-SAN'S UNSEXY SEXY POSE AND IT'S OVER?!
THEY'RE NOT THAT STUPID!!
I wouldn't even put that in my newspaper!!
AND YOU DON'T HAVE ANY OTHER IDEAS?
UM ...
NO, I DON'T KNOW...
IF THEY COULD BE BROKEN UP THAT EASILY, MY LIFE WOULDN'T BE THIS HARD!!
THAT'S RIGHT, SO WHY AM I FREAKING OUT?!
THERE IS NOTHING TO WORRY ABOUT!!
I MEAN, WHO WOULD WORRY ABOUT STUPID OLD ASAHI AND SHIRAGAMI-SAN ANY--
OH!
MAYBE ...

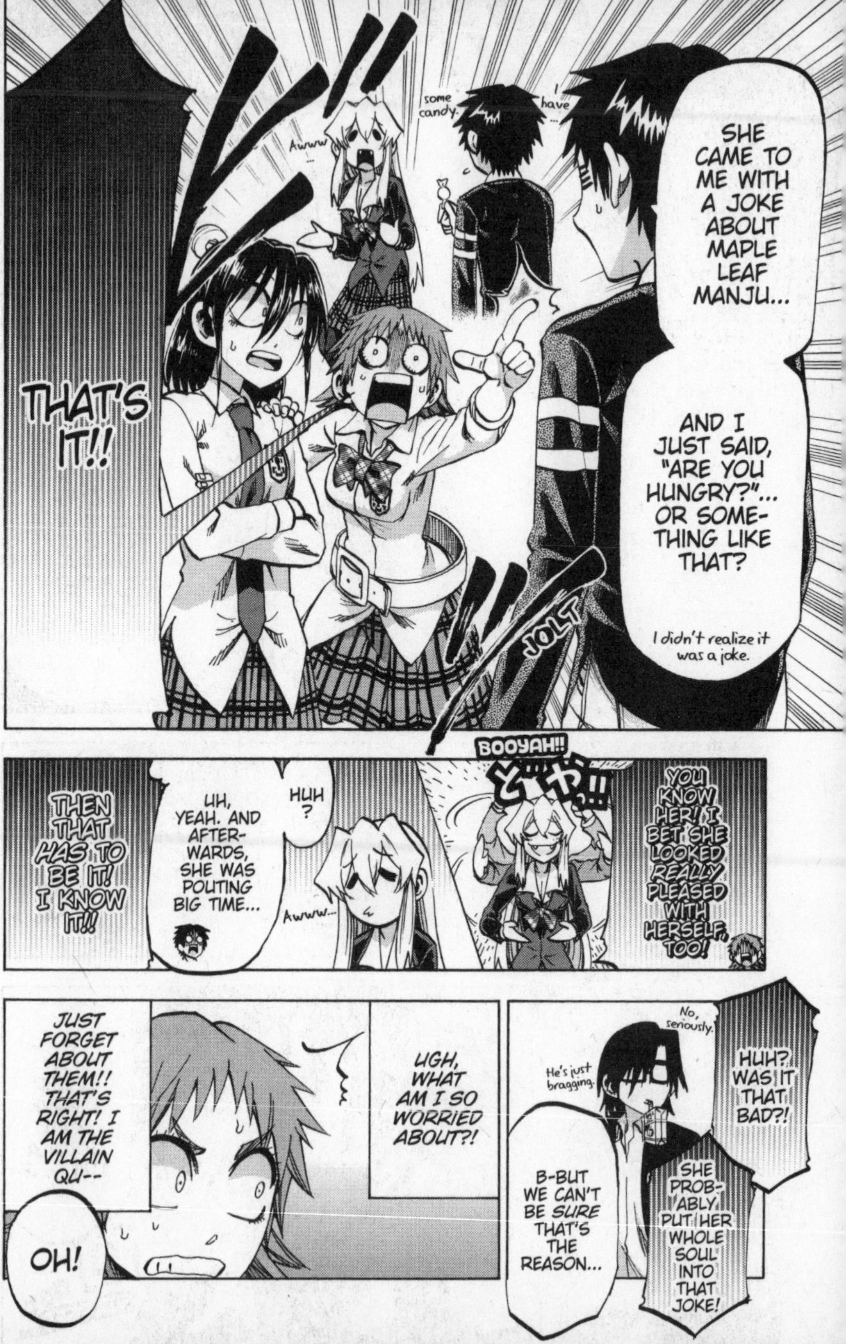
SHE CAME TO ME WITH A JOKE ABOUT MAPLE LEAF MANJU...
AND I JUST SAID, "ARE YOU HUNGRY?"... OR SOMETHING LIKE THAT?
I didn't realize it was a joke.
I have...
some candy.
Awww...
JOLT
THAT'S IT!!
BOOYAH!!
どや!!
YOU KNOW HER! I BET SHE LOOKED REALLY PLEASED WITH HERSELF, TOO!
HUH?
Awww...
UH, YEAH. AND AFTERWARDS, SHE WAS POUTING BIG TIME...
THEN THAT HAS TO BE IT! I KNOW IT!!
No, seriously.
HUH? WAS IT THAT BAD?!
He's just bragging.
SHE PROBABLY PUT HER WHOLE SOUL INTO THAT JOKE!
B-BUT WE CAN'T BE SURE THAT'S THE REASON...
UGH, WHAT AM I SO WORRIED ABOUT?!
JUST FORGET ABOUT THEM!! THAT'S RIGHT! I AM THE VILLAIN QU--
OH!

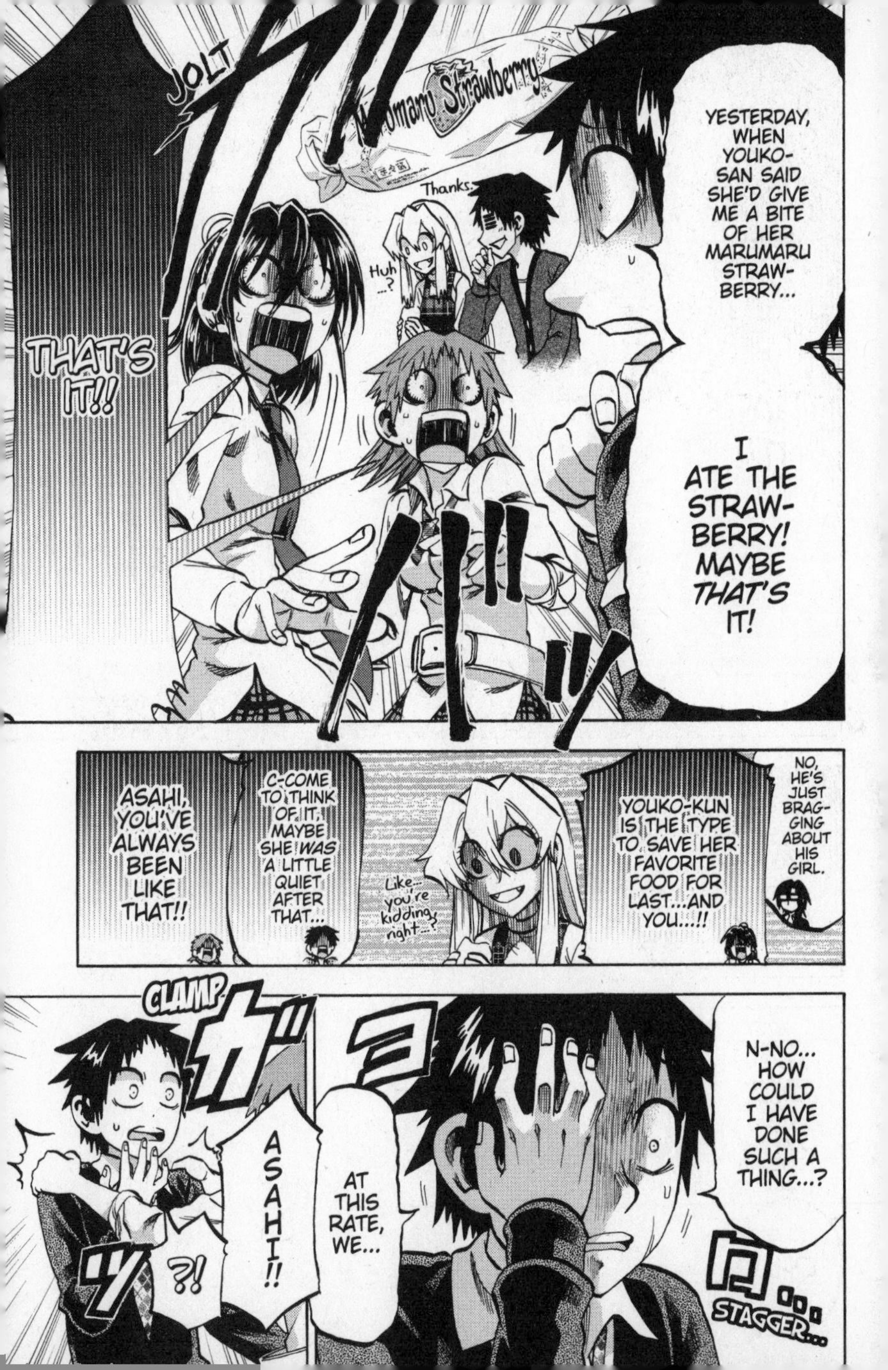
YESTERDAY, WHEN YOUKO-SAN SAID SHE'D GIVE ME A BITE OF HER MARUMARU STRAWBERRY...
I ATE THE STRAWBERRY! MAYBE *THAT'S* IT!
Strawberry
Thanks.
Huh ...?
JOLT
THAT'S IT!!
NO, HE'S JUST BRAGGING ABOUT HIS GIRL.
YOUKO-KUN IS THE TYPE TO SAVE HER FAVORITE FOOD FOR LAST...AND YOU...!!
Like... you're kidding right...?
C-COME TO THINK OF IT, MAYBE SHE *WAS* A LITTLE QUIET AFTER THAT...
ASAHI, YOU'VE ALWAYS BEEN LIKE THAT!!
N-NO... HOW COULD I HAVE DONE SUCH A THING...?
STAGGER...
AT THIS RATE, WE...
ASAHI!!
CLAMP
?!

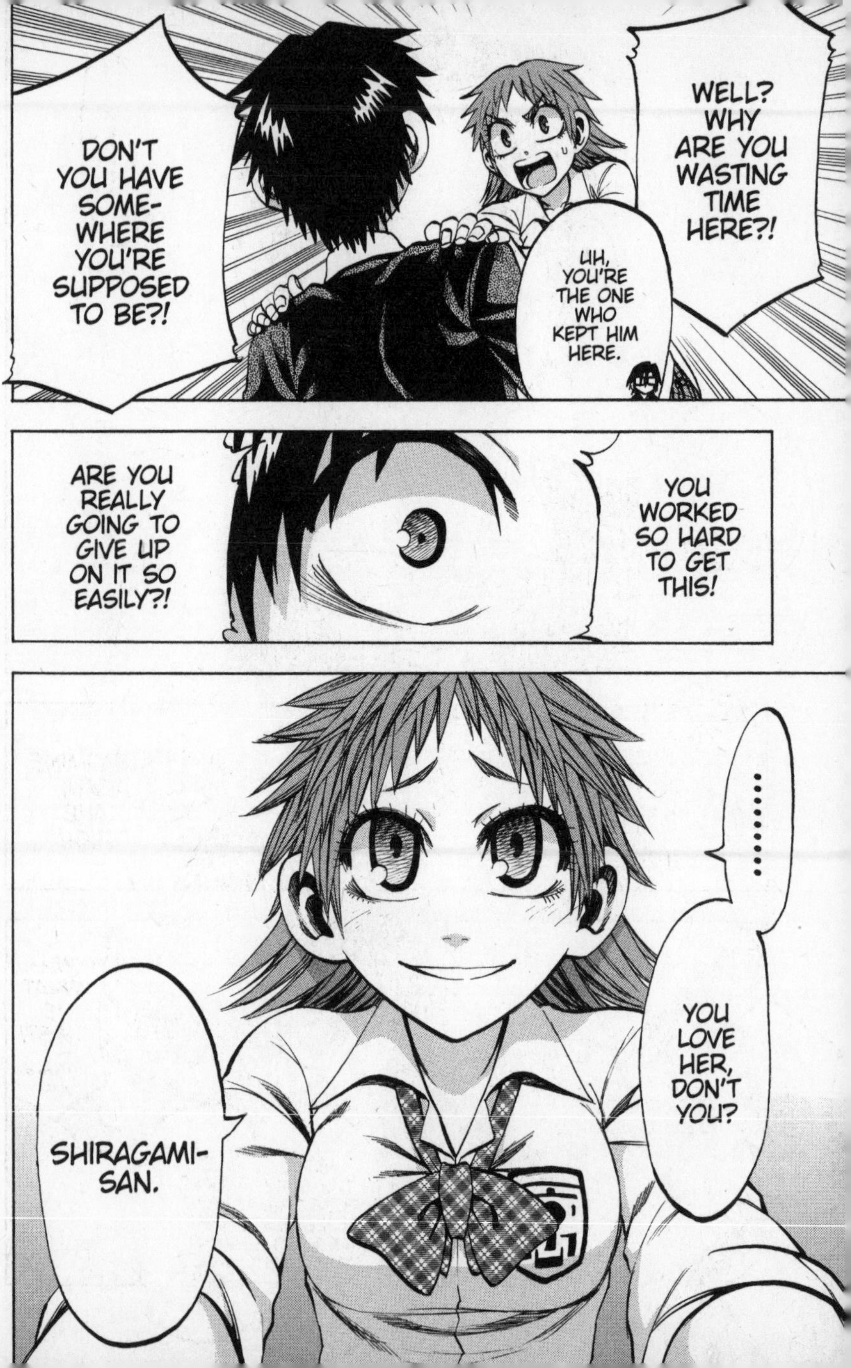
WELL? WHY ARE YOU WASTING TIME HERE?!
DON'T YOU HAVE SOME-WHERE YOU'RE SUPPOSED TO BE?!
UH, YOU'RE THE ONE WHO KEPT HIM HERE.
YOU WORKED SO HARD TO GET THIS!
ARE YOU REALLY GOING TO GIVE UP ON IT SO EASILY?!
......
YOU LOVE HER, DON'T YOU?
SHIRAGAMI-SAN.

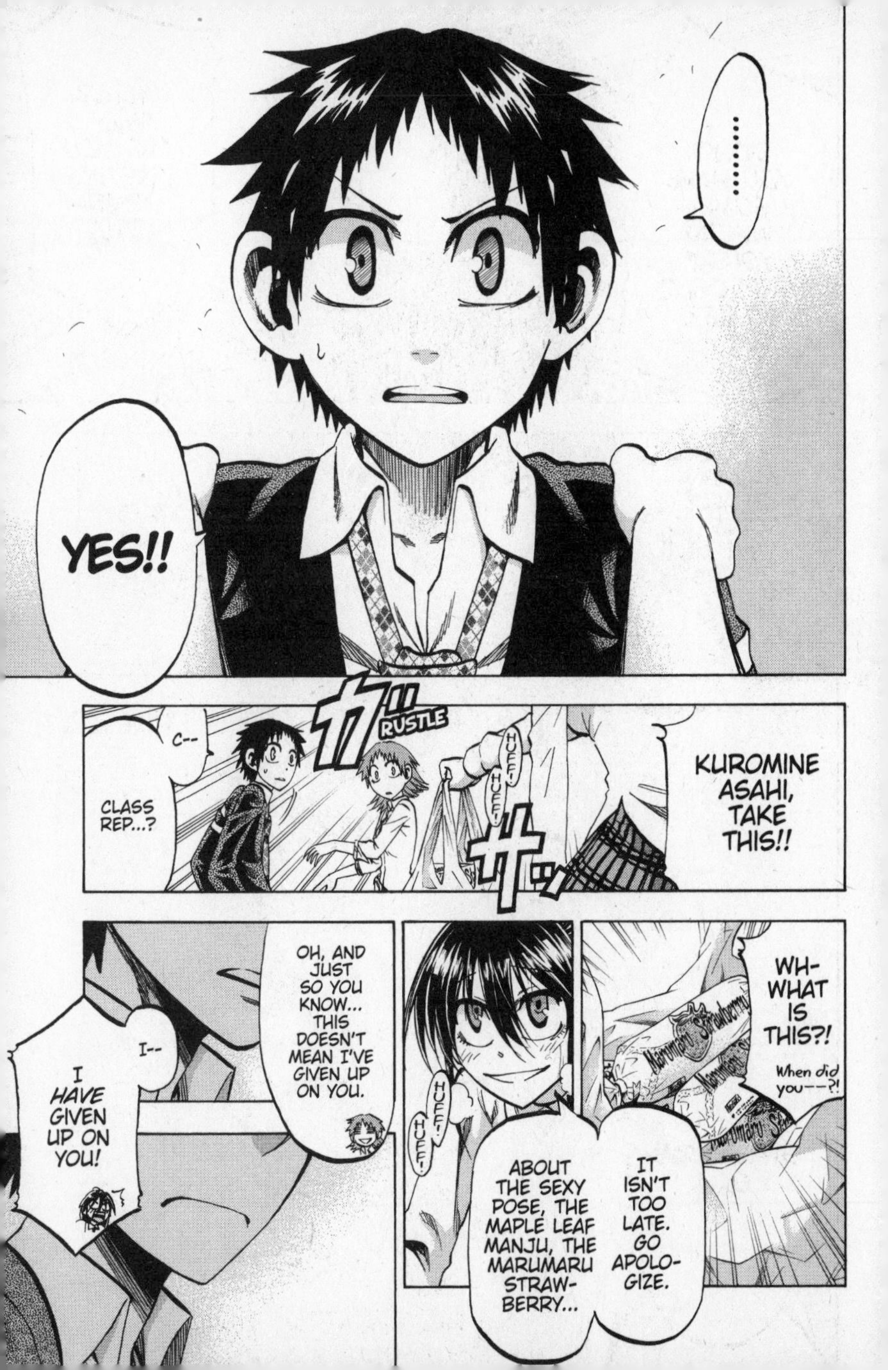
……
YES!!
KUROMINE ASAHI, TAKE THIS!!
HUFF! HUFF!
RUSTLE
C-- CLASS REP...?
WH- WHAT IS THIS?!
When did you--?!
Marumaru Strawberry
HUFF! HUFF!
IT ISN'T TOO LATE. GO APOLO-GIZE.
ABOUT THE SEXY POSE, THE MAPLE LEAF MANJU, THE MARUMARU STRAW-BERRY...
OH, AND JUST SO YOU KNOW... THIS DOESN'T MEAN I'VE GIVEN UP ON YOU.
I--
I HAVE GIVEN UP ON YOU!

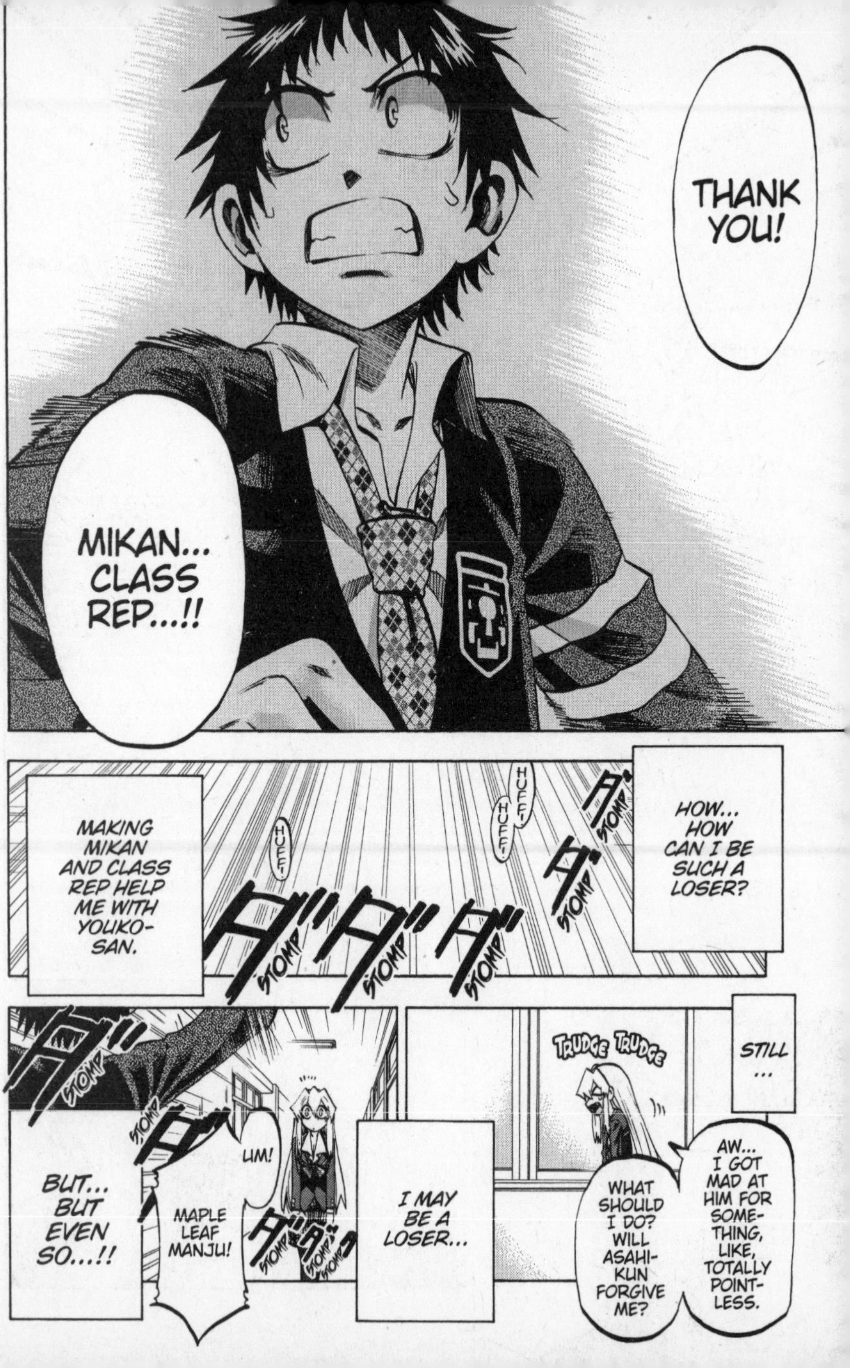
THANK YOU!
MIKAN... CLASS REP...!!
HOW... HOW CAN I BE SUCH A LOSER?
HUFF! HUFF!
HUFF!
STOMP STOMP STOMP STOMP STOMP
MAKING MIKAN AND CLASS REP HELP ME WITH YOUKO-SAN.
STILL...
TRUDGE TRUDGE
AW... I GOT MAD AT HIM FOR SOMETHING, LIKE, TOTALLY POINTLESS.
WHAT SHOULD I DO? WILL ASAHI-KUN FORGIVE ME?
I MAY BE A LOSER...
UM!
MAPLE LEAF MANJU!
STOMP STOMP STOMP STOMP
BUT... BUT EVEN SO...!!

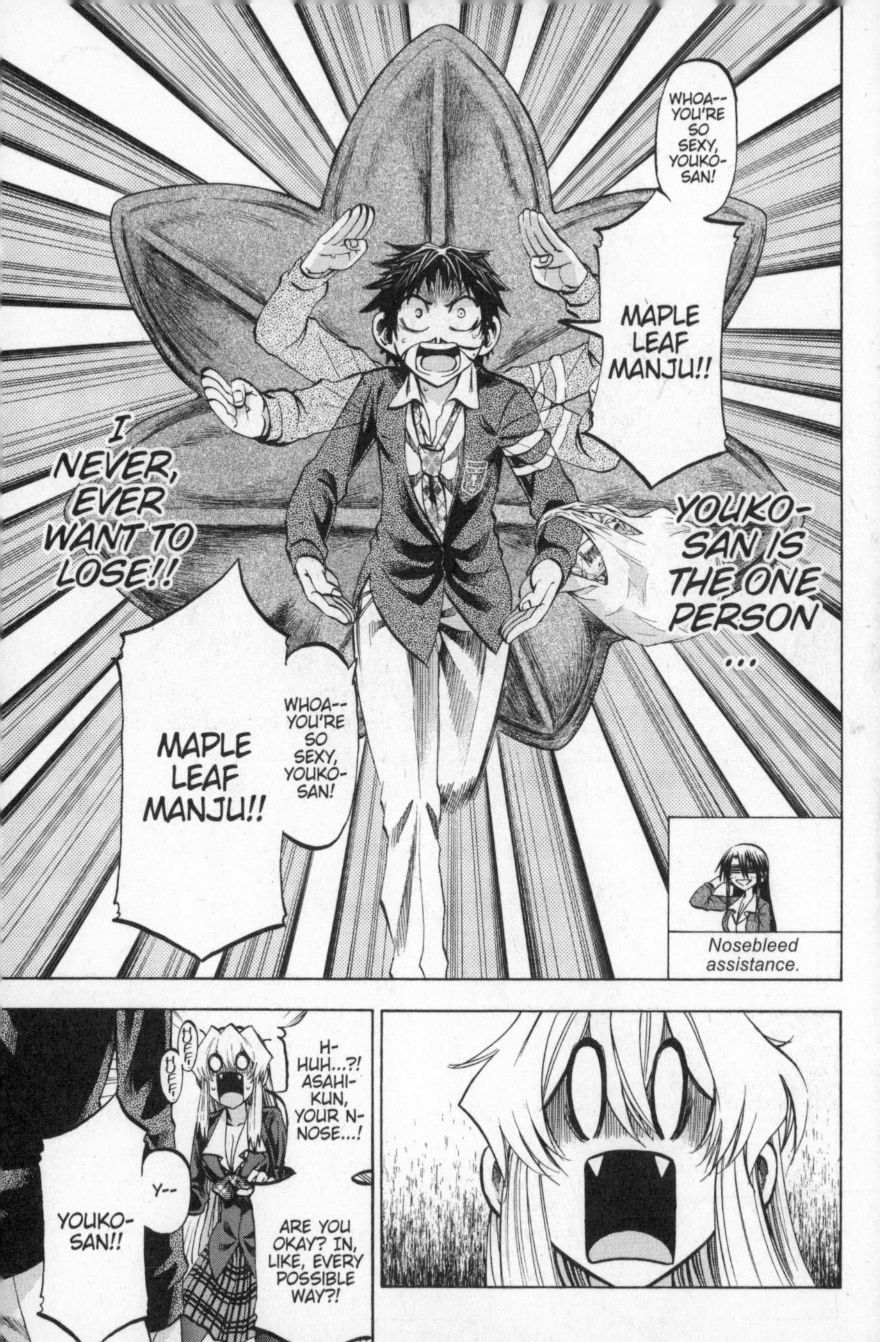
WHOA-- YOU'RE SO SEXY, YOUKO-SAN!
MAPLE LEAF MANJU!!
YOUKO-SAN IS THE ONE PERSON...
I NEVER, EVER WANT TO LOSE!!
WHOA-- YOU'RE SO SEXY, YOUKO-SAN!
MAPLE LEAF MANJU!!
Nosebleed assistance.
HUFF! HUFF!
H-HUH...?! ASAHI-KUN, YOUR N-NOSE...!
ARE YOU OKAY? IN, LIKE, EVERY POSSIBLE WAY?!
Y--
YOUKO-SAN!!

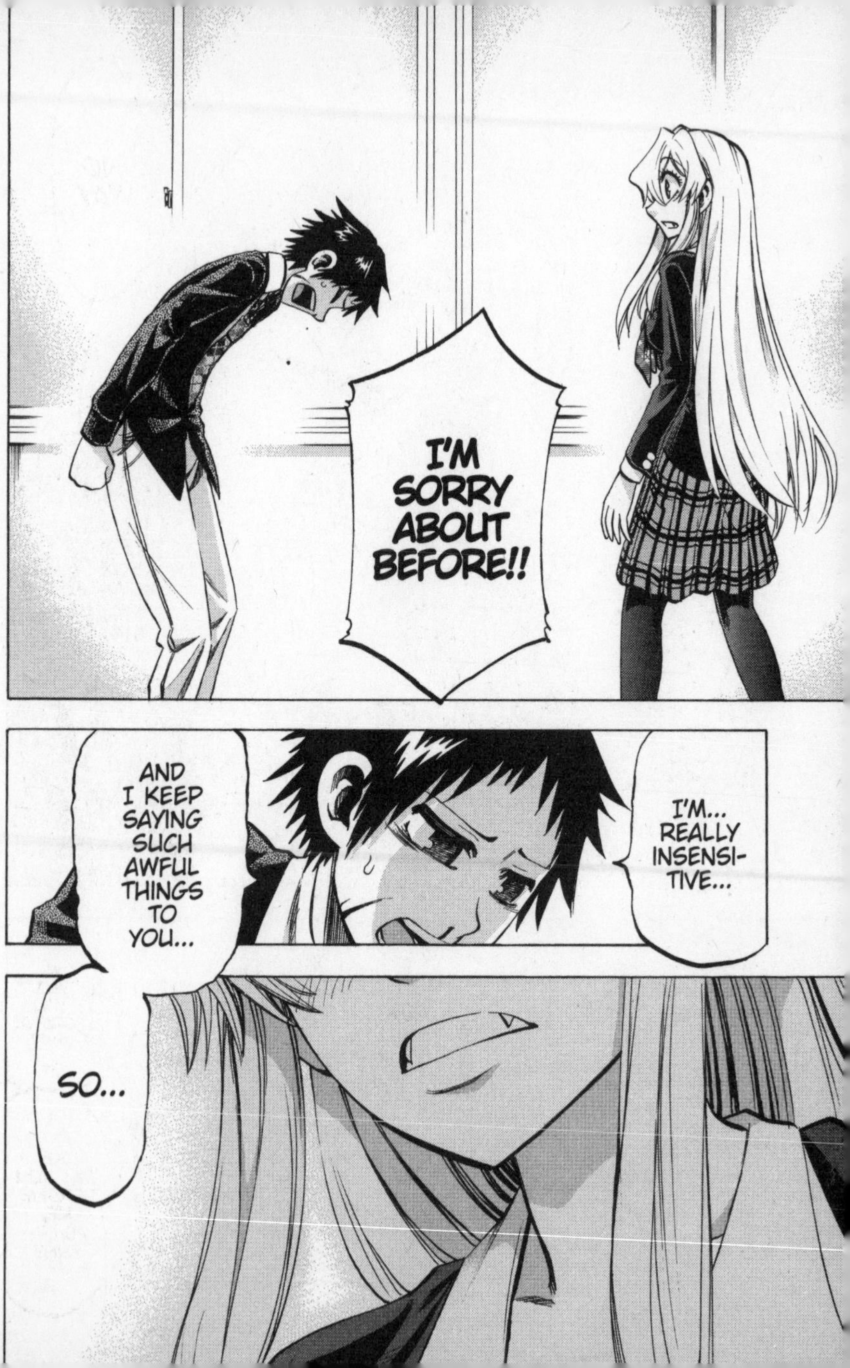
I'M SORRY ABOUT BEFORE!!
I'M... REALLY INSENSI-TIVE...
AND I KEEP SAYING SUCH AWFUL THINGS TO YOU...
SO...

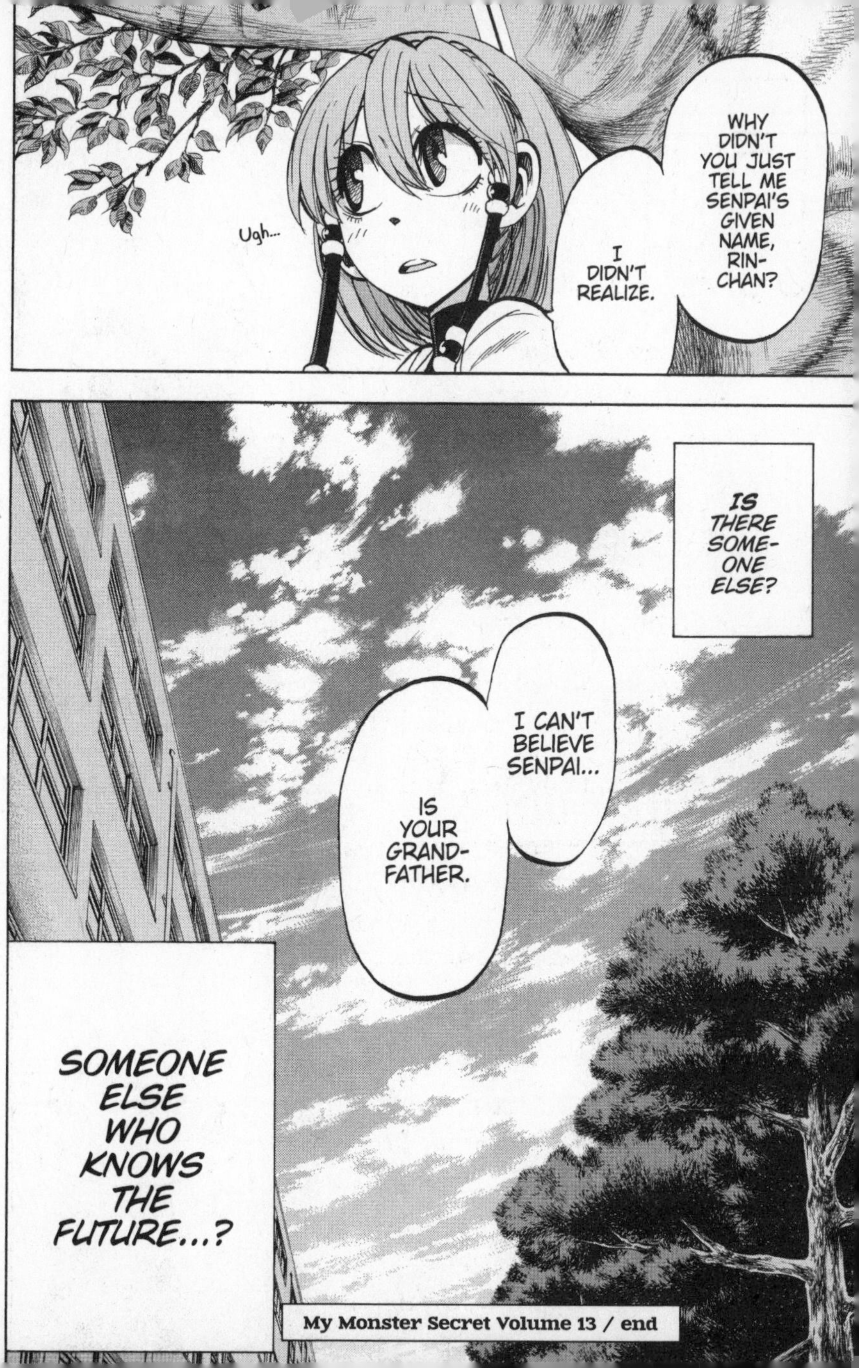
WHY DIDN'T YOU JUST TELL ME SENPAI'S GIVEN NAME, RIN-CHAN?
I DIDN'T REALIZE.
Ugh...
IS THERE SOMEONE-ONE ELSE?
I CAN'T BELIEVE SENPAI...
IS YOUR GRAND-FATHER.
SOMEONE ELSE WHO KNOWS THE FUTURE...?
My Monster Secret Volume 13 / end

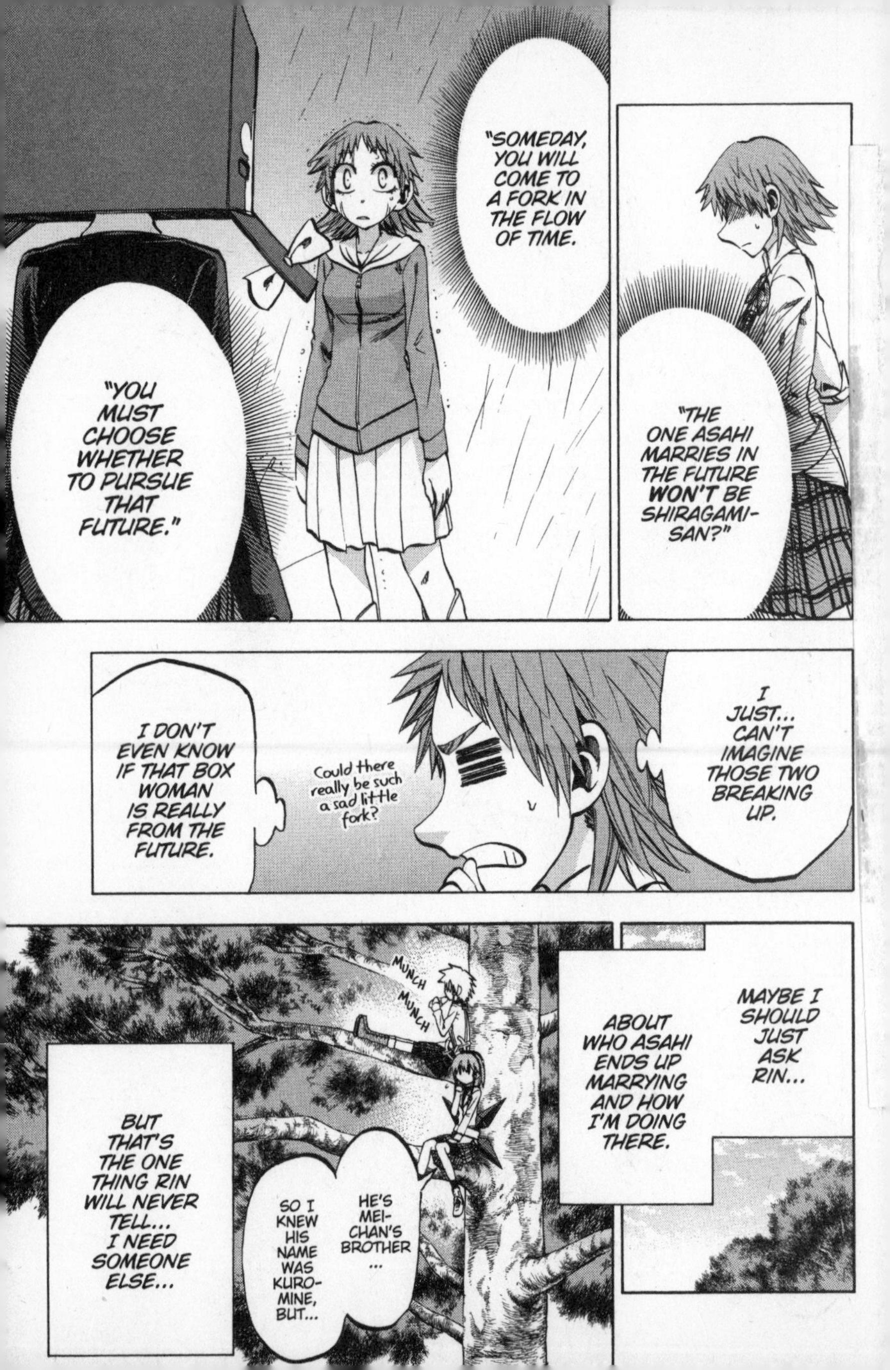
"THE ONE ASAHI MARRIES IN THE FUTURE WON'T BE SHIRAGAMI-SAN?"
"SOMEDAY, YOU WILL COME TO A FORK IN THE FLOW OF TIME.
"YOU MUST CHOOSE WHETHER TO PURSUE THAT FUTURE."
I JUST... CAN'T IMAGINE THOSE TWO BREAKING UP.
Could there really be such a sad little fork?
I DON'T EVEN KNOW IF THAT BOX WOMAN IS REALLY FROM THE FUTURE.
MAYBE I SHOULD JUST ASK RIN...
ABOUT WHO ASAHI ENDS UP MARRYING AND HOW I'M DOING THERE.
MUNCH
MUNCH
BUT THAT'S THE ONE THING RIN WILL NEVER TELL... I NEED SOMEONE ELSE...
HE'S MEI-CHAN'S BROTHER ...
SO I KNEW HIS NAME WAS KURO-MINE, BUT...

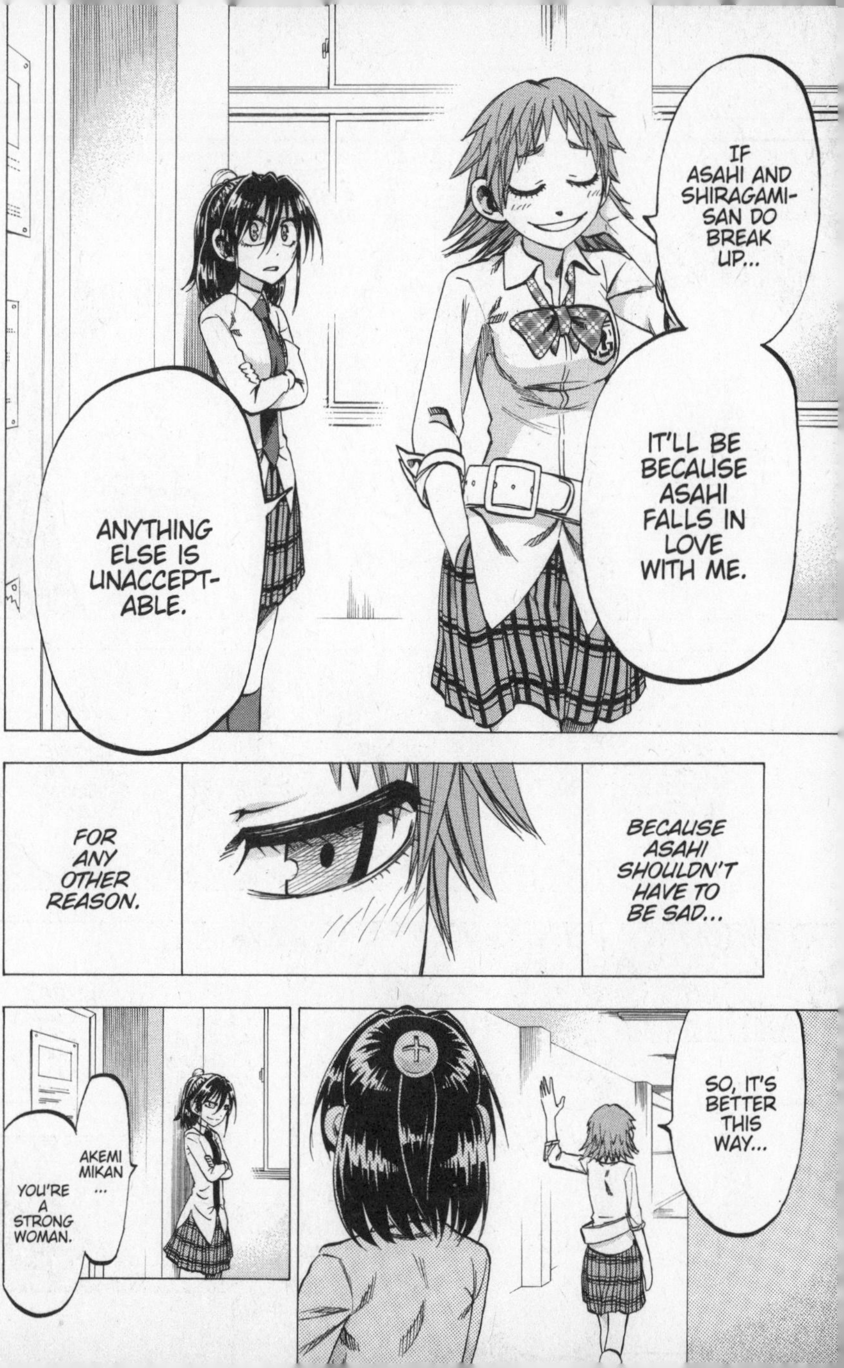
IF ASAHI AND SHIRAGAMI-SAN DO BREAK UP...
IT'LL BE BECAUSE ASAHI FALLS IN LOVE WITH ME.
ANYTHING ELSE IS UNACCEPT-ABLE.
BECAUSE ASAHI SHOULDN'T HAVE TO BE SAD...
FOR ANY OTHER REASON.
SO, IT'S BETTER THIS WAY...
AKEMI MIKAN ...
YOU'RE A STRONG WOMAN.

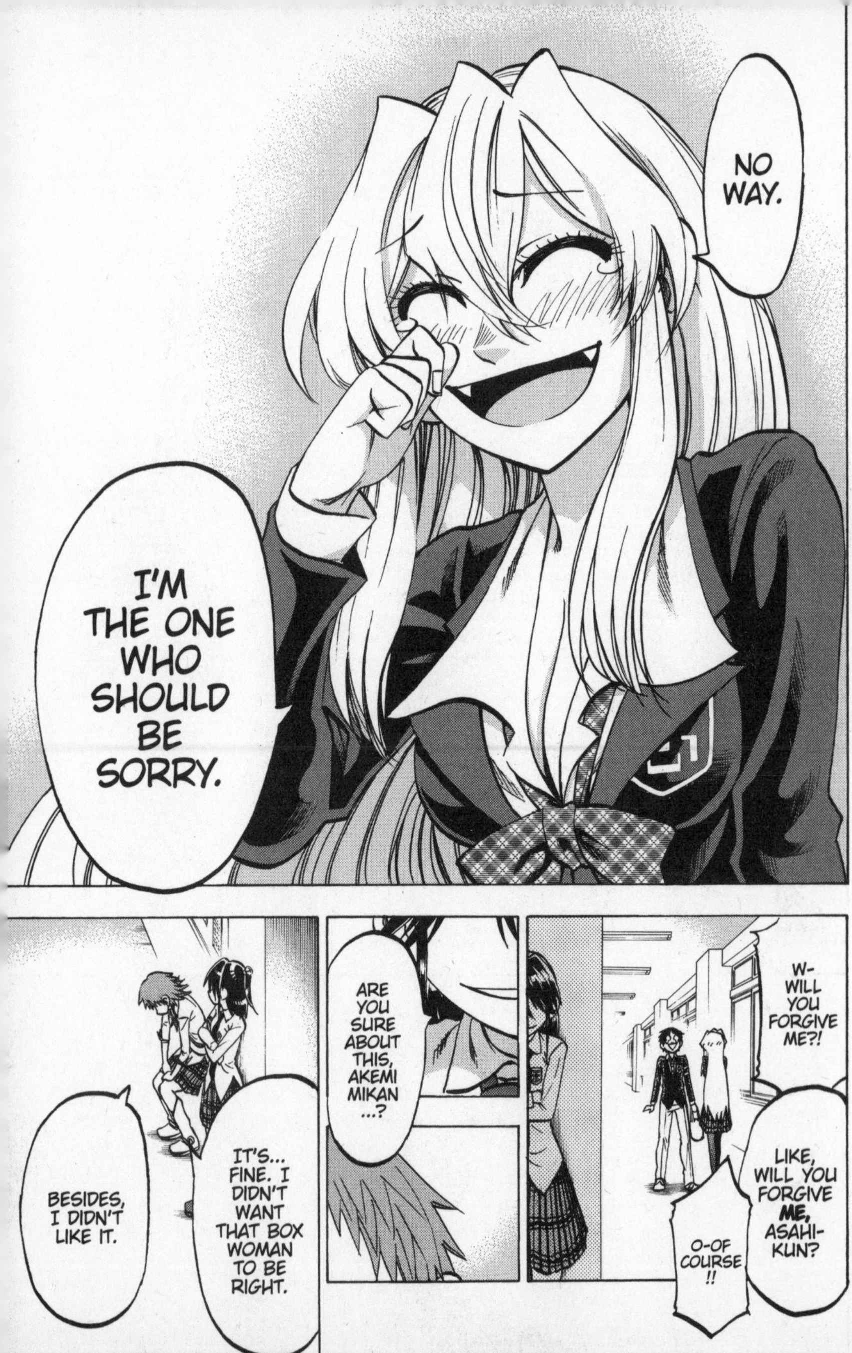
NO WAY.
I'M THE ONE WHO SHOULD BE SORRY.
W- WILL YOU FORGIVE ME?!
LIKE, WILL YOU FORGIVE **ME,** ASAHI-KUN?
O-OF COURSE!!
ARE YOU SURE ABOUT THIS, AKEMI MIKAN...?
IT'S... FINE. I DIDN'T WANT THAT BOX WOMAN TO BE RIGHT.
BESIDES, I DIDN'T LIKE IT.

CLINK...
HEH... TO DROWN IN DRINK AND WOMEN.
THAT TOO IS A MAN'S PLEASURE.

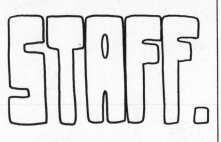

STAFF.

- Garage Okada-san
- Shuumeigiku-san
- Suzuki Seijun-san
- Daifuku Mochiko-san
- Nakamura Yuji-san
- Hayashi Rie-san
- Mana Haruki-san
- Minemura Hiroki-san
- Mori Keiko-san (in syllabary order)

SPECIAL THANKS.

- Inayama Kakuya-sensei
  Thank you for drawing the anime voice-recording report manga!
- Adachi-san
- Araki Nozomu-san
- Katou Shinichi-san
- Kawaji-san
- Nakano Akari-san
- Yuoka Youko-san

Editor: Mukawa-san,
Otsuka-san

Thanks to you, the one holding this book right now, everyone who watched the anime, and everyone who let me and my work be a part of their lives.

Eiji Masuda

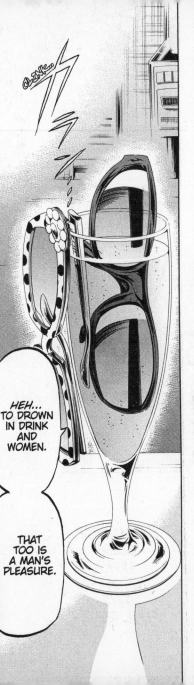

I am 13...

Dentist

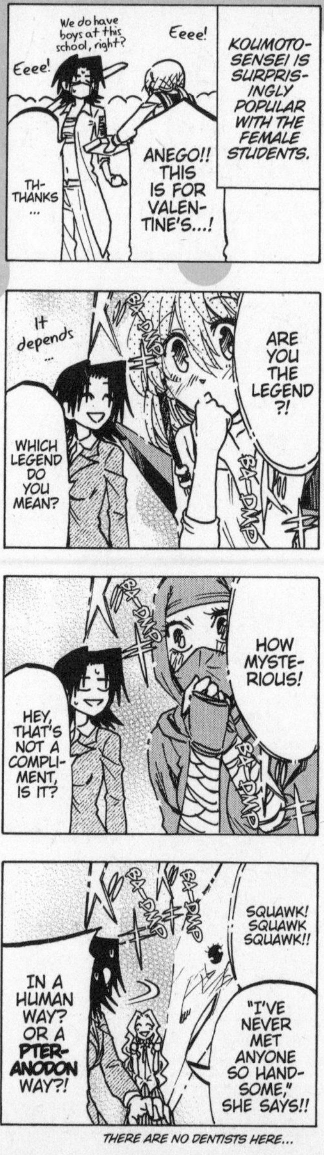
KOUMOTO-SENSEI IS SURPRISINGLY POPULAR WITH THE FEMALE STUDENTS.
Eeee!
We do have boys at this school, right?
ANEGO!! THIS IS FOR VALENTINE'S...!
Eeee!
TH-THANKS...
ARE YOU THE LEGEND?!
BA-DMP
It depends...
WHICH LEGEND DO YOU MEAN?
BA-DMP
HOW MYSTERIOUS!
BA-DMP
HEY, THAT'S NOT A COMPLIMENT, IS IT?
BA-DMP
SQUAWK! SQUAWK SQUAWK!!
BA-DMP
"I'VE NEVER MET ANYONE SO HANDSOME," SHE SAYS!!
IN A HUMAN WAY? OR A **PTERANODON** WAY?!

THERE ARE NO DENTISTS HERE...

After Running Away

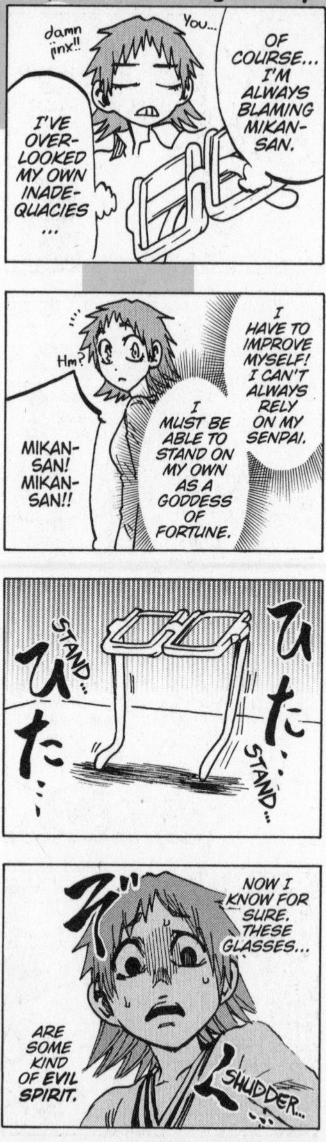
OF COURSE... I'M ALWAYS BLAMING MIKAN-SAN.
You...
damn jinx!!
I'VE OVERLOOKED MY OWN INADEQUACIES...
I HAVE TO IMPROVE MYSELF! I CAN'T ALWAYS RELY ON MY SENPAI.
I MUST BE ABLE TO STAND ON MY OWN AS A GODDESS OF FORTUNE.
Hm?
MIKAN-SAN! MIKAN-SAN!!
ひた…
STAND...
ひた…
STAND...
NOW I KNOW FOR SURE. THESE GLASSES...
ARE SOME KIND OF **EVIL SPIRIT.**
SHUDDER...

I am... 13

After Superhero Part ①

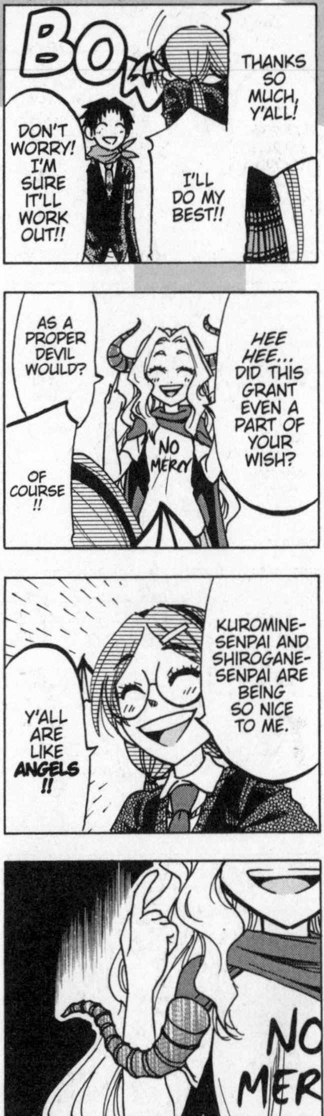
THANKS SO MUCH, Y'ALL!
BOW
I'LL DO MY BEST!!
DON'T WORRY! I'M SURE IT'LL WORK OUT!!
HEE HEE... DID THIS GRANT EVEN A PART OF YOUR WISH?
AS A PROPER DEVIL WOULD?
NO MERCY
OF COURSE !!
KUROMINE-SENPAI AND SHIROGANE-SENPAI ARE BEING SO NICE TO ME.
Y'ALL ARE LIKE **ANGELS** !!
NO MER

After Superhero Part ②

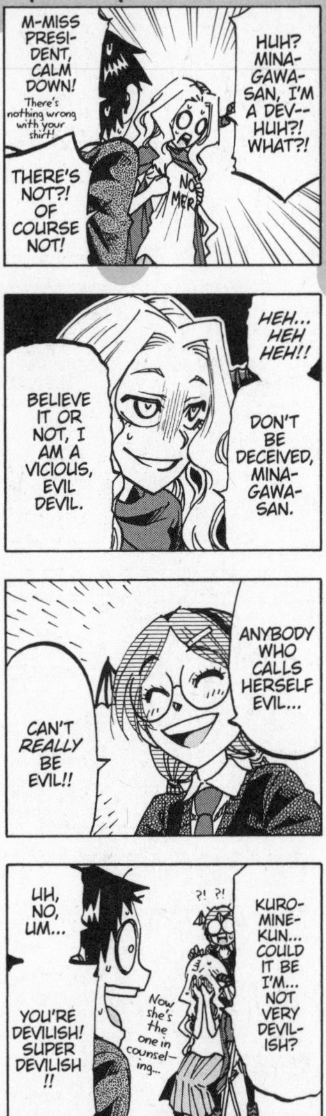
HUH? MINAGAWA-SAN, I'M A DEV-- HUH?! WHAT?!
M-MISS PRESIDENT, CALM DOWN!
There's nothing wrong with your shirt!
NO MER
THERE'S NOT?! OF COURSE NOT!
HEH... HEH HEH!!
DON'T BE DECEIVED, MINAGAWA-SAN.
BELIEVE IT OR NOT, I AM A VICIOUS, EVIL DEVIL.
ANYBODY WHO CALLS HERSELF EVIL...
CAN'T *REALLY* BE EVIL!!
KUROMINE-KUN... COULD IT BE I'M... NOT VERY DEVILISH?
?! ?!
Now she's the one in counseling...
UH, NO, UM...
YOU'RE DEVILISH! SUPER DEVILISH !!

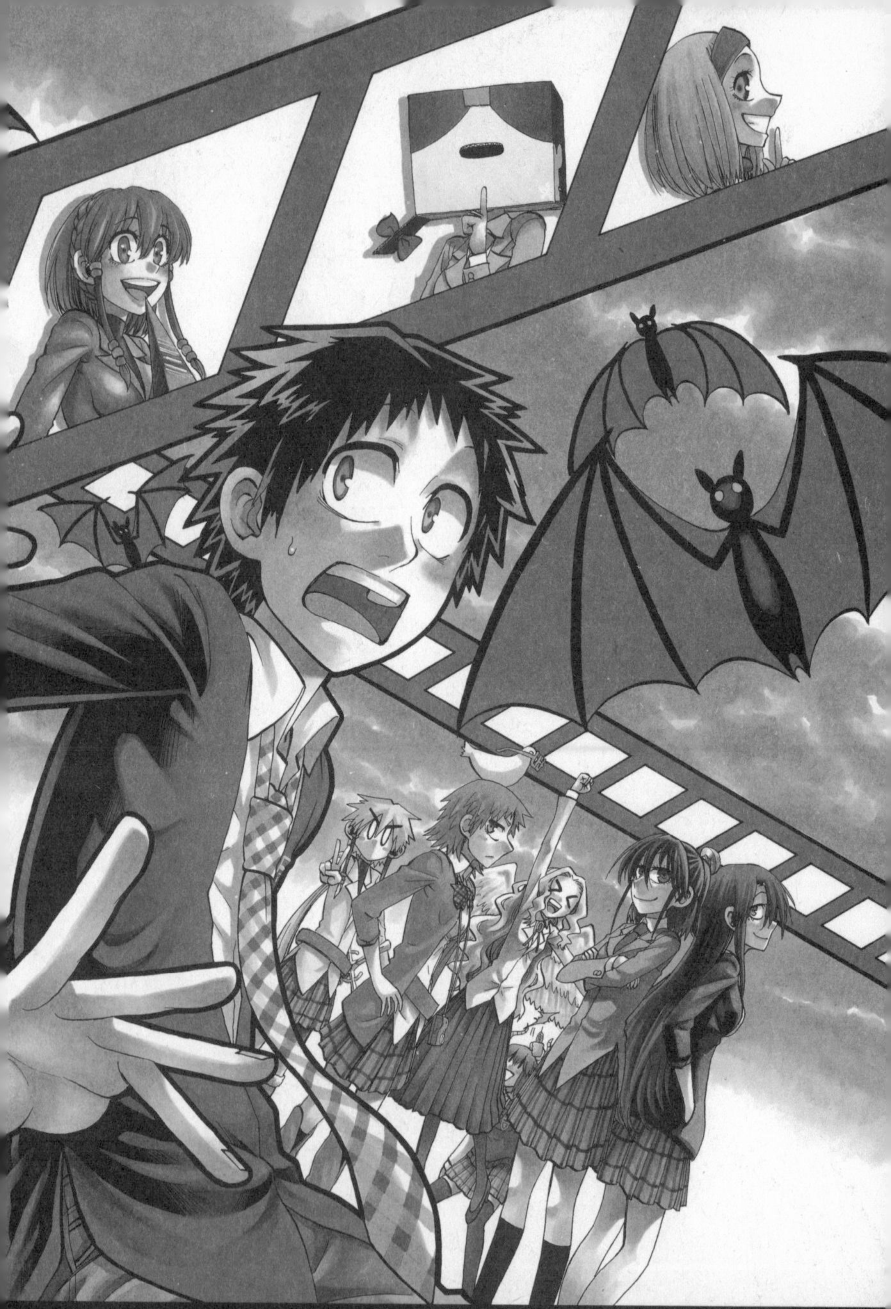

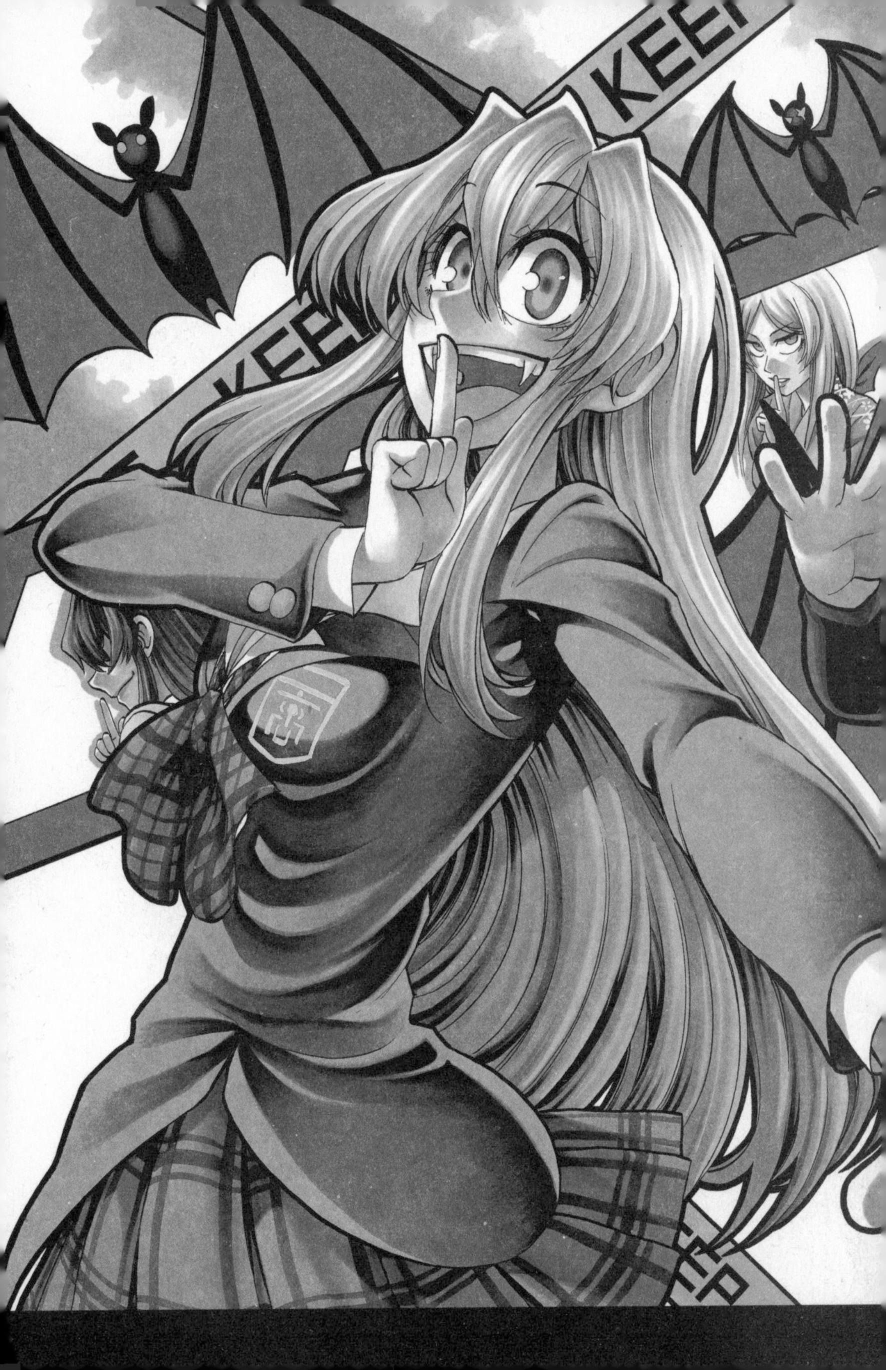

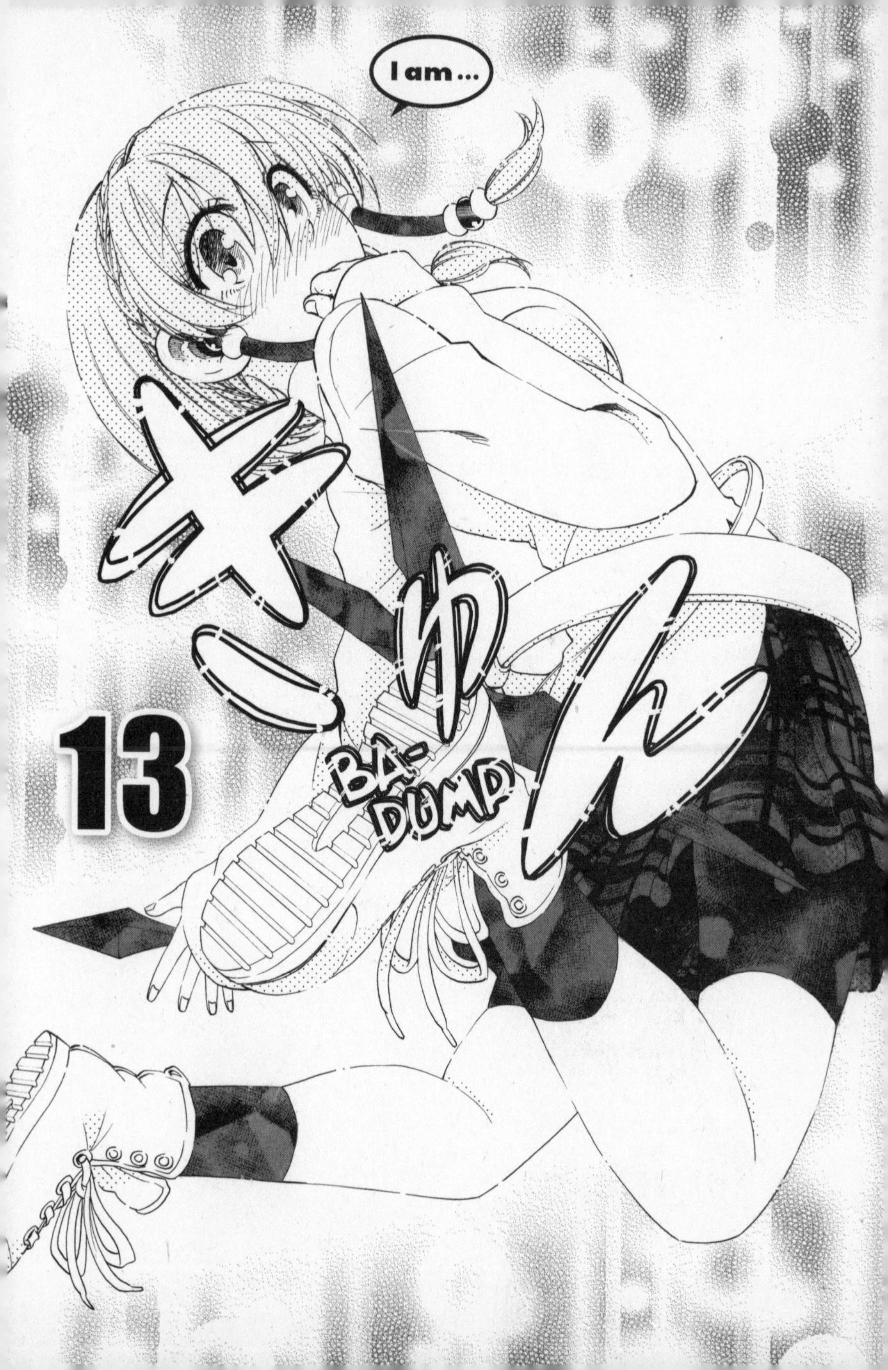
I am ...
13
BA-DUMP

I am... a Ninja

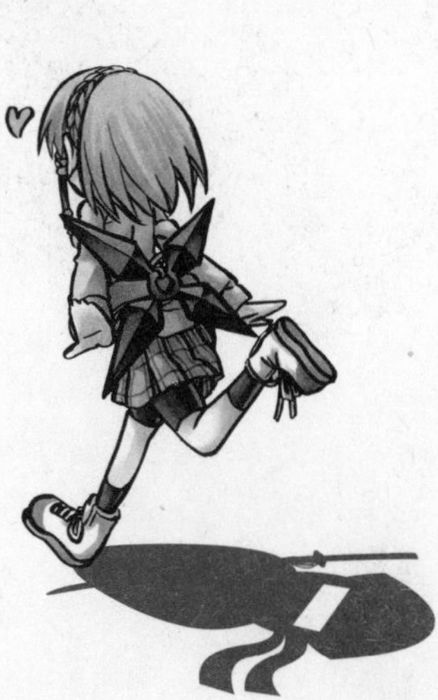

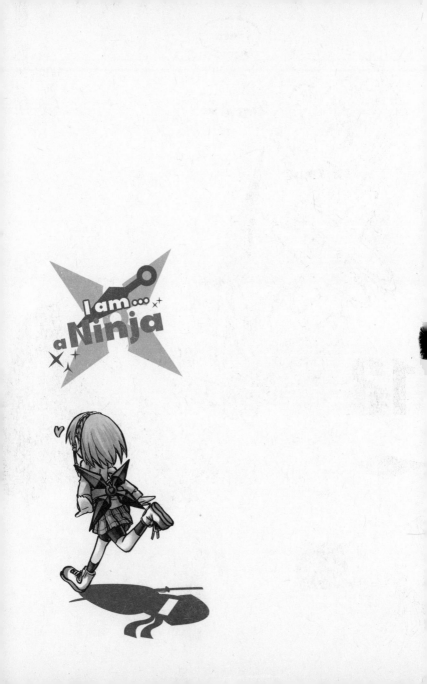

My Monster Secret

"Actually, I am..."